ON 11 APRIL 2006, AFTER OVER FORTY-TWO YEARS SPENT AS A FUGITIVE from justice, Bernardo 'the Tractor' Provenzano, Cosa Nostra's boss of all bosses, was arrested near his home town of Corleone. The event brought the attention of the world's media more intensely to bear on the problem of the Sicilian mafia than at any time since the murders of magistrates Giovanni Falcone and Paolo Borsellino in 1992. Such an epoch-making coup by the Sicilian forces of order raises many questions. It will also bring change to the world's most infamous criminal organization. Indeed dramatic changes have already begun to unfold, now that the foreign media's interest has moved elsewhere.

THE ENTIRELY NEW CHAPTER WRITTEN SPECIALLY FOR THIS REVISED EDITION of *Cosa Nostra* delves into the dark background to Provenzano's arrest to answer some of those questions and survey those changes. It does so with a fundamental principle in mind: that we cannot understand the Sicilian mafia's present without understanding its past.

John Dickie is senior lecturer in Italian studies at University College, London. In 2005 the Italian government made him a Commendatore dell'ordine della stella della solidarieta italiana for his work. He lives in London with his wife and son.

D0652804

'The first truly definitive English-language study of this myth-laden subject, and it is a pleasure to read . . . notable for shrewd judgements couched in language that is vibrantly memorable. His acquaintance with the island and his immersion in the wider modern Italian culture also allow him to convey the noxious atmosphere of corruption with flair.'
The Sunday Times

'Lucid . . . grimly readable.'
Daily Telegraph

'Dogged . . . a brave work.'
Mail on Sunday

'Highly readable . . . compelling. The narrative is entertaining and, at times, as chilling as the darkest crime fiction. It combines compelling horror with clear, rational analysis.'
Glasgow Herald

'A fascinating book. *Cosa Nostra* combines scholarship with a rip-roaring read.'
Sunday Herald

'Well-written . . . convincing . . . supported by careful research and copious documentation. The book contains some powerful stories, scenes and surprises.'
Irish Times

'Reads like a novel. When I finished Dickie's book I did not know what to praise most: his care, precision and intelligence as a historian; or his agility, pace and fluidity as a narrator.'
Andrea Camilleri

'No other book on the mafia is so persuasive, so comprehensive and so readable.'
Denis Mack Smith

'Five hundred pages that you literally devour. A history book written with the skill of a ruthless thriller-writer.'
Salvatore Ferlita, *La Repubblica*

COSA NOSTRA

JOHN DICKIE

NOSTRA

A HISTORY OF THE SICILIAN MAFIA

HODDER

Copyright © 2004, 2007 by John Dickie

First published in Great Britain in 2004 by Hodder and Stoughton
A division of Hodder Headline
This edition published in 2007

The right of John Dickie to be identified as the Author of
the Work has been asserted by him in accordance with the
Copyright, Designs and Patents Act 1988.

A Hodder paperback

13

All rights reserved. No part of this publication may be
reproduced, stored in a retrieval system, or transmitted,
in any form or by any means without the prior written
permission of the publisher, nor be otherwise circulated
in any form of binding or cover other than that in which
it is published and without a similar condition being
imposed on the subsequent purchaser.

A CIP catalogue record for this title
is available from the British Library

Maps by Neil Gower

ISBN 978 0 340 93526 2
ISBN 0 340 93526 X

Set in Monotype Sabon
Typeset by Rowland Phototypesetting Ltd,
Bury St Edmunds, Suffolk

Printed and bound in the UK by
CPI Mackays, Chatham ME5 8TD

Hodder Headline's policy is to use papers that are natural, renewable and recyclable
products and made from wood grown in sustainable forests. The logging and
manufacturing processes are expected to conform to the environmental regulations of the
country of origin

Hodder and Stoughton
A division of Hodder Headline
338 Euston Road
London NW1 3BH

Contents

Prologue xiii

Introduction 1

Men of Honour 9

1 The Genesis of the Mafia 1860–1876

Sicily's Two Colours 21

Dr Galati and the Lemon Garden 26

Initiation 34

Baron Turrisi Colonna and the 'Sect' 39

The Violence Industry 47

'The So-Called Maffia': How the Mafia Got its Name 55

2 The Mafia Enters the Italian System 1876–1890

'An Instrument of Local Government' 67

The Favara Brotherhood: the Mafia in Sulphur Country 79

Primitives 87

3 Corruption in High Places 1890–1904

A New Breed of Politician 95

The Sangiorgi Report 100

The Notarbartolo Murder 128

4 Socialism, Fascism, Mafia 1893–1943

Corleone 155

The Man with Hair on His Heart 172

5 The Mafia Establishes Itself in America 1900–1941

Joe Petrosino 195

Cola Gentile's America 213

6 War and Rebirth 1943–1950

*Don Calò and the Rebirth of the
Honoured Society* 235

Meet the Grecos 254

The Last Bandit 260

7 God, Concrete, Heroin, and Cosa Nostra 1950–1963

The Early Life of Tommaso Buscetta 271

The Sack of Palermo 277

Joe Bananas Goes on Holiday 289

8 The 'First' Mafia War and its Consequences 1962–1969

The Ciaculli Bomb 305

*Like Chicago in the Twenties? The First
Mafia War* 309

The Antimafia 319

'A Phenomenon of Collective Criminality' 325

9 The Origins of the Second Mafia War 1970–1982

*Rise of the Corleonesi: 1 – Luciano Leggio
(1943–1970)* 331

Leonardo Vitale's Spiritual Crisis 340

*Death of a 'Leftist Fanatic':
Peppino Impastato* 344

Heroin: The Pizza Connection 356

Bankers, Masons, Tax Collectors, Mafiosi 362

*Rise of the Corleonesi: 2 – Towards the
Mattanza (1970–1983)* 367

10 Terra Infidelium 1983–1992

The Virtuous Minority 379
Eminent Corpses 383
Watching the Bullfight 391
The Fate of the Maxi-Trial 397

11 Bombs and Submersion 1992–2003

Totò Riina's Villa 407
After Capaci 410
'Uncle Giulio' 418
Enter the Tractor 426
The Major-Domo and the Ad Man 434

12 Ricotta Cheese and Ghosts

A Chronicle of Cosa Nostra since the
Summer of 2003 445

Acknowledgements 461
Picture Acknowledgements 464
Bibliography 465
Notes on Sources Quoted 481
Index 487

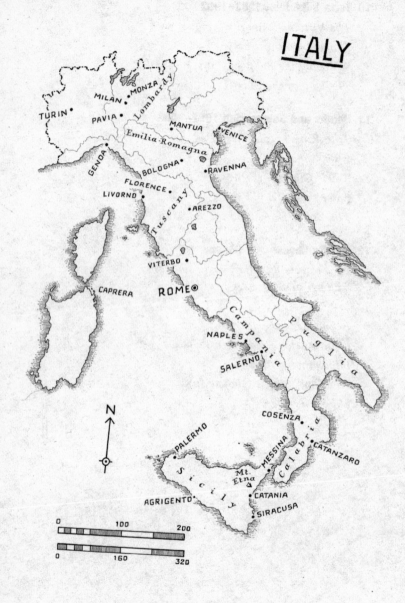

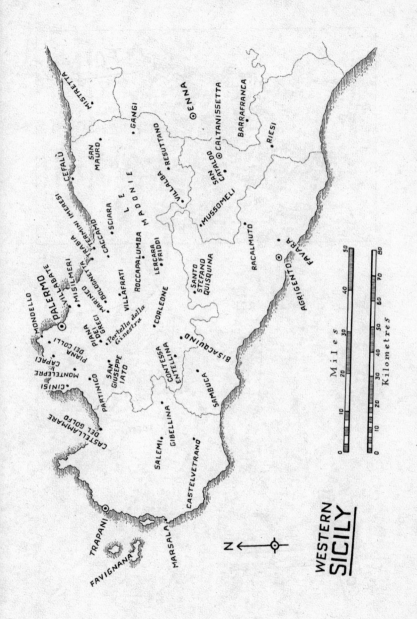

WESTERN
SICILY

N

Miles

Kilometres

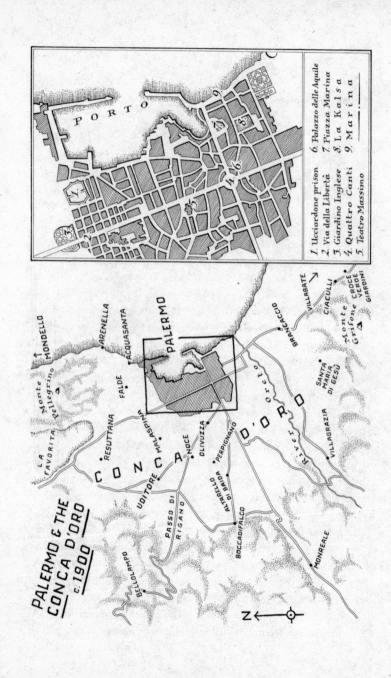

PALERMO & THE
CONCA D'ORO
c. 1900

PORTO

PALERMO

MONDELLO
Monte Pellegrino
ARENELLA
ACQUASANTA
FALDE
LA FAVORITA
RESUTTANA
UDITORE
MALASPINA
NOCE
OLIVUZZA
PERPIGNANO
ALTARELLO
DI BAIDA
PASSO DI RIGANO
BOCCADIFALCO
BELLOLAMPO
MONREALE

C O N C A   D' O R O

Riviera   Oreto

BRANCACCIO
VILLABATE
CIACULLI
Monte Grifone
CROCE VERDE
GIARDINI
SANTA MARIA DI GESÙ
VILLAGRAZIA

N

1. Ucciardone prison
2. Via della Libertà
3. Giardino Inglese
4. Quattro Canti
5. Teatro Massimo
6. Palazzo delle Aquile
7. Piazza Marina
8. La Kalsa
9. M a r i n a

As will quickly become evident, these pages inevitably refer to serious allegations relating to certain individuals. It is essential therefore that no one should read the book without keeping the following points in mind:

Mafia Families and blood families are distinct entities. The fact that one or several members of any blood family mentioned in this book are initiated into the mafia in no way entails that their relatives by birth or marriage are affiliates of the mafia, working in its interests, or are even aware that their relatives are or were affiliated. Indeed, since Cosa Nostra is a secret organization, it has a rule that its members must not tell their blood family members anything about its affairs. For the same reason, *a fortiori*, it should not be inferred that any descendants of now dead individuals about whom suspicions of complicity with the mafia are raised in this book are in any way themselves complicit.

Throughout their history, the Sicilian mafia and the American mafia have established relationships with individual business people, politicians and members of organizations such as trade unions. Equally, both the Sicilian and the American mafias have established relationships with companies, trade unions, political parties or groups within those parties. The available historical evidence strongly suggests that one of the primary characteristics of those relationships is their variety. For example, in cases in which protection money is paid to the mafia, the organizations and individuals involved may be entirely innocent victims of extortion, or willing collaborators with organized crime. Comments about such organizations and individuals in this book are in no way intended to prejudge the specific nature of single cases in this regard. Nor should it be inferred that such organizations and individuals that have, at one time, had a relationship with the mafia continue to do so. Furthermore, no inference should be drawn from what is written in this book about any organizations and individuals whose names, by pure coincidence, happen to be the same as those mentioned here.

This book, like many other studies of the mafia, identifies a broad historical pattern in which members of the mafia have tended to escape prosecution more often than would be expected. Within this broad pattern, individual cases have very varied characteristics; there are by no means always grounds for suspicion of any wrongdoing or incompetence on the part of any members of law enforcement agencies, members of the judiciary, witnesses or jurors. Accordingly no inference about any such wrongdoing or incompetence should be drawn unless explicitly stated.

Many people throughout history have denied the existence of the mafia or sought to downplay its influence. Very many of these people were speaking and acting in perfectly good faith. Similarly, many people have expressed honest, reasonable, and sometimes absolutely justified doubts about the reliability of evidence from individual mafia *pentiti* (defectors) or *pentiti* collectively. In the absence of explicit statements to the contrary in these pages, no inference should be made about a person's complicity with the mafia merely from the fact that someone is reported as denying or downplaying the existence of the mafia or expressing doubts about *pentiti* of the kind outlined.

In instances where, as related in these pages, members of the mafia met in hotels, restaurants, shops or other public places, no inference should be made that the proprietors, management or staff of the places mentioned were in any way complicit with the mafia, or aware of the meeting, of the criminal calibre of participants in the meeting, or of the criminal nature of the business conducted at the meeting.

For practical reasons it has not been possible to interview all of the people still living whose spoken words are quoted here from written sources such as interviews in books and newspapers. In each case the author has made an assumption that the words in such books and newspapers have been transcribed with accuracy and good faith.

Prologue

Two stories, two days in May, separated by a century of history. Each story – the first a melodramatic fiction, the second a tragic reality – reveals something important about the Sicilian mafia, and about why, at last, the history of the mafia can now be written.

The first story was introduced to the world at the Teatro Costanzi in Rome on 17 May 1890 at what many people believe was the most successful opera première of all time. Pietro Mascagni's *Cavalleria rusticana* ('rustic chivalry') put plangent melody at the service of a simple tale of jealousy, honour, and vengeance set among the peasants of Sicily. It was greeted with wild enthusiasm. There were thirty curtain calls; the Queen of Italy was present and apparently applauded all evening. *Cavalleria* rapidly became an international hit. A few months after that night in Rome, Mascagni wrote to a friend that his one-act opera had made him, at the age of twenty-six, rich for life.

Everyone knows at least some of the music of *Cavalleria rusticana*, and everyone recognizes its associations with Sicily. Its intermezzo is played over the famous slow-motion title sequence of *Raging Bull*, Martin Scorsese's dissection of Italian-American machismo, pride and jealousy. The opera also runs through Francis Ford Coppola's *The Godfather Part III*. In the climactic scene, a mafia killer disguised as a priest stalks his victim through the sumptuous Teatro Massimo in Palermo as *Cavalleria* is performed on stage. Don Michael Corleone's son is singing the lead tenor role of Turiddu. At the end of the film, the intermezzo makes a return to accompany the solitary death of the aged don played by Al Pacino.

What is less well known about *Cavalleria* is that its story is the purest, most anodyne form of a myth about Sicily and the mafia, a myth that was something akin to the official ideology of the Sicilian mafia for nearly a century and a half. The mafia was not an organization, it was believed, but a sense of defiant pride and honour, rooted deep in the identity of every Sicilian. The notion of 'rustic chivalry' stood square against the idea that the mafia might even have a history worthy of the name. Today, it is impossible to tell the story of the mafia without reckoning with the power of that same myth.

The second story takes us to a hill above the road that leads back towards Palermo from the city's airport. It is nearly 6 p.m. on 23 May 1992 and Giovanni Brusca, a stocky, bearded young man of honour, is watching a short stretch of motorway just before the turn-off to the small town of Capaci. At that point his men have used a skateboard to fill a drainage pipe with thirteen small barrels containing nearly 400 kilos of explosives.

A few metres behind Brusca, another, older mafioso is smoking and talking on his mobile phone. Abruptly, he breaks off and leans forward to look at the road through a telescope propped on a stool. When he sees a convoy of three cars approach the spot, he hisses, 'Vai!' ('Go on!') Nothing happens. 'Vai!' he urges again.

Brusca has noticed that the convoy is travelling more slowly than expected. He waits for brief seconds that seem interminable, even allowing the cars to pass an old fridge that he has placed by the roadside as a marker. Only when he hears a third, almost panicked 'Vai!' from behind him does he press the switch.

There is a deep, tripping drum roll of detonations. A colossal explosion tears upwards through the tarmac, hurling the first car into the air. It lands sixty or seventy metres away in a field of olive trees. The second car is a white, bulletproof Fiat Croma; its engine is blown away and the car crashes, shattered, into the deep crater. The third is damaged but intact.

The victims of the explosion were leading antimafia investigating magistrate Giovanni Falcone and his wife (in the white Fiat Croma), and three members of their escort (in the lead car). In murdering Falcone, the Sicilian mafia rid itself of its most dangerous enemy, the symbol of the fight against it.

The Capaci bomb brought Italy to a standstill. Most people remember exactly where they were when they heard the news, and in its aftermath several public figures declared themselves ashamed to be Italian. To some, the tragedy at Capaci was the supreme demonstration of the mafia's arrogance and power. Yet the attack also marked the demise of the myth crystallized in *Cavalleria rusticana*; the mafia's official ideology was now officially bankrupt. It is no coincidence that the first credible history of the mafia ever to be written in Italian was only published after Capaci.

The little love-triangle narrative that is *Cavalleria rusticana* reaches its climax in a Sicilian town square when the tough cart driver, Alfio, refuses a drink offered by a young soldier, Turiddu. No explicit accusations are exchanged, but both men know that this little slight will have deadly consequences, for Alfio has been told that Turiddu has dishonest intentions towards his wife. A whole primitive value system is compressed into their brief exchange. Both men recognize that honour has been offended, that vendetta is a right, and that a duel is the only way to settle the debt. As custom dictates, the two embrace and Turiddu grips Alfio's right ear between his teeth as a sign that the challenge has been accepted. Turiddu tearfully kisses his mother farewell and leaves the stage to meet Alfio in a nearby orchard. Then, from a distance, comes a woman's shriek, 'Turiddu has been killed!' The curtain drops as the peasants wail in dismay.

Mascagni, who was from Tuscany, had never been to Sicily when he set the *Cavalleria* story to music. In rehearsal the tenor changed the words of his opening song because the librettists, both from Mascagni's home town, had not been able to make it sound Sicilian enough. But it mattered little. Sicily – or at least a certain image of it – was in fashion in 1890. What the audience at the Teatro Costanzi expected – and got – was the picturesque island as packaged for them by their illustrated magazines: an exotic land of sun and passion inhabited by brooding, dark-skinned peasants.

In 1890, the mafia was already a murderous and sophisticated criminal association with powerful political connections and an international reach. In the Sicilian capital, Palermo, local politicians were engaged in banking and share fraud, and were stealing urban renewal funds allocated to municipal government; among them were mafiosi. Yet the widespread image of the mafia was very different. Mascagni's audience would have viewed Turiddu, and particularly the cart driver Alfio – for all the countrified pathos of their tale – not just as typical Sicilians, but as typical mafiosi. For 'mafia' was widely taken to refer not to an organization, but to a mixture of violent passion and 'Arabic' pride that supposedly dictated Sicilian behaviour. 'Mafia', as viewed by many, was a primitive notion of honour, a rudimentary code of chivalry obeyed by the backward people of the Sicilian countryside.

Nor was this just a misunderstanding propagated by supercilious northern Italians. Seven years after the staggering success of Mascagni's opera, a precocious Sicilian sociologist, Alfredo Niceforo, wrote *Contemporary Barbarian Italy*, a study of southern Italy's 'backward races'. Niceforo gave a pejorative colouring to some *Cavalleria*-style commonplaces about the Sicilian psyche: 'Sicilian man . . . eternally has rebellion and the unbounded passion of his own ego in his bloodstream – the *mafioso* in a nutshell.' Niceforo, *Cavalleria rusticana*, and much of Italian culture at that time systematically confuse Sicilians and the mafia. Since then, generations of observers, whether Sicilians, Italians, or foreigners, have made the same mistake, blurring any clear distinction between the mafia and what one English travel writer of the 1960s called the 'primeval mentality' of the 'Sicilian subconscious'.

Sicilian culture was for too long confused with *mafiosità* ('mafia-ness'), and that confusion served the interests of organized crime. Needless to say, it was a great help to the illegal organization known as the mafia when people thought it did not exist. 'There is no secret criminal society,' the argument went; 'that is just a conspiracy theory dreamed up by people who do not understand the way Sicilians think.' Countless writers have rehashed the same misguided argument: that centuries of invasion have made Sicilians suspicious of outsiders, and so they naturally prefer to settle disputes among themselves without involving the police or the courts.

Smudging the line between the mafia and Sicilians could also make legal measures against the mob look futile. If the supposedly primitive Sicilian mentality was to blame, how could the mafia be prosecuted, short of putting the whole island in the dock? 'Tutti colpevoli, nessuno colpevole,' as the Italian saying has it: 'If everyone is guilty, no one is guilty.'

The mafia had great success in peddling this family of falsehoods for a century and a half. The most insidious effect was simply to create muddle and doubt. As a result the existence of the mafia remained no more than a suspicion, a theory, a point of view – until surprisingly recently. And the notion of writing a history of the 'mafia mentality' often seemed pointless, hardly more worthwhile than writing a history of Gallic flair or the British stiff upper lip.

We owe it to Falcone and his colleagues if the myth of rustic chivalry has now, at last, been dispelled. The story of the Capaci bomb began in the early 1980s when, in less than two years, as many as 1,000 people were murdered – men of honour, their relatives and friends, police, and innocent bystanders. People were shot down in the street, or taken to secret locations to be strangled; their bodies were dissolved in acid, buried in concrete, dumped in the sea, or cut up and fed to the pigs. This was the bloodiest mafia conflict in history, but it was not a war; it was a campaign of extermination. The perpetrators were an alliance of mafiosi grouped around the leadership of the Corleone mafia. They were using secret death squads to hunt down their enemies and establish a well-nigh dictatorial power over the mafia across Sicily.

Among the victims of the slaughter were two sons, a brother, a nephew, a brother-in-law, and a son-in-law of a well-connected man of honour, Tommaso Buscetta. The papers dubbed him the 'boss of two worlds' because of his interests on both sides of the Atlantic. When the Corleonesi mounted their assault, neither of his worlds was safe for him any more. Buscetta was arrested in Brazil. When he was extradited to Italy, he tried to commit suicide by swallowing the strychnine he always kept with him. He survived the attempt – just. On recovering, Buscetta decided to tell what he knew about the secret society into which he had been initiated when he was seventeen. And it was to Giovanni Falcone, and to him alone, that he wanted to speak.

Falcone was the bright son of a middle-class family from the then crumbling la Kalsa area of central Palermo. He once said that he had breathed in the smell of mafia since he was a boy. At the local Catholic youth club he played table tennis with Tommaso Spadaro, later to become a notorious mafioso and heroin trafficker. Falcone's family insulated him from these influences, bringing him up under a code of duty, church, and patriotism.

Falcone's early career as an investigating magistrate was in the bankruptcy court, where he developed his skills in hunting down obscure financial records. These skills became the first ingredient in what came to be known as the 'Falcone method' of mafia investigation. It was first applied to a big heroin smuggling case in 1980 after Falcone was transferred to the criminal investigative office in Palermo. In 1982, Falcone secured seventy-four convictions in the heroin case: a prodigious success on an island where the terrorizing of witnesses, judges, and juries had caused the failure of innumerable previous prosecutions.

Buscetta provided Falcone for the first time with access to the Sicilian mafia from the inside. 'For us he was like a language professor who allows you to go to Turkey without having to communicate with your hands,' said Falcone. In many hours of interviews with Buscetta, Falcone and his team developed their understanding of the organization, and patiently mapped the connections between faces, names, and crimes. They assembled a completely new picture of its command structure, methods, and mindset.

It is hard now to realize how much was *not* known about the mafia before Tommaso Buscetta sat down with Giovanni Falcone. The first revelation was the name given to the organization by its members: Cosa Nostra – 'our thing'. Until then, even the few investigators and police who had taken this name seriously had assumed that it only applied to the American mob.

Buscetta also told Falcone about Cosa Nostra's pyramidal command structure. The soldiers at the lowest level are supervised in groups of ten or so by a *capodecina* (head of ten). Each *capodecina* reports upwards to the elected boss of a local gang or 'Family', who is flanked by a deputy and one or more *consiglieri* (advisers). Three families with adjoining territories are organized into a *mandamento* (district). The head of each *mandamento* is a member of the Commission, Cosa Nostra's parliament or board of management for the province of Palermo. In theory, above this provincial level there is a regional body made up of mafia bosses from the whole of Sicily. But in practice Palermo dominates the Sicilian mafia: nearly 50 per cent of the approximately 100 Families in Sicily have their territory in Palermo and its province, and the boss of the Palermo Commission has a leadership role within the Sicilian mafia as a whole.

At the time of Buscetta's revelations, some 5,000 men of honour were members of a single criminal organization. Significant murders – of policemen, politicians, or other mafiosi – had to be approved and planned at the highest level to make sure that they were compatible with the organization's overall strategy. With the aim of creating stability, the Commission also issued rulings on disputes within the families and *mandamenti* over which it presided. This level of internal discipline astonished investigators.

'The boss of two worlds' also knew the American Cosa Nostra well. He told Falcone that the Sicilian mafia, and the American mafia to which it had given birth, had a similar structure. But they were separate organizations; being a member in Sicily did not mean that you also became a member in the US. The strong links between the two were blood and business ties rather than organizational ones.

Other men of honour followed Buscetta's example as they turned to the state for protection from the Corleonesi and their death squads. Together with his close colleague Paolo Borsellino, Falcone meticulously checked their testimonies and assembled 8,607 pages of evidence – the prosecution case for the famous 'maxi-trial', which was held in a specially built bombproof bunker courthouse in Palermo.

On 16 December 1987, after proceedings lasting twenty-two months, the judge in the maxi-trial handed down guilty verdicts on 342 mafiosi and sentenced them to a total of 2,665 years in prison. Just as importantly, what sceptics had dismissed as the 'Buscetta theorem' on the structure of Cosa Nostra had withstood a stiff judicial examination.

Final legal confirmation of the Buscetta theorem had to wait until January 1992 when, contrary to Cosa Nostra's hopes and expectations, the Court of Cassation – Italy's Supreme Court – set a seal on the initial verdicts. It was the worst legal defeat the Sicilian mafia had ever suffered. In response, the Corleonesi put their death squads on the trail of the investigating magistrates. Falcone was murdered within a few months of the verdict. Less than two months after Falcone's death, disbelief and indignation swept across Italy once more when Paolo Borsellino and five members of his escort were killed by a massive car bomb outside his mother's house.

The tragic deaths of Falcone and Borsellino had profound effects that are still unfolding today. The first of those effects was simply to reinforce the fact that the antimafia magistrates had won a momentous victory; the existence of a centralized criminal organization called Cosa Nostra is no longer just a theory.

If Cosa Nostra exists, then it has a history; and if it has a history then, as Falcone often said, it had a beginning and it will have an end. Because of the work of Falcone, Borsellino, and their colleagues, as well as the collapse of the cluster of untruths surrounding the notion of 'rustic chivalry', historians can now research the history of the mafia with more confidence and insight than has ever been the case.

As the reality about Cosa Nostra emerged through Buscetta's testimony and the maxi-trial, a few historians, most of them Sicilians, took their cue from the investigating magistrates: they began to look back at neglected records and unearth new evidence. A whole field of study was slowly opening up. Then, in 1992, when the Court of Cassation's verdict confirmed the Buscetta theorem – and in so doing triggered the murders of Falcone and Borsellino – writing the history of the mafia suddenly became far more than an academic pursuit: it was now part of an urgent imperative to understand a deadly threat to society, and to show the remaining antimafia magistrates that they were not alone in their struggle.

A pioneering history of the Sicilian mafia was published in Italian the following year. It was updated in 1996, and further discoveries have been made since then. The drive to tell the mafia's story has progressed in tandem with the drive to combat Cosa Nostra in the wake of the atrocities of 1992. In Sicily, history counts.

It may also count for something if the history of the mafia is told to the world beyond Italy. While Falcone's epic confrontation with Cosa Nostra in the 1980s became the subject of some superb accounts in English, the totally new perspective on the mafia's history that Falcone opened up remains almost totally unknown. This book is the first history of the Sicilian mafia, from its origins to the present day, to be written in any language other than Italian. It presents the findings of the latest research and tells the story of the mafia as the Italian specialists now tell it. It also contains some completely new findings. What has emerged in the last few years is a much fuller historical description of the Sicilian mafia than was thought possible even a short time ago. A picture that used to be drawn in the fuzzy lines of sociological jargon – 'mentalities', 'para-state functions', 'violent mediators' – now contains real people, places, dates, and crimes. And the clearer the picture becomes, the more disturbing are its implications: a secret society that has murder as its very *raison d'être* has been an integral part of the way Italy has been run since the middle of the nineteenth century.

Introduction

'Mafia' is now one of a long list of words – like 'pizza', 'spa-ghetti', 'opera', and 'disaster' – that Italian has given to many other languages across the world. It is commonly applied to criminals far beyond Sicily and the United States, which are the places where the mafia in the strict sense is based. 'Mafia' has become an umbrella label for a whole world panoply of gangs – Chinese, Japanese, Russian, Chechen, Albanian, Turkish, and so on – that have little or nothing to do with the Sicilian original.

There are other criminal associations based in other regions of southern Italy, and all of them are sometimes called 'mafia': the Sacra Corona Unita, in Puglia (the heel of the Italian boot); the 'Ndrangheta, in Calabria (the toe); and the Camorra, in the city of Naples and its environs (located on the shin). These other associations all have a fascinating history of their own – one of them, the Camorra, is a little older than the mafia – but they will only be touched on here when relevant to the history of the Sicilian Cosa Nostra. The reason is simply that no other Italian illegal society is nearly as powerful, as well organized, or as successful as the mafia. It is not by chance that it is this Sicilian word that has become the most widely used.

This book is selective in that it is a history of the mafia of Sicily. Some of the most famous American mafiosi, men like Lucky Luciano and Al Capone, also people these pages because the history of the Sicilian mafia cannot be told without also telling the story of the American mafia to which it gave birth. The United States has been a thriving environment for organized criminals over the past two centuries, but only a part of organized crime in the US has been mafia crime. Accordingly, the American mafia is here placed in its proper and most illuminating perspective. It is only when viewed from the coast of a small, triangular island in the Mediterranean that the history of the mafia in the USA, at least in its early stages, can begin to make sense.

The mafia of Sicily pursues power and money by cultivating the art of killing people and getting away with it, and by organizing itself in a unique way that combines the attributes of a shadow state, an illegal business, and a sworn secret society like the Freemasons.

Cosa Nostra is like a state because it aims to control territory. With the agreement of the mafia as a whole, each mafia Family (the Italian word used through much of the mafia's history is *cosca*) exercises a shadow government over the people within its territory. Protection rackets are for a mafia Family what taxes are for a legal government. There is a difference, in that the mafia tries to 'tax' all economic activity, whether it is legal or illegal: retailers and robbers alike pay what is known as the *pizzo*. A mafioso may well end up protecting both the owner of a car showroom and the gang of car thieves who prey on him. So the only party absolutely guaranteed to benefit from any given protection deal is the mafia. Like a state, the mafia also arrogates to itself the power of life and death over its subjects. But the mafia is not an alternative government; it exists by infiltrating the legal state and twisting it to its own purposes.

Cosa Nostra is a business because it tries to make a profit – albeit by intimidation. But it rarely clears large margins from its 'governmental' activities. Most of the income from protection rackets tends to get ploughed back into maintaining its murder capability: it buys lawyers, judges, policemen, journalists, politicians, and casual labour, and it supports mafiosi unlucky enough to end up in prison. Cosa Nostra pays these overheads in order to build what some 'mafiologists' think of as a brand of intimidation. The mafia brand can be deployed in all sorts of markets, like construction fraud or tobacco smuggling. As a general rule, the more treacherous, violent, and profitable a market is – the obvious case is narcotics trafficking and dealing

– the more mafiosi who enter that market benefit from having a world-renowned and utterly reliable brand of blood-curdling intimidation behind them.

Cosa Nostra is an exclusive secret society because it needs to select its affiliates very carefully and impose restrictions on their behaviour in return for the benefits of membership. The chief demands that Cosa Nostra makes of its members are that they be discreet, obedient, and ruthlessly violent.

The history of this organization is fascinating in its own right. But the history of the mafia cannot *just* be about the mafia, about the deeds of men of honour. Before Falcone and Borsellino, a great many other people died fighting the mafia. Some of them are characters in the drama recounted here, because an integral part of the story of the mafia is the tale of its struggle with the Sicilians and others who have opposed it from the outset. The mafia's story also embraces the people who, for an assortment of motives ranging from rational fear, through political cynicism, to downright complicity, have favoured the organization's cause.

But even a history of the mafia that included all these things would still leave many questions unanswered. Because everyone outside Italy knows what the mafia is, or at least thinks they do, it still seems baffling that it took until 1992 for the full truth about the Sicilian mafia to be confirmed. How could an illegal organization remain so powerful and so difficult to understand for so long? Part of the explanation was a lack of evidence. The mafia survived and prospered because it intimidated witnesses, and confounded or corrupted the police and courts. All too often in the past, the authorities (and so, after them, the historians) were left to count the dead bodies and wonder what strange logic underlay all the bloodshed.

The problem was even more deep-seated; indeed, it went to the heart of the Italian system of government. At the very least, the Italian state has been extremely absent-minded about the Sicilian mafia over the past century and more. On the few occasions when an understanding of the mafia penetrated government institutions, it was swiftly forgotten. And even when it was remembered for a while, it was not put to good use. Italy repeatedly missed opportunities to grasp some of the truths that judges Falcone and Borsellino finally paid with their lives to prove. The mafia was a secret hidden in plain view. For that reason, Italy's recurring failure to understand the mafia makes for a much richer story than would be the case if it were all down to some cloak-and-dagger conspiracy by a few individuals bent on keeping the truth concealed. For that reason too, as well as being a history of the mafia, this book is a history of Italy's failure to comprehend and combat what was visible all the while.

There are plenty of contemporary examples that suggest that Italy's deeply rooted mafia problem is still very much alive. At the time of writing, the seven-times Prime Minister of Italy, Life Senator Giulio Andreotti, has been convicted for arranging to have the mafia murder a journalist who was blackmailing him. (Supergrass Tommaso Buscetta, the former 'boss of two worlds', was a key witness.) Andreotti has lodged an appeal to the Court of Cassation. Another high-profile mafia case involves the advertising executive who in 1993 founded Forza Italia, the political party of the current Prime Minister, media tycoon Silvio Berlusconi. A recent mafia defector has alleged that there were high-level meetings to seal a pact between Cosa Nostra and Forza Italia. The allegations are strongly denied and one should not rush to draw conclusions about these individual trials, none of which has yet reached a definitive verdict. But as well as raising eyebrows, they also raise historical questions about how Italy managed to get itself into such a predicament.

The historians who first attempted to answer those questions in the wake of Buscetta's evidence quickly made a remarkable find that only deepened the mystery of why Italy had failed properly to understand the mafia before. Buscetta was, in fact, far from the first man of honour to break the mafia's famous code of silence known as *omertà*; he was not even the first to be believed when he did so. There have been mafia informants for almost as long as there have been mafiosi. In addition, there existed from the outset a furtive and often intimate dialogue between men of honour and the powers that be – police, magistrates, politicians. Historians can now eavesdrop on passages of that dialogue; it makes for fascinating and uneasy listening because it reveals the extent of the Italian state's complicity with murderers.

Even after the discovery of these earlier mafia defectors, there remained the profound problem of how to interpret what they said; police and magistrates had wrestled with this from the beginning of the mafia's history, right up to Falcone's and Borsellino's maxi-trial. Why should anyone believe professional criminals who have any number of reasons to lie? The evidence of mafia informers was often dismissed as simply not reliable enough to be used in court – or in a history book. The testimonies of men of honour, even of *pentiti*, are always hard to read. In fact the word *pentito* is deceptive: true repentance in a man of honour is comparatively rare. Throughout the association's history, members of the mafia have generally given their testimonies to the state as a way of getting back at other mafiosi who have betrayed them and defeated them in a war. Confessions turn up when the losers have no other weapons left. Buscetta was a loser and, like other *pentiti*, his testimony is skewed in parts as a consequence.

Yet there is something else about Buscetta's evidence, something that made it more than just a subjective version of events, and turned it instead into the Rosetta Stone of mafia testimonies. Buscetta explained exactly how men of honour *think* because he set out both the strange rules that they follow and the reasons why they often break them. The 'boss of two worlds' himself still felt the power of these rules and always denied that he had become a *pentito* instead of a man of honour. Buscetta's great lesson to magistrates and historians alike is that the mafia's rules need to be taken seriously – which is by no means the same thing as assuming that they are always obeyed.

Tommaso Buscetta never ceased to stress the importance of one particular rule within Cosa Nostra. It relates to truth.

Thanks to Buscetta we now know that the truth is a peculiarly precious and dangerous commodity for mafiosi. When a man of honour is initiated into the Sicilian mafia, one of the things he swears is never to lie to other 'made men', whether or not they are from the same Family. Thereafter, any man of honour who tells a lie can easily find that he has taken a short cut to the acid bath. Yet at the same time, a well-disguised lie can also be a very powerful weapon in the permanent struggle for power within Cosa Nostra. The upshot is simple: acute paranoia. As Buscetta explained, 'A *mafioso* lives in terror of being judged – not by the laws of men, but by the malicious gossip internal to Cosa Nostra. The fear that someone could be speaking ill of him is constant.'

In the circumstances, it is not surprising to learn that all men of honour are prodigiously good at keeping their mouths shut. Before turning state's evidence, Buscetta once spent three years in the same prison cell as a man of honour who had recently carried out an order to kill a third mafioso – a close friend of Buscetta's. Throughout those three years the two enemies did not exchange a single hostile word, and even shared Christmas dinner. Buscetta knew that his cellmate had already been condemned to death by Cosa Nostra; it is not known whether the cellmate was also aware that he had been marked down for execution. He was duly murdered on his release.

Men of honour prefer not to say anything to anyone who does not already know what they are talking about; they communicate in codes, hints, fragments of phrases, stony stares, significant silences. In Cosa Nostra, no one asks or says more than they absolutely have to; nobody ever wonders out loud. Judge Falcone observed that 'the interpretation of signs, gestures, messages and silences is one of a man of honour's main activities'. Buscetta was particularly eloquent in explaining what it feels like to live in such a world:

In Cosa Nostra there is an obligation to tell the truth, but there is also great reserve. And this reserve, the things that are not said, rule like an irrevocable curse over all men of honour. It makes all relationships profoundly false, absurd.

For the same reason that they are so reluctant to speak openly, when men of honour do tell each other things, what they say is never idle chat. For example, if mafioso A tells mafioso B that he has murdered entrepreneur X or that politician Y is on Cosa Nostra's paybook, what he says is probably true; if it is not, then it is a tactical lie that, in its own way, is every bit as significant as the truth. Thus, since Buscetta, mafiosi have no longer been viewed as inherently unreliable witnesses. Interpreting the testimonies of mafiosi, whether they have 'repented' or not, is now seen to be about making out a pattern among the truths and the tactical lies, and finding other evidence to corroborate that pattern. This has important consequences for the history of the mafia. It is a history built from all the usual sources – from police files, government inquiries, newspaper reports, memoirs, confessions, and so on. But running like a blood-tinged watermark through many of those documents, whether they directly reproduce the words of men of honour or only contain their faded traces, are the signs of the deadly truth game that is life within the mafia.

Because an element of uncertainty is bound to remain in any history, let alone a history that ventures into the devious world of the Sicilian mafia, this book cannot give the final word on the guilt or innocence of the characters whose stories appear here; the history of the mafia is not a retrospective trial. But it is not mere guesswork either. Although it would be both wrong and futile to try to lock long-dead historical figures in an imaginary prison, what we can do is sample the pungent 'smell of mafia' – as the Italian phrase would have it – that they still give off.

The history of the mafia thus has many characters and many layers. Accordingly, the different chapters of this book tell different kinds of story. They move between the soldiers and the bosses, but they also step into the mafia's penumbra to tell of its victims, enemies, and friends – from the poorest in society to the most powerful. In one or two of these chapters, because of a lack of historical evidence, the mafia must remain what it often seemed to be at the time: a malevolent, spectral presence.

Before telling of the mafia's genesis, this history gives an account of what life is like inside Cosa Nostra today, with the code of honour obeyed by the men who are members of it. Recent defectors have provided an insight into how mafiosi think and feel now, which is simply not possible for earlier periods. And of course it would be simplistic to use what we know about things like the code of honour today to fill in the inevitable blind spots in the mafia's history. All the same, as the mafia's story unfolds, what becomes clear is that Sicily's famous criminal association has changed surprisingly little since it began around 140 years ago. There never was a good mafia that at some point became corrupt and violent. There never was a traditional mafia that then became modern, organized, and business-minded. The world has changed but the Sicilian mafia has merely adapted; it is today what it has been since it was born: a sworn secret society that pursues power and money by cultivating the art of killing people and getting away with it.

Men of Honour

Countless films and novels have helped lend a sinister glamour to the mafia. These mafia stories are so compelling because they dramatize the everyday by adding the hair-trigger thrill that comes when danger is mixed with unscrupulous cunning. The world of the cinematic mafia is one where the conflicts that everyone feels – between the competing claims of ambition, responsibility, and family – become matters of life and death.

It would be both pious and untrue to say that the mafia presented in fiction is simply false – it is stylized. And mafiosi are like everyone else in that they like to watch television and go to the cinema to see a stylized version of their own daily dramas represented on-screen. Tommaso Buscetta was a fan of *The Godfather*, although he thought the scene at the end where the other mafiosi kiss Michael Corleone's hand was unrealistic. The conflicting demands that lie behind the motivation of a fictional character like Al Pacino's Michael Corleone – ambition, responsibility, family – are indeed the same ones that are central to the lives of real mafiosi.

One obvious thing that *is* different is that none of the glamour of the cinema can survive an encounter with the horrific reality of Cosa Nostra. A less obvious, but in the end more important, difference is that whereas Michael Corleone's story is about the moral dangers of unchecked power, real Sicilian mafiosi are obsessed with the rules of honour that limit their actions. A man of honour may dodge, manipulate, and rewrite those rules, but he is nonetheless always aware that they shape how he is perceived by his peers. That is not to say that the values of mafia honour have much that is conventionally 'honourable' about them. Honour has a specific meaning within Cosa Nostra that informs even its members' most execrable actions, as the unsettling case of Giovanni Brusca, the man who pressed the detonator on the Capaci bomb, goes to show.

Brusca was known in Cosa Nostra circles as 'lo scannacristiani', 'the man who cuts Christians' throats'. In Sicily, 'a Christian' means 'a human being'; in the mafia, it means 'a man of honour'. Brusca was part of a death squad reporting directly to the boss of bosses, the leader of the Corleonesi, Totò 'Shorty' Riina. After the Capaci bombing Giovanni Brusca was not idle. He killed the boss of the Alcamo Family who had begun to resent Riina's authority. A few days after that, members of Brusca's team strangled the same man's pregnant partner. Brusca then killed a spectacularly wealthy businessman and man of honour who had failed to use his political contacts to protect the mafia from the maxi-trial.

Worse followed. 'Lo scannacristiani' was the friend of another man of honour, Santino Di Matteo, whose little son Giuseppe would play with Brusca in the family garden. That was all before Santino Di Matteo decided to betray Cosa Nostra's secrets to the state; he was the first mafioso to tell the authorities how the killing of Falcone had been carried out. Brusca's response was to kidnap little Giuseppe Di Matteo at a gymkhana and hold him captive in a cellar for twenty-six months. Finally, in January 1996, when Giuseppe was fourteen, Brusca ordered him to be strangled and his body dissolved in acid.

'Lo scannacristiani' was captured on 20 May 1996 in the countryside near Agrigento. Four hundred police surrounded the box-like two-storey house where he was hiding. At about 9 p.m., a team of thirty broke in through the doors and windows. They found Brusca and his family at table watching a television programme about Giovanni Falcone – the fourth anniversary of his murder was only two days away. In the bedroom police discovered a wardrobe full of Versace and Armani clothes, and a big red bag containing some $15,000 in Italian and US currency, two GSM cellphones, and jewellery including Cartier watches. On the dining-room table they found a short-barrelled pistol; it was made of plastic and belonged to Brusca's young son Davide.

Brusca is now collaborating with justice. By his own disturbingly imprecise confession, he has killed 'many more than one hundred but less than two hundred people'. Here is what he says about the murder of Giuseppe Di Matteo:

If I'd had a moment longer to reflect, a bit more calm to think, as I did with other crimes, then maybe there would be a hope in a thousand, a million, that the child would be alive today. But today it would be useless to try and justify it. I just didn't think it through at the time.

The terrifying thing about the Sicilian mafia is that men like 'lo scannacristiani' are not deranged. Nor are their actions at all incompatible with the code of honour or, indeed, with being a husband and father in Cosa Nostra's view. Until the day he decided to turn state's evidence and tell his story, nothing that Brusca did, including murdering a child not much older than his own, was considered by mafiosi to be inherently dishonourable.

In the wake of the Capaci bomb, more mafiosi turned state's evidence, and some of these 'penitents' justified their decision by saying that killers like 'lo scannacristiani' had betrayed traditional values, the code of honour. Tommaso Buscetta had used the same argument, along the lines of 'I did not leave Cosa Nostra, Cosa Nostra left me'. But this is a flimsy claim, historically speaking, because within the mafia betrayal and brutality have been compatible with honour since the beginning. Giovanni Brusca is more typical than some mafia defectors would have the world believe.

This new post-Capaci wave of *pentiti* has allowed researchers to flesh out the evidence about the mafia's internal culture that had been provided by the earlier generation of defectors, including Buscetta. What is now clear is that the code of honour is much more than a list of rules. Becoming a man of honour means taking on a whole new identity, entering a different moral universe. A mafioso's honour is the mark of that new identity, that new moral sensibility.

Tommaso Buscetta first outlined Cosa Nostra's code of honour to Falcone back in 1984. He told of its initiation rite in which the candidate for membership holds a burning picture – usually of the Madonna of the Annunciation – while swearing allegiance and silence until death. Rumours of this quaint ritual had previously been dismissed as folklore, and it is still a part of Buscetta's evidence that seems to run counter to common sense. Yet it has become abundantly clear from the testimonies of Buscetta, 'lo scannacristiani', and others that mafiosi take such things in deadly earnest, as matters of honour.

The initiation ritual shows that honour is a status that has to be earned. Until he becomes a man of honour, an aspiring mafioso is carefully watched, supervised, put to the test; committing murder is almost always a prerequisite for admission. During this period of preparation, he is constantly reminded that until he goes through the ritual of affiliation he is a nonentity, 'nothing mixed with nil'. And when initiation arrives, it is often the most important moment in a mafioso's life. The burning of the sacred image symbolizes his death as an ordinary man and his rebirth as a man of honour.

At initiation, the new mafioso swears obedience – the first pillar of the code of honour. A 'made' man is always obedient to his capo; he never asks, 'Why?' One way to understand the implications of this obligation involves what is also a crucial test case for the code of honour as a whole: the murder of women and children. This has always been something of a delicate issue for the Sicilian mafia; indeed, mafiosi have frequently made the claim that they never touch women and children. It has to be said that many men of honour hold to that principle for as long as they can. Cosa Nostra certainly does not murder babies willy-nilly, not least because to do so would damage its image and alienate some of its closest supporters.

Yet Giuseppe Di Matteo was far from being the first child whose life had been very deliberately ended by men of honour. For eliminating women and children is only deemed dishonourable if it is unnecessary; it can become necessary when a mafioso's survival is at stake; and simply by being a member of Cosa Nostra, a mafioso often puts his life in danger.

Like nearly all mafia killings, the murder of Giuseppe Di Matteo was committed after it was collectively decided that it was necessary. The boy's death was part of a strategy adopted by some of Cosa Nostra's leaders vis-à-vis the families of mafia defectors who were putting the whole organization at risk. Once such a decision became policy, it would have been considered dishonourable not to put it into effect.

Which is where obedience comes in. The mafioso who actually implemented that policy and strangled Giuseppe Di Matteo on Brusca's orders later explained his thinking to a court:

If someone wants to have a good career [in Cosa Nostra] he must always be available . . . I wanted a career, and I'd accepted this from the outset because I was walking on air. At that time I was a soldier in Cosa Nostra, I obeyed orders, and I knew that by strangling a little boy I would make a career for myself. I was walking on air.

Honour accumulates through obedience: in return for what they call 'availability', individual mafiosi can increase their stock of honour and in doing so gain access to more money, information, and power. Belonging to Cosa Nostra offers the same advantages as does belonging to other organizations, including the achievement of aspirations, an exhilarating sense of status and comradeship, and the chance to pass responsibility, moral or otherwise, upwards in the direction of their bosses. All of these things are ingredients of mafia honour.

Honour also involves the obligation to tell the truth to other men of honour and, therefore, the notoriously elliptical way in which mafiosi talk. Giovanni Brusca relates that, when he visited American mafiosi in New Jersey, he was appalled by how talkative his hosts were by comparison. A dinner was held to welcome him, yet on entering the restaurant Brusca was astonished to see that the mafiosi had all brought their mistresses, and that they chatted openly about which Families various mobsters belonged to. 'In Sicily, none of us would dream of talking that way in public. Or even in private. Everyone knows what needs to be known.' Brusca claims he was so embarrassed that he made his excuses and left. 'It's a different mentality,' he concluded about his American experience. 'They live out in the light of day. They only commit murders in exceptional circumstances. They never carry out massacres like we have in Sicily.'

The mafioso's duty to tell the truth is partly a way of promoting the kind of mutual trust that is in short supply among outlaws. This need for trust also explains the components of mafia honour that relate to sex and marriage. Newly 'made' mobsters swear not to take income from prostitution, and if they sleep with another mafioso's wife they face a death sentence. Moreover, if a mafioso gambles, womanizes, and parades his wealth, he is likely to be considered unreliable and therefore expendable. Keeping to these rules is an important way of showing your fellow men of honour that you can be trusted. For the same reason, the mafia's top management makes a virtue of getting its hands dirty, and old-school patriarchal machismo is crucial to the company culture. For example, there are work social events that usually revolve around manly pursuits like hunting parties and banquets.

Honour is also about loyalty. Membership of what mafiosi used to call the 'honoured society' brings new loyalties that are more important than blood ties. Honour implies that a mafioso must put Cosa Nostra's interests above those of his kin. Enzo Brusca, brother of 'lo scannacristiani', worked for the organization, took part in killings, but was never made into a man of honour. As was appropriate, he did not ask questions. What he knew about his relatives in Cosa Nostra he gleaned from hearsay, and from the media; thus he was unaware for a long time that his father was boss of the local *mandamento* (district). So although Enzo Brusca was part of the mafia's operations and was a member of the same *family* as men of honour, this did not entitle him to know about *Family* business.

The reverse is not true, in the sense that a mafia boss has an absolute right to keep watch over the personal lives of his men.

For example, a mafioso will often have to ask his capo's permission to marry. It is crucial that individual mafiosi make a sensible choice of marital partner and behave honourably within marriage. Mafiosi have an even greater need than other husbands to keep their spouses sweet, simply because a disgruntled mafia wife could do extensive damage to the whole Family by talking to the police. Members of Cosa Nostra have to be careful to preserve their women's prestige; a major reason for the taboo against pimping is to ensure that the wives of men of honour, as Judge Falcone explained, 'are not humiliated in their own social environment'. Mafiosi often marry the sisters and daughters of other men of honour, women who have lived in a mafia environment all their lives and are therefore more likely to have the kind of discretion and/or submissiveness that the organization requires of them. Women may also actively support the work of their men, albeit in a subordinate role. Women cannot formally be admitted to the mafia and honour is exclusively a male quality. Nevertheless a mafioso's honour brings prestige to his spouse, and his spouse's good behaviour feeds back into his stock of honour.

Judge Falcone once compared entering the mafia to being a convert to a religion: 'You never stop being a priest. Or a mafioso.' The parallels between religion and the mafia do not end there, largely because many men of honour are believers. Catania boss Nitto Santapaola had an altar and a little chapel constructed in his villa; according to one *pentito*, he also once had four kids garrotted and thrown in a well for mugging his mother. The current boss of bosses, Bernardo 'the Tractor' Provenzano, communicates from his place in hiding by little notes, some of which have recently been intercepted; they always contain blessings and invocations of divine protection – 'By the will of God I want to be a servant'. One senior boss who led a death squad like 'lo scannacristiani' would pray before every action: 'God knows that it is they who want to get themselves killed, and that I carry no blame.'

Sentiments like these are partly a result of the tolerance towards the mafia that was displayed for a long time by the Catholic Church. Clergymen have often treated men whose power is based on routine murder as if they were sinners of the same ilk as everyone else. They have overlooked the evil influence of the mafia because it seems to share the same values of deference, humility, tradition, and family as the Church. They have accepted donations drawn from criminal wealth for processions and charity. They have been content to see *cosche* (plural of *cosca*) disguise themselves as religious confraternities, and to entrust the administration of charity funds to dignitaries with blood on their hands. Some churchmen have even been killers. The story of the Church's relationship with the mafia is filled with episodes like these.

But the point is not, as some would wish to claim, that the mafia is little more than a branch of the Catholic Church. A mafioso's religion has nothing to do with the Church as an institution. In fact, the secret of mafia religion is that it serves the same purposes as the code of honour; it merely expresses the same things in a different language. Mafia religion generates a sense of belonging, trust, and a set of flexible rules by borrowing words from the Catholic creed, just as the code of honour does so by aping the chivalric terms that were still used by the nobility when the mafia began.

Like mafia honour, mafia religion helps mafiosi justify their actions – to themselves, to each other, and to their families. Mafiosi often like to think that they are killing in the name of something higher than money and power, and the two names they usually come up with are 'honour' and 'God'. Indeed, the religion professed by mafiosi and their families is like so much else in the moral universe of mafia honour, in that it is difficult to tell where genuine – if misguided – belief ends, and cynical deceit begins. Understanding how the mafia thinks means understanding that the rules of honour mesh with calculated deceit and heartless savagery in the mind of every member.

So 'honour' translates as a sense of professional worth, a value system, and a totem of group identity for an association that regards itself as being beyond good and evil. As such, it has nothing to do with Sicilian traditions, or chivalry, or Catholicism. Whether it is expressed in religious terms, or in the pseudo-aristocratic language of 'honour', the code is there to ensure that every aspect of a mafioso's life is completely subordinated to the interests of 'our thing'.

When it is working well, the code produces a proud sense of fellowship. Catania mafioso Antonino Calderone spoke for the whole organization when he said, 'We're mafiosi, all the others are just men.' But for that very reason a mafioso without honour is no one; he is a dead man. For a member of Cosa Nostra, being defeated in one of the organization's internecine wars and losing honour can amount to exactly the same thing.

It is no wonder, then, that the decision to break the code of honour and turn state's evidence is traumatic for some mafiosi. It means abandoning both an identity and a dense fabric of friendships and family ties; it means trying to find a way of coming to terms with a life built on murder; it means incurring an automatic death sentence. Giovanni Brusca maintains that it took more courage for him to turn state's evidence than it did to kill.

Nino Gioè was the mafioso who shouted 'Vai!' to Brusca when he pressed the detonator on the Capaci bomb. Soon after being captured and placed in solitary confinement in the summer of 1993, Gioè began to feel the accumulated pressure of long years lived by Cosa Nostra's rules. He knew that some of his conversations had been bugged by the police, and that he had probably given away evidence that would count heavily against other men of honour; unwittingly, he had broken the most sacred of Cosa Nostra's tenets. He sensed the suspicion growing among the mafiosi held in cells on the same wing. As the pressure mounted, it began to show – he let his beard grow and neglected to clean his clothes. Men of honour are expected to maintain the dignity of their bearing in prison, so the decline in his appearance only increased the fears of those around him that he was about to break and tell what he knew to the state. Instead, on 28 July 1993, he used the laces of his tennis shoes to hang himself in his cell. Although it is very rare for men of honour to end their own lives, Gioè's suicide note can serve as the final word on what it means to live and die by the code of honour:

This evening I will find the peace and serenity that I lost some seventeen years ago [at initiation into Cosa Nostra]. When I lost them, I became a monster. I was a monster until I took pen in hand to write these lines . . . Before I go, I ask for forgiveness from my mother and from God, because their love has no limits. The whole of the rest of the world will never be able to forgive me.

The historical question raised by this picture of life inside Cosa Nostra is simply: 'Was it always like this?' The equally simple answer is that no one will ever know for sure. *Pentiti* may have talked to the police on many occasions, but when they did, they tended to talk about specific crimes and not about what it felt like to be a mafioso. But what evidence there is does suggest that something along the same lines as this code of honour existed all along. After all, if it had not existed, then the mafia would not have survived so long; in fact, it might never even have emerged at all.

The Genesis of
the Mafia
1860–1876

Sicily's Two Colours

Palermo became an Italian city on 7 June 1860 when, under the terms of a ceasefire, two long columns of defeated troops snaked out from its eastern edges, and doubled back round outside the walls to await the ships that would ferry them home to Naples. Their withdrawal was the culmination of one of the most famous military achievements of the century, a feat of patriotic heroism that astonished the rest of Europe. Until that day, Sicily had been ruled from Naples as part of the Bourbon kingdom that encompassed most of southern Italy. Then, in May 1860, Giuseppe Garibaldi and around 1,000 volunteers – the famous Redshirts – invaded the island with the aim of uniting it with the new nation of Italy. Under Garibaldi's leadership, this ragged but zealous force disorientated and defeated a far larger Neapolitan army. Palermo was conquered after three days of intense street fighting during which the Bourbon navy bombarded the city.

With Palermo liberated, Garibaldi then led his men – who were now growing in number and becoming an army in their own right – east towards the Italian mainland. On 6 September, the hero was welcomed into Naples itself by cheering crowds, and the following month he handed over his conquests to the King of Italy. He refused to take any reward, and headed back to his island home of Caprera with little more than his poncho, some basic supplies, and seed for his garden. A plebiscite quickly confirmed that Garibaldi had made Sicily and southern Italy into an integral part of the nation of Italy.

Even contemporaries thought Garibaldi's achievements were 'epic' and 'legendary'. But they soon came to seem like nothing more substantial than a dream, so tormented and violent did Sicily's relationship with the Italian kingdom turn out to be.

The mountainous island had a long-standing reputation as a revolutionary powder keg. Garibaldi had succeeded largely because his expedition had triggered another uprising; the Bourbon regime rapidly collapsed in the face of it. It now became clear that the revolt of 1860 had been only the beginning of the trouble. The incorporation of 2.4 million Sicilians into the new nation brought in its wake an epidemic of conspiracy, robbery, murder, and score-settling.

The King's Ministers, mostly men from the north of Italy, had hoped to find partners in government from among the upper echelons of the Sicilian population, people who looked like themselves: conservative landowners with a sense of good government and a desire for ordered economic progress. What they found instead – they would often protest – looked like the face of anarchy: republican revolutionaries with strong links to semi-criminal gangs; aristocrats and churchmen with a nostalgia for the old Bourbon regime or a hankering for Sicilian autonomy; local politicians who were killing and kidnapping in a struggle for power with equally unscrupulous opponents. There was massive and enraged popular resistance to the introduction of conscription, previously unknown in Sicily. Many people also seemed to think that the patriotic revolution had entitled them not to pay any tax.

The Sicilians who had invested their political ambitions in the patriotic revolution were infuriated by what they saw as the government's arrogant refusal to allow them access to power – the power they needed to address the island's problems. In 1862, Garibaldi himself so despaired at the state of the new Italy that he came out of retirement and used Sicily as a base to launch another invasion of the mainland. His objective was to conquer Rome, which still remained under the authority of the Pope. But an Italian army stopped him in the mountains of Calabria, and he was even shot and wounded in the foot. (Rome would not become the capital of Italy until 1870.)

The Italian government responded to the crisis provoked by Garibaldi's new invasion by declaring martial law in Sicily. In so doing it set a pattern for the coming years. Unwilling or unable to find the support to pacify Sicily politically, the government repeatedly tried the military solution: mobile columns of troops, sieges of entire towns, mass arrests, imprisonment without trial. But the situation failed to improve. In 1866, there was another revolt in Palermo, similar in some respects to the one that had overthrown the Bourbons. As they had done when Garibaldi attacked in 1860, revolutionary gangs descended on the city from the surrounding hills. There were unsubstantiated rumours of cannibalism and blood drinking by the rebels; martial law was once again the response. The 1866 revolt was quelled, but it was only after ten more years of turmoil and repression that Sicily settled into life as part of Italy. In 1876, for the first time, politicians from the island entered a new coalition government in Rome.

A constant counterpoint to the strife in Sicily between 1860 and 1876 was the impression that the island's splendours made on the visitors who arrived in the aftermath of Italian unification. Palermo's extraordinarily beautiful setting could not help but strike new arrivals. One *garibaldino* who approached Palermo for the first time from the sea said it looked like a city built to fit a child's poetic vision. Its walls were enclosed by a band of olive and lemon groves, behind which lay an amphitheatre of hills and mountains. There was the same simplicity to its layout: Palermo had two straight, perpendicular main roads that met at the Quattro Canti ('Four Corners'), a piazza built in the seventeenth century. At each corner of the Quattro Canti, an elaborate façade of balconies, cornices, and niches symbolized the four quarters of the city.

Despite the damage caused by the Bourbon shelling, Palermo in the 1860s offered numerous attractions for residents and out-siders alike; foremost among them perhaps was the famous sea front. During the seemingly endless summers, once the intense heat of the day had faded, genteel Palermitani took moonlit carriage rides along the Marina, perfumed by its flowering trees; or they sampled ice creams and sorbets while promenading to the sound of favourite opera melodies played by the city band.

In the narrow, tortuous alleys off the main streets and away from the Marina, aristocratic palaces competed for space with markets, artisans' workshops, hovels, and no fewer than 194 places of worship. Visitors in the early 1860s were often struck by the sheer number of monks and nuns in the streets. Palermo also seemed like a stone palimpsest of cultures stretching back over many hundreds of years. Like the rest of the island, it was layered with the monuments left by countless invaders. For since the ancient Greeks, virtually every Mediterranean power from the Romans to the Bourbons had made Sicily its own. The island seemed to many as if it were a fabulous display case of Greek amphitheatres and temples, Roman villas, Arab mosques and gardens, Norman cathedrals, Renaissance palaces, baroque churches . . .

Sicily was also imagined in two colours. It had once been the granary of ancient Rome. For hundreds of years thereafter, wheat grown on vast estates painted the imposing highlands of the interior in golden yellow. The island's other colour had more recent origins. When the Arabs conquered Sicily in the ninth century, they brought new irrigation techniques and introduced the groves of citrus fruit trees that tinted the northern and eastern coastal strip with dark green leaves.

It was during the troubled years of the 1860s that the Italian kingdom's ruling class first heard talk of the mafia in Sicily. Without having a clear idea of what it was, the first people to study the problem assumed that it must be archaic, a leftover from the Middle Ages, some symptom of the centuries of foreign misrule that had kept the island in a backward condition. Accordingly their first instinct was to look for its source in the golden yellow of the interior highlands, among the ancient grain-producing estates. For all its desolate beauty, the interior of Sicily was a metaphor for everything Italy wanted to leave behind. The great estates were worked by droves of hungry peasants who were exploited by brutal bosses. Many Italians hoped and believed that the mafia was a symptom of this kind of backwardness and poverty, that it was destined to disappear as soon as Sicily emerged from its isolation and caught up with the historical timetable. One optimist even claimed that the mafia would disappear 'with the whistle of the locomotive'. This kind of belief in the mafia's antiquity has never quite died, not least because many men of honour keep resuscitating it. Tommaso Buscetta, too, thought that the mafia began in the Middle Ages as a way of resisting French invaders.

But the mafia's origins are not ancient. The mafia began at roughly the time when beleaguered Italian government officials first heard talk of it. The mafia and the new nation of Italy were born together. In fact, the way that the word 'mafia' surfaced and became widely used is a curious affair, not least because the Italian government that discovered the name also played a part in nurturing the association that bore it.

As perhaps befits the mafia's own fiendish ingenuity, its genesis involves not just one story, but a knot of them. Untying those narrative threads and laying them out in the following chapters requires a little chronological dexterity; it means moving back and forth in the turbulent period from 1860 to 1876, and a brief loop back through the half-century before then. It also means borrowing the testimonies of the people caught up in the story, the people who were participants and onlookers in the mafia's beginnings.

It is best to start not with the word 'mafia' – for reasons that will become clear – but with what the early mafia did and, just as importantly, where it did it. For if the mafia was not ancient, then neither was the golden yellow of the interior the place where it was born. The mafia emerged in an area that is still its heartland; it was developed where Sicily's wealth was concentrated, in the dark green coastal strip, among modern capitalist export businesses based in the idyllic orange and lemon groves just outside Palermo.

Dr Galati and the Lemon Garden

The mafia's methods were honed during a period of rapid growth in the citrus fruit industry. Lemons had first become prized as an export crop in the late 1700s. Then a long citrus fruit boom in the mid-nineteenth century thickened Sicily's dark green hem. Two pillars of the British way of life played their part in this boom. From 1795, the Royal Navy made their crews take lemons as a cure for scurvy. On a much smaller scale the oil of the bergamot, another citrus fruit, was used to flavour Earl Grey tea; commercial production began in the 1840s.

Sicilian oranges and lemons were shipped to New York and London when they were still virtually unknown in the mountains of the Sicilian interior. In 1834, over 400,000 cases of lemons were exported. By 1850, it was 750,000. In the mid-1880s an astonishing 2.5 million cases of Italian citrus fruit arrived in New York every year, most of them from Palermo. In 1860, the year of Garibaldi's expedition, it was calculated that Sicily's lemon groves were the most profitable agricultural land in Europe, out-earning even the fruit orchards around Paris. In 1876, citrus cultivation yielded more than sixty times the average profit per hectare for the rest of the island.

Nineteenth-century citrus fruit gardens were modern businesses that required a high level of initial investment. Land needed to be cleared of stones and terraced; storehouses and roads had to be built; surrounding walls had to be erected to protect the crop from both the wind and thieves; irrigation channels had to be dug and sluices installed. Even once the trees had been planted, it took about eight years for them to start producing fruit. Profitability followed several years after that.

As well as being investment-intensive, lemon trees are also

highly vulnerable. Even a short interruption to water supplies can be devastating. Vandalism, whether directed at the trees or the fruit, is a constant risk. It was this combination of vulnerability and high profit that created the perfect environment for the mafia's protection rackets.

Although there were and are lemon groves in many coastal regions of Sicily, the mafia was, until relatively recently, overwhelmingly a *western* Sicilian phenomenon. It emerged in the area immediately surrounding Palermo. With nearly 200,000 inhabitants in 1861, Palermo was the political, legal, and banking centre of western Sicily. More money circulated in the property and rental sectors than anywhere else on the island. Palermo was the centre for wholesale and consumer markets, and it was the major port. It was here that much of the farmland in the surrounding province and beyond was bought, sold, and rented. Palermo also set the political agenda. The mafia was born not of poverty and isolation, but of power and wealth.

The lemon groves just outside Palermo were the setting for the story of the first person persecuted by the mafia ever to leave a detailed account of his misfortunes. He was a respected surgeon, Gaspare Galati. Almost everything that is known about Dr Galati as a person – his courage most notably – emerges from the testimony he would later submit to the authorities, who subsequently confirmed the authenticity of what he wrote.

In 1872, Dr Galati came to manage an inheritance on behalf of his daughters and their maternal aunt. The centrepiece of the inheritance was the Fondo Riella, a four-hectare lemon and tangerine fruit farm, or 'garden', in Malaspina, which was only a fifteen-minute walk from the edge of Palermo. The *fondo* was a model enterprise: its trees were watered using a modern three-horsepower steam pump that required a specialist operator. But when he took control of it, Gaspare Galati was well aware that the huge investment in the business was in danger.

The previous owner of the Fondo Riella, Dr Galati's brother-in-law, had died of a heart attack following a series of threatening letters. Two months before his death, he had learned from the steam-pump operator that the sender of the letters was the warden on the *fondo*, Benedetto Carollo, who had dictated them to someone who knew how to read and write. Carollo may have been uneducated, but he had attitude: Galati describes him swaggering about as if he owned the farm, and it was widespread knowledge that he creamed 20–25 per cent off the sale price of its produce; he even stole the coal intended for the steam engine. But it was the way Carollo stole that had caused most worry for Dr Galati's brother-in-law; it showed that he understood the citrus fruit business well, and was intent on running the Fondo Riella into the ground.

Between the Sicilian groves where the lemons grew, and the shops in northern Europe and America where consumers bought them, a host of agents, wholesale merchants, packagers, and transporters plied their trade. Financial speculation lubricated every stage of the process, beginning while the lemons were still on the trees; as a way of offsetting the high initial costs and spreading the risk of a poor harvest, citrus businesses usually sold the crop well before the fruit was ripe.

Dr Galati's brother-in-law had followed this common practice on the Fondo Riella. However, when brokers bought options on the farm's produce in the early 1870s, they found that the lemons and tangerines that they had already paid for began to disappear from the trees. The Fondo Riella quickly acquired a very bad business reputation. There seemed no doubt that the warden Carollo was responsible for the thefts, and that the young man's intention was to drive down the price of the business so that he could then buy it out.

Upon taking control of the Riella fruit farm from his brother-in-law, Dr Galati resolved to save himself trouble and lease it to someone else. Carollo had other ideas. When prospective tenants came to view the *fondo*, he made his views abundantly clear to them as he showed them round: 'By Judas's blood this garden will never be leased or sold.' It was too much for Dr Galati; he sacked Carollo and hired a replacement.

Dr Galati soon came to know how the young warden felt

about having 'the bread taken out of his mouth', as he was heard to say. Disconcertingly, some of Dr Galati's close friends, men who had no reason to know anything about his business, came to him and advised him in confidence to take Carollo back. The doctor stood firm.

At around 10 p.m. on 2 July 1874, the man whom Dr Galati had hired to replace Carollo as the warden on the Fondo Riella was shot several times in the back as he travelled along one of the narrow roads that passed between the lemon groves. The attackers had made a terraced platform out of stones inside another grove so that they could shoot him from behind the surrounding wall – a method used in many early mafia hits. The victim died in hospital in Palermo a few hours later.

Dr Galati's son went to the local police station to report the family's suspicion that Carollo was behind the murder. An inspector ignored this lead and arrested two men who had no connection with the victim. Subsequently they were released when no evidence was found against them.

Despite this lack of support from the police, Dr Galati hired another warden. He and his family then received a series of letters, which said he had been wrong to sack a 'man of honour' like Carollo and hire an 'abject spy' instead. They threatened that if he did not re-employ Carollo, he was going to meet the same end as his warden – only 'in a more barbarous manner'. Looking back a year later, by which time he had found out exactly what he was up against, Dr Galati was able to explain this new terminology: 'In the mafia's language, a thief and a murderer is a "man of honour"; a victim is an "abject spy".'

The doctor returned to the police with the threatening letters – seven in all. He was promised that Carollo and his associates, who included an adopted son, would be arrested. But the inspector – the same man who earlier had sent the investigation down a false trail – was not so keen. Three weeks passed before he took Carollo and his son into custody, and even then they were released after two hours on the grounds that they had nothing to do with the crime. Galati became convinced that the inspector was in league with the criminals.

As he fought to save his business, Dr Galati began to build up a picture of how the local mafia worked. The *cosca* was based in the neighbouring village of Uditore and operated behind the façade of a religious organization. A priest and former Capuchin monk known as Father Rosario ran a small confraternity in the village, the 'Tertiaries of Saint Francis of Assisi', ostensibly devoted to charity and assisting the Church in its work. Father Rosario, a man with a record as a police spy under the old Bourbon regime, was also a prison chaplain and took advantage of his role to ferry messages to and from inmates.

But Father Rosario was not the leader of the gang. The president of the 'Tertiaries of Saint Francis', and the mafia boss of Uditore, was Antonino Giammona. He had been born into a desperately poor peasant family and had started his working life as a labourer. His rise to wealth and influence coincided with the revolutions that accompanied Sicily's integration into the Italian nation. The revolts of 1848 and 1860 gave him the chance he needed to show his mettle and win important friends. By 1875, at the age of fifty-five, Giammona was a man of status; he owned property worth some 150,000 lire, the Chief of Police of Palermo reported. He was strongly suspected of having executed several fugitives from justice to whom he had at first given shelter. Their deaths became necessary, the police thought, when they started to steal from local properties while under his protection. Giammona was also known to have received a sum of money along with instructions to carry out mysterious business on behalf of a criminal from near Corleone who had fled to the United States to escape prosecution.

Dr Galati summed up Antonino Giammona's character as 'taciturn, puffed up, and wary'. There is good reason to believe him because the two men knew each other; several members of the Giammona family were clients of Dr Galati who, on one occasion, had pulled two musket balls out of Giammona's brother's thigh.

The Uditore mafia based their power on running protection rackets in the lemon groves. They could force landowners to accept their men as stewards, wardens, and brokers. Their network of contacts with cart drivers, wholesalers, and dockers could either threaten a farm's produce, or ensure its safe arrival at the market; when astutely applied, violence allowed the mafia to set up miniature cartels and monopolies. Once in control of a *fondo*, the mafiosi could steal as much as they liked, whether with the aim of raking off a comfortable parasitic 'tax', or in order to buy it for themselves at an artificially low price. Giammona was not just picking on Dr Galati; he was orchestrating a concerted campaign to control the citrus fruit industry of the whole Uditore area.

Now that he was alert to the fact that the mafia also had an influence over the local police, Dr Galati decided to report his evidence about the murder directly to an investigating magistrate. His resolve was strengthened when the police returned only six of the seven threatening letters to him – the most explicit one had been 'lost'. From the investigating magistrate, Dr Galati heard that such 'incompetence' was common in that police station.

New threatening letters arrived: Dr Galati was given a week to replace his new warden with a 'man of honour'. But he was fortified by the knowledge that his complaints had led to the removal of the police inspector whom he suspected of collusion with the mafia. Dr Galati also reasoned that the mafia was unlikely to take the risk of killing a man of property and status like himself, so he decided to ignore the ultimatum. Just after the deadline passed, in January 1875, his new warden was shot three times in broad daylight. Benedetto Carollo and two other former workers on the *fondo* were arrested on suspicion.

The attack brought Dr Galati's first stroke of luck. Before the warden collapsed from his wounds, he was able to see and identify his attackers. At first, lying in hospital, he did not respond to police questions. Then, as his fever rose and death seemed near, he called for the investigating magistrate and gave a statement: the men who had fired on him were indeed the three who had just been arrested.

Encouraged by the magistrate, Dr Galati treated the wounded warden himself, tending him day and night. He never went out without his revolver and kept his wife and daughters at home. The family's health had begun to suffer as threatening letters continued to arrive. Dr Galati was told that he, his wife and daughters would be stabbed, perhaps on their way out of the theatre; the blackmailers clearly knew that Dr Galati had a season ticket. The doctor learned that there was also a mafia spy in the magistrate's office since the mafiosi let it be known that they had access to the details of his statements. Nevertheless there seemed to be a hint of desperation to these latest blackmail letters. Dr Galati became more hopeful that, with a case being prepared and a witness ready to testify, Benedetto Carollo had finally been cornered.

Then the wounded warden under the doctor's care took matters into his own hands. As soon as he was well enough to move, he went to Antonino Giammona and asked to make peace. He was invited to celebrate the deal at a banquet, after which he changed his statement and the case against Carollo collapsed.

Without even waiting to say goodbye to his relatives and friends, Dr Galati took his family and fled to Naples, leaving behind his property and a client list that he had taken a quarter of a century to build up. All that he could then do was to send a memorandum to the Minister of the Interior in Rome in August 1875. He reported that Uditore was a village of only 800 souls yet, in 1874 alone, he knew of at least twenty-three people who had been murdered – the victims included two women and two children – and a further ten who had been seriously wounded. Nothing had been done to investigate these crimes. A war to control the citrus fruit industry in the area was going on while the police force remained impassive.

The Minister of the Interior ordered the Chief of Police in Palermo to look into the matter. A capable young police officer was put to work on the Galati case. It turned out that, like his murdered predecessor, the second replacement warden was a fearsome character. Although Dr Galati either did not know it or would not admit it, the likelihood is that *both* of the wardens he employed were also affiliated to the mafia. He was probably being used all along in a war between rival mafia *cosche*.

The Uditore mafia responded to the new investigation by showing off its friends. Benedetto Carollo made an application for permission to go hunting in the Fondo Riella; his partner for the day's shoot was to be a judge at the Palermo Court of Appeal. A series of landowners and politicians lined up behind Antonino Giammona. Lawyers prepared a statement to the effect that Giammona and his son had been persecuted merely because they 'lived from their own means and would not let themselves be robbed or bullied'. In the end, a police caution and intensified surveillance were the only response that the authorities could muster.

Evidently Dr Galati's problems were not just the fault of a bunch of criminals; they came in large part because he could not trust the police, the judiciary, or even his fellow landowners. Thus Dr Galati's story picks out another important strand in the story of the mafia's origins. As will become clear later, the origins of the mafia are closely related to the origins of an untrustworthy state – the Italian state.

Protection rackets, murder, territorial dominance, competition and collaboration between gangs, and even a hint of a code of 'honour': enough clues emerge from Dr Galati's memoir to reach the conclusion that many of the central components of the mafia method were being employed in the lemon groves in the early 1870s. The case also produced evidence of the most distinctive component of all: the mafia's initiation ritual.

Initiation

Although the police did not manage to bring the mafiosi of Uditore to justice following Dr Galati's memorandum on his unfortunate dealings with Antonino Giammona's *cosca*, the case did bring to light the first signs that the mafia was a secret association bound by a blood oath. Remarkably, the men under Antonino Giammona's command not only had an initiation ritual, but it was virtually identical to the one that men of honour still undergo today.

When Dr Giuseppe Galati sent his memorandum to the Minister of the Interior in 1875, he provoked the Minister into asking for a report from the Chief of Police of Palermo. It is in this report that the Chief of Police revealed the mafia initiation ritual for the first time. His source for this discovery was reliable; it was probably the police themselves who, as is apparent from Dr Galati's story, had a close and ambiguous relationship with the mafia from the outset.

According to the Chief of Police's account, in the mafia of the 1870s any man of honour due to be initiated would be led into the presence of a group of bosses and underbosses. One of these men would then prick the would-be mafioso's arm or hand and tell him to smear blood from the wound on to a sacred image. Then the oath of loyalty would be taken as the image was burned and its ashes scattered, thus symbolizing the annihilation of all traitors.

A special government envoy on his way to Sicily replied to the Chief of Police on the Minister's behalf: 'Congratulations! Now a huge and intricate field of investigation has opened up for the authorities.' Doubtless the envoy would have been taken aback to learn that his 'field of investigation' would still be huge and intricate a century later, in May 1976, when Giovanni 'lo scannacristiani' Brusca was 'made'. (The term Brusca himself uses is 'combinato', a vague, unexceptional Italian word that means 'arranged' or 'got together'.) The ritual undergone by Brusca makes for a striking comparison with the 1875 version, and that comparison creates a better understanding of how and why it made sense for the mafia to be a secret association right from the outset.

The man who would later blow up Judge Falcone at Capaci was initiated young, at nineteen. The fact that his father was a boss had helped put him on the fast track; his first murder was already behind him. One day Brusca was taken to a house in the countryside on the understanding that one of the organization's periodic banquets was to take place. Many men of honour were present, including the superboss, Totò 'Shorty' Riina, whom the young man already called *padrino* (godfather). Some of the men there began to ask Brusca, 'How would you feel about killing a man? About committing crimes?' This seemed rather odd; he had already killed, yet they were asking him how he *would* feel. He did not know it but the initiation had already begun.

At a certain point, the others gathered in a room, leaving Brusca outside. When he was called in a little while later, he saw that his father had withdrawn and that the other mobsters were sitting at a large round table which had a pistol, a dagger, and a small image of a saint placed at its centre. The men of honour began to fire questions at Brusca: 'If you end up in jail will you be faithful and not a traitor?'

'Do you want to be part of the association called Cosa Nostra?'

As he gained confidence, he began to reply with enthusiasm: 'I like these friendships, I like the crimes.'

One of the men of honour then took his finger and pricked it with a pin; Brusca smeared the blood on the saint's image, which he then held in his cupped hands while Riina himself set light to it. The godfather spoke the words, 'If you betray Cosa Nostra, your flesh will burn like this saint,' cupping his own hands over the flame as he did so, to prevent the initiate from dropping it.

Among the statutes of the organization that Riina set out to Brusca that day was the now famous one relating to introductions. No one is allowed to introduce himself as a mafioso, even to another man of honour. Instead, a third party, who has also been initiated, has to present one to another using a formula like 'He is a friend of ours' or 'You two are the same thing as me'. This was even the phrase spoken by Riina when, after Brusca's father was readmitted to the room to offer congratulations, he 'introduced' father and son as men of honour.

The rules on introductions as they were explained to Brusca betray some interesting differences from the original version contained in the Chief of Police's 1875 report. A century before Brusca was 'made', mafiosi used a much more elaborate recognition system, a coded dialogue that began with a conversation about 'toothache':

A: God's blood! My tooth hurts! (*pointing to one of the upper canines*)

B: Mine too.

A: When did yours hurt?

B: On the day of Our Lady of the Annunciation.

A: Where were you?

B: Passo di Rigano.

A: And who was there?

B: Nice people.

A: Who were they?

B: Antonino Giammona, number 1. Alfonso Spatola, number 2, etc.

A: And how did they do the bad deed?

B: They drew lots and Alfonso Spatola won. He took a saint, coloured it with my blood, put it in the palm of my hand, and burned it. He threw the ashes in the air.

A: Who did they tell you to adore?

B: The sun and the moon.

A: And who is your god?

B: An 'Air'.
A: What kingdom do you belong to?
B: The index finger.

Passo di Rigano, mentioned here, is another village on the out-skirts of Palermo. The references to 'the sun and moon', 'Air' and the 'index finger' are clearly designations of the mafia family into which mafioso B was initiated.

This original recognition ceremony is more cumbersome and less reliable than the contemporary version explained to Gio-vanni Brusca. (One wonders how the two mobsters know which of them is supposed to take the lead.) All the same, for the first time this strange dialogue confirms something very simple and very important about the early mafia: it was an association so extensive that its members did not always know each other. 'Mafia' was already more than a name for isolated local gangs, or a face-to-face criminal network.

More than anything else about the mafia, the initiation ritual bolsters widespread myths about how ancient the organization is. In reality, it is as modern as everything else about the mafia. It was almost certainly borrowed originally from the Masons. Masonic secret societies, which were imported to Sicily from France via Naples around 1820, rapidly became very popular among ambitious middle-class opponents of the Bourbon regime. The societies had initiation ceremonies, of course, and some of their meeting rooms were adorned with bloody daggers as a warning to potential traitors. A Masonic sect called the *carbonari* ('charcoal burners') also had patriotic revolution as its aim. In Sicily such groups sometimes developed into political factions and even criminal gangs; one official report from 1830 tells of a *carbonaro* circle involved in cornering local government contracts.

Becoming a single, secret association using Masonic-style rites of this kind offered many advantages to the mafia. Creating a sinister ceremony, and a constitution that has the punishment of traitors as its first article, helped create trust because it was a sensible way of putting up the price of betrayal among criminals who might normally betray each other without a second thought. In that way, the high risks involved in running protection rackets would be reduced for everyone who joined. The ritual was probably particularly effective in keeping ambitious and aggressive younger members in line. The secret society also offered a system of mutual guarantees with neighbouring gangs that would allow each *cosca* to operate relatively unmolested on its own patch. There were also great advantages vis-à-vis criminals outside the association, who would have to gain the mafia's approval to operate – or face its united opposition. Many illegal activities, like cattle rustling and smuggling, involved not only travelling across territories ruled by other gangs but also finding trustworthy business partners all the way along the route. Membership of the association offered the guarantees required by all parties involved in these activities.

By the time the Minister of the Interior heard of Dr Galati's encounter with the Uditore *cosca* in 1875, the story of the mafia's genesis was nearly complete. Yet it still remains to explain where the mafia came from. There is more to discover about the 'taciturn, puffed up, and wary' Antonino Giammona, and finding it entails taking a step back into the decade before the story of the Fondo Riella.

Baron Turrisi Colonna and the 'Sect'

In the early summer of 1863 – three years after Garibaldi's expedition – a Sicilian nobleman who was soon to write the first ever study of the mafia was the target of a well-planned assassination attempt. Nicolò Turrisi Colonna, Baron of Buonvicino, was returning one evening to Palermo from one of his estates. The road he travelled ran through the prosperous countryside just outside the city walls; it was lined with lemon trees. At a point between the villages of Noce and Olivuzza, five men firing from different points at the roadside shot down the horses of his carriage before taking aim at the occupant. Turrisi Colonna and his driver were quick to pull out their revolvers and return fire while they ran for cover. The noise attracted one of Turrisi Colonna's own wardens. A blast of his shotgun was followed by a scream of pain from the roadside greenery. The would-be assassins gave up and dragged their wounded companion away.

Turrisi Colonna wrote a study titled *Public Security in Sicily* the year after he was attacked. It was the first of many books published after the unification of Italy that made the Sicilian mafia a subject of analysis, controversy, and confusion. With the benefit of hindsight afforded by the work of Judge Falcone, historians now also have a good idea of which participants in the earliest debates about the mafia to believe. Turrisi Colonna turns out to have provided a peculiarly well-informed and credible account.

Part of the reason why Turrisi Colonna is such a good witness derives from his status and the important role he played in the dramas of the early 1860s. He had an impeccable record as an Italian patriot. In 1860, through his efforts as a leader of the new Palermo National Guard, Turrisi Colonna did his bit to try and ensure that the revolution did not lead to anarchy. He was already a member of the Italian parliament when he wrote his little book on the crime issue in 1864. Much later, in the 1880s, Turrisi Colonna would serve twice as mayor of Palermo. Even today he is honoured with a marble bust in the committee room of the Palazzo delle Aquile, the seat of the Palermo city council. His stern features are adorned with one of those beards – it seems resolutely glued on below the nose – that signified 'august' and 'statesman' to his contemporaries even more clearly than the medals on his chest.

Turrisi Colonna had an equanimity equal to his status. Law and order was a burning political issue when he wrote his pamphlet in 1864. The government was trying to claim that the opposition was conspiring against the new Italian state and was bent on causing disorder to further its aims. Opposition politicians maintained that the government was amplifying the law and order crisis in an effort to brand them as criminals. Turrisi Colonna took a careful line that would have pleased neither camp: he pointed out that organized criminals were a powerful force in Sicily, and had been for many years, but he also argued that the new government's tough measures had only made the situation worse.

Turrisi Colonna's study hinged on a sombre observation: the newspapers were full of extortions, robberies, and murders, he explained, but only a fraction of the crimes committed around Palermo were reported because the problem went beyond ordinary lawlessness.

We should not delude ourselves any more. In Sicily there is a sect of thieves that has ties across the whole island . . . The sect protects and is protected by everyone who has to live in the countryside, like the lease-holding farmers and herdsmen. It gives protection to and gets help from traders. The police hold little or no fear for the sect because it is confident that it will have no trouble in slipping away from any police hunt. The courts too hold little fear for the sect: it takes pride in the fact that evidence for the prosecution is rarely produced because of the pressure it puts on witnesses.

This sect, Turrisi Colonna guessed, was about twenty years old. In each area it recruited its affiliates from the brightest peasants, the wardens who guarded estates around Palermo, and the legions of smugglers who brought grain and other heavily taxed items past the customs posts that the city depended on for its income. The sect's members had special signals that they used to recognize each other when they were transporting stolen cattle through the countryside to city butchers. Some of the sect members specialized in rustling cattle, others in transporting the animals and removing identifying brands, still others in illegal butchery. In some places the sect was so well organized, receiving political protection from the disreputable factions that dominated local government, that it could frighten any citizen. Even some honest men found themselves turning to the sect in the hope that it might be able to bring some semblance of safety to the countryside.

Driven by its hatred of the brutal and corrupt Bourbon police, the sect had offered its services to the revolutions of 1848 and 1860. Like many men of violence, the sect's members had an interest in revolution because it offered the chance to open prisons, burn police records, and kill off police and informers in the confusion. A revolutionary government would – the sect hoped – grant an amnesty to people 'persecuted' by the old regime; it would form new militias that needed tough recruits, and give jobs to the heroes of the struggle to overthrow the old order. But the 1860 revolution had brought few of these benefits, and the new Italian government's indiscriminately harsh response to the crime wave that followed only made the sect more eager to cause trouble.

It was only four months after the publication of Turrisi Colonna's report that the sect would acquire its name when the word 'mafia' was written down for the first time. And given what is now known about the mafia, Turrisi Colonna's account of the sect is strikingly familiar. He mentions the kind of kanga-roo court that can be found in many later tales of mafia business; the sect members meet to decide the fate of any of their number who has broken the rules – with a death sentence a frequent outcome. Turrisi Colonna goes on to describe the sect's code of silence and loyalty in terms that chime rather eerily with current knowledge:

In its rules, this evil sect regards any citizen who approaches a *carabi-niere* [military policeman] and talks to him, or even exchanges a word or a greeting with him, as a villain to be punished with death. Such a man is guilty of a horrendous crime against 'humility'.

'Humility' involves respect and devotion towards the sect. No one must commit any act that could directly or indirectly harm the members' interests. No one should provide the police or judiciary with facts that help uncover any crime whatsoever.

Humility – *umiltà* in Italian or *umirtà* in Sicilian – is a word that jumps off the page. It is now considered to be the most likely origin for the word *omertà*. *Omertà* is the mafia's code of silence, and the obligation not to speak to the police that it imposes on those within its sphere of influence. Evidently *omertà* was originally a code of submission.

Turrisi Colonna advised the government not to respond to the sect by ruling 'with the scaffold and the torturer'. Instead he offered some well-thought-through reforms of policing that would, he hoped, change the behaviour of the people of Sicily, giving them 'a second, civil baptism'. The balance, astuteness, and honesty that Turrisi Colonna demonstrated in his account of the sect was matched by his gentlemanly reserve. He was too modest even to mention the assassination attempt that he himself had suffered only the previous year; it was, after all, only one of many violent episodes in the countryside around Palermo in the difficult years that followed Garibaldi's expedition. Turrisi Colonna's discretion means that it is not known who ambushed him and why, or what later happened to the attackers. But reasons have now emerged for suspecting that they may not have lived for very long afterwards.

A dozen years later, on 1 March 1876, Leopoldo Franchetti and Sidney Sonnino, two wealthy, high-minded young Jewish intellectuals from Tuscany, arrived in Palermo with a friend and their manservant to conduct a private investigation into the state of Sicilian society. By this time – the year after Dr Galati wrote his memorandum – the word 'mafia' had been on everyone's lips for a decade, but there was great confusion about what it meant, if, indeed, it meant anything at all. (There was even uncertainty about how to spell it: in the nineteenth century, mafia was sometimes written with one F, sometimes with two, without any difference in meaning.) Franchetti and Sonnino had no doubts that the mafia was a dangerous form of criminality, and intended to blow away the mist of different opinions that enveloped it.

The day after reaching Sicily, Sonnino wrote to a friend, asking her to arrange letters of introduction to Nicolò Turrisi Colonna, Baron of Buonvicino and expert on the sect:

Here they say he is linked to the mafia. But that doesn't matter to us. We want to hear what he has to say ... Mind you do not tell *anyone* what I have told you about Baron Turrisi Colonna and his supposed links with the maffia. Some friend of his could write to him about it and that would do us a nasty service.

There is a deal of evidence to suggest that Turrisi Colonna, author of the analysis of the sect, was indeed the strategic political protector of the most important and ruthless mafiosi in Palermo. Rumours of his mafia connections were widespread; even members of his own political grouping were expressing their concerns about him at court in Rome.

In 1860, Turrisi Colonna had made a leading sect member into a captain of his National Guard unit. The man was chosen because of his authority and military experience; earlier he had led one of the revolutionary gangs that descended on Palermo from the surrounding countryside as the patriotic revolution spread. The man in question was a canny thug named Antonino Giammona – the same Antonino Giammona who would later orchestrate the takeover of the Fondo Riella from Dr Galati. Turrisi Colonna was one of the landowners who supported Giammona when the Ministry of the Interior looked into Dr Galati's allegations; it was Turrisi Colonna's lawyers who prepared Giammona's defence statement. According to the Chief of Police's 1875 report, the mafia's initiation rituals took place on one of Turrisi Colonna's estates.

In three separate interviews with Franchetti and Sonnino in 1876, Turrisi Colonna was his usual lucid self on matters of economics. In addition to his interest in the sect, he was a forward-thinking farmer and an agronomist with a long list of academic publications on the citrus fruit business to his name. But he was uncharacteristically evasive on the crime issue. Two years previously, four of his men had been arrested on his estate near Cefalù. To Franchetti and Sonnino he protested their innocence, as, indeed, he had done at the time of the arrests. Landowners like him were the victims, he complained; out on their country estates they were forced to deal with bandits because otherwise they would be unable to protect their valuable crops and trees. He made no mention of a sect.

When Franchetti and Sonnino later interviewed the Palermo Chief of Police they found him pessimistic about a prosecution against Turrisi Colonna's men because the baron had the political connections to undermine the trial. Other interviewees quickly changed the subject when asked for an opinion of him.

Turrisi Colonna embodies the puzzles of the violent years that saw the mafia appear. He probably based his 1864 pamphlet about the sect on inside sources – perhaps even on what he was told by Antonino Giammona himself. When he wrote it, he may also genuinely have hoped that unification with Italy could normalize Sicily. He may have been a victim of mafia intimidation, who wanted a powerful, efficient new state to help land-owners like himself put the mafiosi in their place. Perhaps he saw himself as reluctantly collaborating with men like Giammona on a short-term basis, while he waited for the Italian government to take the violence out of Sicilian society. If so, these were hopes that he had lost long before he was interviewed by Franchetti and Sonnino in 1876.

A less generous interpretation is that Turrisi Colonna was never a victim at all. Giammona's relationship with him may have been based more on deference than intimidation. Perhaps Turrisi Colonna was simply the first of many Italian politicians whose pronouncements on the mafia did not match their actions. For all the sophistication of its structure and the insidious grip of its code of honour, the Sicilian mafia would be nothing with-out its links to politicians like Turrisi Colonna. Ultimately, there would be little point in the mafia's corrupting policemen and magistrates if the dignitaries to whom those officials are answer-able were still intent on impartially upholding the rule of law. And in the mafia's account book, a friendly politician is more useful the more credibility he has. If credibility has to be bought with thundering speeches against crime, or with learned diag-noses of the state of law and order in Sicily, then so be it.

The mafia deals with politicians in a currency that is rarely printed on the paper of parliamentary proceedings and law books. Rather it is stamped on the solid gold of small favours: news of government contracts or land sales leaked, overzealous investigators made to pursue their careers away from the island, jobs in local government given to friends. Thus, in public, Turrisi Colonna could take a detached, scientific interest in the sect, gazing down on it from the height of his intellectual and social prestige. In private, away from the domain of open debate, a close relationship with men like Giammona was integral to his business interests and political support.

Whatever went on between Giammona the mafia boss and Turrisi Colonna the politician, intellectual, and landowner, the Palermo revolt that took place two years after the publication of Turrisi Colonna's pamphlet was probably an important stage in their relationship. In September 1866, armed gangs once again marched on the city from the surrounding villages. Turrisi Colonna's National Guard, captained by Antonino Giammona, opposed the revolt. Whereas Giammona, like many other men of violence, had speculated on revolution in the past, he now realized that the Italian state was a body with which he could do business. Key members of the sect like Giammona were beginning to put their revolutionary past behind them, and as they did so the sect began to enter the bloodstream of the new Italy. Like other leading defenders of order, Turrisi Colonna was interviewed during a government inquiry into the trouble of 1866, and he had no hesitation in using the new word 'mafia' to describe some of the troublemakers who caused the revolt: 'Trials cannot be brought to a conclusion because the witnesses are not sincere. They will only start to tell the truth when the nightmare of the Mafia comes to an end.' 'Mafia', Turrisi Colonna had evidently decided, only meant criminals he did not know personally.

The question that still remains is how the 'nightmare of the mafia' began. In 1877, the two men who interviewed Turrisi Colonna published their own research on Sicily in a substantial two-part report. In the first part, Sidney Sonnino, a profoundly melancholic character who would later become Prime Minister of Italy, analysed the lives of the island's landless peasants. Leopoldo Franchetti's half of the report bears the less than racy title, *Political and Administrative Conditions in Sicily*. But it has a unique stature; it is an analysis of the mafia in the nineteenth century that is still considered an authority in the twenty-first. Franchetti would ultimately influence thinking about the mafia more than anyone else until Giovanni Falcone over a hundred years later. *Political and Administrative Conditions in Sicily* is the first convincing explanation of how the mafia came to be.

The Violence Industry

There was something rather English about the investigation mounted by Leopoldo Franchetti and Sidney Sonnino. Both men were great admirers of British liberalism and Sonnino owed his first name to his English mother. When they travelled to Sicily they were entering a land where the vast majority of the population spoke a dialect they could not understand. In the university and salon milieu that Sonnino and Franchetti left behind, the island was still a mysterious place known primarily from ancient Greek myths and sinister newspaper reports. So they planned for the considerable stresses and dangers of their journey with the resolve of explorers setting off for uncharted territory. Among the equipment they took on their journey in the spring of 1876 were repeating rifles, large-calibre pistols, and four copper basins each. The plan was to fill the basins with water and stand the legs of their camp-beds in them to keep insects away. Because roads were poor or non-existent in the interior of the island, the two researchers often travelled on horseback, choosing their routes and guides at the last possible moment to avoid brigand attacks.

Franchetti in particular was far from entirely naive when he went to Sicily; two years earlier he had hacked across large areas of the mainland of southern Italy on a similar expedition. Yet what he found on the island caused him to feel overcome by 'a profound tenderness' towards the rifle he carried across his saddle. 'The nightmare of a mysterious, evil force is weighing down on this naked, monotonous land,' he later wrote. The notes that Franchetti actually took during the journey have only recently been published; two of the many stories that emerge from those notes can serve to explain the shock of his encounter with Sicily.

Franchetti recorded that, on 24 March 1876, he and Sonnino rode into the central Sicilian city of Caltanissetta. Two days earlier, a priest had been shot dead in the nearby village of Barrafranca, a mafia stronghold, according to the authorities who informed them of what had happened. Sixty metres from where the priest lay dying stood a witness, a new arrival in Sicily, a government inspector from the northern city of Turin whose job was to supervise the collection of taxes on milled flour. This honest functionary ran to the priest's side in time to hear his dying words of accusation: his own cousin was the murderer.

Profoundly disturbed, the tax inspector jumped on his horse and rode off to tell the *carabinieri*. He then went to inform the victim's family. Not wanting to upset them by blurting out what he knew, he told them to follow him to where the priest needed help. Along the way, he gently broke the news. Grateful for his sensitivity, they told him that the murder was the culmination of a twelve-year feud between the priest and his cousin. The priest himself was a wealthy man with a fearsome reputation for violence and corruption.

Twenty-four hours later local police arrested the tax inspector, threw him in jail, and charged him with the murder. The witnesses against him included the priest's cousin. But the people of Barrafranca, including the murdered man's family, kept quiet. Mercifully for the tax inspector, the government authorities in Caltanissetta got wind of the case; when he was released the real murderer went into hiding.

A week after hearing of this episode, Franchetti and Sonnino arrived in Agrigento, a town on Sicily's southern coast famous for its ancient Greek temples. Franchetti's notebooks tell another story he learned there, of a woman who had taken 500 lire from the police in exchange for information on two criminals; they were in league with a local boss, a man with a hefty share of government road-building contracts. Soon after she accepted the money, the woman's son returned to his village after a decade in jail. He was carrying a letter from the local mafia detailing what his mother had done. When he confronted her and asked for money to buy some new clothes, her evasive response triggered a furious row after which the man stormed out. He returned shortly afterwards with his cousin and together they stabbed his mother ten times – the son six times and his cousin four. They then threw her body out of the window into the street before giving themselves up.

As they journeyed round Sicily, Franchetti and Sonnino also encountered the seemingly hopeless confusion that had set in around the word 'mafia' during the ten years since it had first been heard. Everyone the travellers interviewed during the two months they were in Sicily seemed to have a different understanding of the new buzzword; everyone seemed to accuse everyone else of being a mafioso. The authorities in some places were confused. As one lieutenant in the *carabinieri* lamely told them: 'Mafia is an extremely difficult thing to define; you would need to live in Sambuca to get an idea.'

When he subsequently published his findings, Franchetti explained how perplexed he had been to find that the situation was most worrying not in the treeless, yellow interior of the island, where most people would have expected there to be backwardness and crime, but in the citrus groves around Palermo. On the surface, this was the centre of a thriving industry in which the locals took great pride: 'Every tree is looked after as if it were a rare plant specimen.' These initial perceptions, Franchetti wrote, were soon changed by the hair-raising tales of murder and intimidation in the area: 'After a certain number of these stories, the scent of orange and lemon blossom starts to smell of corpses.' The presence of endemic violence in such a modern setting ran counter to one of the beliefs most cherished by Italy's rulers: that economic, political, and social progress all marched in step. Franchetti began to wonder whether the principles of justice and freedom he so cherished 'might just amount to nothing more than well-planned speeches to disguise ailments that Italy cannot cure; they are a layer of gloss to make the dead bodies gleam.'

It was a bleak and perplexing spectacle. But Leopoldo Franchetti was intellectually tenacious as well as brave; he passionately believed in a hands-on engagement with the nation's problems. A patriotic shame burned within him at the thought that foreigners seemed to know Sicily much better than did the Italians. By patiently covering the territory and by studying its history, Franchetti overcame his doubts and confusion. He produced an account of the mafia business that is starkly systematic. Sicily was not chaotic; on the contrary, its law and order problems had an underlying and very modern rationality to them. The island, Franchetti argued, had become home to 'the violence industry'.

Franchetti's account of the genesis of the mafia opens in 1812 when the British, who occupied Sicily during the Napoleonic wars, began the process of abolishing feudalism on the island. The feudal system had been based on a form of joint land ownership: the king granted land in trust to a nobleman and his descendants; in return, the noble put his private army at the service of the king when the need arose. Within the nobleman's territory, termed a 'fief' or 'feud', his word was law.

Until the abolition of feudalism, Sicilian history was shaped by tussles between a long series of foreign monarchs and the feudal barons. The monarchs tried to draw more power towards the centre; the feudal barons resisted the monarchy's interference in the running of their estates. In this tug-of-war, it was the nobles who usually had the advantage, not least because Sicily's mountainous geography and atrocious transport infrastructure made it impossible for central government to rule without letting the barons have their way.

Baronial privileges were wide-ranging and long-lasting. A custom dictating that vassals should greet their feudal lord with a kiss on the hand was only formally abolished by Garibaldi in 1860. The title of 'don', which was originally given to the Spanish noblemen who had ruled Sicily, was applied to any man of status for many years after that. (These practices were widespread in Sicily, and were not just mafia habits.)

The abolition of feudalism did not immediately do more than change the rules of the tug-of-war between the centre and the provinces. (The power of the landowners was slow to fade; the last of the great estates was only broken up in the 1950s.) However, forces for long-term change were set loose when feudalism ended; the legal preconditions were put in place for a property market. Quite simply, bits of the estates could now be bought and sold. And land that is acquired rather than inherited needs to be paid for; it is an investment that has to be put to profitable use. Capitalism had arrived in Sicily.

Capitalism runs on investment, and lawlessness puts investment at risk. No one wants to buy new machinery or more land to plant with commercial crops when there is a strong risk that those machines or crops will be stolen or vandalized by competitors. When it supplanted feudalism, the modern state was supposed to establish a monopoly on violence, on the power to wage war and punish criminals. When the modern state monopolizes violence in this way, it helps create the conditions in which commerce can flourish. The barons' ramshackle, unruly private militias were scheduled to disappear.

Franchetti argued that the key to the development of the mafia in Sicily was that the state had fallen catastrophically short of this ideal. It was untrustworthy because, after 1812, it failed to establish its monopoly on the use of violence. The barons' power on the ground was such that the central state's courts and policemen could be pressurized into doing what the local lord wanted. Worse still, it was now no longer only the barons who felt they had the right to use force. Violence became 'democratized', as Franchetti put it. As feudalism declined, a whole range of men seized the opportunity to shoot and stab their way into the developing economy. Some of the feudal lords' private heavies were now acting in their own interests, roaming the countryside as brigand bands that were sheltered by the landlords either out of fear or complicity. The formidable managers called *gabelloti*, who often rented bits of the landowners' estates from them, were also adept at using violence to defend their interests. In the city of Palermo, societies of artisans demanded the right to carry arms so that they could police the streets (and force up prices or run extortion operations).

When modern local government institutions were set up in the towns of the Sicilian provinces, groups that were part armed criminal gang, part commercial enterprise, and part political clique, quickly organized themselves to get their hands on the spoils. Officials complained that what they called these 'sects' or 'parties' – sometimes they were merely extended families with guns – were making many areas of Sicily ungovernable.

The state also set up its courts, but soon found that they were subject to control by anyone who was tough and well organized enough to impose his will. Even the police became corrupted. Instead of reporting crime to the authorities, they would often broker or impose deals between the victims and perpetrators of theft. For example, rather than send stolen cattle along the long chain of intermediaries to the butchers, rustlers could simply ask the captain of the local police to mediate. He would arrange for the stolen animals to be handed back to the original owner in return for money passed on to the rustlers. Naturally the captain would get a percentage of the deal.

In a hellish parody of the capitalist economy, the law was parcelled up and privatized just like the land. Franchetti saw Sicily as being in the grip of a bastard form of capitalist competition. It was a violent market in which there were only notional boundaries between economics, politics, and crime. In this situation, people hoping to run a business could not rely on the law to protect them, their families, and their economic interests. Violence was an essential asset in any enterprise; the ability to use force was as important as having capital to invest. Indeed, Franchetti thought that in Sicily violence itself had become a form of capital.

Mafiosi, for Franchetti, were entrepreneurs in violence,

specialists who had developed what today would be called the most sophisticated business model in the marketplace. Under the leadership of their bosses, mafia bands 'invested' violence in various commercial spheres in order to extort protection money and guarantee monopolies. This was what he called the violence industry. As Franchetti wrote,

[in the violence industry] the mafia boss . . . acts as capitalist, impresario and manager. He unifies the management of the crimes committed . . . he regulates the way labour and duties are divided out, and controls discipline amongst the workers. (Discipline is indispensable in this as in any other industry if abundant and constant profits are to be obtained.) It is the mafia boss's job to judge from circumstances whether the acts of violence should be suspended for a while, or multiplied and made fiercer. He has to adapt to market conditions to choose which operations to carry out, which people to exploit, which form of violence to use.

Men with commercial or political ambitions in Sicily were faced with two alternatives: either to arm themselves; or, more likely, to buy in protection from a specialist in violence, a mafioso. If Franchetti were around today, he might say that threats and murder belonged to the service sector of the Sicilian economy.

Franchetti seems to have seen himself as a kind of Charles Darwin for a delinquent ecosystem, and as such he gives us a powerful insight into the laws of Sicily's rich criminal habitat. Yet in doing so he makes Sicily sound like a complete anomaly. In fact all capitalism has a bit of the bastard in it, particularly in the early stages. Even the English society that Franchetti so admired had had its violent entrepreneurs. In Sussex in the 1740s, for example, semi-militarized gangs made huge profits for themselves and their contacts by smuggling tea. They caused a breakdown in law and order by corrupting customs officials, directly confronting troops, and performing armed robberies as a sideline. One historian has described England in the 1720s as resembling a banana republic, its politicians masters in the arts of patronage, nepotism, and the systematic pillaging of the public revenue. Franchetti's analysis is also limited by the fact that he did not believe that the mafia was a sworn secret association.

Political and Administrative Conditions in Sicily met with a mixture of hostility and indifference on its release. Many Sicilian reviewers berated its author for ignorant prejudice. In part this poor reception was Franchetti's own fault. For one thing, his proposals for solving the mafia problem were outlandish and authoritarian: Sicilians were not to be allowed any say at all in how their island was policed. Franchetti even thought that their whole outlook was so perverted that they gave violence a 'moral value' and considered it ethically wrong to be honest. He seemed not to realize that people very often went along with the mafiosi simply because they were intimidated and did not know whom to trust.

Thus a pioneering account of the 'violence industry' failed to make an impact during Franchetti's lifetime. After publishing his research in Sicily, he went on to serve as a backbench MP, but his political career did not take off. In the end, it was the very same grim patriotism that had impelled him to investigate the mafia in 1876 that eventually killed him. (Even friends thought there was something dark and excessive about Franchetti's love of his country.) During the First World War he was tormented by the thought that he had not been called to an important office in the nation's hour of need. In October 1917, when news came through of Italy's catastrophic defeat at the battle of Caporetto, he became so depressed that he shot himself.

'The So-Called Maffia':
How the Mafia Got its Name

In Palermo dialect the adjective 'mafioso' once meant 'beautiful', 'bold', 'self-confident'. Anyone who was worthy of being described as mafioso therefore had a certain something, an attribute called 'mafia'. 'Cool' is about the closest modern English equivalent; a mafioso was someone who fancied himself.

The word mafioso began to have criminal connotations because of a hugely successful play written in Sicilian dialect, *I mafiusi di la Vicaria* ('The mafiosi of Vicaria Prison'), which was first performed in 1863. The *mafiusi* are a gang of prison inmates whose habits look very familiar in retrospect. They have a boss and an initiation ritual, and there is much talk in the play of 'respect' and 'humility'. The characters use the term *pizzu* for protection payments as do today's mafiosi – the word means 'beak' in Sicilian. By paying the *pizzu* you are allowing someone to 'wet their beak'. If this use of *pizzu* started life as jailhouse slang, it almost certainly entered general use because of the play; an 1857 Sicilian dictionary lists only the 'beak' meaning; an 1868 dictionary explains the alternative sense of extortion money.

The fact that *I mafiusi di la Vicaria* is set in Palermo prison also squares with what we know about the jail, which was soon to be confirmed as Sicilian organized crime's business school, think-tank, language laboratory, and communications centre. One observer at the time called it 'a kind of government' for the criminal gangs.

I mafiusi di la Vicaria is at heart a sentimental fable about the redemption of criminals. This first ever literary representation of the mafia is also the first ever version of the myth of the good mafia, a mafia that is honourable and protects the weak. The gang's boss stops his men picking on defenceless prisoners and kneels in prayer to beg for forgiveness after a man who had spoken to the police is killed, seemingly by mistake. In an implausible denouement, the capo leaves the gang and joins a workers' self-help group.

Next to nothing is known about the two authors of *I mafiusi*, other than that they were members of a troupe of travelling players. Sicilian theatrical legend has it that they based *I mafiusi* on inside information given them by a Palermo tavern owner involved in organized crime. The character of the gang boss in the play is supposed to be based on this real-life mobster. There is no way of confirming this story, and *I mafiusi* is consequently destined to remain an enigmatic historical document.

The word 'mafiosi' is only used once, in the title of *I mafiusi di la Vicaria* (it was probably inserted at the last minute to help give the piece the kind of local flavour that a Palermo audience would expect) and the term 'mafia' never appears at all. All the same, it was following the great success of *I mafiusi* that the words 'mafia' and 'mafioso' began to be applied to criminals who seemed to operate in a way similar to the characters in the play. From the stage, the word's new connotations filtered into the streets.

But a play alone was not enough to give the mafia its name. Baron Turrisi Colonna would certainly have known *I mafiusi* when he wrote his report at the end of 1864; the King of Italy's son and heir even came to Palermo to see a gala performance in the spring of that same year. Yet Turrisi Colonna referred only to the 'sect', and not to either the mafia or mafiosi. The criminals and enforcers he knew did not call themselves mafiosi, or name their sect 'the mafia'.

In fact it was only when the Italian authorities picked up on 'mafia' that the term entered general use and became a significant part of the sect's own story. Although it was *I mafiusi di la Vicaria* that began to give 'mafia' its criminal meaning on the streets of Palermo, it was the government that turned the word into a subject of national debate.

The story of how it did so reveals what a devious and violent business ruling Sicily was in the years immediately following Garibaldi's heroic expedition of 1860. Many Sicilians thought that the challenges of ruling their island had led the Italian government completely to abandon its liberal principles. The government's critics pointed to two cases in particular: the 'stabbers' conspiracy', and the torture of Antonio Cappello. It was cases like these that completely robbed the state of its credibility, and made many Sicilians very reluctant to trust it on any matter, let alone when it started to complain about the mafia.

Perhaps the strangest crime in Palermo's long history of misdeeds was referred to by the press as the 'stabbers' conspiracy'. On the evening of 1 October 1862, in an apparently synchronized operation carried out within the same small area of Palermo, thugs emerged from the shadows to knife thirteen randomly chosen citizens, one of whom subsequently died of his wounds. Police on the spot only caught one of the perpetrators, a shoeshiner and pedlar who also had a record as a police spy under the old Bourbon regime. His confession led to the arrest of the other eleven 'stabbers', who had been paid for their work.

The attacks caused consternation in Palermo. When the stabbers' trial took place early in 1863, there was huge public interest. Only the twelve men who were believed to have actually carried out the attacks were in the dock. The judge handed down death sentences to three ringleaders; the other nine got hard labour.

Yet the court showed a curious lack of interest in discovering who had funded the conspiracy and what its aims were. A Sicilian nobleman called Sant' Elia who was close to the Italian royal family had been named by one of the stabbers as the man behind the plot, but he was not even questioned. Opposition newspapers were scornful: evidence weighty enough to condemn three poor wretches to death was apparently not considered sufficiently substantial to set in motion preliminary inquiries into a member of the new Italian establishment. (Sant' Elia was also, as it happened, the head of a Masonic lodge.)

Sporadic stabbings that bore similarities to the events of

1 October 1862 continued. Whoever had set the plot in motion had clearly not yet achieved his aim. A second investigation began, and this time the nobleman Sant' Elia was named as the chief suspect and his palace was searched. In response, the authorities rapidly closed ranks and the King pointedly chose Sant' Elia to represent him at the Easter celebrations in Palermo. The case lost momentum, the stabbings ceased, and the investigators left Sicily.

It is still a mystery whether Sant' Elia was really behind the stabbers' conspiracy, although the balance of evidence currently suggests that he was not. What is certain is that the conspiracy came from within the institutions. Either it was dreamed up by interests in Palermo as a way of convincing the national government to put more power in their hands; or the national government was using terror tactics to try to create panic, accuse the opposition of the crimes, and generate the climate for a clampdown. Later in Italian history this move would be called the 'strategy of tension'.

The year after the first stabbings, another episode cast further suspicion over the authorities. The political climate at the time – late in 1863 – was fiery even by the standards of post-unification Sicily because a brutal campaign was being conducted to round up the estimated 26,000 deserters and draft dodgers at large in the island. In late October an opposition journalist went to follow up a story about a young man who was being held against his will in the military hospital in Palermo. The journalist found workman Antonio Cappello bedridden, with more than 150 small circular burns on his body. Doctors claimed that the burns were part of Cappello's treatment, and their highly implausible theory was later backed up by a judicial inquiry.

The truth was that Cappello had entered the hospital a well man. Three military doctors from northern Italy had starved, beaten, and tortured him by placing red-hot metal buttons on his back. Their aim was to get him to confess that he was a deserter.

In the end, Cappello managed to convince the doctors that

he had been a deaf-mute since birth and was not faking the condition to avoid conscription. Soon after he was released on 1 January 1864, photos of his tortured body were circulating in the streets of Palermo with a caption written by the journalist, accusing the government of being barbarians. Within three weeks, on the prompting of the Minister of War, the prison doctor was awarded the Cross of Saints Maurice and Lazarus by the King. At the end of March it was announced that the torturers would face no charges.

For a decade and a half after the unification of Italy, the authorities repeatedly lurched towards a blindly repressive response to the unruly island, only to stagger back towards decent principles that they were unable to uphold, or to sink into complicity with shady local enforcers. This toing and froing helped them pull off an extraordinary feat of political image-making: the Italian state managed to look brutal, naive, hypocritical, incompetent, and sinister all at the same time.

It is hard not to have some sympathy for the government's plight as it faced a number of huge tasks: building a new state virtually from scratch while also dealing with a civil war on the southern Italian mainland, crippling debt, the prospect of an attack by Austria, and a population of which over 95 per cent spoke a variety of dialects and languages other than Italian. To a government so starved of credibility, the notion that there might be a devilish secret conspiracy against it was manna. So it was that a government conspiracy theorist gave the world the first written use of the term 'mafia'.

On 25 April 1865, two years after the torture of Antonio Cappello, the recently appointed prefect of Palermo, the Marquis Filippo Antonio Gualterio, sent an alarming secret report to his boss, the Minister of the Interior. Prefects like Gualterio were key officers of Italy's new administrative system; they were the eyes and ears of the government in the cities, with responsibility for monitoring opposition and supervising the maintenance of law and order. In his report, Gualterio spoke of 'a serious and long-standing lack of understanding between the Country and the Authorities'. This breakdown resulted in a situation that enabled 'the so-called Maffia or criminal association to grow more daring'. During the periodic revolutions in mid-nineteenth-century Palermo, wrote Gualterio, the 'Maffia' had developed the habit of offering its muscle to different political groupings as a way of increasing its leverage; now it was on the side of whoever opposed the government. Thus, with Gualterio's report, the Palermo street rumours about the mafia reached the ears of Italy's rulers for the first time.

Prefect Gualterio was quite explicit about what a good occasion for a clampdown the 'Maffia' offered. The government, he explained, could legitimately send in the army to deal with the crime emergency, and in doing so land a fatal blow against the opposition – or so it hoped. As a result of Gualterio's report, 15,000 troops spent nearly six months trying to disarm the population, arrest draft-dodgers, round up criminals on the run, and track down the mafia. The details of this military campaign (the third in a few short years) are not important here; suffice it to say that it failed.

Gualterio was a conspiracy theorist, but he was not a fantasist. He did not conjure up the mafia out of nothing with the sole purpose of justifying repression. In some respects, his analysis of 'the so-called Maffia' ran along the same lines as Turrisi Colonna's. Organized crime was an integral part of politics on the island. Gualterio's convenient 'mistake' was simply to claim that all the villains were on one side of the political spectrum – the opposition's. As the revolt of 1866 subsequently proved, some of the most important mafiosi, like Antonino Giammona, were now partisans of order and no longer revolutionaries.

From the day of Gualterio's report, the word 'mafia' rapidly entered general use and simultaneously became the subject of furious controversy. For every person who used 'mafia' to mean a criminal conspiracy, there were others who maintained that it still meant nothing more menacing than a peculiarly Sicilian form of self-confident pride. Gualterio thus began to kick up the same dust cloud of bewilderment about what the term 'mafia' meant that Franchetti and Sonnino would encounter on their travels round Sicily a decade later – a dust cloud that would only finally be dispersed by Judge Giovanni Falcone.

By giving the mafia a name in these circumstances, Gualterio made a crucial contribution to its image. For since then the mafia and its politicians have frequently claimed that Sicily has been victimized and misrepresented. The government, they protest, has invented the idea that the mafia is a criminal organization as a pretext to oppress Sicilians – yet another version of the 'rustic chivalry' theory. One reason that these protests have won support over the past 140 years is that they have sometimes been true. Officials were constantly tempted to pin the label of mafioso on anyone who disagreed with them.

When the Italian government acted in this hypocritical way, it boosted the mafia's reputation. Thus, unwittingly, when Gualterio gave the mafia its name, he set in place what could be called the mafia 'brand's' positioning strategy vis-à-vis its main competitor. After Gualterio, every blind crackdown that failed to prosecute the mafia – whatever the government happened to take that word to mean – served further to undermine the state's trustworthiness, and thus to boost the real mafia's reputation not only for being smart and immune from prosecution, but also for being more efficient and even 'fairer' than the state.

More than a century would pass after Gualterio's report before anyone would write perceptively about the mafia's own attitude to its name. The writer in question was novelist Leonardo Sciascia, whose 1973 short story 'Philology' has a contemporary setting and takes the form of an imagined dialogue between two anonymous Sicilians about the meaning of the word 'mafia'. The more educated of the two, evidently a politician, is intent first and foremost on displaying his erudition, citing a century-long list of conflicting dictionary definitions, and explaining that 'mafia' probably derives from Arabic. With the indecision proper to a gentleman scholar – one imagines him as a portly man in his late sixties, dressed in a crumpled suit – he refuses to settle on one meaning for the word.

The younger man is much more down-to-earth – the picture in the reader's mind is of a chunky, middle-aged, flat-faced character in Ray Bans. Despite the respect that he evidently has for his partner in discussion, he cannot disguise that all the scholarly debate just makes him edgy. He prefers to hear that 'mafia' is the manly swagger of someone who knows how to look after his own interests.

It turns out, of course, that both men in Sciascia's story are mafiosi and that their dialogue is a rehearsal in case they are called before a parliamentary commission of inquiry. The older man says he is so confident that he will even ask the commission to let him make his 'little contribution' – 'a contribution to the confusion, you understand'. At some point after 1865, Sciascia is suggesting, the name 'mafia' became the Sicilian mafia's own little joke at the state's expense.

If the sources we have are to be believed – and, in the history of a secret society like the mafia, that 'if' is inevitably quite large – then the sect emerged in the Palermo hinterland when the toughest and smartest bandits, members of 'parties', *gabelloti*, smugglers, livestock rustlers, estate wardens, farmers, and lawyers came together to specialize in the violence industry and to share a method for building power and wealth that was perfected in the lemon business. These men extended their method to family members and business contacts. When they spent time in jail, they would also extend it to their fellow inmates. This sect became the mafia when the new Italian state made ham-fisted attempts to repress it. Thus by the mid-1870s at the very latest, and in the Palermo area at the very least, the most important components of the mafia method were firmly in place. The mafia had the protection rackets and the powerful political friends, and it also had its cellular structure, its name, its rituals, and an untrustworthy state as a competitor.

The great imponderable is whether, at this moment in history, there was one mafia or many. It is not clear how many of the 'mafias' referred to by the authorities in different parts of Sicily in the 1860s and 1870s were just autonomous gangs; they may have been copying methods that were widespread anyway, or may actually have recognized themselves as forming part of the same brotherhood as Uditore boss Antonino Giammona. The problem is how to interpret the historical documents. The authorities often referred to the mafia, but by no means everything that they called 'mafia' really was the mafia. Some policemen were evidently too keen to twist the facts to fit the conspiracy stories that their political masters needed to brandish against rivals.

Baron Turrisi Colonna's 1864 account of the sect carries a great deal of weight on this question because of his close relationship with the mafia – and Turrisi Colonna definitely talked only of a single 'great sect'. But this belief may derive from his Palermo-based perspective and may not be valid for the rest of western Sicily. There are also, by way of contrast, numerous police reports from the 1860–76 period that tell of different gangs locked in combat against each other in many towns and villages. But these are not a reliable indication that there were different mafias; the disputes referred to could just as easily have been generated within a single association in the same way that Cosa Nostra has internal wars today.

However all this evidence is interpreted, its very existence raises a question. If the mafia was around in the 1860s and 1870s, and if today's historians have been able to find evidence of it, then all the information needed to understand the mafia and to oppose it must have been available to people at the time. By 1877, Italy had Turrisi Colonna's pamphlet, the parliamentary inquiry into the 1866 revolt, Franchetti's report on the 'violence industry', Dr Galati's memorandum to the Minister of the Interior, and much more. The question is therefore why no one was able to stop the mafia. Part of the answer is that the Italian state simply had too many other troubles to cope with at the same time. But the main reason is far more sordid. For 1876 marks the point where the mafia became integral to Italy's system of government.

The Mafia Enters the Italian System
1876–1890

'An Instrument of Local Government'

The evidence of Dr Galati's misfortunes at the hands of the Uditore mafia was not allowed to gather dust; it was included in papers submitted to a full-scale parliamentary inquiry into law and order in Sicily that was set up in the summer of 1875, but only delivered its findings in January 1877. The story of the parliamentary inquiry – the first explicitly to address the mafia issue – demonstrates just how much Italy's rulers knew about the mafia problem in Sicily. It is also part of a much bigger political drama that took place between 1875 and 1877, illustrating how the Italian political system not only failed to combat the mafia in its early years, but actively contributed to its development.

The map of Italian politics after unification was a little like the map of Palermo at the time: a maze of little alleyways within the simple outlines of the main streets. Italy was ruled for a decade and a half after unification by a loose coalition called the Right; at its core were conservative landowners from northern Italy. The opposition, an even looser grouping called the Left, with strongholds in the South and Sicily, was in favour of higher government spending and more democracy. But the differences between the two coalitions were as much cultural as they were political. It often seemed to the Right – with no little justification, it must be said – that many southern and Sicilian members of parliament owed their election to boss politics, and to electoral machines that bribed supporters and bullied opponents. In the eyes of the Left, the Right seemed haughty and hypocritical; it had betrayed the ideals that had led to the foundation of the Italian state and it had badly neglected the South.

The story of the parliamentary inquiry begins in 1874 at a

time when the Right coalition began to run into serious trouble. Sicily – where there had always been few Right supporters – was the primary cause of the government's difficulties. By 1874, for a number of reasons (tax policy was top of the list), Sicily was slipping completely from the Right's political grasp. In the November elections of that year, forty out of forty-eight Sicilian constituencies returned opposition MPs to the national parliament in Rome. And expert on the 'sect', Nicolò Turrisi Colonna was among the leading campaign managers for the Left. His work was assisted by Antonino Giammona – his favourite mafia boss and the persecutor of Dr Galati. Giammona had a political following that brought some fifty votes under his direct control – this at a time when only 2 per cent of the population were enfranchised and a few hundred votes were regularly enough to win a constituency.

In Rome, following the November 1874 elections, the Right clung to power. During and after the election campaign, it resorted to a tactic that it had used previously: stoking up the crime issue to discredit the opposition. In more strident tones than ever, the Right accused the Sicilian Left MPs of wanting to undermine the country's unity, of being corrupt, of using bandits to rake in votes, of being mafiosi.

As part of this strategy, the government put forward some highly repressive legislation soon after the elections: it was proposed that suspected members of criminal associations and their political patrons could be imprisoned without trial for as much as five years. A wealth of compelling evidence garnered from prefects, investigating magistrates, and the police was presented to the committee examining the draft laws. It was pointed out that during 1873 there had been one murder for every 44,674 inhabitants in the northern region of Lombardy; in Sicily the figure was one murder for every 3,194 inhabitants. Official reports indicated that the mafia now reached right across western Sicily and even into some cities in the east like Messina – a major port for the citrus fruit industry. The prefects' opinions were divided on whether the mafia was a united organization, and on what role the Sicilian mentality played in it. But most of them were clear that the mafia based its power on extortion rackets and the intimidation of witnesses, and that its recruits included Sicilians of all social classes. The prefect of Agrigento, in the south-west of Sicily, believed that mafiosi were a special 'grade' of man:

The grade of *Mafioso* is acquired by giving evidence of personal courage; by carrying prohibited arms; by fighting a duel through whatever pretence; by stabbing or betraying someone; by pretending to forgive an offence in order to take vengeance for it at some other time or place (to take personal vengeance for injuries received is the first canon law of the *Mafia*); by keeping absolute silence regarding some crime; by denying before all the authorities and the magistrates the knowledge of any crime he has seen committed; by bearing false witness in order to procure the acquittal of the guilty; by swindling in whatever way.

The sober and well-informed Rome correspondent of *The Times* read through some of this material and concluded in alarm that the mafia was an 'intangible sect whose organization is as perfect as that of the Jesuits or the Freemasons, and whose secrets are more impenetrable'.

In producing all this evidence and putting forward its new anti-crime legislation, the Right was making a last-ditch bid to create the impression that it was an antimafia government facing up to a pro-mafia opposition. To the Left it seemed that the Right had overreached itself. Not only were men like Turrisi Colonna being directly targeted by the government's proposals, but a great many Sicilian property-owners who were simply victims of the mafia also felt threatened. Since unification they had been hoping in vain that the government would help them lever themselves from the clutches of organized crime. But now that their patience was entirely exhausted and they had voted for opposition candidates, they found that they were becoming potential targets for the police. The scene was set for a crucial political confrontation between the two sides.

The confrontation came during a tense debate in parliament about the proposed reforms over ten days in June 1875. When the discussion began, one Sicilian MP after another stood up to defend the island's reputation. Some denied that the mafia existed; it was just a pretext for putting down the opposition, they claimed. They pointed to the venomous anti-Sicilian prejudices displayed by one prefect who had asserted in a leaked report that Sicilians were a 'morally perverted' people who could only be governed by force.

One speech finally detonated the controversy; because of it the debate would be remembered as the rowdiest since the Italian parliament was founded in 1861. During the early exchanges, various speakers from the Left began to wonder out loud why a man sitting on their own benches had not yet intervened. A wiry, balding, bespectacled MP from southern Italy, Diego Tajani had been chief prosecutor at the Palermo Court of Appeal between 1868 and 1872, and he therefore knew a great deal about how the Right itself had ruled Sicily. The Left MPs regarded him as their secret weapon against the government, and their asides were intended to provoke him into telling what he knew. As a former public servant, Tajani was reluctant to speak about the duties he had once performed. But eventually, stung both by the comments from his colleagues on the Left benches, and by the government's attempts to capture the moral high ground on the crime question, he stood up to address the chamber.

Tajani's speech began with a gibe directed at the men of the Left sitting alongside him: denying the existence of the mafia, he said, was like denying the existence of the sun. Then he turned much sharper barbs against the Right. With what one pro-government newspaper called a 'cold smile' on his lips, Tajani revealed that, following the revolt of 1866, the Right had encouraged the police to collaborate with the mafia. Mafiosi, he alleged, were given freedom to operate in return for supplying information to the authorities on unauthorized criminals and on anyone the government regarded as a subversive.

Tajani had been personally involved in the most scandalous

cases, which centred on the figure of Giuseppe Albanese, the Palermo Chief of Police appointed in 1867. Albanese had no qualms about admitting that he was an admirer of a Bourbon official who had 'got the mafia interested in keeping the peace'. This was what one contemporary called the 'homoeopathic' approach to law and order. It involved making friends with the mafiosi, using them as vote-gatherers and unofficial police agents, and in return helping them to keep their rivals in check.

In 1869, Tajani explained, Chief of Police Albanese had been stabbed by a mafioso in a Palermo piazza. It turned out that he had been attacked because he had been trying to blackmail his assailant. Albanese also had links with a criminal band that had broken into the offices of the Court of Appeal, tunnelled under a main street to rob a savings institute, and stolen a number of precious objects from the Palermo museum. All of the objects were subsequently found in the home of a man who worked in Albanese's office at police headquarters.

Chief of Police Albanese, Tajani asserted to parliament, was more than an isolated corrupt policeman. In 1869, in the course of his duties as chief prosecutor, Tajani had learned that crimes in Monreale near Palermo were committed with the approval of the commander of the National Guard. Soon after the story emerged, two criminals who seemed prepared to give evidence about the case were ambushed and murdered. Albanese himself, despite being Chief of Police, not only discouraged an investigation into why and how the two men had died, he even told the magistrate responsible that 'reasons of public order had induced the authorities to order their deaths'. In 1871, on Tajani's orders, Albanese was charged with the murder of the informants in the Monreale case. It was when the Chief of Police was released for lack of evidence that Tajani resigned in disgust and stood for election under the Left banner.

Before Tajani could finish his speech to parliament, he was angrily interrupted by Giovanni Lanza, a gaunt man in his mid-sixties. Lanza had been Prime Minister and Minister of the Interior at the time of the alleged policy of collusion with the mafia. The austere, self-made son of a blacksmith, he embodied the Right's claims to moral superiority over the Left. But he had hardly begun to vent his rage in response to Tajani's accusations when his words were drowned out by shouts, boos, and whistles. What had already been a rowdy sitting descended into chaos as supporters of the two men jostled each other and traded insults. Tajani remained motionless, his cold smile still fixed on his face as he watched four of Lanza's friends drag the former Prime Minister from the chamber for his own good. The turmoil spilled out into the corridors of parliament and the session had to be abandoned.

It was only the following day that Tajani was able to bring his speech to its stark conclusion: 'The mafia in Sicily is not dangerous or invincible in itself. It is dangerous and invincible because it is an instrument of local government.' Having recovered his calm, Lanza tabled a demand for an inquiry into the accusations, but the political damage to the government was already done. The Right's law-and-order platform had collapsed. Nobody could now believe that parliament was divided between pro-mafia and antimafia politicians. It would prove easier for both sides to just drop the whole subject. So, when the repressive laws were passed (they were destined to remain a dead letter), both Left and Right agreed on what for politicians the world over is the preferred means of smoothing over a controversial issue: they set up a parliamentary commission of inquiry. The mafia was included within the inquiry's terms of reference, but so much else about Sicilian society was also included that the real contours of the mafia issue would almost certainly be blurred.

It is no wonder that the two 'English' intellectuals Franchetti and Sonnino did not trust the parliamentary inquiry to be incisive and they subsequently decided to mount their own private one instead. The people to whom Franchetti and Sonnino spoke, after the parliamentary inquiry had finished gathering evidence in Sicily, would confirm the account of events that Tajani had given to parliament. It is also now known that, with Tajani's arrest warrant hanging over him, Chief of Police Albanese fled

Sicily and was only persuaded to return by the then Prime Minister Lanza, who received him in his house and assured him of the government's support. It is also thought that an attempt to assassinate Tajani was being prepared just before he left office.

The nine members of the parliamentary commission of inquiry made their way round Sicily in the winter of 1875–6. Each town welcomed them warmly – municipal or military bands would accompany them to their hotels – and they held their interviews in the town hall. Various Senators and MPs used their interviews with the commissioners as a chance to explain away the crime problem: 'What is this maffia then? First of all, there is a benign maffia. The benign maffia is a kind of spirit of defiance . . . So I too could be a benign *maffioso*. I am not one, of course. But anyone who respects themselves could be.' Less cynical politicians, lawyers, police officers, and administrators, as well as ordinary citizens like Dr Gaspare Galati, also submitted evidence. Plenty of witnesses spoke of the mafia's role in the citrus fruit industry and in the revolts of 1860 and 1866. Together all these testimonies provided a confused but deeply worrying portrait of organized crime and political corruption. Italian politicians now had at their disposal even more evidence about the mafia.

The papers of the inquiry were never published. When the time came for the commission to submit its findings to parliament early in 1877, the Right coalition had already fallen. What little will there had been to make political use of the mafia issue was now gone. Neither the Right nor the Left had much interest in a serious understanding of organized crime in Sicily. (Hence also the poor reception given at the same time to Franchetti's work on the violence industry.)

The parliamentary commission's final report was delivered to an almost empty Chamber of Deputies. The conclusion it reached was both bland and wrong: the mafia was defined as 'an instinctive, brutal, biased form of solidarity between those individuals and lower social groups who prefer to live off violence rather than hard work. It unites them against the state, the

73

law and regular bodies.' In short, the mafia was conveniently dismissed as a disorganized bunch of poor, lazy crooks – enemies of the state rather than 'instruments of local government'. By 1877, Italy's politicians had most of the knowledge they needed about the mafia in order to fight it, and all of the reasons they needed to forget what they knew. The first stage of the process by which the mafia entered the Italian system was complete.

The second stage began when a Left coalition government was formed in March 1876. It was joined, cautiously, by the Sicilian MPs who had been elected with the opposition in 1874. The new Minister of the Interior was Giovanni Nicotera, a lawyer who had fought with Garibaldi and who understood southern Italian boss politics better than anyone – for the simple reason that he was its leading exponent. Nicotera set about turning the Ministry of the Interior building off Piazza Navona into a formidable vote-farming machine for the Left. Opposition supporters were cut from the electoral roll or harassed by the police; government funds and jobs were placed at the disposal of friendly candidates. In November 1876, Nicotera managed the elections so successfully that the Left won 414 parliamentary seats, leaving only 94 to the Right. He was returned in his own Salerno constituency with 1,184 votes to his opponent's 1; it is to be hoped that members of the poor man's family were at least allowed to abstain.

Nicotera approached the crime issue with the same gusto. The state of law and order in Sicily was still intolerable in 1876. For one thing, it was an international embarrassment. On 13 November, the young English manager of a sulphur company, John Forester Rose, was kidnapped just outside the mining town of Lercara Friddi. *The Times* reported that he was treated well before a ransom was surrendered and he was freed, although the American press subsequently said that his wife received his ears in the post before she was persuaded to pay up. It was clear, all the same, that the kidnappers had informers among the well-to-do Palermo circles that Mr Rose frequented, and that the ransom was paid through a mafia intermediary.

Nicotera knew that something had to be done. He was clearly no political ingénu: the sources of support that he drew on in his own fiefdom included the Freemasons and – it is suspected – the Camorra, the Neapolitan equivalent of the mafia. But he did not know Sicily well and did not have a power base there. So when he took office even he was genuinely taken aback by what his civil servants told him about the mafia's ties with the most powerful people in Sicily and about its far-reaching influence over the police and magistrature. He concluded that the wealthy classes in Sicily were 'heavily compromised with the mafia'.

A month after the Rose kidnapping, and without bothering to propose authoritarian legislation along the lines that the Right had wanted two years earlier, Nicotera appointed yet another tough prefect of Palermo and gave him instructions to implement yet another brutal crackdown on crime. Just as had happened under the Right, towns were encircled at night and suspects deported en masse. Just as they had done under the Right, the police colluded with some criminals against others. Just as under the Right, the repression produced howls of protest from some Sicilian politicians – including the friend of the 'sect', Baron Turrisi Colonna – about the illegal means used by the police. And, just as his Right predecessor Lanza had done, Nicotera used the repression to hit anyone he regarded as subversive and to bring potential allies to heel. When one Sicilian landowner who was heavily suspected of links with mafiosi wrote a newspaper article critical of Nicotera's antimafia campaign, the brother of the newspaper's editor was arrested and only freed in return for a promise to change the paper's uncooperative line.

But unlike the Right's campaigns of repression, Nicotera's proved to be successful. In November 1877, a year after his electoral triumph, he was able to announce the total defeat of the 'bandits' who had terrorized the countryside in Sicily since

1860. Even the man who had kidnapped the unfortunate Mr Rose was shot down. Nicotera's secret was that he had offered politicians in Sicily an implicit bargain: they would be looked on favourably by the government as long as they handed over the bandits. 'Bandits', in this case, often meant mafiosi who created problems for the government or who did not have the right political protection. The politicians were being asked to make sure that their friends in the violence industry kept crimes like kidnapping down to politically acceptable levels. Only the most flagrant aspects of the deep-seated crime issue were to be addressed in the process of, finally, making the island governable. To demonstrate that the bargain had been accepted, seventy town councils in the province of Palermo sent letters and petitions in support of Nicotera and the police. This warm demonstration of loyalty was probably orchestrated by Nicotera's prefect, but it did at least show that, seventeen years after Garibaldi invaded Sicily in the name of the Italian nation, some sort of political consensus between Rome and Sicily was finally taking shape.

A month after proclaiming the total defeat of Sicilian 'banditry', Nicotera was removed from office. His shameless authoritarianism had made him both a threat and an easy target for rival faction leaders on the Left. Before then, his dragnet had hauled in some mafia-like criminal associations, and operations against them did not stop with Nicotera's departure. Over the coming years, a series of high-profile trials followed investigations into groups like the 'Stuppagghieri' ('Fuse Burners') in Monreale, the 'Brothers' in Bagheria, the 'Fontana Nuova' in Misilmeri, and a gang of extortionist millers in Palermo. (The story of one such association, the 'Fratellanza' – or 'Brotherhood' – from Favara, is told in the next chapter.)

The picture of organized crime that emerged from these trials was predictably murky. Some *pentiti* came forward, and one or two were murdered. But for every witness whose credibility was confirmed posthumously in this way, another turned out to be too close to the authorities to be reliable, and still another turned out to have important political friends shielding him from prosecution. Whereas some policemen were overzealous in their hunt for evidence of secret societies, others were themselves linked to gangs. Accordingly the verdicts varied from complete acquittal on appeal, as in the case of the 'Stuppagghieri', to the twelve death sentences handed down in 1883 to the Piazza Montalto *cosca*, which was based on the south-eastern edge of Palermo. The few high-level suspects arrested for their connections with organized crime escaped conviction. Many mafiosi were left untouched by the repression – as long as they had the right political cover.

As the trials followed one another in the late 1870s and early 1880s, it became clear that the bargain pioneered by Nicotera was proving to be a turning point. Governments in Rome were resigning themselves to working with Sicilian politicians who had mafia support. Mafiosi were gradually becoming part of a new political normality. The men of honour built up their extortion rackets and other business interests, but they also learned that political friendships had become more important than ever to their survival. For their part, Sicilian politicians were given the opportunity that the Right had denied them for so long: they could now launch themselves into the national arena, into the mysterious dance of coalition partners that determined how power and resources were distributed from Rome. There was a bonus in that the Left spent much more public money in Sicily than the Right had done – on roads, bridges, harbours, hospitals, schools, sanitation, slum clearance, and asylums. All of these were potential sources of income and power for politicians and criminals alike. Thus mafiosi found that the Left was willing to use them as 'an instrument of local government', just as the Right had done, only in a slightly different way. Whereas the Right had tried to run Sicily by oiling guns, the Left preferred to grease palms. Under the Left, the mafia and the politicians it dealt with began to sink their arms deep into the Roman pork barrel.

Nicotera's bargain thus created a blueprint for governing

Sicily that would remain more or less in place for the next forty years. Indeed, even today, the mafia aims to be an 'instrument of local government' of the kind that it became under the Left. And today, as during the critical years of 1875–7, men of honour do not set the political agenda; only very rarely do they have either the inclination or the power to turn the tide of Italian politics. They merely adapt to circumstances by striking bargains with politicians of all colours.

The Favara Brotherhood: the Mafia in Sulphur Country

In the early nineteenth century blemishes of a more sickly shade of yellow began to appear in the grain-coloured highlands of the Sicilian interior. The island had a virtual natural monopoly in an element that was an essential raw material of the industrial revolution: sulphur, used in the production of a host of things from fungicides and fertilizers to paper, pigments, and explosives. The plains and hillsides of the south-western and central provinces of Agrigento and Caltanissetta were torn open to expose the precious element that lay in thick seams below the surface. It was as if a congenital geological illness were finally beginning to make its symptoms manifest. In the mining regions, unearthly bluish smoke could often be seen emanating from the *calcaroni*, huge buried mounds of sulphur-bearing rock that were slowly burned to release a brown liquid. The fumes poisoned the countryside around and ruined the health of men and animals alike. And life in the sulphur mines was more infernal even than the landscape: collapses were common, and any fire would create lethal sulphur dioxide fumes. One hundred men were killed in 1883 – by no means an untypical year.

Sicily's sulphur mines were a running national scandal, and not just because of the physical risks. Italian public opinion was most concerned about the little boys, some as young as seven or eight, who were hired in small teams to carry the rock from the workface to the *calcaroni*. These children led a wretched life. Their miserable pay went straight to their parents; they often saw no more than the odd cigar or cup of wine as a reward for their efforts. The huge baskets of rock they carried deformed their bodies. Worse still, concerned observers talked darkly of their 'wild instincts of wickedness and immorality'; pederasty was endemic in the sulphur mines.

In March 1883 in Favara, a town in the heart of sulphur country not far from the south-western coast of Sicily, a railway worker came to the police to say that he had been invited to join a secret republican society called la Fratellanza – the Brotherhood. He had been approached by a builder who told him that the society had special recognition signals that he would have to use if he wanted to avoid being attacked by other members. The railwayman felt he was being threatened, and guessed that there was a criminal intent behind the association.

The railwayman's evidence came soon after what had been weeks of tension and violence in Favara. The trouble began on the evening of 1 February when a man was shot dead by two hooded assailants outside a tavern where a christening was being celebrated. The police assumed that the killing was the conclusion of a fight in the tavern and interpreted the guests' blanket failure to recognize the killers as a sign that they were complicit. Everyone at the celebration was arrested.

The rumours in Favara were that the victim was a member of a criminal association. And those rumours became more credible the following day when a member of a rival gang was found dead outside the town. He had been shot in the back and his right ear was missing. Favara was suddenly on the verge of civil war. In the following days men from the two factions went about the town in groups, armed and wary. But then, just as suddenly, the tension dissipated and the threatened fighting between the two gangs failed to materialize. It was only when the railwayman told his story that the police began to reconstruct what had happened.

Between March and May 1883, more than 200 people were arrested in Favara and the surrounding area. One of the Brotherhood's leaders was actually caught in the act of initiating two hooded brothers. Extraordinarily, he even had a written copy of the association's statutes in his possession. He confessed, explaining that members would draw lots to decide who was to perform any killing that the leaders deemed necessary to the Brotherhood's interests. More confessions followed. Skeletons were recovered from remote grottoes, dried-up wells, and abandoned sulphur mines. Further versions of the statutes and a diagram of the Brotherhood's organization were recovered.

The trial of the Brotherhood took place in the specially adapted church of St Anne in Agrigento in 1885. One hundred and seven men were led in four chained lines into the dock. Many now denied the charges, claiming that they had confessed under torture. But the tactic did not work. The Brothers were convicted and imprisoned – a rare success against such a criminal association.

The case of the Favara Brotherhood gave the police a unique insight into the kind of mafia organization that grew up away from Palermo, in the sulphur regions of Agrigento and Caltanissetta provinces. But just as significant as the investigators' discoveries, which they proved in court, is what they failed to see about the Brotherhood's profound hold on the society around them. Historians now believe that the Brotherhood was a much more sophisticated and dangerous organization than the authorities realized. And if the mafia has survived so long in sulphur country, just as it has in the rest of western Sicily, it is partly because of the way that, like the Brotherhood in Favara, it has consistently been underestimated.

The Brotherhood was, in fact, only a few weeks old when police learned of its existence. It was formed when the bosses of Favara's two factions met to discuss the escalating violence in the town following the murder at the christening. Remarkably, given the interests at stake and the violence of the conflict, the two sides not only agreed a peace but decided to merge and form a single association.

The Brotherhood's rules were older than the association; they were followed by both of the gangs that came together to form it. And to anyone familiar with the story of Dr Galati and the Uditore mafia, those rules are strikingly familiar. The initiation ritual, for example: new members had their index finger pricked so that blood could be smeared on a sacred image. As the image was burned, the initiate recited an oath: 'I swear on my honour to be faithful to the Brotherhood, as the Brotherhood is faithful to me. As this saint and these few drops of my blood burn, so I will spill all my blood for the Brotherhood. As this ash and this blood can never return to their original state, so I can never leave the Brotherhood.' Because the Brotherhood had some 500 members recruited from several sulphur towns near Favara, a recognition ritual was also necessary. Like the Palermo version, it began with an inquiry about a sore tooth and proceeded with a similar exchange. (A report by the Palermo Chief Prosecutor to the Minister of Justice in 1877 claimed that this ritual was recognized across the island.)

The structure of the Brotherhood even bears similarities with the structure of Cosa Nostra that Tommaso Buscetta would first describe a century later. Members of the Brotherhood were divided into *decine* – groups of ten. Each *decina* had a commander known only to its members but secret from the rest of the brotherhood except for a single boss.

Investigators also learned that the Brotherhood regarded the bond between its members as more sacred than family ties. One member of the Brotherhood of Favara, Rosario Alaimo, told police how the Brothers had called him to a tavern to tell him that his nephew was a traitor; they then gave him a choice between killing his own nephew and being killed himself. When he accepted the first option, fear drove him to demonstrate his resolve with a toast: 'Wine is sweet, but the blood of a man is sweeter.' A few days later he helped lure his nephew into a trap so that other Brothers could murder him. As proof of his confession, Alaimo took the police to the ruined castle where his nephew's body was hidden. On returning to his cell, he hanged himself. It was said that he wanted his own end to mirror as closely as possible the way his nephew had been killed – by garrotting.

Even today, the mafia takes great care to manage blood relationships between its members. Because kinship can help the cohesion of a Family, nephews, brothers, and sons are often brought into the organization. But affection for a relative can also be destabilizing if it interferes with the first duty of obedience to the capo. So mafiosi are sometimes forced to show in dramatic fashion where their loyalty ultimately lies. If you, as a mafioso, have a brother who is also a man of honour and he breaks the rules, you may well be offered the same stark choice as the Brothers offered Alaimo: either you kill him or you both die. In such cases the firm has to be seen to come first. The elimination of a family member may become a point of pride for some men of honour. As captive mafioso Salvatore 'Totuccio' Contorno boasted in the 1980s, 'I'm the only one who can bathe my hands in my own blood.'

The similarity between the Brotherhood's rules and the ones adopted by the *cosche* around Palermo was striking even in 1883. Yet its significance seems largely to have escaped the magistrates and criminologists of the day. Favara and Palermo are on opposite coasts. One hundred kilometres of Sicily's mountainous interior, with its terrible roads, lie between them. That the mafia in two such distant places should share the same rules is probably explained by the fact that, before 1879, some of the leading Brothers had been confined on prison islands like Ustica with mafiosi from Palermo. It was in prison that these men were first told of the mafia and, quite possibly, initiated into it. They maintained links with mafiosi from other parts of Sicily once they were released. Being part of the early mafia meant joining a local gang; but it was also a passport to a wider world of criminal connections.

The prosecutors in the Favara Brotherhood case thought that the rituals binding the association together were merely 'primitive'. They suggested that crude instincts for vendetta and *omertà* were the Brotherhood's main motives. One magistrate talked of the 'barbarous mysticism' of the initiation ceremony; 'pure cannibalism' was his comment on the toast that Alaimo had drunk after agreeing to help murder his own nephew.

Words like 'primitive' and 'backward' mark one of the great

blind spots in nineteenth-century Italy's understanding of the mafia, as will become apparent in the next chapter. In this case they helped turn attention away from what was almost certainly the Brotherhood's tactically astute role within the local sulphur economy. Of the 107 men tried for membership of the gang, 72 worked in the sulphur industry. In addition to miners there were overseers and even small-time mine owners. These shared mining interests probably explain why the two rival gangs successfully united as la Fratellanza: economic rationality won out over the desire for vendetta. The trial also brought the Brotherhood's network of protectors out into the open: landowners, noblemen, and former mayors submitted character references. No one thought to ask exactly why these notables were seeking to protect the 'primitives'.

For all their hellishness, Sicily's sulphur mines were operated in almost as sophisticated a way as the lemon groves. The young boys who were treated as little more than beasts of burden in the industry were at the bottom of a long chain of contractors and subcontractors. The landed gentry leased out mining rights to entrepreneurs; the entrepreneurs hired overseers on commission; the overseers in turn engaged surveyors, guards, and miners. As the chain became longer, the risks of dealing in a commodity that was traded on international markets were spread more thinly.

The miners themselves – known as 'pickmen' – were paid piece rates. It was they who hired the teams of boys. They were a notoriously hard and quarrelsome crew known for their murderous drinking bouts. By the standards of their time and place they were far from poor; indeed, they were entrepreneurs of a kind. Some of them were in charge of three or four other miners. Many were keen to flaunt their hard-won social status. One observer, an Englishwoman who married a landowner in a sulphur region, wrote of the typical pickman: 'He is very ambitious in his way of dressing, and is often seen on Sundays arrayed in fine black cloth, with patent-leather top-boots and a large hooded cloak of fine dark cloth lined with green.' (It is not clear whether the hoods worn by the Brothers had a ritual significance, or were badges of the pickmen's status, or both.)

Sulphur was a highly competitive business for everyone involved. And, as in most of western Sicily, violence could give an edge over the competition. At every tier in the hierarchy running from the landowner down to the miner, the ability to use force in an organized and tactically astute way was a key economic asset. Entrepreneurs, managers, overseers, guards, and pickmen could form cartels to force out rivals. Like the lemon groves around Palermo, the sulphur mines were a breeding ground for criminal associations.

Viewed without 'primitivist' preconceptions, the Favara Brotherhood case also provides an early hint of what it means to be a godfather within the mafia. It is far from incidental that the murder which ultimately led to the foundation of the Brotherhood was carried out at a christening. Killing a man at a christening was a calculated offence aimed not just at a family, but at a whole enemy gang. That is why the murder brought an equally calculated retort when the second victim had his ear cut off after being shot in the back.

In Sicily as in much of southern Italy, christenings were important less because of the child's baptism than because the ceremony also meant welcoming a new godfather into the family. Baptizing the child made the father and godfather into *compari* – 'co-fathers'. It was a solemn undertaking: even brothers who became *compari* had to stop using the familiar 'tu' form of address and speak to each other with the formal 'voi' instead. For the rest of their lives, the two 'co-fathers' would be obliged to respond to each other's requests, of whatever kind. Peasants and sulphur miners told many hair-raising folk tales about the terrible vengeance that John the Baptist, the patron saint of *compari*, wrought on any man who betrayed his 'co-father'.

The institution known as *comparatico* was a kind of social glue; it extended the family bond further out into society, encouraging peace and cooperation. Two men at daggers drawn might decide to bury their differences and become *compari* in order to avoid a violent dispute that would only harm both of their families. A labourer might enlist a more influential man as the godfather of his child, offering him deference and loyalty in the hope of favours in return. Choosing a powerful godfather for your child could bring a job in the sulphur mine, some land to cultivate, a loan, charity.

But becoming a godfather sometimes had another side to it. The Sicilian phrase 'fari u cumpari' ('to act like a co-father') also meant to be an accomplice, to help someone commit an illegal deed. If the link between *compari* could help keep society together, it could also bind men into a criminal pact. Mafiosi frequently strengthened the bonds between them by becoming *compari*. Senior men of honour were sometimes called 'godfather' in imitation of the prestige with which the title was endowed in society. Even today, just as a *compare* oversees a baby's baptism, so a mafia godfather presides over a young recruit's initiation – his rebirth as a man of honour.

The mafia has, from the outset, been highly sophisticated in the way that it infiltrates the leading sectors of the Sicilian economy, and equally sophisticated in adopting and adapting any sources of loyalty within Sicilian culture that it can use for its own murderous purposes. The mafia, in other words, is anything but backward.

Primitives

By the time the Favara Brotherhood was discovered, the mafia had left the headlines and entered the quieter domain of academic debate. The chief prosecutor in the Favara case sent an account of the Brotherhood's deeds to an academic journal, *The Archive of Psychiatry, Penal Sciences and Criminal Anthropology to Serve the Study of Deranged and Delinquent Man*. It was edited by leading criminologist Cesare Lombroso who, outside Italy, was the most famous Italian intellectual of his day. The book that made his reputation was *Delinquent Man*, first published in 1876. In it he argued that criminals could be identified by certain physical deformities: jug-handle ears, low foreheads, long arms, and so on. He termed these physical signs 'criminal stigmata'. What they demonstrated, according to Lombroso, was that crooks were actually biological anachronisms, accidental throwbacks to an earlier stage in human evolution. That is why they looked like 'primitive' non-European peoples and even animals. Non-Europeans were, Lombroso confidently assumed, stationed at a lower rung on the ladder of racial development and were therefore inherently criminal. Pushing his own logic through to breaking point, Lombroso also thought that all animals were criminal too.

The lunacy of what Lombroso called his 'criminal anthropology' is considerably more apparent today than it was then. Italians were the anxious citizens of a fragile new state and, since unification, had been the victims of an alarming crime wave. As a result, many of them found Lombroso's ideas reassuring. The implication of his theory was that it was not Italy's fault if it had so many wrongdoers – biology makes a good scapegoat. As well as offering political comfort, the many new editions of *Delinquent Man* (and its even racier sequel, *Delinquent Woman*) gave Lombroso's readers a prurient thrill with their copious illustrations of criminal ears, delinquent genitalia, and so on. To the large audiences that came to his lectures at Turin University, Lombroso – a tubby, squirrel-like man – would demonstrate the presence of the stigmata of delinquency on the bodies of live felons.

Lombroso's thinking on the mafia was more than usually muddled; he attributed it to a bundle of causes including race, weather, 'social hybridism' – whatever that was – and the fact that monasteries had promoted idleness by doling out soup. He had plenty of critics ready to point out that his theories were contradictory and unsupported by any evidence. But many of those critics also seriously underestimated the mafia. Crime had social causes, they argued. It was poverty that led peasants and workers to form secret societies. The mafia was primitive, certainly, but it was socially primitive. It existed because Sicily was still stuck in the Middle Ages. Some left-wing thinkers saw the Favara Brotherhood as a very rudimentary trade union. They trusted that economic modernization and the advance of the working class would soon bring an end to all symptoms of backwardness like the mafia. (This illusion would hamstring left-wing thinking on the mafia for decades to come.)

In the 1880s, the new ideals of scientific criminology and social progress inspired a generation of policemen who were beginning to build up considerable expertise in fighting organized crime. One such policeman, who was a follower of Lombroso, was Giuseppe Alongi. His 1886 book, *The Maffia in its Factors and Manifestations*, lays great stress on the ethnic psychology of Sicilians. They displayed 'an unbounded egotism', 'an exaggerated sense of themselves', 'a capacity for violent, tenacious disdain and hatred that are implacable until *vendetta* is achieved'. Alongi did not believe that such people could create a large criminal association that had fixed rules. The mafia, he maintained, was nothing more than a label for disparate, self-contained *cosche* in individual neighbourhoods and villages. He saw the Favara Brotherhood as an example. Alongi may have been right to discount the theory that the mafia was a centralized conspiracy. But he was almost certainly wrong to discount the possibility that many local *cosche* were part of a bigger network.

Despite his primitivist preconceptions, Alongi was an astute observer of the lifestyles of families who benefited from the trickle-down profits of crime in areas of mafia activity. He saw that money was spent conspicuously in the villages around Palermo. The men wore expensive hats, boots, and gloves, and had thick gold watch chains and rings. On Sundays the women donned silk dresses and little plumed hats. Feast days saw a heavy consumption of meat and desserts. The families of doctors, professionals, and bureaucrats could not compete with the sartorial display mounted by their social inferiors.

Alongi also noted that pawnbrokers did a good trade. As Dr Galati had observed of the Uditore *cosca* a decade before, only the mafia bosses became truly rich. 'Most of them squander the fruit of their thieving. They spend it on living it up, and engage in debauchery, gluttony, and every kind of vice.' The excess of these lifestyles was not reflected in the way the men of honour themselves talked and behaved, according to Alongi:

These people are imaginative and their villages hot; their day-to-day language is mellifluous, exaggerated, full of images. Yet the *maffioso*'s language is short, sober, clipped . . . The phrase *lassalu iri* ('let him go') has a disdainful meaning along the following lines: 'My dear chap, the man you are dealing with is an imbecile. You only compromise your dignity by picking him as an enemy' . . . Another phrase – *be' lassalu stari* ('let him be') – seems identical, but has the opposite meaning. It translates as, 'That man deserves a severe lesson. But now is not the time. Let us wait. Then, when he is least expecting it, we will get him' . . . The true *maffioso* dresses modestly. He affects a brotherly bonhomie in his attitude and speech. He makes himself seem naïve, stupidly attentive to what you are saying. He endures insults and slaps with patience. Then, the same evening, he shoots you.

Alongi's book helped him make an outstanding career. His insistence that the mafia was a primitive gang and the fact that he was very reticent about its connections among politicians, policemen, and magistrates probably had something to do with his success.

Italy's fascination with its 'primitives' also had a softer and yet ultimately more sinister side to it. For more than four decades before the First World War, Giuseppe Pitrè, a lean, high-browed doctor, toured Palermo and its environs in a battered carriage that doubled as an office – papers and notes permanently littered its interior. As he went he collected peasant sayings, fables, songs, customs, rituals, and superstitions. Pitrè, who liked to think of himself as a 'demo-psychologist', was building up a vast portrait of the collective Sicilian mentality. The result was an invaluable, if sentimental, archive of a disappearing 'primitive' world. Almost everything that people have thought about Sicilian folklore since the late nineteenth century – and almost every stereotype about the Sicilian character – can be traced back to it.

Here is how the professor of 'demo-psychology' defined 'mafia' in 1889:

Mafia is neither a sect nor an association, it has no regulations or statutes. The *mafioso* is not a thief or a criminal ... *Mafia* is the awareness of one's own being, an exaggerated notion of one's own individual strength ... The *mafioso* is someone who always wants to give and receive respect. If someone offends him, he does not turn to the Law.

When *Cavalleria rusticana* met with its astounding success the year after Pitrè published these words, he could have been justified in feeling a certain pride. The opera that peddled the myth of rustic chivalry to the world is based on a short story and a one-act play by the leading Sicilian author of the era, Giovanni

Verga, who drew heavily on Pitrè's work. Although it is filtered through the words of other men, the Sicily that Mascagni set to music, and set in stone, is in good measure Pitrè's Sicily.

Pitrè became a talisman for Sicilian gangsters and their lawyers for a long time afterwards; his cosy definition of the mafia was even quoted in court in the mid-1970s by fearsome Corleone boss Luciano Leggio. It is unlikely that Pitrè was actually a member of the mafia. Yet at the time of the first performance of *Cavalleria* in 1890, he was working closely in local government in Palermo with a member of parliament whom he gushingly proclaimed was 'a real gentleman . . . an extremely upright and honest administrator'. That 'honest administrator' was in fact the most notorious mafioso of the turn-of-the-century era, a man who belied any notion that the mafia was backward: Don Raffaele Palizzolo. When the public came to learn more about Don Raffaele, it would also learn just how deep into Italy's system of government the mafia had extended its power – at the very time when the country was busy convincing itself that men of honour were nothing more than primitives.

3

Corruption in High Places
1890–1904

A New Breed of Politician

Don Raffaele Palizzolo would receive his clients in the morning in his Palermo home in the Palazzo Villarosa, in via Ruggiero Settimo. They approached him bearing flowers or other gifts as he sat up in bed with a blanket round his shoulders. Some were seeking a job with the municipality. Others might be magistrates or police officials who wanted a transfer, a promotion, a pay rise. Or they might be suspects in need of a gun licence or of protection from police harassment; councillors looking for a position of influence on a commission or committee; high-school or university students looking to be forgiven poor grades that threatened their progress.

Don Raffaele was not haughty and would listen to everyone indulgently; he would chat, ask after relatives, offer sympathy, promise help. The audiences continued as he washed, tended to the jaunty upward curls at the tips of his moustache, and slipped into the long, close-fitting, double-breasted jacket the Italians called a *redingote* (from 'riding coat').

In the afternoons, Palizzolo would take care of his interests and bestow favours. He was an owner of land and a holder of leases, a councillor in local and provincial government, a charity and bank trustee. He managed the merchant navy's health insurance fund, and presided over the administration of the lunatic asylum. As a member of parliament he was a staunch supporter of the government, whoever was in power.

Palizzolo's morning receptions, which were held throughout a forty-year political career, had a distinctively shameless style. But there is nothing exclusively mafioso, or exclusively Sicilian, about this kind of patronage and clientele building in politics. The same basic mechanisms are still found in many places in

95

Italy, to say nothing of other countries across the world. Votes are exchanged for favours: politicians and state officials appropriate public resources – jobs, contracts, licences, pensions, grants – and reinvest them privately, in their personal support networks or clienteles.

Patronage, clientelism, and corruption are not the same thing as the mafia. In fact, the mafia would not have come into being if a modern state had not at least tried, however cack-handedly, to impose the rule of law in Sicily. In other words, the mafia does not grow naturally from a mulch of sleaze. There are plenty of places in the world where there is political corruption, and not all of them produce mafia-like organizations. Nor does the patronage factor in politics mean that the big issues like economics, democracy, and foreign policy count for nothing. That said, Palizzolo was certainly in league with the mafia, and the power of the mafia cannot be understood without grasping the patronage politics of which he came to be the most notorious exponent of his era.

Patronage is costly. Until 1882, the costs were relatively contained: only some 2 per cent of the population, all property-owning male adults, were entitled to participate in the Italian political process. The electorate in any given constituency might well consist of only a few hundred people. In those circumstances, the packet of fifty votes controlled by Antonino Giammona could make all the difference. In 1882, things changed when the franchise was extended to include one quarter of the adult male population. The era of mass politics was on its way. Elections suddenly became more expensive. It was a time of risk and opportunity both for politicians and mafiosi.

Don Raffaele Palizzolo rose to the challenge and devoted his life to brokering favours. His record was long and crooked: he defrauded charities, protected and used bandits, testified in favour of mafiosi. His domain had its nerve centre in the suburban township of Villabate, but it extended far to the city's south-east, taking in Caccamo, Termini Imerese, and Cefalù. He was the protector of the Villabate *cosca*, the guest of honour at their banquets, the man who helped them turn their territory into an important terminal for the cattle-rustling routes leading from the great estates of the interior towards Palermo. He also had a strong enough support network in Palermo and its outskirts to get himself elected three times as MP for a constituency there in the 1890s.

Gun licences are a good example of the chain of favours linking men like Palizzolo and the mafia. They could only be obtained with a reference from a leading citizen, such as a politician. This was an obvious opportunity to curry favour. In the run-up to elections the deal became more systematic. On the order of the Minister of the Interior, the prefect could withdraw all gun permits. His declared aim was to prevent the political contest spilling over into violence, but the real aim was to influence the vote. Only sponsoring letters from the central government's favoured electoral candidate would allow the licences to be returned. The politicians would sell such letters for electoral funds, votes, or favours.

The fragmentation of the Italian political system was Don Raffaele's great ally. For much of the history of Italy there have been few clear dividing lines within an unstable mosaic of cliques and interest groups. This has been true from the top to the bottom of the state, in the council chambers of provincial towns as in national assemblies. Amid the fragmentation, strategically placed minorities have been able to exert great leverage. In most cases, the mafia and its politicians have constituted a strategically placed minority.

Under normal circumstances in the late nineteenth century, Italy could not muster the political resolve and vigilance needed to expose the likes of Don Raffaele. The country's quarrel-racked coalition governments were held in place for only a few months at a time with the support of Sicilian MPs. But in the 1890s Italy was swept by a crisis so grave that for a while it seemed as if the country might fall apart. The political turmoil was to lead to the most serious threat the mafia had faced since its birth.

In 1892, the two major Italian credit institutions folded. Later that year it was revealed that the Banca Romana, one of several banks that had the right to produce currency, had been effectively forging millions of lire; 'genuine' bills were found with duplicate serial numbers. The cash was channelled to some of the country's leading politicians who used it to fund their political campaigns. The weakness of the lira precipitated a massive exportation of metal currency; silver and even bronze coins became so scarce that mutual aid societies and shop-keepers' associations in northern Italy had to issue their own tokens. With the economy already at the bottom of a long depressive cycle, it looked as if the whole financial system was about to collapse. Martial law was declared in Sicily in January 1894 to quell violent confrontations between labourers and land-owners. The Socialist Party was banned later the same year.

Under its first Sicilian Prime Minister, Francesco Crispi, the government responded to the crisis in the worst possible way: by staging a lunatic drive for colonial glory in Ethiopia. The result was inevitable. At the battle of Adowa in March 1896, a force of 17,500 Italian troops and locally recruited askari was destroyed by a better-armed and better-led Ethiopian army numbering over 120,000. It was the worst defeat ever suffered by a European colonial power. Fifty per cent of the Italian force was killed, wounded, or led away into captivity.

The country stumbled from crisis to crisis. In May 1898, mar-tial law was declared even in Milan, the country's economic capital: at least eighty people were killed by troops. Cannons bombarded Milan's Capuchin monastery where rebels were thought to be hiding. When the smoke cleared, only a few friars were found, along with some beggars who had been waiting for their soup.

A month after the events in Milan a military man was appointed as the new Prime Minister. General Luigi Pelloux, who had served his king as a soldier since he was little more than a boy, has a bad reputation today because his period in office is associated with an attempt to pass a package of highly authoritarian reforms; they would have curtailed press freedom, banned unions in the public services, and allowed the government to send suspects into internal exile without trial. Nonetheless, Pelloux was no blind reactionary by the standards of the moment. His government was appointed with the aim of managing a transition back to something more like normality from what had been the most turbulent years in the short history of the Italian state. An attack on corruption in Sicily was a part of this programme. Thus it was that in August 1898, General Pelloux appointed a new Chief of Police in Palermo with instructions to tackle the mafia. In 1900, the Chief of Police described Don Raffaele Palizzolo's political supporters as follows:

[they are] the *mafiosi*, the men with criminal records, the sort who are a permanent danger to public safety because they are engaged in all manner of crimes against people and property. None of them spares threats, violence and intimidation to force honest electors to vote for their candidate . . . To this end they use the same methods that the mafia uses to impose wardens on the owners of fruit farms and extort tributes from rich landowners.

Palizzolo would be worthy of his place in this book if he were only the prime representative of a new breed of mafia politician. But he also became the subject of the biggest mafia trial of the era; with Don Raffaele, the mafia returned to the national headlines for the first time in twenty-five years. Much less well known than Palizzolo – but just as important to the history of the mafia – was his adversary, the Chief of Police of Palermo appointed by General Pelloux. His name was Ermanno Sangiorgi and his story has only recently surfaced from the archives.

The Sangiorgi Report

Among the innumerable documents now held in Italy's Central State Archive in Rome is a restricted file containing a report, submitted to the Ministry of the Interior in instalments between November 1898 and January 1900. The report was written by Ermanno Sangiorgi, Chief of Police of Palermo, and addressed to the city's chief prosecuting magistrate as part of the preparations for a trial. Reading its 485 yellowing, handwritten pages today feels rather like working away at the contours of a buried vase with an archaeologist's probes and brushes, only to realize in the end that what has been exhumed is an unexploded bomb.

The report begins with the first complete picture of the Sicilian mafia ever produced. Earlier evidence about the mafia of the Palermo area always comes in scattered fragments. Here the information is explicit, detailed, and systematic. There is an organizational plan of the eight mafia *cosche* ruling the suburbs and satellite villages to Palermo's north and west: Piana dei Colli, Acquasanta, Falde, Malaspina, Uditore, Passo di Rigano, Perpignano, Olivuzza. The boss and underboss of each *cosca* are named, and there are personal details on many of the rank-and-file members. In all, there are profiles of 218 men of honour, men who own land, who work in and guard the citrus groves, who broker fruit deals. The report tells of the mafia's initiation ritual and code of behaviour. It sets out its business methods, how it infiltrates and controls the market gardens, how it forges money, commits robberies, terrifies and murders witnesses. It explains that the mafia has centralized funds to support the families of men in prison and to pay lawyers. It tells how the bosses of mafia *cosche* work together to manage the association's affairs and control territory.

This diagram of the mafia is impressive enough; it chimes almost precisely with what Tommaso Buscetta sat down to reveal to Judge Falcone decades later. There is no more riveting illustration of Italy's long-standing failure to see the truth about the mafia. But more riveting still is the sense that this dull-looking document – reference DGPS, aa.gg.rr. Atti speciali (1898–1940), b.1, f.1 – could have changed history. It could have done as much damage to the mafia as Falcone's maxi-trial of 1987. If the report had achieved its aim, the mafia would have suffered a devastating defeat only a few decades after it emerged.

The report's author, Ermanno Sangiorgi, was a stern, square-jawed career policeman. The newspapers of the time say that he cut an unmistakable figure in Palermo. Although he was nearer sixty than fifty, and his hair had receded to the crown of his head, his striking blond beard was only just beginning to grey. His accent clearly betrayed his origins in the Romagna region of northern–central Italy. Sangiorgi was and remains all but unknown, and as a result there is precious little information available about him. Yet he understood the Sicilian mafia better than anyone. It was Sangiorgi who was called in to conduct the operation against the Uditore *cosca* when Dr Galati reported his story to the Minister of the Interior in 1875. It was Sangiorgi who led the round-up of the Favara Brotherhood in 1883. His appointment as Chief of Police in Palermo in August 1898 was the culmination of his career, a chance to use his patiently accumulated expertise to bring Sicily's secret criminal association to its knees.

Sangiorgi wrote his report with attention to detail and no little passion. He was tackling head on the scepticism and complicity in the institutions, and he sensed that he was within reach of a landmark prosecution. He wrote his report at a time when it was difficult, but by no means impossible, to convict mafiosi for single crimes, or even bring isolated *cosche* like the Favara Brotherhood to book. Witnesses had to be convinced to take the stand and tell the truth; mafia informers had to be kept alive long enough to testify; judge and jury had to be protected from reprisals and insulated from bribery. Sangiorgi faced all of these problems, but he knew that the real challenge was to convict the mafia per se, and to base that prosecution on the protection rackets and political contacts that underlay its method.

For that reason he aimed to use a specific legal instrument: a law that proscribed criminal associations. Although this law did not bring particularly heavy penalties, a conviction based on his report would have a profound political significance. It would prove the seemingly outlandish theory that a secret, highly sophisticated criminal society had extended its influence across western Sicily and even overseas. Quite simply, if Sangiorgi had been successful, no one would ever again have been able to deny that the mafia existed.

But Sangiorgi failed. If his report constitutes startling proof that in 1898 Italy's rulers knew precisely what the mafia was, then his failure, and the way that his precious knowledge came to be forgotten, is a disquieting lesson in how the country's political system has helped the mafia survive up to the present day.

Sangiorgi was not just a good cop; he was also something of a storyteller in his own right. From among the hundreds of names, the dozens of carefully cross-checked witness statements, his policework slowly exposed an intricate pattern of crimes, a series of interlocking tales of murder and deception that illustrated the brutality and labyrinthine complexity of mafia influence at every level of Sicilian society. The Chief of Police even has moments of genuine narrative verve.

Most of Sangiorgi's stories are set in the western part of the Conca d'Oro, the 'golden basin' curving around the outskirts of Palermo. The area has been famous for its beauty and fertility since Roman times. In 1890, the magazine *Illustrazione Italiana* portrayed it as a place where 'the imagination catches fire and takes flight', as 'a whole oriental vision, an enchantment'. Here was proof that 'poetry blossoms generous and abundant in the Sicilian people'. Palermo's moneyed elite built out-of-town residences among the lemon groves of the Conca d'Oro. Spring was the season of *villeggiatura*, when the wealthy would abandon their city homes and head for huge villas, set in exotic gardens and tended by armies of servants. At the turn of the century, Palermo's eighty barons, fifty dukes, and seventy princes mingled with Europe's crowned heads and plutocrats in the city's villas, clubs, theatres, salons, and boulevards. By the time of Sangiorgi's appointment in Palermo, the yacht set had made the Sicilian capital into a favourite resort, a Paris by the sea. In his drive to discover the mafia's secrets, Sangiorgi followed men of honour along winding Stygian channels that connected the ordinary people of Palermo with the gilded lives of Sicily's internationally celebrated high society.

Much of Sangiorgi's work revolved around a murder mystery that had already been vexing the police in Palermo for a year before he arrived. The papers called it the 'case of the four missing men', and it centred on a typical lemon business, the Fondo Laganà, that lay not far from the cemetery in Arenella, a village squeezed between the echoing shadow of Monte Pellegrino and the sea just to the north of Palermo. It was a place where, after dark, even the cries of the fishermen on the beach hundreds of metres away could be heard distinctly. Across the road from the main building on the *fondo* stood a shop where they made pasta in night shifts. Nearby was a post occupied twenty-four hours a day by customs guards. Yet nobody confessed to noticing anything unusual there in September and October of 1897 until a smell betrayed the fact that all was not right. The unmistakable sweet stench of rotting flesh had been drifting over the walls of the Fondo Laganà for several days before customs guards timidly alerted the police. And when the police broke into the *fondo*, they uncovered a mafia killing factory. The interior walls of the farm building, little more than a one-room brick box, were pocked with bullet holes and spattered with blood. The unholy odour came from a narrow, deep grotto nearby. Firefighters were called in to reach the bottom. There they found human remains in an advanced stage of decomposition – they had been sprinkled with quicklime. Within the space of six weeks, four men had died of multiple gunshot wounds on the Fondo Laganà.

The case of the four missing men was still unsolved when Sangiorgi arrived in Palermo to begin his duties as Chief of Police the following August. When he did, there was also a mafia war under way: men with fearsome reputations were found dead in the lanes and streets of the Conca d'Oro; others were disappearing without trace. The detectives under Sangiorgi's command had their sources, but knew little about how the battle lines were drawn up, or whether the war and the four murders on the Fondo Laganà were connected. Then as now, not only was knowledge of mafia affairs hard to come by, but there was also a sizeable gap between knowledge and proof. The problem that the authorities faced was how to convince sources to become witnesses. For that reason, in his report Sangiorgi does not name most of the people who gave him his information. Terrified by the organization's proven ability to punish anyone who gave evidence to the police, and suspecting that the mafia had agents among the police and prosecutors, people would only speak off the record. Sangiorgi's journey towards the secrets of the Fondo Laganà only began when he found a courageous exception to this rule.

On 19 November 1898, Sangiorgi arranged for his detectives to interview Giuseppa Di Sano. As later newspaper reports suggest, Giuseppa was a plump, robust woman with plenty of grit and not too much imagination. But in many senses she is the quiet heroine of the Sangiorgi report. The story she told began two years before she gave her evidence to Sangiorgi, and nine months before the murders on the Fondo Laganà.

She was then struggling to make ends meet selling food and other supplies to the neighbourhood near the Giardino Inglese park. But she also had more than her usual lot of cares. The local commander of the *carabinieri* was visiting her store too often. More often, that is, than was strictly necessary to follow up his station's orders for food and wine. The trade was more than welcome, of course. What concerned Giuseppa was the gossip: the quarter was alive with rumours that the officer was trying to persuade her eighteen-year-old daughter Emanuela to begin an affair. This was a big problem for a small business-woman in a community not famous for its good relations with the forces of law and order. The rumours had to be dampened down – without offending the officer.

Giuseppa's troubles did not end there. The owner of a local tannery had been sending his sons to her for supplies. They kept trying to pay in notes and coins that she knew were false. She also knew that the businessman and his sons had dangerous friends. When she politely turned down the proffered money, the tannery owner's sons persisted. Finally one large-denomination note got past her husband. Giuseppa sent him off, ears still ringing, to sort the matter out. The tannery owner fobbed him off with only part of the debt, protesting that his boys had not known that the money was false.

Then came the most worrying episode of all. In late December 1896, the local women suddenly began looking askance at Giuseppa and avoiding her shop. Finally a housewife came in and complained audibly about 'cheap women' in the neighbourhood. Giuseppa challenged the housewife to spell out what was on her mind, assuming that this gibe was aimed at her daughter. The woman replied sharply that she was talking about police spies. Giuseppa was perplexed and afraid. There was something going on that was far more ominous than the rumours about her daughter or even the dispute over the phoney money.

On 27 December two suspicious-looking men, one of them barely out of his teens, came into her store. Across the street from the entrance was a wall surrounding a lemon grove. The wall now had a small hole knocked through it not far above the ground. In retrospect, Giuseppa realized that the two men were checking that the hole offered a clear line of fire into the shop. She recalled that the older man stopped long enough to say, out loud, apropos of nothing, 'If I do something stupid there's always my mother who will look after me, my wife and my children.' A statement so oblique could only be read one way, as a threat. Giuseppa's anxiety turned to alarm.

At eight o'clock the same evening a slim, pale young stranger entered and asked for half a litre of fuel oil. Picking up the container, he went to the door. Then he stretched out his right arm and made a gesture towards the other side of the street. Through the hole in the wall two shots were fired. Giuseppa was hit in the shoulder and side. As she fell, her daughter Emanuela came towards her to help. A third shot was fired, hitting Emanuela and killing her instantly.

When Chief of Police Sangiorgi asked Giuseppa Di Sano to come in to be interviewed, he was revisiting an old crime – one of the guilty men had already been caught. But, as antimafia investigators often have to do, Sangiorgi was reinterpreting an earlier episode, looking for loose ends, fitting them into a bigger pattern of intrigue. Crucially, for the progress of Sangiorgi's investigations, Giuseppa was prepared to testify that her daughter's murder was a mafia affair. Her words would allow Sangiorgi to turn this isolated case into evidence that the mafia was indeed a criminal organization with its own rules, its own structure and, most important of all, its own way of killing.

Sangiorgi's underworld sources also told him that Giuseppa's daughter was the first victim – an incidental one – of a sequence of betrayals and murders perpetrated by men of honour in the Conca d'Oro. The sequence was set in motion two weeks before the murder when the *carabinieri* raided a counterfeit currency factory near Giuseppa's store and caught three men at the scene. The mafia suspected a leak. Inquiries were led by man of honour Vincenzo D'Alba; his brother was one of the mafiosi arrested during the raid. He did not take long to put together the various pieces of evidence: Giuseppa Di Sano resented the local mob because of the business of the forged banknotes; she and her daughter were friendly with the *carabinieri*; what is more, Giuseppa's brother-in-law had installed a screw press in the machine shop that was the cover for the forgers' operation. Everything seemed to point in the same direction. Before he even presented his case to the meeting of the *cosca*, Vincenzo D'Alba instructed his mother to orchestrate a gossip campaign by the women of the area. His aim was to ruin both Giuseppa's business and her reputation: the unpopular are less likely to be missed, their deaths less likely to be investigated thoroughly. On 26 December 1896, Giuseppa Di Sano was condemned to death by the Falde *cosca* of the mafia for a crime against *omertà* that she did not commit. Twenty-four hours later D'Alba and his accomplice attempted to carry out the sentence, but only succeeded in killing Giuseppa's daughter.

It was Vincenzo D'Alba who came into Giuseppa's shop both to check the line of fire from the lemon grove across the street and to utter his abstruse threat. For a mafia hit is not just about the practicalities of ending someone's life. It is also brutal, laconic theatre. The local people would have known who controlled the lemon grove opposite, and the hole in the wall was there to be seen. News of Vincenzo D'Alba's threat would have travelled quickly. He came to the shop on the day of the planned murder as much to show his face as to prepare the ground for the attack. Although no casual passer-by would have been able to see the two killers through the hole in the wall, their identity would probably not have been a great mystery in the community. This deliberately public murder defied anyone who saw what happened to go to the police. The Falde *cosca* was parading its dominance over the territory.

It probably needed to. Sangiorgi surmised that the loss of the forgery operation had resonated well beyond the Falde *cosca* on whose territory the phoney mint was located. Just as the counterfeiters needed a wider network to pass their 'money' into circulation, so income from the operation was spread among other *cosche*. As a result, the *cosca*'s prestige had been damaged by the raid; it needed a rapid demonstration to the rest of the organization that everything was still under control.

When the mafia kills, it does so in the name of all its associates.

It consults, it mounts trials, it looks for consensus, it seeks to justify its actions to its supporters and show that it is in charge. This is what Chief of Police Sangiorgi sought to use Giuseppa Di Sano's evidence to prove. Today's antimafia investigators would put it more starkly: the mafia kills in the way a state does; it does not murder, it executes.

Giuseppa's testimony would be crucial evidence that the mafia was far more than just a mentality. Even the way that she had been persecuted since that terrible day in December 1896 showed as much:

It is almost as if I am the guilty one. Everyone shuns me or looks at me with scorn on their faces. Now very few people come and buy things from my shop. The only ones who come are the honest ones who are not receptive to the mafia's influence. So the disaster that struck me did not just hurt me directly, physically (which cost me a huge amount in medical bills). And it has done even more than open up an incurable wound in my heart by killing my poor eighteen-year-old daughter. To all that must now be added the economic harm that the mafia's persecution has brought. The mafia refuses to pardon me for an offence I never committed.

A week after dictating these words to detectives, Giuseppa looked out of the window of her store and saw that a new hole had appeared in the wall opposite. Palermo's shadow state was already taking steps to counteract the threat posed by Chief of Police Sangiorgi.

The murder of Giuseppa Di Sano's daughter also had an intriguing loose end that would lead Sangiorgi to discover how the first of the four missing men met his death on the Fondo Laganà. Remarkably, Vincenzo D'Alba's careful preparations failed to protect him from prosecution. Within days of the murder, his young accomplice, Giuseppe 'Pidduzzo' Buscemi, was questioned by the police. Buscemi, whom Sangiorgi describes as a cocky young man, had his alibi prepared as any mafioso would. Yet he also helped himself to freedom by saying that he had seen Vincenzo D'Alba pale and trembling in a via Falde tobacco shop ten minutes after the killing. As a result of this hint D'Alba was arrested and, with Giuseppa's testimony counting against him, was convicted and sentenced to twenty years. For Sangiorgi, D'Alba's betrayal by Buscemi was an astonishing and therefore highly significant breach of *omertà*.

Whoever Sangiorgi's sources within the mafia were, they told him that Pidduzzo Buscemi's scandalous behaviour enraged mafiosi close to Vincenzo D'Alba. Antonino D'Alba, Vincenzo's cousin, was a tavern owner and an influential man of honour in his forties with a record for fencing stolen goods. He denounced Pidduzzo's betrayal of *omertà* to other senior bosses who agreed to hold a trial. Antonino D'Alba's call for mafia justice was to lead eventually to his murder: he was the first of the four missing men.

Pidduzzo Buscemi's mafia trial did not take place until September 1897; it was postponed until he returned on leave from military service. Standing before the assembled bosses, he still wore the uniform of the 10th regiment of Bersaglieri with its extravagant black plume on a broad-brimmed hat. When called on to explain why he had given evidence to the police, the young soldier nonchalantly claimed he had done so to turn suspicion away from the mafia as a whole, and that he had always planned to change his story later to favour his accomplice and confuse the investigators. Strangely, Sangiorgi learned, the mafia court found his flimsy testimony convincing and acquitted Buscemi.

Something more important than the mafia rulebook was clearly at stake. As so often in mafia wars, that something was territory. Among the 'jurors' at young Buscemi's trial was the capo of the Acquasanta *cosca*, the hefty, walrus-moustached Tommaso D'Aleo, who suspected that Antonino D'Alba had orchestrated a challenge to an established protection racket over two wealthy lemon derivatives dealers; a bomb had even been detonated on the balcony of their house. Tommaso D'Aleo also happened to be Pidduzzo Buscemi's godfather. He was almost certainly using the young soldier to manoeuvre D'Alba into a position where he could be killed.

Soon after Pidduzzo Buscemi was acquitted, another trial was called in secret – mafia justice can be very swift when it needs to be. Antonino D'Alba was found guilty *in absentia*. The sentence was death, and his execution was carefully arranged. This time it was not to be a public affair, as the shooting of Giuseppa Di Sano had been, because D'Alba's punishment was an internal organizational matter.

A few days after the mafia trial that had acquitted him of breaking the code of *omertà*, Pidduzzo Buscemi, still in his dashing uniform, called at the tavern run by D'Alba. He found him washing out a barrel, and invited him outside into a cone of light from a street lamp to discuss their differences. The exchange was curt. Buscemi said he wanted to restore the damage to his honour caused by D'Alba's accusations; he demanded a duel.

D'Alba agreed. But, as he may have suspected, he was being lured into a trap. According to his young son's testimony as recorded by Sangiorgi, on the afternoon of the following day, 12 September 1897, the boss Tommaso D'Aleo and another mafioso came to D'Alba's tavern where they ate, talked, and lingered. They offered a 100-lire note when asked to pay a 3.25 lire bill; it was a carefully pitched gesture of mistrust and hostility. At half past six in the evening D'Alba returned from the nearby shop where he had gone to change the 100-lire note. He took off his two gold rings, gold tie-pin, and other valuables, and placed them safely in a coffee cup on the shelf. Then he picked up his revolver and went out. Tommaso D'Aleo and the other mobster followed him.

Antonino D'Alba was never seen alive again. The mafia gossip mill churned out rumours of sightings in North Africa. A letter purporting to be from him was even sent from Tunis to his father. But by the time the letter arrived, the police had already found out that D'Alba had in fact been gunned down on the night of his disappearance by a large party of mafiosi on the Fondo Laganà.

Through his careful interviews with police informers, and his patient re-examination of evidence, Sangiorgi was beginning to piece together a complete picture of how the mafia operated; how its bitter conflicts were not merely the product of an outlaw sense of pride, but actually involved laws, legal proceedings, and a system of territorial control. The next stage of his investigation reached right from the Fondo Laganà to the domestic lives of the wealthiest and most famous families in Sicily: the Florios and the Whitakers. As Sangiorgi discovered, these two opulent dynasties lived alongside the mafia in contrasting ways. One of them was cynical, the other more resigned and put upon; but both were complicit in perpetuating the mafia's power.

When European kings and princes visited Palermo, as they often did, there was one place where they were always received: a lavish villa set in a private park in Olivuzza in the Conca d'Oro. It belonged to Ignazio Florio Jr. In 1891, at twenty-three, Ignazio inherited the greatest fortune in Italy. It was said that 16,000 people in Palermo alone 'ate his bread'. The Florios had extensive interests in sulphur, light and heavy engineering, tuna fishing, pottery, insurance, finance, Marsala wine and, above all, shipping. The house of Florio was the major shareholder in NGI, Navigazione Generale Italiana, Italy's leading shipping concern and one of the biggest in Europe.

But when Ignazio Jr came into his inheritance, the family's fabulous wealth had already begun to decay from the inside. NGI had grown fat on government contracts and subsidies arranged by his father's carefully cultivated political contacts. Now it was becoming clear how uncompetitive it was. Moreover, the country's political and economic centre of gravity was shifting inexorably northwards, to the cities of Genoa, Turin, and Milan. The Florios' influence slipped away at increasing speed. Before he was forty, Ignazio Jr had lost control of a fortune that it had taken three generations to build. In 1908, he was forced to sell the family's NGI holding; it is as good a date as any to mark the end of the Palermo *belle époque* that began when he became head of the family in 1891. These were the years when Sicilian high society orbited around the dying sun of Florio money. The press called Palermo 'Floriopolis', but this was its last flowering as a great European city.

Ignazio Florio Jr was urbane, gifted, and raffish. The figure of a Japanese woman was tattooed on his arm. His clothes were almost exclusively from London: ties from Moulengham, hats from Locke & Tuss, suits from Meyer & Mortimer – the Prince of Wales's tailor. A flesh-coloured carnation adorned his button-hole in the mornings, a gardenia in the evenings. In 1893, as his father had done, Ignazio consolidated his social status by marrying a titled woman. His bride, Franca Jacona di San Giuliano, was considered one of the most beautiful women in Europe. A few months after the wedding, during Franca's first pregnancy, Ignazio went off to Tunisia on a safari that required the services of fifty porters and tens of camels. Franca found female underwear in his luggage when he got back. She was pacified with a string of fat pearls. The same penitence ritual was to be repeated many times during their marriage; Franca is said to have accumulated thirty kilos of jewels.

Her husband's transgressions notwithstanding, Franca quickly asserted herself as the queen of Palermo high society. She patronized the arts. Her green eyes, olive skin, and rangy figure were celebrated by the poet Gabriele d'Annunzio. She caused a minor scandal by allowing the fashionable artist Giovanni Boldini to sketch her legs. An icon of Liberty style, she wore strings of pearls that almost reached her knees. Money meant display for Franca Florio. To the end of her life, she remained doggedly unmindful of the family's worsening financial situation. When ageing threatened in the 1900s, she underwent pioneering cosmetic surgery by having her face 'porcelainized' in Paris.

Sangiorgi's report relates that, one morning in the early weeks of 1897, Ignazio and Franca Florio were woken early by their servants. Ignazio was outraged to discover that a number of art objects had been stolen from the villa during the night. Nevertheless, the party most offended by this unprecedented burglary was not Commendatore Ignazio Florio Jr, but the man he bawled out and told to put the matter right: his gardener. Francesco Noto, a well-built, bald man with a sharply sloping moustache, would not have accepted this kind of dressing-down from anyone but Florio. For, as Ignazio Jr was well aware, the gardener was actually the capo of the Olivuzza *cosca* of the mafia. His younger brother and underboss, Pietro, was also employed in the Florio villa as a security guard. These lowly job titles should not fool us as to the immense strategic and symbolic importance of protecting the villa owned by the wealthiest family in Sicily, the hub of Palermo high society. The Noto brothers were the real targets of the Olivuzza villa burglary, and they knew who had carried it out.

Chief of Police Sangiorgi traced the reason for the robbery back to the moment a few weeks earlier when ten-year-old Audrey Whitaker was kidnapped by mafiosi under the command of the Noto brothers. Audrey had been out riding in La Favorita, the royal park on the north-western edge of Palermo where the idle wealthy shot quail, or attended horse races and show-jumping. Four men emerged from the bushes to set upon the groom that her family had charged with her protection. He was beaten up and tied to his horse while Audrey was taken away. Her father Joshua ('Joss') received a polite demand for a ransom of 100,000 lire.

Sangiorgi had no need to explain who the Whitakers were. The family belonged to the leading English business dynasty in Sicily. (Palermo's British community had put down strong roots when His Majesty's Forces had occupied the island during the Napoleonic wars.) Like their friends the Florios, the Whitakers were involved in the Marsala wine business. Along with the Florios, the Whitakers would be invited to London for Queen Victoria's state funeral in 1901.

The extended Whitaker family also lent a strong dose of Englishness to the Palermo *monde*. It was they who introduced garden parties to Sicily; extravagant meals would be served in a marquee attached to the back of the villa. Whitakers also founded a charity for abandoned infants, an animal welfare society, and the Palermo Football and Cricket Club. Little Audrey's mother Effie cultivated an eccentric image. She toured Palermo in her carriage with a parrot on her shoulder. It was fed with sunflower seeds from a silver box, and a silver trowel was kept ready for its droppings. Effie's other passion was lawn tennis. In the Whitakers' garden there were three courts, known as Inferno, Purgatorio, and Paradiso. A visitor's social standing largely determined which court he or she was permitted to use. Effie's parrot was allowed to fly free during games. It was during one such match that Ignazio Florio's teenage brother Vincenzo, not sharing the English sentimentality about animals, shot the pampered bird out of a tree.

Audrey Whitaker's kidnapping was not the first trouble the family had had with the mafia. They were not as well connected as the Florios. As a young man, Joss's brother Joseph ('Pip') had received a series of letters, demanding money and marked with a skull and crossbones. His Harrow masters would have been quietly satisfied with his bluff reaction. 'I knew well enough who was the head of the local *Mafia*,' he recorded, 'so I sent him a message saying that the letters had been deposited at the police station giving the name of the man, in case I was killed. I had no more trouble after this.' Some years later, Joss's sister-in-law was strolling in the garden of the family villa when a severed hand was lobbed over the boundary wall, landing at her feet. This time the family's response was more circumspect: they kept quiet about the incident in case it was a threat. By now mafiosi were 'protecting' some of the family's own property.

Joss Whitaker opted for the same approach after his daughter's kidnapping. He paid up immediately and denied that the whole episode had even happened. Little Audrey was back home within days.

Sangiorgi's mysterious sources not only revealed the secret of Audrey Whitaker's abduction, they also told him that the huge ransom caused friction within the Olivuzza *cosca*. Two of its members, the carriage drivers Vincenzo Lo Porto and Giuseppe Caruso, were not happy with their share of the loot. They decided on a chancy response, a *sfregio*. As Sangiorgi explained, *sfregio* is an important piece of mafia terminology that means two very closely related things. It is a disfiguring wound and, more importantly, it is also an affront, an insulting action designed to make someone lose face. Since, for the mafia, control of territory is all, the most blatant *sfregio* possible is damage caused to property protected by another mafioso. As Sangiorgi puts it, 'One of the mafia's canons is respect for another man's territorial jurisdiction. Flouting that jurisdiction constitutes a personal insult.'

It was Lo Porto and Caruso who stole the art objects from the Florios' villa. The burglary was a *sfregio* aimed at the leadership of the Olivuzza clan. The rollicking that Ignazio Jr gave Francesco Noto was the object of the whole exercise. To quote Sangiorgi again, 'The aim that the two carriage drivers had set themselves, that is to humiliate their boss and underboss, had been achieved.'

The Noto brothers reacted to this *sfregio* with exemplary patience. First, they ensured that the damage to their reputation in Ignazio Florio's eyes was repaired. They promised the two thieves a larger share of the Whitaker kidnapping cash, and even a reward for the return of the booty from the Florio robbery. Thus it was that, a few days later, the Florio family awoke to another, more welcome surprise: every single missing object had been returned to exactly the same place from which it had been stolen.

With the Florios' property restored, their gardener and guard were ready to move against Lo Porto and Caruso. The killing of any man of honour is a potentially destabilizing act that is of concern to the whole mafia organization. The Florio family's involvement in the case heightened its importance. So when the

Notos secretly denounced Lo Porto and Caruso to other bosses, the outcome was a hearing that involved all the capos of the eight *cosche*. It was held on Falde territory rather than in Noto's own Olivuzza domain – another demonstration that the decision had implications for the whole association. The Notos clearly wanted more than a guilty verdict: as Sangiorgi asserted, they were aiming for as wide a consensus as possible for the death penalty. They got what they were after: to avoid suspicion and to make the killings as efficient as possible, the death sentences would not be carried out for several months.

When the time came to carry out the executions, on 24 October 1897, the two carriage drivers were lured to the Fondo Laganà on the pretext that they were going to take part in a robbery. They were met there by a representative firing party comprising men of honour from each of the different *cosche*. Lo Porto and Caruso were shot first by the men who had arrived with them. The other mafiosi waited until the two had pulled themselves back on to their feet before finishing them off. Their bullet-riddled bodies were tossed into the grotto. On top of them fell the fourth and final corpse: that of another young mafioso executed on the *fondo* for stealing from his boss. A week earlier he had been shot several times in the head as he sat down, he thought, to play a game of cards.

It was one thing for Sangiorgi to tell a story of collective executions and protection rackets that explained how the four missing men had ended up on the Fondo Laganà. It was quite another to prove it in court and turn the story into evidence of the existence of what he called the 'shadowy fraternity'. He needed more witnesses. Soon two would come forward and significantly both were, once again, women.

When the two carriage drivers' wives discovered that they were widows, other mafiosi spun them a story that their husbands had died heroically, killed by a rival gang for refusing to take part in a plan to kidnap Ignazio Florio's brother, the parrot-shooting teenager Vincenzo. The widows were told, in other words, that their husbands had died in the Florios' service, and not because they had stolen from their villa.

This fiction was exposed a few weeks later by Ignazio's mother, the formidable Baroness Giovanna d'Ondes Trigona. On 29 November 1897 – not long after the smell of rotting flesh from the Fondo Laganà had led to the discovery of the bodies in the well – the baroness set off from the Florios' Olivuzza villa to a nunnery of which she was a benefactress. Along the way she saw Vincenzo Lo Porto's widow approach her carriage. The widow begged the baroness for help in bringing up her son. But her hopes were dashed by the baroness's reply: 'Don't waste my time. Your husband was a thief who stole from my house with Caruso.'

When both widows came forward to tell what they knew, it was immediately evident to Sangiorgi that the baroness knew the whole story behind the burglary. She believed Lo Porto had got what he deserved. At this point in time, she plainly knew more than did the widows of the murdered mafiosi. She was also better informed than the police, who had by now found the bodies but knew little else about the case of the four missing men. The likely implication is clear: the whole Florio family had been discreetly told that the two men who had stolen the art objects from their home had met with the nasty end that their outrageous impudence merited. Because order had been restored through private channels, it would not have crossed the Florios' minds to inform the police. Indeed, their role in the murders may even have gone deeper. Sangiorgi did not know the substance of Ignazio Jr's conversation with his mafioso gardener on the morning after the robbery. It is legitimate to wonder whether in fact Ignazio actually intimated what he thought would be an appropriate fate for the culprits.

Chief of Police Sangiorgi draws on statements from the widows of both carriage drivers to tell this story with his usual sobriety and attention to detail. He also remarks that the

Baroness Florio could profitably be interviewed by prosecution lawyers. It was his duty to do so. Yet it is hard not to imagine a bitterly ironic smile on Sangiorgi's face as he makes the suggestion:

Signora Florio is a pious, religious noblewoman. It is difficult to tell which is greater: the immense riches she has at her disposal, or the illustrious virtues of her extremely noble, well-born mind. For that reason, if she were invited to testify under oath, it is likely that she would not be willing or able to conceal from justice her encounter with the widow.

There was no hope that Sangiorgi's wish would be granted; the power of the Florio family placed them above the law. Sangiorgi now had three witnesses who were prepared to testify, all of them women, all of them bereaved, yet none of them decisive in his attempts to prove what the mafia really was.

Sangiorgi continued to send in further instalments of his report up to the end of 1898 and through the early months of 1899. At each stage of his work, the mafia took countermeasures. The brother of one of the carriage drivers killed for the Florio burglary was driven to suicide because of suspicions that he had collaborated with the authorities. One mafia informer, probably Sangiorgi's most important internal source on the bodies in the well, emigrated for his own protection under a passport supplied by the police. To no avail: an assassin caught up with him in New Orleans and poisoned him. Sangiorgi confessed his worries about bringing the investigation to a successful conclusion in court. He complained that the investigating magistrate handling the case was a man with 'a pusillanimous character, extremely open to influence'. All the while the mafia war was carrying on in fits and starts. The murders and disappearances continued; fragmentary news also emerged from the underworld of negotiations, shifting alliances, failed truces.

Then on 25 October 1899 came Sangiorgi's big chance. A known man of honour was arrested red-handed at the scene of a shooting. The would-be victim of the attack survived; astonishingly, he turned out to be none other than the mafia's former 'regional or supreme *capo*', as Sangiorgi called him. Francesco Siino, a gaunt man of fifty, capo of the Malaspina *cosca* and a successful lemon trader, had until recently been at the top of the organizational tree that the police had built up from confidential sources.

Sangiorgi grasped his opportunity rapidly and shrewdly, again aiming to exert pressure on what he now knew to be the mafia's potential weakness: its women. He kept Siino hidden and let it be known that the wounded capo was close to death. He then brought Siino's wife face-to-face with the hit man he had arrested. She could not contain herself, shouting, '*Infame! Infame!*' (The term is the habitual mafia insult for a traitor – 'dishonoured scum'.) There and then she accused him and his associates of a series of murders. It was the beginning of her collaboration with justice. Francesco Siino soon learned that his wife had spoken to Sangiorgi and he too started to talk about what he referred to as 'the company of friends'. Sangiorgi had the *pentito* he needed to build his case.

Interviews with the new defector allowed Sangiorgi gradually to understand the mafia war from the inside; just as importantly, they allowed him to demonstrate that the war was not just a chaotic skirmish between separate gangs, but the result of a breakdown within a single organization. Sangiorgi began to grasp that even when it is at war the mafia has its rules, its language, its diplomacy, and even its historical memory.

Francesco Siino's power within the mafia had already been fading when the police learned of his position as 'regional or supreme *capo*'. The dominant wealth and influence, and with it the mafia's centre of gravity, lay not with Siino but with an alliance between the Passo di Rigano, Piana dei Colli, and Perpignano families. The patron of that alliance had a familiar name: Don Antonino Giammona, the 'taciturn, puffed up, and wary' mafioso who rose to power under Baron Nicolò Turrisi Colonna's protection in the 1860s, and who was behind the persecution of Dr Gaspare Galati in the 1870s. In 1898, Giammona had a large house in via Cavallacci in the same suburban village of Passo di Rigano where he had been born seventy-eight years earlier. His son was installed as capo in charge of day-to-day business in the area. But the old man was still the mafia's 'executive mind', according to Sangiorgi. 'He gives direction through advice based on his vast experience and his long criminal record. He offers instructions on the way to carry out crimes and construct a defence, especially alibis.' Old man Giammona's continuing influence was proof that mafiosi were not fly-by-night thugs. By then, the 'shadowy fraternity' had been a settled feature of Palermo society for four decades.

The roots of the fitful mafia war of 1897–9 went back to the police raid on the Falde *cosca*'s counterfeiting operation, the same raid for which Giuseppa Di Sano had been blamed back in late 1896. It was Don Antonino Giammona who sought to manage the knock-on effects of this loss. A summit of the capos of the eight *cosche* – Piana dei Colli, Acquasanta, Falde, Malaspina, Uditore, Passo di Rigano, Perpignano, Olivuzza – was called in January 1897. As normal, Francesco Siino was in the chair. But this time the drop in the mafia's income made the mood tetchy. Giammona detected weakness in Siino and was determined to manipulate the situation to his own advantage. Sensing a challenge to his authority, Siino stood up: 'Well, since I'm no longer respected in the way I ought to be, let every group think and act on its own!' The meeting went on to demarcate each group's area of influence. But not long after the meeting, the Giammonas began making exploratory, symbolic incursions into Siino turf – calculated acts of disrespect. But Siino refused to be provoked. Both sides in the conflict knew that it was risky to be seen to start a conflict.

It took a young hothead to accelerate matters. Francesco Siino's nephew Filippo, 'a very impetuous, cocky and audacious young man' according to Sangiorgi, was underboss in Uditore.

He began to send threatening letters to old man Giammona. In response, some forty senior mafiosi were called to a meeting in the building that contained Don Antonino's olive press. Although nothing explicit was said, the old boss made it plain where he thought blame for the letters was to be placed. Outside the meeting, another boss quietly suggested to Francesco Siino that he should bring his nephew to heel.

Instead the Siinos retaliated by cutting down some prickly pears on Giammona land. These fleshy, fruit-bearing cacti are virtually worthless in themselves, but destroying them was a clear *sfregio*. The Giammonas' response was circumscribed: they vandalized plants on an estate guarded by the young Siino. He responded by again attacking Giammona property.

Don Antonino Giammona was now at a tactical crossroads. Young Filippo Siino did not own any property himself. Sangiorgi explains that, in the formalized language of the *sfregio*, a second reprisal against the estate that the young underboss protected would be interpreted as an insult aimed at the landowner rather than the guard. This was very definitely *not* the message the Giammonas and their allies wanted to give. An offence against a landowner could bring trouble down on the whole organiz-ation. The Giammonas chose instead to damage stock on land leased by Francesco Siino, the former supreme boss; it was still a manifest escalation of the dispute. For a third time, the 'impetu-ous' Filippo Siino destroyed plants on Giammona land in retali-ation. The Giammonas concluded that it was time to go to war.

The conflict went badly for the Siinos from the outset. They lost both men and ground across the Conca d'Oro as the Giam-monas and their allies edged them out of their jobs as wardens within the lemon groves. The decisive moment came at sunset on 8 June 1898, when 'impetuous' Filippo Siino was intercepted and shot dead in the street by four Giammona killers who had been given a tip-off from inside the Siino camp.

Sangiorgi also learned of the war's innocent victims: confir-mation, if confirmation was needed, that mafiosi do not only kill their own. On one occasion, Giammona assassins were sent after a particularly feared Siino killer; happening across his brother, they murdered him instead. As they followed their planned escape route they were spotted by a seventeen-year-old cowherd, Salvatore Di Stefano. Calmly, a month later, they went back to prevent him testifying against them. The killers found Salvatore watering plants with his shoes off and his trousers rolled up. Improvising, they drowned him in a well and put his shoes on the edge to make it look like an accident – which is precisely what the police had believed it to be.

By the time of the luckless cowherd's murder, Francesco Siino had taken refuge in Livorno in Tuscany where he had contacts in the citrus fruit industry. This time he was joined by three of his surviving nephews, who abandoned their strategic jobs in the lemon groves. The Siino power base was crumbling. Following the spate of murders, police confiscated gun licences from all the most prominent mafia families, including the Giammonas and Siinos. The mafia's response was to call in favours from the upper world of politics and high society. A series of distinguished public figures – parliamentarians (including Don Raffaele Palizzolo), businessmen, and even a princess – lined up to provide the character references needed to get the gun licences back. The Giammonas themselves were sponsored by an old family friend, the son of 'sect' expert Baron Nicolò Turrisi Colonna. The Siinos, by contrast, searched in vain for someone to speak in their favour. Word had got around the mafia-friendly sections of Palermo's bourgeoisie that the Siinos had been expelled from the honoured society. They were being abandoned to their fate.

Sangiorgi tells us that in December 1898, Francesco Siino, back in Palermo once more, called his men together to spell out the situation. 'We've counted ourselves and we've counted the others. We total 170, including the *cagnolazzi* ["wild dogs" – young toughs yet to be initiated]. There are five hundred of them. They have got more money. And they have contacts that we don't have. So we've got to make peace.' A truce was negotiated at another meeting of senior bosses at a via Stabile butcher's shop. Siino then departed for Livorno again, followed by his

la Repubblica

Direttore Eugenio Scalfari

Anno 17 - Numero 121 - L. 1200

ROMEO GIGLI

domenica 24 maggio 1992

Una tonnellata di tritolo: 5 morti e 7 feriti. Mea culpa dei partiti a Roma

Falcone assassinato

Strage di mafia, è morta anche la moglie

Shock a Montecitorio: oggi il Presidente

Non c'è più tempo

di EUGENIO SCALFARI

L ASCIA allibiti l'attentato che è costato la vita al giudice Falcone, a sua moglie e agli uomini della scorta. Incute sgomento e paura. Ancora sangue in Sicilia, ancora morti, ancora mistero sugli esecutori e i mandanti) quali avevano comunque perfetta cognizione dei movimenti delle loro vittime e sono stati in grado di programmarne la strage con cronometrica esattezza.

All'apertura della campagna elettorale fu ucciso a Palermo Salvo Lima; prima che si concluda l'elezione presidenziale è stato falciato Falcone: è terribile questa scansione che intreccia gli atti della malavita con le scadenze della politica, inquinando e avvelenando l'intera vita pubblica di questo disgraziato paese.

Falcone era il simbolo della lotta contro la mafia. La bomba fatta esplodere contro di lui rivela una gravità addirittura superiore all'assassinio del generale Dalla Chiesa: per le coincidenze con fatti politici di grande rilievo, vien fatto di paragonarla al rapimento di Aldo Moro, consumatosi nel momento stesso in cui si presentava in Parlamento il primo governo sostenuto dal partito comunista. Saranno coincidenze fortuite ma danno molto gravemente da pensare su un viluppo di questioni mai veramente rischiarato dalla luce della verità.

Noi ci troviamo ora, nello stesso tempo, di fronte a tre emergenze: quella criminale, quella finanziaria e quella istituzionale. Mai la vita di questo paese era arrivata, al '45 in poi, a un punto così drammatico e cruciale. Mai come ora è necessario che la rappresentanza politica dia segno di estrema responsabilità e faccia prevalere gli interessi dello Stato su quelli delle parti e delle fazioni.

Entro oggi il Parlamento deve eleggere il presidente della Repubblica. Possibilmente entro domani il nuovo eletto deve designare il nuovo capo del governo.

SEGUE A PAGINA 6

Edizione speciale domani Repubblica sarà in edicola

Il giudice Giovanni Falcone

Uccisi anche i tre agenti di scorta
"Mi hanno delegittimato. Ora Cosa Nostra è pronta per vendicarsi..."
Scalfaro o Spadolini al Quirinale?

Una tonnellata di esplosivo sull'autostrada, un cratere di venti metri, cinque morti: il giudice Giovanni Falcone, la moglie, i tre agenti di scorta. Sette i feriti

Nell'ultima intervista a "Repubblica" aveva detto: "Cosa Nostra non dimentica, non è una piovra, è una pantera feroce. Con la memoria di un elefante"

Martelli è in lacrime: "Giovanni era il migliore, ed ora è morto". Il ministro lo aveva scelto come Super Procuratore nazionale antimafia, contro il Csm

Montecitorio è sotto shock. Appena appresa la notizia i partiti si sono impegnati in frenetiche trattative per eleggere già oggi il Presidente: Spadolini o Scalfaro

Adesso i partiti recitano il "mea culpa". Per il vuoto di potere in cui la Repubblica, per la crisi delle istituzioni che aiuta la mafia. Spadolini sarà oggi a Palermo

Forlani dopo le dimissioni si sfoga con "Repubblica" contro i parlamentari dc: "Che cosa vogliono? Che la gente dica: se è così è meglio che torni Mussolini?"

DA PAGINA 2 A PAGINA 11 i servizi di ATTILIO BOLZONI, SANDRA BONSANTI, ANTONELLO CAPORALE, GIUSEPPE D'AVANZO FEDERICO GEREMICCA, ALESSANDRA LONGO, GIANLUCA LUZI GIOVANNI MARINO, STEFANO MARRONI, SILVANA MAZZOCCHI SEBASTIANO MESSINA, BARBARA PALOMBELLI, UMBERTO ROSSO FRANCESCO VIVIANO e ALESSANDRA ZINITI

1. May 1992. A disbelieving Italian public absorbs the news that judge Giovanni Falcone, Cosa Nostra's greatest enemy, has been murdered. Writing a history of the Sicilian mafia would be unthinkable without Falcone's investigations.

2. The mafioso who revealed Cosa Nostra's secrets to judge Falcone: Tommaso Buscetta (right), with his third wife and father-in-law, in a picture taken in Brazil in 1971 or 1972.

3. 'The man who cuts Christians' throats': Giovanni 'lo scannacristiani' Brusca soon after his arrest in May 1996. Brusca pressed the detonator on the bomb that killed judge Falcone.

4. Nicolò Turrisi Colonna, Baron of Buonvicino and enigmatic expert on the 'Sect'. His bust stands in the Palazzo delle Aquile, seat of Palermo city council.

5. Sidney Sonnino (seated), Leopoldo Franchetti (right) and their travelling companion Enea Cavalieri on the eve of the expedition to Sicily in 1876.

6. The gate of the Fondo Favarella in Ciaculli, where Michele 'the Pope' Greco once produced both tangerines and heroin. The mafia's roots, and its recent history, are to be found within the walls of the citrus fruit groves around Palermo.

8. The only known likeness of Chief of Police of Palermo Ermanno Sangiorgi, taken from a newspaper in 1901. Sangiorgi knew more than anyone about the early mafia.

7. The accused in the 1901 trial based on Chief of Police Sangiorgi's report on the mafia. From a contemporary newspaper.

9. Media interest in the mafia, 1901. 'An exciting session of the Notarbartolo murder trial in Bologna. The accused, Palizzolo, speaks in his own defence.'

10. Corleone, 1915. Police photo of Bernardino Verro's body lying where it fell. Some of the shots that killed him were fired from the doorway on the left.

11. Hero of the fight against the Corleone mafia, Bernardino Verro. This bust was set so that it faced up the street where he died. It was stolen in 1925.

12. Fascism's 'Iron Prefect': Cesare Mori.

13. Joe Petrosino, scourge of the mafia in early twentieth-century New York city.

14. Giuseppe 'Piddu' Morello, one-fingered leader of the mafia in the USA. Press photo from the time of the 'body in the barrel' case, 1903.

15. Little Italy in the early years of the twentieth century.

Vedi giudizio umano, come spesso erra !

Comm. **CALOGERO VIZZINI**

N. 24 - 7 - 1877   M. 11 - 7 - 1954

VILLALBA

———

POCO GENEROSI
SE LA SUA BARA NON ANCORA CHIUSA
INVANO TIRARONO GLI ULTIMI STRALI
L'ODIO E L'INVIDIA
IN QUELLA ESTREMA ORA DI PIANTO
FU PIÙ FORTE L'AMORE
E CON VOCE DI VASTA RISONANZA
DISSE
A TUTTI GLI ONESTI
LA GENTILEZZA SUA DEL TRATTO
LA NOBILTÀ DEL CUORE.

DI VEDUTE LARGHE
NEI COMMERCI NELL'INDUSTRIA
RAGGIUNSE ALTEZZE MAI TOCCATE
CON FELICE INTUITO
PRECORSE ED ATTUÒ LA RIFORMA AGRARIA
SOLLEVÒ LE SORTI
DEGLI OSCURI OPERAI DELLA MINIERA
E RACCOLSE SIMPATIE E PRESTIGIO
NEMICO DI TUTTE LE INGIUSTIZIE
UMILE CON GLI UMILI
GRANDE CON I PIÙ GRANDI
DIMOSTRÒ
CON LE PAROLE CON LE OPERE
CHE LA MAFIA SUA NON FU DELINQUENZA
MA RISPETTO ALLA LEGGE
DIFESA DI OGNI DIRITTO
GRANDEZZA DI ANIMO
FU AMORE

16. Don Calò Vizzini's funeral notice. The text begins: 'In vain did ungenerous hatred and envy shoot their last barbs at his coffin before its lid was even closed. But in that last hour of weeping, love proved stronger and with a resounding voice spoke to all honest men of the kindness of his features and the nobility of his heart.' It concludes, 'He showed with words and deeds that his mafia was not criminal. It stood for respect for the law, defence of all rights, greatness of character: it was love.'

17. The photogenic last bandit, Salvatore Giuliano.

18. Poster advertising Francesco Rosi's 1961 masterpiece _Salvatore Giuliano_. It shows how the film reproduces the scene of Giuliano's death which was itself faked by the authorities.

whole family; he had been bested both militarily and politically. It only remained for the Giammonas to mop up the remaining pockets of resistance.

If Siino had stayed away from Palermo, he would never have become the witness Sangiorgi so desperately needed. But the following autumn he was drawn back for one last visit – just long enough for the Giammona faction to mount an attempt on his life. Sangiorgi had his breakthrough. The time had finally come when he could stop writing his report and start making arrests.

On the night of 27–8 April 1900, Sangiorgi ordered a round-up of mafiosi listed in his report. The police and *carabinieri* involved were not told of their duties that night until the last minute so as to prevent leaks. Thirty-three suspects were immediately arrested, as were many more over the coming months. In October 1900, the prefect of Palermo reported that Sangiorgi had reduced the mafia to 'silence and inactivity'.

As a veteran mafia fighter, Sangiorgi had always known how difficult it would be for his investigations to bring results. He knew too that he would need political support if he were to have any chance of success. The instalments of his report were addressed to the prosecuting authorities in Palermo, but he also wanted the government, in the person of General Luigi Pelloux, to know what he had found. He made sure that a copy of each instalment reached Pelloux via the prefect of Palermo. Back in November 1898, Sangiorgi wrote a covering letter that was addressed to the prefect but intended for the Prime Minister's eyes:

I especially need your respected and legitimate intervention, your good offices with the judicial authorities. And I need your support in dealings with the government. This is because, regrettably, the mafia's bosses act under the safeguard of Senators, MPs, and other influential figures who protect them and defend them and who are, in their turn, protected and defended by the *mafiosi*.

The mafia had created a system of complicity to shield it from people like Sangiorgi, a system that stretched from the wealthy Florios down to the women of the Giardino Inglese neighbour- hood who boycotted Giuseppa Di Sano's store. For Sangiorgi to combat that system effectively he would need a determined government behind him. But unfortunately for Sangiorgi and for Sicily, the window of political opportunity for a decisive strike against the mafia closed at the very moment that his months of work seemed to be producing results.

The crisis of the late 1890s that had brought General Pelloux to power in Rome produced its final drama in the summer following Sangiorgi's round-up of mafia suspects. In July 1900, the King paid for the corruption and inept brutality of his governments when an anarchist shot him dead near the royal palace in Monza. By that time the economy was picking up and the crisis was at its end. A month before the King's death, a more liberal government was established when General Pelloux resigned; with him went support in Rome for the Palermo Chief of Police.

The first sign of the opposition to Sangiorgi was simply how slowly the case was progressing. The chief prosecutor of the city was proving to be very pernickety. He was the man to whom Sangiorgi's report had been officially addressed. Yet, after each new arrest, the prosecutor's office sent the whole case back to the investigating magistrate who was working with Sangiorgi so that the evidence could be updated. It took until May 1901 – a year after the first arrests – for Sangiorgi's trial to begin. Of the hundreds of members of the mafia, only eighty-nine were in the dock charged with belonging to the criminal association that had committed the murders of the four missing men. The chief prosecutor did not consider the evidence to be strong enough to bring the others to trial. The most notable of those released was Don Antonino Giammona; once again the earliest-known mafia capo went free and was left to live out his remaining years in peace.

Sangiorgi never complains about the chief prosecutor, a man from Naples whose name was Vincenzo Cosenza. Yet it seems likely that, in sending a copy of his report to the government in Rome, Sangiorgi was specifically hoping for backing against Cosenza. He would not therefore have been surprised if he had known that, in the month before the trial began, and nearly two and a half years since Sangiorgi had sent him the first instalment of his report, Cosenza had written to the new Minister of the Interior and declared, 'During the course of performing my duties I have never noticed the mafia.' The suspicion must be that Chief Prosecutor Cosenza was the key component in the system that the mafia created to protect itself from the law. It is perhaps a mark of his success that very little is now known about him. Just as Chief of Police Sangiorgi is a hidden hero of the history of the mafia, so Chief Prosecutor Cosenza is probably a hidden villain.

When it finally began in May 1901, the trial that Sangiorgi had been working towards for so long was eagerly followed, both by huge crowds at court and through extensive reports in the press. The whole of Palermo saw the Chief of Police's work unravel before his eyes. The star witness was former 'supreme boss' Francesco Siino. It is impossible to know for certain, but it is likely that Siino intuited the change in the political climate, realized which way the trial was likely to go, and decided to make a peace offering to his former colleagues in the mafia. From their cage, the defendants all watched him in silent intensity as he spoke to the court. He denied that he had ever spoken to Sangiorgi of a criminal association *as such*.

Further witnesses followed. A man who owned land next to the Giammonas testified that they 'have always been generous with everyone who has done business with them. No one has anything but good to say of them.' Joss Whitaker was called into the witness box and denied that his little daughter Audrey had ever been kidnapped. Ignazio Florio Jr did not even deign to come to court; he sent a statement denying that he had ever had a discussion with the Noto brothers about the burglary at his Olivuzza villa. An employee of the Florio household did testify and asserted that the guard (and mafia underboss) Pietro Noto was 'a real gentleman' who deservedly enjoyed the respect of the Florios; he had even been entrusted on several occasions with transporting Franca's jewels, valued at 800,000 lire.

At least one witness did not fail Sangiorgi. Despite the threats she faced – she had been forced to flee by night from her shop – Giuseppa Di Sano mustered her courage once again and told the story of her daughter's murder. The two carriage drivers' widows also bravely took the stand.

The tens of defence lawyers outdid each other in arabesques of oratory when it came to their summings-up. The case against a great number of mafiosi had not even been allowed to reach court, they pointed out, so surely this demonstrated the overall weakness of the prosecution's evidence? What kind of criminal association could this be, they argued, if its members were constantly involved in bloody disputes among themselves? One advocate argued eloquently that the word 'mafia' came from the Arabic 'ma-af' and meant merely 'an exaggerated concept of one's own individual identity'; the attitude was a leftover from the Middle Ages – all Sicilians had it in some measure. Proceedings were regularly interrupted by the wolf-like howling of one of the accused who had entered an insanity plea.

In June 1901, only thirty-two of Sangiorgi's mafiosi – including the Noto brothers, Antonino Giammona's son, and Tommaso D'Aleo – were convicted for forming a criminal association. Given the time that they had already spent in custody, most of them were released immediately. For Sangiorgi, it was a victory so small that it felt like a defeat. Interviewed about the case, he uncharacteristically betrayed his bitterness: 'It was never going to turn out any other way, as long as people who denounced the mafia in the evening then went along and defended it the following morning.'

With Sangiorgi's trial producing such mediocre results, it

would have taken a determined political effort to take further action against the mafia and its system of protection. But Italian politics was returning to normal after the dramas of the 1890s. For the politicians in Rome, fighting the mafia was once again an unwelcome hindrance to the central business of government: building rickety pacts between factions. Allies had to be obtained wherever they could. If they were from western Sicily, and especially if they were close to the Florio shipping lobby, it was counterproductive to ask questions about their unsavoury friends. The Sangiorgi report was consigned to the archives.

But the case of the four missing men was not the only strand of Chief of Police Sangiorgi's investigations. When he had been sent to Palermo by General Pelloux in August 1898 he was also given a brief to look into the affairs of one particularly prominent individual: Don Raffaele Palizzolo.

The Notarbartolo Murder

Marquis Emanuele Notarbartolo di San Giovanni was the mafia's first 'eminent corpse', its first victim among Sicily's social elite. In the century that followed its emergence, the mafia killed no one else with the stature of Emanuele Notarbartolo. He was one of Sicily's outstanding citizens. He served a three-year term as mayor of Palermo in the 1870s that was marked by his uncompromising honesty: he made himself the mafia's enemy by tackling corruption in the customs service. He was then appointed governor of the Bank of Sicily, a job he held until 1890. The integrity and energy with which he applied himself to that task would ultimately cost him his life. His assassination in 1893, and the sensational series of trials that resulted over the following decade, split Sicilian society in two and astonished public opinion across Italy by exposing the mafia's relationship with politicians, legal officials, and police. The Sangiorgi trial was a local drama whose importance was lost on the national press; the Notarbartolo case, by contrast, was Italy's first mafia media circus.

Many years later, Notarbartolo's son Leopoldo, a naval officer, wrote a moving biography of his father. It told how his own role in the Notarbartolo tragedy began in the terrible days following the murder. Crushed by grief, and assailed by fond memories, Leopoldo – a lieutenant of only twenty-three at the time – looked back over the previous three months, which he had spent on leave with his family, for any hint as to who might have killed his father. He kept returning in his mind to their time together on the family estate at Mendolilla. The estate symbolized everything about his father's values, his capacity for hard work. It had been his refuge from the troubles of the city forty kilometres to the north-west. It would now be his monument.

Emanuele Notarbartolo had bought Mendolilla when Leopoldo was little more than a baby. It was a barren place then; its arid 125 hectares rose steeply on the left bank of the Torto from a rocky triangle of land where only wild oleander flourished. (The Torto is a typical Sicilian river – a torrent in winter and a dry, rocky ravine in summer.) The estate's only building was a stone shack that lay two hours' ride from the nearest railway station. Bandits haunted the area's uncommonly bad roads.

As Leopoldo grew up he watched his father transform Mendolilla into a model farm. Despite his daunting workload at the Banco di Sicilia, Emanuele Notarbartolo ploughed into the farm all his spare time and all the money left over from his salary after his first priority: educating his children. He approached the task in a pioneering spirit, refusing to be an absentee landlord like most of his peers in Palermo. He also refused to use workers from the nearest town of Caccamo, a notorious mafia stronghold. Gradually winning the trust of the local peasants, he hired them to build a river defence that he planted with wych elm and cactus. The crumbling slope down to the Torto was stabilized with sumac, tough-rooted shrubs that in spring would cover the hillside with cones of tiny yellowish flowers. In summer the peasants would harvest the leaves to be dried and chopped for use in Palermo tanneries.

The estate was endowed with water supplies drawn from underground sources discovered at several points across the farm. Lemon trees, olives, and vines were planted. The oil and wine were stored in a vast cellar under the new farmhouse, built on the highest point of the property. Every single brick had had to be carried by mule from Sciara station. Just before his death, Emanuele Notarbartolo was working on plans to build a chapel for his peasants. Mendolilla was the local realization of a Utopian vision. (This was a dream that enlightened conservatives like Notarbartolo wanted to reproduce across the whole of Italy. They were aware of the new country's poverty and instability, of the lawlessness of much of the southern Italian countryside, and yet they feared the social conflict that industrialization was bringing to northern Europe. As a result, they sought a more paternalistic, rural capitalism, a sheltered path to modernity. Mendolilla was more than an investment for Notarbartolo; it was a school of hard work and loyalty for the lower orders and middle classes alike.)

On 13 January 1893, as Leopoldo recalled, his father and he had spent what was to be their last full day together, riding across the estate to visit its every corner. Since leaving his job at the Bank of Sicily, his father had had more time to devote to his land. That evening he sat at his big square table taking notes of what he had seen during the day. As he worked, Leopoldo idly opened a drawer and came across a large tin box containing revolver shells and a great many packets of rifle cartridges. 'It looks like the magazine on a battleship,' he said.

His father smiled, put down his pen, and began to demonstrate the security measures in his room. The roof was built from fireproof bricks supported by steel beams. The exceptionally heavy door had the latest English lock. One window gave a view across a wide section of countryside, the other commanded the only entrance to the farmyard. 'When I'm in here,' he concluded, 'I fear no one. With my weapons and a brave and trustworthy companion I can hold my own against twenty criminals.' Mendolilla was a Utopia that had to be stoutly defended. He paused. Then, with a shrug of the shoulders, he added: 'Anyway, it's all nonsense. If they want to hurt me, they'll do it through treachery, just as they did the first time.'

It was a phrase that lodged itself in Leopoldo's memory. His father was referring to the time back in 1882 when he had been kidnapped by bandits in mysterious circumstances. This was the episode that had made Emanuele Notarbartolo so concerned about his safety; he had been kept for six days in a tiny cave in the hills while the ransom was negotiated and handed over. Paying the money was the only alternative to the crude frontal assault that the authorities threatened to launch. A few days after his father's release, the chief kidnapper was found dead along the road to Caccamo, shot several times in the back. The others were captured after an anonymous tip-off to the police and a shoot-out in an empty villa belonging to a baroness in Villabate – the notoriously mafia-infested Palermo satellite town. The mystery of the kidnapping was never solved, but Emanuele Notarbartolo had strong suspicions. Thinking back on the terrible days after his father's death, Leopoldo began to wonder whether the kidnapping and the murder were linked.

It was in Palermo harbour less than a week later – 18 January – that Leopoldo set eyes on his father for the last time. He remembered being aboard the steamer for Naples; this was to be the first stage of a journey that would take him to Venice where he was to join a ship bound for the United States. The last three months spent with his family had been his first extended stay at home since he went away to naval college. It was also the first time that he and his father had been able to relate to each other on an equal footing, man to man, sharing ideas about business, politics, and careers. Leopoldo stood on the poop of the steamer as it slipped its moorings. He searched the busy harbour until his gaze found the familiar, upright figure of his father in a small boat. A brief glimpse, then the boat slid between two larger vessels and disappeared.

In the late morning of 1 February 1893, after a two-hour journey on horseback from Mendolilla, Emanuele Notarbartolo climbed into an empty first-class compartment of the Palermo service at Sciara station. It was only then that he could relax. In the ten years since the kidnapping he had been very cautious – he never travelled in the countryside without a gun – but it was unheard of for bandits to mount an attack on a train, so he unloaded his rifle and set it carefully on the netting of the overhead luggage rack. He slung his raincoat, hat, and body belt on top before settling down to gaze out of the window, waiting for sleep to come, or for the gently darkening Tyrrhenian Sea to appear as the train turned west to follow the coast.

Notarbartolo was alone until the next station, Termini Imerese. There he was seen slumped, half asleep in the corner of the compartment, as if the stop had stirred him. The train left Termini Imerese at twenty-three minutes past six, thirteen minutes late. Not long before it pulled away, two men in dark coats and bowler hats got on.

The deputy stationmaster gave the signal for departure. As the carriages began to slide past, he looked carefully into the first-class compartments – he knew his friend, a railway engineer, would be travelling in one of them. Yet his attention was drawn by someone else standing in the compartment immediately before his friend's. It was a well-dressed, thick-set, powerful man. Under his hat he had a broad, pale face, thick eyebrows, dark eyes, and a black moustache. Struck by the man's sinister appearance and bearing, the deputy stationmaster would later say that he seemed immersed in grim thoughts.

It was only the autopsy and the state that the compartment was in when the train reached Palermo that allowed Emanuele Notarbartolo's terrifying last moments to be reconstructed. As the train entered the tunnel between Termini and Trabia, he was attacked by two men, one wielding a stiletto, the other a bone-handled, double-edged dagger. Shocked from his half-sleep, he thrashed and leapt to avoid the flurry of blows. Some of them missed and cut deep into the seat and headrest. Notarbartolo was nearly fifty-nine, but he was a big man and a former soldier. With the din of the train in the tunnel drowning out his cries, he managed to grab one of the blades. Then he lunged desperately up towards his rifle in the rack above his head. A knife bit into his groin. Both his hand and the netting were slashed. He left a bloody palm-print on the window pane. At this point, Notarbartolo was held from behind by one of the men while the other planted four deep wounds in his chest. He was stabbed twenty-seven times in all.

The train drew towards Trabia station. Covered in blood and breathless from the struggle, the killers pulled Notarbartolo's belongings down from the rack and searched him for anything that would make for an easy identification: the gold watch with the family crest; the wallet with business cards and gun licence. It was not yet dark, but rather than make a getaway at the first opportunity, the killers crouched below the window during the brief stop at Trabia. The place they had in mind to dispose of their victim was just two minutes further along the track. Once the train cleared the station, they propped the body against the door and then bundled it out as they crossed the Curreri bridge. But they did not throw it quite far enough to tumble into the ravine below and be washed out to sea. Instead it struck the parapet and fell by the track.

The two men got out at the next station, leaving the compartment blood-spattered and empty behind them.

The city of Milan had some unusual visitors in the winter of 1899–1900. Hunched and cloaked against the cold, dozens of short, raven-haired men in caps tramped the northern Italian city's foggy streets, struggling to feed themselves on the pittance that the authorities provided for their upkeep. They were the Sicilian witnesses for the Notarbartolo murder trial. The two extremes of Italy met in Milan's Court of Assizes. The jury had to listen to many of the testimonies through interpreters.

The first scandal surrounding the Notarbartolo murder is that it took nearly seven years for the case to come to court. The reasons for that extraordinary delay were to be dramatically revealed before the jury. But in the meantime, even before the trial began it had become clear that robbery could not have been the killers' intention. They evidently had an extensive organization behind them, including accomplices among the railway staff. A possible motive had also emerged; it promised to link the case to financial and political corruption. Not long before Notarbartolo's murder, an inquiry found evidence of serious misconduct at the Banco di Sicilia under his successor as governor. The bank's money was being used to protect the share price of NGI, the Florios' shipping company, during delicate contract negotiations with the government. It was a simple scam. Loans were granted to intermediaries who bought NGI stock that was then deposited with the bank as security for the loan. The real borrowers, who included the bank governor and Ignazio Florio, remained anonymous – in contravention of bank regulations.

The same fraudulent method was then used as a more direct way of making money by other people connected to the bank. If the value of the shares went up, the borrower was able to emerge from anonymity, ask the bank to sell them off, and take the profit. If the shares went down, the bank would be stuck with the devalued shares and no one to turn to when it came to exacting repayment of the advance. The anonymous borrowers could only win; the Banco di Sicilia could only lose. The inquiry also raised suspicions of mafia infiltration.

In the weeks before the murder, with news of the banking inquiry leaking out, there had been rumours that Emanuele Notarbartolo would return once more to the Banco di Sicilia. It was said that Notarbartolo himself had been influential in instigating the investigation into the bank's affairs. Many senior figures connected to the Bank of Sicily would have had much to fear from a return to the old financial rigour. Could Notarbartolo have been murdered to protect these corrupt interests within the bank?

This scent of scandal in high places created considerable public interest in the Notarbartolo case as the hearings began in the Milan Court of Assizes on 11 November 1899. Yet only two railwaymen were in the dock. Pancrazio Garufi was the brakeman in the last carriage. Part of his job was to check that nothing fell from the train, but he claimed not to have seen anything amiss. The police asserted that the killers would not have thrown Notarbartolo's body from the train without being sure that Garufi would look the other way. Even more suspicion surrounded the ticket collector, Giuseppe Carollo. He was unlikely to have been one of the killers because one of his duties was to walk along the platform at each stop calling out the station's name. But the assassins would not have got on the train without tickets, performed a gruesome murder, and waited in the compartment at Trabia with the body if they had not been sure that there was someone – Carollo, the prosecution alleged – whose task it was to prevent their work being disturbed.

The first five days of the trial were a muddle. The two railwaymen floundered, had inexplicable lapses of memory, contradicted themselves. They even denied knowing each other when they lived fifty metres apart. The ticket collector Carollo, who had changed his story several times, made a particularly bad impression. One correspondent at the trial described his shifting eyes set in a 'gaunt, yellowish face with muscles shaped into a fox-like snout'. To most lay observers it seemed a hopeless task to decide whether the two accused were killers, accomplices, or just innocent witnesses who feared the consequences of incriminating anyone far more than they feared prison.

The contrast was stark when the victim's son, Leopoldo Notarbartolo, took the stand on 16 November. He stood tall and erect in naval uniform in the witness box, his head held so high that he seemed to be looking at the court down his strikingly long nose; like his dark, heavy-lidded eyes, it was a trait inherited from his murdered father. He delivered his evidence in a deep voice with a calm and speedy assurance that observers found disconcerting at first. Then, gradually, his honesty and directness made a profound impression. What Leopoldo Notarbartolo said stunned the court, made him a celebrity, and turned the case into one of the most famous trials in Italian history. 'I believe that the murder was a vendetta and that the only man who hated my father is Commendatore Raffaele Palizzolo, the member of parliament. I accuse him of being the instigator of the crime, of commissioning these and other killers.'

Leopoldo then began to paint a portrait of Don Raffaele Palizzolo and to tell the story of his long battle with his father. The two had first become acquainted when they were young men – Palermo is a small place. The animosity between them had been sparked soon after Notarbartolo became mayor in 1873 when he forced Palizzolo to pay back money he had spirited from a fund intended to subsidize bread for the poor.

As mayor, Notarbartolo was in regular contact with the public prosecutors who suspected that Palizzolo was a protector of a notorious brigand; it seemed that Don Raffaele relied on his influence at election time in Caccamo. The enmity between Notarbartolo and Palizzolo became personal. Wherever possible, Notarbartolo avoided places frequented by Palizzolo. He loathed his unmanly bearing, his cowardice, his smarm. Notarbartolo made no effort to hide his revulsion on those occasions where Palizzolo's company could not be avoided.

It was Palizzolo that Emanuele Notarbartolo had suspected of being behind his 1882 kidnapping. The empty villa where some of the kidnappers were captured was on land bordering Palizzolo's own estate; both properties were in Villabate – the fiefdom of his favourite *cosca*. The abduction itself had taken place near Caccamo, which was ruled by another *cosca* sponsored by Palizzolo.

By the time of the kidnapping, the theatre of the conflict between the two men had shifted to the Banco di Sicilia; Notarbartolo was its director and Palizzolo a leading member of its governing body. Leopoldo's account of his father's time at the bank did not disappoint those who had been hoping to hear some scandal emerge from the trial. He explained how his father had fought a losing battle to stop the Banco di Sicilia being used as a great sluice-gate of favours, the most powerful clientele-building instrument on the island. Large sums were found to have been loaned to, and never recovered from, children, janitors, boatmen, the dead, and individuals who had been entirely invented.

Throughout the 1880s, Notarbartolo strove to clean up the bank's affairs while Palizzolo made himself a constant nuisance.

Notarbartolo tried to pilot reforms in the bank's constitution that would reduce the influence of the politicians who made up two thirds of its governing body. In 1889, he sent the government a damning confidential report on the bank's workings. With it went an ultimatum: back my reforms or I resign. These letters were stolen from the office of the Minister of Agriculture, Industry, and Commerce. A few weeks later they were shown to a meeting of the bank's general council, which had been held while Notarbartolo was away in Rome on business. The meeting passed a vote of censure against him. Although nothing was ever proved, suspicions over the theft of the letters centred on Palizzolo. A registered package from a false address in Rome had been sent to his house on the day that the documents disappeared. The package was sealed with wax, bearing only the impress of a button from a particular Roman tailor. Palizzolo was among the tailor's customers.

The whole situation presented the government with a dilemma: it could either back the bank's council, which was increasingly dominated by crooks and clearly complicit in the theft of the letters; or it could back a principled, competent, but politically unreliable governor. It dithered for several months, and then took the first option. Notarbartolo was asked to resign. The bank's administration was dissolved, but most of the old members were subsequently re-elected. After Notarbartolo's enforced resignation, corrupt interests swooped on the bank to engineer the NGI share swindle. The subsequent investigation revealed that Palizzolo was one of the anonymous borrowers involved.

Leopoldo concluded his testimony to the Milan court with a solemn denunciation of the way the investigation into his father's murder had been handled. 'I repeatedly told the authorities all of these things. And yet Raffaele Palizzolo was never questioned. Perhaps they were afraid.'

The reports from Milan of Leopoldo Notarbartolo's evidence caused consternation in political circles in Rome. The trial had been intended to offer up small fry to quell the increasing demand for justice in the Notarbartolo case. Now Don Raffaele

Palizzolo suddenly became a huge political embarrassment. He wrote a letter to the press, claiming that he had always had a good working relationship with Notarbartolo. Then, as the atmosphere darkened around him in Rome, he scuttled back to Palermo.

Palizzolo's parliamentary immunity from prosecution was removed when Prime Minister General Luigi Pelloux arranged a rapid vote in the Chamber of Deputies. Because of rumours that the controversial MP was preparing to escape abroad, telegraph communications between Sicily and the mainland were suspended so that he did not hear the news of the parliamentary vote. With the legal authorities in Palermo still dithering, Chief of Police Sangiorgi was given direct authorization by General Pelloux to go ahead and arrest Palizzolo that very evening. Officers found him relaxing on the same bed around which his clients used to cluster each morning.

A few days later in Palermo 30,000 people marched to place a wreath on a new bust of Emanuele Notarbartolo that had been set on a small Corinthian altar in Politeama Square. Palizzolo appeared to be finished. 'The mafia is in its death throes,' opined one commentator.

Leopoldo Notarbartolo was using the Milan courtroom as a stage; it was his chance to expose the whole affair to the glare of publicity – his father's murder, the mishandled investigation, Palizzolo and the NGI share scandal. One of the striking aspects of his testimony was that he was not a witness for the prosecution. In Italy victims can pursue actions for damages during criminal trials, and they can even play a role in arguing the case for the prosecution. The young naval officer was one such 'civil complainant'. He had good reason for wanting to drive the prosecution: he had become convinced that the prosecuting magistrates who were supposed to prepare the case against the killers were complicit in a cover-up. His suspicions centred on Vincenzo Cosenza – the same chief prosecutor in Palermo who would later do his best to undermine Sangiorgi's prosecution of the mafia of the Conca d'Oro.

Over the six years since his father's murder Leopoldo had done a great deal of investigative work himself. He had met opposition and indifference at every turn. In 1896, an old personal and political friend of his father's, Antonio di Rudinì, became Prime Minister. Leopoldo went to see him, revealed his suspicions about Palizzolo, and asked for help. Rudinì was less than understanding: 'If you really believe he did it, why don't you just hire some good mafioso to kill him for you?'

It was only under Rudinì's successor, General Pelloux (another family friend of the Notarbartolos), that enough political momentum was built up for any kind of trial, even one that only inculpated the two railwaymen. Under Pelloux's influence, the murder trial was switched from Palermo to Milan where there was less likelihood that witnesses would be intimidated.

Following Leopoldo Notarbartolo's testimony, the Milan trial continued and the reasons for the delay in bringing the case to court began to emerge. Witness after witness fuelled the scandal. The local army commander in Milan ordered his officers not to attend the trial because of the stream of subversive revelations. The Minister of War, who had been Royal Commissar in Sicily, testified that 'the prosecution evidence for the Notarbartolo murder was prepared extremely negligently, extremely sloppily; indeed, it was carried out in a culpable way.' A few days later the same Minister was forced to resign when a newspaper published a letter from him, asking the judicial authorities to release a politically influential mafioso in time to help a government candidate during elections.

From the moment that the body on the tracks over the Curreri ravine was identified as being that of Emanuele Notarbartolo, the whole of Palermo had been alive with rumours that Palizzolo was behind the murder. Yet it emerged in court that the chief investigating magistrate in Palermo at the time had been transferred, apparently for suggesting that the rumours might well have some substance to them.

One police inspector, after asking to take charge of the case, had hidden evidence, including a pair of blood-caked socks. He had also sent the investigation along a series of patently false trails, each of them based on hypotheses that cast a shadow over the murdered banker's reputation. In Milan, to loud applause from the public gallery, the inspector was arrested in court. He turned out to be a close ally of Palizzolo's; he had acted as his electoral 'agent'.

The name of one of the men whom Leopoldo Notarbartolo believed had actually carried out the assassination also came out before the Milan jury. The deputy stationmaster at Termini Imerese – who had seen the sinister figure in Notarbartolo's compartment – was called to the stand. After repeating his account of that night back in February 1893, he said that he had not managed to recognize the same man in an identity parade.

Then the advocate representing the Notarbartolo family began to probe: was it not true that he *had* recognized the man, but had told the police he was afraid of saying so in public because of the mafia? The witness began to tremble, but stuck to his story. Then he was brought face to face with one of Ermanno Sangiorgi's predecessors as Chief of Police of Palermo – the very man who had conducted the identity parade. The stationmaster blushed and squirmed. There was considerable sympathy for his distress in the public gallery because he was evidently an honest man in fear for his life. Finally he cracked, and said in barely more than a whisper, 'I confirm everything he says; it's true; it really was the same man.'

The man he had identified was Giuseppe Fontana, age forty-seven, from Villabate. The former Chief of Police outlined for the court the suspect's background. He was a member of the Villabate *cosca* of the mafia. Only a few years before, he had been released from the charge of counterfeiting money because of the connections he was able to mobilize. 'I think that in this trial too, Fontana has been protected by a magical, powerful, and mysterious hand.'

As soon as these revelations were made in Milan, the order went out to arrest Fontana, who went into hiding. The rumour was that he was being sheltered by a prince and member of parliament whose estate he protected. The prince was interviewed by Chief of Police Sangiorgi who intimated that he might be accused of harbouring the criminal. The prince reported back to Fontana who dictated the conditions under which he would give himself up. Sangiorgi wearily agreed. The *Times* reporter in Italy was horrified at the deal:

Fontana . . . was driven into Palermo in the Prince's carriage, accompanied by the Prince's lawyers, interrogated at [Sangiorgi's] private house instead of being taken ignominiously to the police station, allowed to pay a farewell visit to his family, and, without being handcuffed, was considerately conducted . . . to the chief prison, where he was placed in a comfortable cell. Yet this is a man who has on his record four murders and various attempts at murder and theft of all of which charges he has been acquitted for 'insufficient proof', or, in other words, on account of the impossibility of inducing magistrates and witnesses to rise above the terrorism of the Maffia.

Giuseppe Fontana was making a point when he gave himself up in this fashion. His was a world of relationships between men. In that world, institutions, like the state, were meaningless. His arrest was a personal matter between himself and a respected adversary, Chief of Police Ermanno Sangiorgi.

With both Palizzolo and Fontana now under arrest, the Milan trial was abandoned on 10 January 1900 to allow further investigations to be carried out. The judicial marathon was only just beginning.

Even after the revelations in Milan, Palizzolo was not without friends while in custody. Indeed, he nearly managed to avoid being brought to trial at all.

In June 1900, Palizzolo's people put him forward for re-election to his central Palermo parliamentary constituency. The mafia, facing Sangiorgi's trial, needed all the political help it could get. With Sicilian influence on the wane in the national political arena, NGI also needed its old friends. If Palizzolo had been elected, he would again have been given parliamentary immunity. Florio money funded the election campaign, and even Ignazio's mother, the Baroness Giovanna d'Ondes, signed up to a ladies' support association started by Palizzolo's sisters. This local backing was not enough; the government supported his opponent, and Don Raffaele failed to secure victory.

Palizzolo's supporters in the magistrature also nearly stopped the case coming to court. Chief Prosecutor Cosenza drew up a report advising that there was not enough evidence for a trial. Only direct pressure from the King forced him to change his conclusion, although he still called the evidence 'slight'.

Before the second trial started, Fontana's cause was also helped by the death – from cirrhosis of the liver – of the shifty ticket collector, Giuseppe Carollo.

The second trial was held in what was probably Italy's most imposing courthouse, a palace in Bologna whose courtyard and noble façade were designed by Palladio. Its lavish interior was baroque, with the huge courtroom itself panelled in elaborately carved dark wood. Bologna was a politically conservative city, which would not give a sympathetic hearing to anyone trying to take advantage of the case's subversive implications.

Don Raffaele Palizzolo was one of the first witnesses called from the cage where the defendants were held. The time spent in custody had aged him; he looked thin and grey, the flesh sagging around his prominent jaw. He was still dressed immaculately, peering at his notes through an elegant pince-nez. He gave evidence for two days in a tragic pose, leaning on the back of a chair, punctuating his testimony with sobs and flourishing gestures, his voice alternating between a piteous murmur and a defiant boom.

Members of the jury, I am sure that you have not discovered in me any trace of inborn ferocity. What you have seen instead . . . are the deep, ineradicable marks left by the inhuman, barbaric treatment to which I have unjustly been subjected by the factional hatred, vendetta and anger that have formed a pact with fear on the part of the strong and cowardice on the part of the weak. So, let scorned, outraged humanity speak! . . . I am alone, I am poor, and I do not belong to any party factions. My dead brother said to me with his last kiss, 'Defend yourself, and defend your family's honour.'

Exhausted by the strain of delivering his evidence, Don Raffaele succumbed to a chronic nosebleed.

Giuseppe Fontana, the man accused of actually carrying out the Notarbartolo murder, was as composed and concise in the witness box as Don Raffaele had been prolix. He was relaxed and well groomed. Dressed in a dark blue suit, he looked just like the upstanding citrus fruit entrepreneur he claimed to be. Journalists present noted his powerful physique, and the sunken slits of his eyes, 'like two deep finger holes in a head modelled in clay'. Fontana had a characteristic way of pausing for reflection, head back and lips pursed, before continuing his statement with calm assurance. It seemed at times as if the evidence he was giving related to someone else and not to him. He even managed to raise a laugh from the courtroom when he said, with a smile, that if he had been a mafia boss as the prosecution claimed, then he would have sent one of his men to carry out the killing rather than do it himself.

It was an extraordinarily accomplished performance. As a member of the mafia's military organization, Fontana was more exposed than his *cosca*'s political patron. Even politicians prepared to embrace Palizzolo as one of their own were edgy about spending any of their political credibility on protecting a thug.

Much attention in court was focused on the alibi that had helped Fontana avoid prosecution for so long. He provided plentiful company records to show that he had in fact been in Tunisia on the day of the murder. With no little courage, Leopoldo

Notarbartolo had gone to North Africa on the mafioso's trail in the spring of 1895. (Sangiorgi believed that there was a whole *cosca* operating there.) The Sicilians whom Leopoldo encountered in and around Hammamet confirmed Fontana's alibi 'with the uniformity of a phonograph'. But by meticulously comparing Tunisian post-office money order registers with those in Palermo, Leopoldo and his lawyers raised doubts about the alibi. It was quite possible for one of Fontana's associates to have sent and received the money orders that supposedly proved that he had been away from Sicily at the time of the murder.

There had been sightings of the mafioso at key times, such as on the very evening of the murder in Altavilla where the two bowler-hatted suspects alighted from the train. In court, however, the witnesses who had earlier claimed to have seen Fontana made uneasy, contradictory denials.

Palizzolo's response to cross-examination stood as one long proof of the truism that one excuse is better than many. In the teeth of the most evident implausibility, Don Raffaele portrayed himself as the victim of a political plot, and denied even the most trivial of the prosecution's assertions. Far from being the leader of the mafia, he said, he was one of its victims. Fontana and he denied knowing each other. Yet it turned out that Palizzolo's intermediary in the NGI share swindle was also Fontana's business partner – a man who had provided a great deal of evidence in support of the Tunisian alibi.

One witness whose statement was followed with particular interest was Giuseppe Pitrè, the famous folklore expert. The professor of 'demo-psychology' gave a glowing account of Palizzolo's character – the accused was a close colleague of his in local government. Pitrè asserted that the fact that Palizzolo had written a novel in his youth revealed that he had 'a noble mind, devoted to virtue, averse to vice'. When asked to define the mafia, Pitrè explained that its origins lay in the Arabic word 'mascias'. It meant an exaggerated awareness of one's own personality, a reluctance to submit to bullying; in the lower social classes it could lead to criminal activity.

Chief of Police Ermanno Sangiorgi took a less bookish approach when called to the witness stand. The mafia, he said, was a sworn criminal organization based on protection rackets. It had bases across western Sicily and even in other countries. Sangiorgi was suffering from a bad cold at the time, and to many in court his hoarse voice was nearly inaudible. Advocates for the defence countered by pointing out that the recent trial in Palermo hardly gave convincing backing to his theory.

The Bologna jury retired to consider its verdict on the Notarbartolo murder at a quarter to ten on the evening of 30 July 1902. The sense of expectation matched the scale of the trial. It had lasted nearly eleven months. Fifty fat volumes of evidence were submitted; 503 witnesses were heard, whether in person or by sworn statement. They included three former government ministers, seven senators, eleven members of parliament, and five chiefs of police. The trial transcripts recorded fifty-four 'tumults'. On six occasions the court had to be completely cleared to restore order. Several times the lawyers on both sides had to be separated before they came to blows. One of the presiding judges died during the trial; two jurors had to be substituted because of ill health. The numerous advocates on both sides performed feats of forensic oratory: one of the Notarbartolo family lawyers delivered a concluding speech that lasted eight days; another spoke for four and a half.

The night of 30 July was one of the hottest of the year. The gas lamps burning inside the packed courtroom made the atmosphere unbreatheable. The streets outside were crowded. The court was guarded by half a company of infantrymen, fifty police, and forty-five *carabinieri*, many of whom formed a rank around the dock with bayonets fixed. Rumours of a mafia plot to kill one of the Notarbartolos' lawyers had spread during the judge's summing-up.

At twenty-five past eleven the jury filed back into the court-room. The foreman, an elementary school teacher, stood up and placed his hand on his heart. There was evident emotion in his voice as he listened to the judge's list of questions.

'Is the accused, Raffaele Palizzolo, guilty of having caused others to commit the murder of Commendatore Emanuele Notarbartolo?'

The 'Yes' response was greeted with applause and cries of astonishment. Fontana was also convicted of carrying out the Notarbartolo murder.

After the judge had issued the sentences – the accused were given thirty years each – Palizzolo demanded to say a word: 'You have been deceived, I swear it, as I said from day one. I am innocent. There is a God who will avenge me. Not on you, the jury, but on those who have assassinated me despite knowing that I am innocent.'

Fontana chipped in with, 'On my mother's tomb, I am innocent too.' They were led away.

The defence lawyers left the court to deafening whistles from the public gallery. Leopoldo Notarbartolo and his lawyers were already being mobbed to repeated cries: 'Long live the jury!' 'Long live Bolognese justice!' 'Long live the civil complainant.' They were unable to make it through the throng outside to their hotels, and had to take refuge in a nearby lawyer's office. There, in answer to shouted pleas, they spoke of their gratitude from the balcony.

In Palermo the scene could hardly have been more different. Huge numbers had gathered before the telegraph and newspaper offices. Within fifty minutes of the news arriving, special editions were on the street. By then the crowd was already thinning out in silence. The next day signs reading 'City in mourning' appeared in some Palermo shop windows. Chief of Police Sangiorgi reported that they were printed and distributed by mafiosi. *L'Ora*, a newspaper owned by Ignazio Florio, declared its perplexity at the verdict and asked what concrete proof there had been of Palizzolo's guilt.

In an article much quoted in the press across Italy, *The Times* too expressed surprise:

In view of the shuffling evidence of intimidated witnesses and of the testimony favourable to the character of Palizzolo given by several Sicilian magnates, it was expected that the jury would profit by the lack of material proof of the guilt of the accused to give them the benefit of the doubt.

Nevertheless, the article concluded, 'Broad justice has been done, and done courageously.'

The tone in some papers was celebratory. 'Glory and honour to the twelve men of the jury,' proclaimed *La Nazione*. The Socialist *Avanti!* hailed a defeat for 'one of the most barbaric and poisonous forms of delinquency – the maffia'. Sicily was still divided by the case. The *Giornale di Sicilia*, which had looked favourably on Leopoldo Notarbartolo's cause through-out the trial, called the result a blow struck against 'the mafia's principal champion, political power'. Many papers joined Bologna's *Resto del Carlino* in expressing pleasure that justice had prevailed, but also in drawing sombre lessons from the proven complicity of the authorities in protecting the guilty: 'Let us hope that we have all learned something from this mon-strous court case and that we never see its like again under an Italian sky.'

Six months later, the Court of Cassation in Rome quashed the whole Bologna trial on a technicality.

A minor witness had been called to give evidence. No sooner had he taken the oath than he had to withdraw while lawyers argued over whether he needed to testify at all. The next day he appeared in the witness box again, but made his statement without renewing the oath. Leopoldo Notarbartolo understand-ably thought that the episode had been deliberately arranged as a fail-safe for the defence.

In Sicily the Bologna verdict had given rise to a coordinated political response. Following the initiative of the 'demo-psychologist' Giuseppe Pitrè, a 'Pro Sicilia' committee was formed to express 'public indignation' at Palizzolo's conviction, which was seen as an attack on the island as a whole. Two hundred thousand people signed up to show their support.

When things periodically go against them at the national level, the mafia and its politicians fall back on complaints of this kind, and even start to make noises about Sicilian independence. This tactic seeks to draw on some powerful 'Sicilianist' feelings on the island. During the Notarbartolo trials, there certainly had been some prejudiced interventions in the press. 'Sicily is a cancer on Italy's foot,' one commentator proclaimed. These were also the years in which some academics were arguing that southern Italians were a backward race with oddly shaped heads and an innate proclivity for crime.

More importantly, what Palizzolo called his 'martyrdom' galvanized a powerful coalition of conservative political and business interests behind 'Pro Sicilia', which was much more than a mafia front organization, and more even than an extension of the NGI lobby. The Palizzolo case had come at a time when important right-wing Sicilian politicians were no longer influential in Rome. Now the liberal government was even making overtures to the Socialist Party. 'Pro Sicilia' was Sicilian conservatives' reaction to their perceived powerlessness. The pressure group did not last long, but it did manage to get the government to listen. A grouping of this kind could be an important component of any governing coalition. The quashing of the Bologna trial may well have been a peace offering to the powers organized around 'Pro Sicilia'.

The retrial began in Florence on 5 September 1903, more than a decade after the murder on the Termini–Palermo train. Now only Fontana and Palizzolo were in the dock. (Those acquitted in Bologna, including the brake operator on the train, were not asked to face the same charges again.) Nevertheless, the Florence trial lasted only two weeks less than the previous one, which it resembled in many ways.

Leopoldo Notarbartolo's lawyers did call on a new and potentially very important witness. Matteo Filippello was reputed to be the man who liaised with Palizzolo on behalf of the Villabate *cosca*. In 1896, he had been wounded in a dispute thought to have arisen from the division of the payment for Notarbartolo's murder. Early rumours in Palermo had named him as one of the assassins.

Filippello had to be threatened with arrest before agreeing to travel to the hearing. Once in Florence, he was arrested for intimidating another witness, and pretended that he was losing his sanity. The day before he was scheduled to appear in court, he disappeared. He was found hanging from the banisters in his boarding house near Santa Croce basilica. Suicide, the inquiry decided.

But by now public opinion had grown bored and sceptical. Nearly four years had passed since Leopoldo Notarbartolo's stunning revelations in Milan. The case had at first triggered a huge public debate on the mafia. Some valuable accounts were published, including two by Sicilian police inspectors. Yet for every useful study of the famous criminal organization, there were two or three that helped confuse the issue. There were still many voices – including prestigious witnesses – denying that the mafia existed. It was an exaggerated sense of personal pride, a product of the way the islanders had been oppressed throughout history. Others suggested that it was simply the Sicilian name for a type of underworld that could be found in every modern city in Europe and the United States.

Strikingly, even Leopoldo Notarbartolo's advocates in Bologna followed this line. In western Sicily, they argued, there were only isolated *cosche* that sometimes shared the same protector. 'What is the mafia today? Is it, as some people believe, an organization with bosses and underbosses? No. That only exists in the dreams of the odd Chief of Police.' There were obvious reasons for saying this. It would have been very unwise to pin the chances of a conviction in the Notarbartolo case on Sangiorgi's misfired efforts to mount a prosecution of the whole mafia. Nonetheless the statement stirred even more sediment into the debate.

Thus, despite the spotlight of Milan and Bologna, 'mafia' remained a turbid and formless concept. Mafia fatigue was bound to set in. When it did, it diminished the risk of a politically disruptive bout of public indignation following an acquittal.

With the benefit of the Bologna dress rehearsal behind them, the defence lawyers in Florence gave a much better account of themselves. Don Raffaele abandoned the mawkish oratory of his earlier performances and adopted the submissive pose of an invalid who had to be helped into the witness stand by a *carabiniere*.

The prosecution case failed to gain the same momentum it had in Bologna, the same sense that all the contradiction and confusion in the defence testimonies added up to proof of guilt. On 23 July 1904, an 8–4 majority of the jury acquitted the accused for lack of sufficient evidence. Palizzolo fainted on hearing the verdict.

Despite a surprisingly rapid improvement in his health over the week following the trial, Don Raffaele swooned again on 1 August when he stepped off the gangplank in Palermo harbour as a free man. The 'Pro Sicilia' committee had hired an NGI steamer to bring him back in triumph from the mainland.

It was the culmination of days of celebration. The Florio newspaper *L'Ora* said the city had been liberated from a nightmare by the Florentine jury. Palizzolo supporters had pictures of him on their lapels. The festival of the Madonna del Carmine had been postponed to allow the returning hero to take part. When Palizzolo came to his senses again, he was accompanied home by a cheering, disorderly crowd. He found his house

decked in lights spelling out 'Viva Palizzolo!' As he appeared
on his balcony, a band struck up a specially composed hymn to
his victory. One sycophant committed the shrill mood to paper:

After 56 months of harrowing martyrdom, Raffaele Palizzolo
emerged triumphant, bathed by the light of his dazzling halo of Pain
and Virtue. His Pain and Virtue were consecrated by the sublime
self-denial he showed through five years of unparalleled torment.
To pass the cheerless hours of imprisonment, in homage to Sicily,
mistreated Sicily, he plaited Pain and Virtue like tear-sprinkled
blossoms into garlands of harsh suffering.

Restraint has rarely been a strength of the mafia lobby. Many
Sicilians, even those who thought that the evidence against Don
Raffaele was not strong enough to merit a conviction, were
disgusted.

Yet the jubilation did not last long. In the November parliamentary elections, the martyr of Bologna was soundly beaten.
Despite his triumph, he was now too compromised and his
powerful friends abandoned him. The bedside audiences resumed, for Palizzolo continued to hold office in local government, but his days as Sicily's supreme clientele-builder were
behind him.

A short time before Palizzolo's apotheosis, Leopoldo Notarbartolo slipped back into Palermo aboard the postal steamer.
Only a small party of friends were there to greet him in silence,
hats in hands. There were tears as he was reunited with his
sister. Taking on the legacy of his father's struggle with Palizzolo
had cost him dearly. The Mendolilla estate would have to be
sold to pay legal costs.

Over the years that followed, Leopoldo's naval career
took him mercifully far from the island. He reached the rank
of admiral, but faded from public memory. From the day of
Palizzolo's acquittal he had resolved not to lose faith in progress,
not to collapse into a resigned vision of the world as evil and
chaotic. The only way that he found to continue the fight for
justice, to which he had dedicated the best years of his life, was

to record the story of his father's life. The long sea voyages afforded him plenty of time to write a biography that systematically understated his own role in the dramas of 1893–1904. His father would have approved of his modesty. In 1947, after a long and painful illness, Leopoldo died, childless, in his adopted home city of Florence. His wife published the biography two years later.

Giuseppe Fontana also left Sicily after the trial. Taking his four little daughters with him, he emigrated to New York to pursue his career in extortion and murder on the mafia's new frontier.

4

Socialism, Fascism, Mafia
1893–1943

Corleone

As the crow flies, it is only some thirty-five kilometres from Palermo to Corleone. Yet when Adolfo Rossi made the journey on 17 October 1893 – eight months after the Notarbartolo murder – the little train took its usual four and a quarter hours to wind a path through the treeless mountains. Much of the landscape traversed by the train was still parched by the Sicilian summer; bleached and rocky, it was marked only by the occasional ruined watchtower or the dark green of the sparsely scattered olive and lemon groves.

Adolfo Rossi was a journalist working for the liberal Roman daily *La Tribuna*. He had not long returned from the United States where he had spent a dozen years crossing the continent in search of his fortune. By the end of his time in America he had become editor of *Il Progresso Italo-Americano*, the leading organ of New York City's growing Italian population. Rossi returned to Europe with a passionate enthusiasm for the openness and speed of life in the United States. He claimed that by comparison Italy seemed as closed and static as a cemetery.

Riding in the same compartment as Rossi was another man from the mainland, a young army officer. They began to talk about the subject on everyone's lips: the desperate living conditions of Sicilian peasants. Rossi recorded the typical story that the officer told him:

It hurts to see some of the scenes you come across when you live here like I do. One hot day in July, I remember, I was on a long march with my men. We stopped for a rest by a farmyard where they were dividing out the grain harvest. I went in to ask for some water. The measuring had just finished, and the peasant had been left with no more than a small mound. Everything else had gone to his boss. The peasant stood with his hands and chin planted on the long handle of a shovel. At first, as if stunned, he stared at his share. Then he looked at his wife and four or five small children, thinking that after a year of sweat and hardship all he had left to feed his family with was that heap of grain. He seemed like a man set in stone. Except that a tear was sliding silently down from each eye.

For nearly two decades Italian reformers had in vain been denouncing the plight of the peasantry of the Sicilian interior: malnutrition, illiteracy, malaria, debt slavery, appalling working conditions, exploitation backed by mafia violence, theft justified by bought lawyers.

In Corleone, the peasants said that honest bosses were as rare as white flies. Many of the town's 16,000 inhabitants were labourers whose meagre existence depended on the great grain farms that stretched far into the hills below its narrow streets, its tiny squares, and its baroque churches. Corleone existed to feed Palermo, yet it did not always seem able to feed its own people. One English traveller of the 1890s found the town inhabited by 'pale, anaemic women, hollow-eyed men, ragged weird children who begged for bread, croaking in hoarse accents like weary old people tired of the world'.

Rossi had come to Corleone to interview a man who had devoted his life to changing these conditions, a man who would become a symbol of the struggle against both privation and the mafia.

The poverty of the peasants of the Sicilian interior had simple causes. The big landowners of Corleone and towns like it typically spent their time in Palermo and leased out their estates on short-term contracts to middlemen or *gabelloti*. The short leases meant that the *gabelloti* had to wring money out of the peasants quickly. The average *gabelloto* was a ruthless, self-made man; this was a job you could not do without making enemies. The *gabelloti* often had to protect themselves and their assets, notably cattle, from bandits and rustlers. Frequently the *gabelloti* were in league with or controlled the bandits. The *gabelloti* often needed friends in the legal business too; the abolition of the feudal system and the periodic auctions of church and state property had left thickets of red tape going back decades.

Gabelloti were such pivotal figures in Sicily's violent economy that it was often assumed that being a mafioso and being a *gabelloto* were the same thing. It is more accurate to say that joining the mafia enabled a *gabelloto* to do his job better. For one thing, the mafia had contacts in Palermo where many of the lease deals were made. For another, membership of the honoured society offered the military power needed to combat unruly peasants.

That power was to be called on when, as if from nowhere, in the autumn before Adolfo Rossi's journey to Corleone, the oppressed peasants of western and central Sicily began to form new organizations called Fasci. The Fasci had nothing in common with the militaristic, anti-democratic Fascist movement founded by Benito Mussolini a generation later. A *fascio* is simply a bundle, an image of solidarity; the Sicilian Fasci were brotherhoods that united the peasants against the landowners and the *gabelloti*.

For a few months in 1893 the Fasci movement made Corleone the focus of the nation's attention. The local *Fascio*, founded and led by Bernardino Verro, was one of the first and best-organized groups on the island. The previous year, Verro had been a lowly municipal bureaucrat with only an unfinished education behind him – he had been expelled from secondary school. There were thousands of anonymous functionaries like him across Italy, men who were forced to rely on patronage to obtain administrative jobs that barely paid enough to feed their families. Verro, infuriated by the injustices he witnessed around him, rebelled.

When he became leader of the Corleone *Fascio*, Verro was sacked for his political beliefs. By then he was past caring. He made flaming speeches to the peasants in their own dialect with examples drawn from the fables they knew. With Utopian fervour he preached cooperation, discipline, and women's rights. The future was socialist, he explained; the capitalist system was powerful because the power of love had waned, but the time was coming when the whole of humanity would be held in one loving embrace. Travelling by mule from Corleone, Verro spread the message through the nearby towns. Fasci formed wherever he spoke. Verro and the movement's leaders were impassioned lay evangelists. 'Like real brothers', they would kiss each other on the mouth when they met.

It was Verro that the journalist Adolfo Rossi had come to Corleone to interview. By the time Rossi made his journey into the Sicilian interior, Verro was at the head of the first mass peasant strike in Italian history, a leader talking on equal terms with top politicians and officials, a man who had won sympathy from almost all sections of Italian society for the peasants he led.

The meeting between Rossi and Verro produced one of the few first-hand portraits of the Fasci leader. It is an interview influenced by Rossi's acquired New World prejudices, as well as his readiness to indulge his Italian readers' sentimental view of Sicily. For all that, it reveals much about what Verro and the Fasci were really like.

Other people who knew Verro describe him as a bear of a man, energetic and short-tempered with an absolute devotion to his cause. Rossi, in contrast, had a metropolitan eye for the outlandish: 'The president of the *Fascio* is a young man of twenty-seven or twenty-eight. He genuinely has a touch of the Arab in his face, his beard, and especially his large, bulging eyes.'

Nevertheless Verro's hope and enthusiasm shone through his responses to Rossi's questions. 'Our *Fascio* has about six thousand members, men and women . . . Our women have understood the advantages of a union of poor people so well that they now teach their children socialism.' Rossi also discerned Verro's political acumen. The demands set forth in Corleone had become the template for every *Fascio* on the island. They were clear and moderate: new contracts that stipulated an even split of produce between the proprietor and the peasants who rented small plots of land. Even many conservatives saw this as a fair and efficient arrangement. Most of the landowners in Corleone had accepted the deal. 'The richest ones have not given in yet,' Verro explained to Rossi. 'Not so much for economic reasons; it is more out of pique. They don't want to look as if they have given in to the *Fasci*.'

Verro proudly showed the journalist round the large vaulted hall that served as the headquarters of the *Fascio*. At one end, above a table, was a terracotta bust of Marx flanked by portraits of the patriotic heroes Mazzini and Garibaldi. Underneath the table there was a display of superannuated weapons: sabres, muskets, and a blunderbuss.

Rossi interviewed some of the peasants there. They explained how the members who could read and write kept the illiterate up to date with news from the rest of the island. The old soldiers among the membership had formed a uniformed band to play patriotic songs and the workers' hymn that was the Fasci anthem. Rossi asked the peasants what they meant by socialism. 'Revolution!' came one reply; 'Putting property together and all eating the same,' came another. 'I am fifty years old,' explained a third peasant, 'and I have never eaten meat.'

Rossi saved until last the most sensitive issue, the one his readers were most curious about: the relationship between the Fasci and crime. Italians would remember the role that gangs of gunmen had played in the many revolutionary episodes in recent Sicilian history; the mafia was little understood, but widely feared. The Sicilian landowners tried to claim that the Fasci were just the latest disguise for the island's savage pica-roons and wreckers. 'What attitude have you taken to people with criminal records?' Rossi asked Verro. The reply was strenu-ously upbeat:

There are only a few, and they have been convicted of minor things like stealing from fields, so we accept them into the *Fascio* as a way of improving them. Since the *Fascio* started the crime rate has dropped. There are hardly any more disputes, because any issues are sorted out through the *Fascio*: we often act like magistrates or arbitrators. The real criminals are some of the landowners: loan sharks, former protectors of brigands; they rape young peasant girls and thrash the workers. If you only knew what these bullies get away with! It is still like the Middle Ages here!

Rossi was evidently touched; he had also got the simple story he came to Corleone to write. To outsiders like him, it sometimes seemed as if nothing in the Sicilian countryside had changed since Roman times when slaves worked the wheat fields. So on his return he gave his readers a fable of good and evil set in a timeless faraway land:

In this island, in the middle of areas that are heaven on earth, there are others that seem like Africa, where thousands of slaves labour on land belonging to a handful of great lords. Indeed they are worse off than those ancient slaves, who at least had their bread guaranteed.

Verro was written up as a noble barbarian, a latter-day Spartacus.

Reading Rossi's reports, it is tempting to think that his lazy fondness for certain stereotypical ideas about Sicily may just have cost him the story of his career. For what he did not realize is quite how complicated it is to be a hero in western Sicily.

Unbeknown to Rossi, only six months earlier Verro had been woken at dawn by a handful of gravel thrown against the window of his house in via San Nicolò. As agreed, he dressed quickly. Once outside, he was led the short distance through narrow streets to the house of a man he knew, a *gabelloto* on one of the estates that surrounded the town. There he was shown into a room where he found a group of men around a table. At its centre were three rifles and a piece of paper with a skull drawn on it.

The presiding boss began by explaining that the purpose of the meeting was to examine a proposal to admit Verro to the secret association – the members called themselves the Fratuzzi ('the Brothers'). When prompted, the initiate Verro explained how the social movement he had founded in Corleone aimed to champion the interests of the oppressed proletarian masses. Satisfied with this account, the boss warned of the dangers that faced any man who did not keep the society secret.

Verro was asked to repeat the Fratuzzi oath of loyalty before holding out his right hand for the thumb to be pricked with a pin. The blood was smeared on the image of the skull, which was then burned. In the light of the flames, Verro exchanged a fraternal kiss with each of the mafiosi in turn. He was told that, to introduce himself as a member of the Fratuzzi, he was to touch his incisors and complain of a toothache. He was now a member of the Corleone *cosca* of the mafia.

In becoming a mafioso Bernardino Verro was far from typical of Fasci leaders; and in leaving a written account of how he became one, he was unique among mafia initiates at the time. But Verro's story – which would only come to light after his murder – is nonetheless highly significant. For a long time it was treated with perplexed scepticism by left-wing writers, and not just because most people did not believe in such a thing as a mafia initiation ritual. Over the sixty years and more that followed the flowering of the Fasci movement, mafiosi would intimidate and murder countless socialists, Communists, and trade union leaders – so many, in fact, that it came to seem as if the mafia's very purpose was to batter the organized working class in the countryside into submission. And yet here, at the very origins of Italian peasant socialism, was a socialist hero consorting with the mafia.

Verro's initiation is easy to explain from the Corleone *cosca*'s point of view. Men of honour never set themselves square against change – their aim is to steer it in the direction they want – and in 1892–3 the situation was highly unpredictable. The Fasci could end up turning the peasants into a new force in the Sicilian countryside, changing the way land was owned and worked; or they could fail and be sucked back into clannish local politics. The *gabelloti* affiliated to the mafia were unsure whether to oppose the Fasci or use them to get better lease terms out of the landlords. By approaching the Fasci leaders, the mafia was trying to make sure that it would be able to maintain its influence whatever the future held.

The mafia has a serenely unscrupulous attitude to political ideologies. It has no guiding political ideas, only tactics. Opportunism is its masthead value. For that reason, no social or political movement, of whatever colour, is born immune to mafia influence. The mafia's unscrupulousness even extends to its own traditions. The initiation is not quite as hallowed a rite as is often believed, even by many mafiosi. If it is cheaper, less risky, and more effective to offer someone membership than it is to buy or bully them, then senior bosses will run through the necessary ritual performance.

As a result, the Fasci had to take constant care to avoid mafia infiltration. Some local groups even had it in their statutes that known mafiosi were barred from membership. Not the least reason for this is that elements in government would have been very happy to have a pretext to suppress the peasant organizations on the grounds that they were merely criminal gangs. As it turned out, a government investigation showed that the Fasci had largely been successful in keeping their ranks free of wrongdoers.

Yet in some places like Corleone the relationship between the Fasci leadership and the mafia had a fearsome intimacy to it. The peasant chiefs and the mafia bosses were competing in the same political marketplace for hearts and minds. The peasants wanted to force a better deal, and some of them were happy to take it from whoever looked most likely to deliver it, be they mafiosi or socialists.

Bernardino Verro's side of the story of his initiation into the Fratuzzi would only come out after his death. The train of events was set in motion during the winter of 1892–3. At this time a low-level campaign of intimidation and provocation against the Fasci was under way. Activists were beaten up and haystacks were burned down so that the socialists could be blamed, thus increasing the chances of a military crackdown. There was police harassment and the Fasci leaders were being arrested on trumped-up charges. Some peasants were also responding to the landowners' intransigence with vandalism. Verro and the other Fasci leaders knew that there were politicians in Rome who were looking for a chance to send the troops into Sicily. Many Fasci leaders believed that a violent confrontation with the state was inevitable, sooner or later. Voices within the movement were airing the possibility of an armed socialist insurrection to pre-empt the repression.

It was during these tense months that Verro heard strong rumours that he was about to be made to disappear. To protect himself he made sure he never walked the streets of Corleone alone. One night he saw – and avoided – three unknown men waiting for him near his house. Then a man from Corleone approached him repeatedly, expressing sympathy for the peasant movement and offering reassurances about his personal safety. He explained that the landowners had ordered his murder, but that there was a secret society in Corleone that was prepared to protect him. The society was even willing to offer him assistance and membership. All they asked was that he modify his hostile attitude to certain local men with great qualities and notable courage.

Verro decided to accept the offer. He, like most other Sicilians, probably had only an imprecise idea of what the mafia really was: perhaps a kind of Masonic league, or something more vague and informal. Understandably enough, the chance that the Corleone mafia offered Verro to save his own life helped him make up his mind to join.

There was also a broader background to Verro's decision. During the same tense months of early 1893 there were exploratory contacts between men of honour and the socialist movement's leadership at a regional level. Both sides were cagey. If there was going to be a revolution, the honoured society in each area had to assess whose side it would fight on. Was it better to back a distant and frail Italian state? Or infiltrate the socialist peasantry? For their part, the peasant leaders began to wonder whether an alliance with the mafia might not be a price worth paying for victory in the coming struggle. A Utopian faith in the power of socialism perhaps even gave them hope that the mafia could be incorporated and neutralized.

At the end of April, Verro and two other senior members of the Fasci umbrella organization met Palermo mafia bosses. The proposal was that a peasant revolution, if it came, would be spearheaded by '200,000 lions' – these lions being the mafiosi and their skirmishers. (The discussion seems to have been marked by a Homeric level of exaggeration.) Not a great deal of progress was made towards a deal. Accounts differ as to why: either the mafiosi reached the conclusion that the Italian state, in the end, was going to prove stronger than the Fasci; or the peasant leaders suspected that the mafia was trying to draw them into an ambush on behalf of the police and the landowners.

Bernardino Verro quickly came to regret accepting membership of the Corleone *cosca*. The Fratuzzi invaded the 'New Era' – a club he had set up as a centre of republican and socialist activity. They ran card games there and used the gambling to pass counterfeit money into circulation. It was obvious to Verro that both he and the Corleone *Fascio* risked being discredited and labelled as criminals by the police, so he stayed away from the 'New Era' club. The distance separating mafiosi and peasant activists in Corleone became wider when the former took over land left uncultivated because of a strike organized by the *Fascio*. Verro rapidly abandoned all hope that the Fratuzzi and the peasants might form a pact. He would spend the rest of his life trying to make amends for joining the mafia – a mistake that would eventually cost him his life.

On 3 January 1894, the hawks in Rome and Sicily finally had their way: 50,000 troops enforced martial law and the dissolution of the Fasci. The crunch had come in December when the Fasci staged tax strikes and demanded that corrupt local councils be dissolved – a direct challenge to the mafia's vital political interests. The level of violence began to rise. The worst incidents occurred when troops fired directly into crowds of demonstrators; eighty-three peasants were killed. In places, the fighting was deliberately provoked when persons unknown fired random shots from low rooftops or windows; with decisive cunning the mafiosi were acting on their decision to back the landowners and the state rather than the Fasci. The discipline that Verro had managed to instil in the peasants of Corleone meant that it was one of the few places where there was no bloodshed.

Bernardino Verro tried to escape Sicily, but was arrested on 16 January 1894 on board a steamer to Tunis and brought before a military tribunal. The charges were of conspiracy to provoke a revolt, incitement to civil war, violence, and destruction. During the trial the authorities banned mainland newspapers from the island. Verro was found guilty and sentenced to twelve years in prison. The harsh penalty shocked even many conservatives. Unexpectedly, in 1896, he was released in an amnesty. But the next decade of his life would be divided between political activism, prison, exile, and persecution by the authorities.

Verro was released at the end of a second prison sentence in the summer of 1907. (He had been convicted of slander after a newspaper that he had set up revealed that a senior local police officer had procured a young woman for the deputy prefect – her husband was in jail. Verro was sentenced to eighteen months when his key defence witnesses retracted.)

Hundreds of socialist peasants from the interior came to Palermo to welcome him on his release. Carrying flags and banners, they arrived early in the morning on a specially chartered train from Corleone. The town band, dressed in red shirts, led a procession through the streets. Women in traditional peasant costume marched under a banner that read 'Corleone women's section'. Heavily guarded, they walked along via Macqueda to the Ucciardone prison and there greeted Bernardino Verro with cheers, embraces, and tears. After a meeting in the Palermo workers' chamber, they took him back to Corleone in triumph.

Now, thirteen years after the repression of the Fasci, morale in the peasant movement had never been higher. There was a more liberal government in power in Rome. The year before Verro's release, a new law made it possible for cooperatives to borrow from the Banco di Sicilia on behalf of the peasants; the money was to be used to rent land directly from the owners. In Corleone, Verro immediately assumed the leadership of a cooperative formed for just this purpose. It had the potential to be the most powerful weapon yet against the mafia. The aim was to cut the middlemen, the *gabelloti*, out of the rural economy. Verro knew that the approaching struggle would probably be violent; two men who worked closely with him had been murdered while he was away. He knew too that the Fratuzzi in Corleone had a personal score to settle with him; he still carried the mortifying secret of his initiation.

The Fratuzzi were cautious at first. They initially attempted to bribe Verro to stop the cooperative taking their leases. Although the mafia managed to infiltrate many peasant associations across western Sicily, Verro resisted and by 1910 his cooperative had taken charge of nine estates, freeing hundreds of labourers from near-serfdom in the process.

But Verro's cooperative also faced political opposition from a Catholic fund, the Cassa Agricola San Leoluca. It was a sign of a fundamental change happening across Italy. When Italian unification was completed in 1870 with the occupation of Rome, the Pope had declared the Church 'despoiled', shut himself in the Vatican, and instructed the faithful not to take any active part in the political life of the godless new country. Only towards the end of the nineteenth century did Catholics, with the approval of the clergy, begin to take political action. What drew them into the public domain was the need to protect the faithful from the subversive materialist creed of socialism.

Mafiosi had always dealt with priests as they did with politicians – man to man, favour for favour. Now the Church and the mafia also had common ideological ground in their hatred of socialism. The priests and lay believers who ran the Cassa Agricola San Leoluca are obscure figures; little is known about the Corleone Church. But some idea of the atmosphere among the local clergy emerges from the letter one canon wrote to the archbishop in 1902, asking him to stop Corleone priests carrying guns 'both by day and by night'. The Catholic cooperative used the Fratuzzi to guard the land it rented. The most deadly phase of Verro's struggle against the mafia was about to begin.

In 1910, Bernardino Verro launched a tax strike in protest at a corrupt Catholic mayor. The municipal administration collapsed. During the subsequent election campaign, Verro gave a speech denouncing the 'mafia affiliated with the Catholics'. The reaction was swift. On the evening of 6 November he was waiting in the pharmacy for voting to finish when someone fired both barrels of a shotgun at him through the window. His hat was blown off and his wrist cut, but astoundingly he was otherwise unhurt. It seems that the would-be killer's aim had been thrown off by the bright lights and reflections in the pharmacy cabinets. When Verro rushed outside to see whether he could identify his would-be assassin, he came face to face with a well-known mafioso who was evidently surprised to see him still alive. 'You see, your boys could only make smoke this time,' Verro said.

If in public he maintained a brave face, in private Verro was terrified. He began to discover just how far the mafia's contacts reached; its links with the local MP, the magistrature, and the clergy. The bullets fired at him, he said, stank of 'mafia and incense'. He was forced to leave his beloved Corleone once again. Although he denounced to the authorities the men he thought had tried to kill him, the case went nowhere because witnesses were afraid to come forward.

In the spring of 1911, Verro wrote to a friend in despair when he heard that his comrade Lorenzo Panepinto, the peasant leader in Santo Stefano Quisquina, had been shot dead on his doorstep:

Have you seen what they did to poor Panepinto? The clerical-mafia *gabelloti* have risen up against the cooperatives. The truth is so terrible that it almost makes me insane with despondency. Every time I look at the wound on my left wrist I see two corpses in the scar: one is my own, and the other belongs to my good friend and comrade Panepinto. I have had to leave Corleone, where the maffia has declared me a traitor. What is there left for me to do? Become a criminal myself, and take vengeance with lead and dynamite? Or wait, like a dead man on holiday, to be murdered?

Troubles continued to pursue Verro. The treasurer of the peasants' cooperative in Corleone was arrested for fraud and falsely stated that he had been working on Verro's orders. (Strong evidence suggests instead that the treasurer had the support of the Fratuzzi.) Although there is now no suspicion that Verro was guilty of deliberate wrongdoing, it does seem that he was naive and lax in supervising the cooperative's accounts. He was arrested and spent nearly two years in jail on remand.

When Verro was finally released in 1913, he still had the fraud charge hanging over him and seemed to his enemies to be a broken man; he was reduced to selling wine and pasta to get by. But his intention was merely to wait until his name was cleared before returning to politics. The peasants, their faith in him unshaken, begged him to head the socialist list in the local elections. They now had the vote at last; universal male suffrage, which had been introduced in 1912, was an unprecedented opportunity to fight for justice and equality by democratic means. Verro knew the dangers he faced; he would say to friends that the mafia was bound to end up killing him because it could not beat him any other way. But he felt it was his duty to accept the peasants' plea. In 1914 he was overwhelmingly elected mayor of Corleone.

Verro's political life in 1914 and early 1915 was dominated by the First World War. Like most socialists, and indeed most

Italians, Verro opposed Italian intervention in the war. Three times in the previous two decades the people of Corleone had seemed to be on the brink of securing a more just future for themselves. In 1894, their Fasci were repressed by martial law; in 1910, their cooperative was checked by intrigue and violence; now, just as a broad-based democracy arrived, their hopes were to be denied by conscription. Italy eventually joined the war in May 1915.

But these were important months in Verro's personal life too. After years on his own, the itinerant activist had settled down, and his partner (the couple were ideologically opposed to marriage) gave birth to a daughter; they named her Giuseppina Pace Umana – 'Josephine Human Peace'. In the autumn of 1915 the fraud trial that had caused Verro so much anxiety also, finally, began to draw near. Having spoken to the lawyers involved, he felt optimistic about his prospects for success.

On the afternoon of 3 November 1915, Verro left the Corleone town hall under a rapidly darkening sky. The downpour began as he turned the corner to climb via Tribuna. Just as he reached a flight of four steps that stretched the full width of the top end of the street, a bullet fired from a stable hit him under the left armpit. He staggered, turned, and pulled out his Browning pistol. He got off one futile shot before it jammed. Five more bullets hit him from two angles. He was probably already dead when he fell face down into the mud.

One of the killers then calmly emerged from cover and, it seems, knelt on the small of Verro's back. He aimed his pistol at the base of his victim's skull and fired four times. He then put the muzzle to Verro's temple and pulled the trigger again. The state of the corpse was to serve as a warning to others.

Reports of the demonstratively savage murder were limited to a few lines in most national newspapers. News of the fighting on the western front, in Serbia, and on Italy's north-eastern borders dominated the nation's interest.

For many years following the failure of Sangiorgi's maxi-trial in 1900 and the acquittal of Palizzolo and Fontana in 1904, it was hugely difficult to raise any interest in the fight against the mafia. Public opinion in Italy was resigned and sceptical; people greeted news of organized crime in Sicily with apathy and distaste. It was taken for granted that the Corleone mayor's death was a mafia affair and that, very probably, no one would be held to account.

Not even the remarkable evidence produced in the trial helped it attract the public attention it deserved. Among Verro's personal papers, the police discovered a testimony in his own hand that added a new layer of intrigue to a life that fully reflected a dramatic period in Sicilian history. It was Verro's posthumous confession. In it he told the full story of his initiation into the Fratuzzi – a secret he had never divulged to anyone before – and gave a detailed account of how the mafia in Corleone operated. The policemen who discovered the document all swore to Verro's absolute integrity and devotion to his cause; they believed that if he had revealed what he knew about the mafia, he would have been killed much earlier.

As expected, despite the highly public nature of the murder, no one was ever convicted; the trial ended after a few days when the chief prosecutor withdrew his evidence, stating that he did not feel it stood up. The collapse of the trial saw to it that, yet again, a reliable witness to the reality of the 'honoured society' was not believed.

The Fratuzzi had plenty of reasons to assassinate Bernardino Verro. The question is why they did it when they did. The police later surmised that the mafia feared Verro would use the fraud trial to expose what he knew about the association. It may also have entered the *cosca*'s thinking that the ongoing war would muffle the publicity surrounding the murder. Over the years, the Fratuzzi had tried without success to coopt Verro, corrupt him, defeat him politically, smear him, and intimidate him. Apparently, by 1915, only one instrument was left.

Even where it is at its most powerful, the mafia cannot just eliminate anyone it wants to without preparing for the consequences. Any killing involves calculating risks, and the killing of a powerful man like Verro, who had many passionate supporters in Corleone and beyond, was a particularly risky undertaking. Tragically, it seems that in this case the mafia had made its calculations accurately.

Verro was far from the last martyr of the peasant movement. Spates of political killings by the mafia followed both world wars. The tactics adopted against the Fasci in Corleone were to be used again; wherever the honoured society could not infiltrate peasant organizations, or create more pliable alternatives, it confronted them with terror. Among the mafia's political victims at around the time that Verro fell were also five brave and honest priests whose names deserve to be recorded: Don Filippo Di Forti, in San Cataldo, 1910; Don Giorgio Gennaro, in Ciaculli, 1916; Don Costantino Stella, in Resuttana, 1919; Don Gaetano Millunzi, in Monreale, 1920; Don Stefano Caronia, in Gibellina, also in 1920. The new socially committed Catholicism was not entirely oblivious to the reality of the mafia, and paid a price in blood as a result.

In 1917, the peasants of Corleone erected a bust of Bernardino Verro in Piazza Nascè where the labourers gathered every morning in the hope of being hired by a *gabelloto* for a day's work. Verro was depicted looking up via Tribuna to the spot where his murder had taken place. In 1925, the bust was stolen; it was never found. In 1992, a courageous young left-wing mayor of Palermo erected another bust as part of his effort to weave into the fabric of the town the memory of the mafia's misdeeds. After being vandalized several times, the monument was finally destroyed in July 1994. The mafia was making the point that it pursues its victims even beyond the grave.

The Man with Hair on His Heart

In January 1925, Prime Minister Benito Mussolini stood up in parliament, assumed personal responsibility for the violence of his Fascist gangs, and launched the process of suppressing all opposition. Mussolini's Fascist Party was no longer a government; it was a regime. A year later the new dictatorship brandished its authority by inaugurating a war on organized crime in Sicily.

The siege of Gangi, the opening showpiece of the war, began on the night of 1 January 1926 as heavy snow fell on the Madonie mountains. In the preceding days police and *carabinieri* in mobile parties of fifty had been gradually narrowing a cordon, arresting all those suspected of collaborating with bandits. The cordon and the cold together forced the bandits themselves back up into Gangi, which was known to be their headquarters. The police occupied hilltops and other strategic points near by. Telephone and telegraph wires were cut. Lorries and armoured cars blocked the access roads below. Then large numbers of police, with a sprinkling of black-shirted militiamen, struggled up the steep and narrow road into Gangi itself.

Gangi had seemed impregnable in its lofty isolation, dominating the landscape of the whole of central Sicily from its position in the Madonie; on a clear day the looming outline of Mount Etna can even be made out half across the island to the east. Locally the bandit leaders were referred to as 'the prefect' or 'the chief of police'. They had been so powerful that they had even succeeded in persuading the mayor to turn down a government street-lighting subsidy on the grounds that the town's steep alleys were actually safer in the dark.

Now the labyrinth was brightly lit and it teemed with uniformed men who were searching and occupying houses, making dozens of arrests. Many of the wanted men had retreated into secret rooms constructed by a local builder who was expert in the siting of false walls and ceilings. Only a few Gangitani risked sneaking out into the snow to take messages and victuals to the men in hiding. The rest huddled in their homes behind barred doors and windows.

The first bandit to give himself up emerged from his hideaway on the morning of 2 January. Gaetano Ferrarello, the 'King of the Madonie', was sixty-three years old and had been a fugitive from justice since the day when he killed his wife and her lover. That was more than half his life ago. It had taken him years to build an extensive network of cattle rustling, estate management, and extortion, and to construct the political protection needed to operate unmolested by the authorities. He let it be known that he would not give himself up to a policeman, but only to the mayor.

In the town hall, the officer commanding the besieging forces simply sat and waited for Ferrarello to appear. He found him to be a tall man with an almost military dignity of bearing and a patriarch's beard that reached his belt. The bandit flung down his decorated stick on the desk and delivered a studied pronouncement: 'My heart is trembling. This is the first time I have ever been in the presence of the law. I am giving myself up to restore peace and serenity to these people who have been so tormented.' Several days later Ferrarello committed suicide in jail by throwing himself down a stairwell. No others were involved in the incident, it seems.

The operation continued. No one was allowed in or out of Gangi while the police mounted a series of stunts designed to humiliate the concealed bandits. Their cattle were confiscated; the most handsome beasts were slaughtered in the town square and offered for sale at token prices. Hostages were taken, including women and children. Policemen slept in bandits' beds and – so strong rumours suggested – abused their women. Then the town crier was ordered to walk through the empty streets, banging a hefty drum at his hip:

Citizens of Gangi! His Excellency Cesare Mori, Prefect of Palermo, has sent the following telegram to the Mayor with the order to make his proclamation public:

I command all fugitives from justice in this territory to give themselves up to the authorities within twelve hours of the moment when this ultimatum is read out. Once that deadline has passed, the severest measures will be taken against their families, their possessions, and anyone who has helped them in any way.

Cesare Mori was the man Mussolini had chosen to lead his war on organized crime. The ultimatum was a typical gesture, demonstratively turning the Gangi operation into a man-to-man confrontation with the criminals.

Mori had been in Palermo during the siege, monitoring the press approval of his 'Herculean labour'. On 10 January, with bandits still hiding in the town, he came to Gangi to proclaim its liberation in person. The piazza was suitably festooned and the band played military marches. Posters displayed Mussolini's congratulatory message to his prefect. 'I express my heartiest satisfaction and urge you to carry on until your work is done without regard for anyone, high or low. Fascism has cured Italy of many of its wounds. It will cauterize the sore of crime in Sicily – with red-hot iron if need be.'

If the Fascist-controlled press are to be believed, speeches were then made from the balcony of the town hall. The young Palermo Fascist chief Alfredo Cucco, a strutting little ophthalmologist in a black shirt and leather flying helmet, led the invited leaders as they echoed the Duce's sentiments. Finally Mori stepped forward. He was just past his fifty-fourth birthday with regular if rather pointed features, an imposing build, and a deep voice. He relished the nicknames he had acquired during the years he had spent fighting crime in Sicily: the 'iron prefect', the 'man with hair on his heart'. The heavy army boots and long thick scarf that he chose to wear with his immaculate suit were intended to reinforce the same message: here was a man of action, a personal enemy of the criminals. That very day one of the bandits still in hiding issued a threat to kill him.

Mori's speech was characteristically far blunter than the ones that preceded it. He talked to Sicilians in what he considered to be their own rudimentary moral language.

Citizens! I will not give up the fight. The government will not give up the fight. You have a right to be freed from these villains. You will be. The operation will carry on until the whole of the province of Palermo is redeemed.

Through me, the government will do its duty to the full. You must do yours. You are not scared of guns. Yet you are afraid to be associated with the name 'cop'. You must get used to thinking of the war on criminals as the duty of every honest citizen.

You are good people. Your bodies are sound and strong. You have all the right virile anatomical attributes. So you are men, and not sheep. Defend yourselves! Counter-attack!

Mori's words sound as if they were meant for the ears of some higher breed of farm animal. Whether or not he actually delivered the speech that the newspapers printed is open to doubt. All the same, they typify the attitude of the man chosen to enact Fascism's authoritarian fantasies in Sicily.

The siege was wound up a few days later; 130 fugitives from justice and some 300 of their accomplices had been arrested.

Militaristic, decisive, tough, spectacular: the siege of Gangi is remembered in more or less the way that Fascist propaganda wanted it to be, the way it very deliberately styled its war on organized crime. When mafia defectors began to talk to Giovanni Falcone in the 1980s, it became clear that mafiosi themselves had similar memories of the Fascist years. Catania man of honour Antonino Calderone, who turned *pentito* in 1986, revealed that, more than forty years after its fall, Benito Mussolini's Fascist regime remained a scar on the mafia's folk memory.

The music changed [under Fascism]. *Mafiosi* had a hard life. Many were sent to a prison island, just from one day to the next ... Mussolini, Mori, the people in charge of justice, they did this: they gave *mafiosi* five years of internal exile without trial, the maximum. And when those five years were over they issued a decree and gave them five more. Just like that. A decree! Five more years ... After the war the mafia hardly existed any more. The Sicilian Families had all been broken up. The mafia was like a plant they don't grow any more. My uncle Luigi, who had been a boss, an authority, was reduced to stealing to earn a crust.

Calderone was only a small boy when his uncle Luigi was suffering these indignities. Although the tales the youngster was told had the simplicity of all family memories, they undoubtedly had a basis in truth. The Fascist crackdown that began with the siege of Gangi allowed some policemen and magistrates who had accumulated years of experience in fighting the *cosche* to go on the offensive. The mafia suffered badly; a great many men of honour were sent to prison, with or without trial, and the rest of the organization went into hibernation.

Fascism claimed that it had solved the mafia problem. But like so much of what Mussolini said, it proved to be a hollow boast. And, although the Duce's control over information still makes it difficult for historians to discern the truth, the real story of 'the man with hair on his heart' – the mafia's most feared enemy – is certainly darker and more intriguing than either Fascist propaganda or mafia memories suggest.

Cesare Mori's parents only recognized his existence at the age of seven; until then he had been in the foundling hospital in Pavia, near Milan. For a bright boy from nowhere, with no contacts, in late-nineteenth-century Italy, the army and police were among the few places to make a career. The secret Interior Ministry files on Mori chart his inexorable rise and leave no doubt as to either his driving ambition – or his courage. In 1896, Mori was awarded a medal for pursuing and apprehending a pimp whom he had seen holding up a young soldier with a revolver while a prostitute tried to stab him in the back. It was to be the first of many face-to-face encounters with violent crime.

Mori's superiors' reports on all aspects of his work are glowing: 'He is energetic, determined, and prudent. He knows every aspect of his job well, especially political policing duties because he knows the doctrines of all the parties and the habits and behaviour of politicians.' Mori was already being marked out for promotion when, in Ravenna in 1903, he frisked a powerful local councillor whom he suspected of carrying a knife. (Sicily was not the only place where council politics could be a dangerous business.) A press campaign was mounted against him. The reward for Mori's cussedness was a transfer to Castelvetrano, Sicily. From this point onwards, his life was entwined with the history of the mafia.

Electoral violence tacitly managed by the authorities, cattle rustling, and organized crime: for most of the next fourteen years Mori had the standard workload for the forces of order in the countryside of western Sicily. He applied himself to it with unstinting vigour. Local people regularly filed accusations that he had abused his authority. In 1906, he was promoted to superintendent. Three years later he was promoted again after killing a bandit during a lengthy firefight. In 1912, he distinguished himself once more by hunting down a ring of extortionists who had demanded money from an MP.

Policing in Italy was always highly politicized. Mori's own political opinions – he was a conservative monarchist – were conventional enough to be subordinated to his ambitions. That meant conforming to the expectations of the powers that be, both in Rome and locally (at least when the two could be reconciled). In Sicily he had followed a line favourable to the most powerful interest group: the landowners.

When the Great War began, Mori was deputy chief of police in the city of Trapani on the western tip of the island. There were no military engagements in Sicily during the war, but everything that happened after Italy joined the fighting in May 1915 conspired to push the island towards an abyss of violence. Over 400,000 Sicilians – equivalent to more than the whole population of Palermo – were drafted. As had happened since the foundation of the Italian state, thousands of recruits avoided the draft by taking to the hills. Large-scale banditry made a comeback in the interior as these runaways turned to crime for survival. Without the hands to sow and harvest grain, the great estates began to convert to pasture for rearing animals. The demand for horses, mules, and meat at the front also meant increased livestock prices. Violent crime increased as competitive forces converged to cash in; cattle rustling increased dramatically, and there were frequent bloody conflicts over contracts to rent, manage, or 'protect' land. In places, the island came close to anarchy.

Mori was relentless in the fight against the rustlers who infested the countryside during the Great War. The horseback patrols that he led covered all terrain, at all hours, and in all weather conditions. He laid siege to villages to force out the fugitives, and on occasion even disguised himself as a monk to surprise his foes.

In 1917, Mori was promoted away from the island to become chief of police in the northern industrial city of Turin at the very time when disastrous military defeat at Caporetto threatened the country with collapse. Mori opposed the city's militant socialist workers with his habitual resolve; many were killed. Three years later, in Rome, Mori ordered his men to charge a right-wing student demonstration; again deaths and injuries resulted.

It was in the years immediately after the First World War that Italy's fledgeling democracy entered what would turn out to be a terminal crisis. The old patronage politicians no longer seemed able to contain the conflicting demands of the Socialists, the Catholics, and the Nationalists (who dreamed of an Italian 'race' devoted to imperial war). In 1918, as a desperate economic crisis took hold, hundreds of thousands of demobilized soldiers began to arrive back home. Many were determined to force a change, whether to the left or the right. The example of the Russian revolution excited many workers and peasants. The peninsula looked to some as if it were becoming ungovernable; revolution, or civil war, seemed imminent.

Sicily did not have a strong workers' movement like the industrial North, but in 1919 and 1920 the island seemed to be consumed by mayhem unlike anything it had seen since the aftermath of Garibaldi's expedition in 1860. The recruits who returned to Sicily reignited the struggle to control the land; the issues that the Fasci had first tried to address in the 1890s had not gone away. Now the ex-combatants felt that they deserved land in return for their sacrifice; in places they occupied estates by force. In Rome several political groupings made noises about helping veterans acquire plots and legalizing the forced occupation of uncultivated fields. Some landlords, feeling abandoned by Rome, began to resort to violence to defend their property. The mafia adopted the same tactics towards the peasant cooperatives that it had developed to cope with the Fasci movement: it variously infiltrated, cajoled, corrupted, and – if all else failed – terrorized and murdered.

It was also a time of numerous mafia wars. One of the most destabilizing influences was simply the return, among the veterans, of battle-hardened and ambitious young men from traditional mafia recruiting grounds. They had missed out on the profiteering and were now keen to make their presence felt – whether within the mafia or in autonomous gang operations. Mori talked of a 'hailstorm' of fighting among mafiosi after the war: 'There were no rules, and no respect for anybody.'

The Fascist movement was founded in Milan in March 1919 by journalist and combat veteran Benito Mussolini. He aimed to institute a 'trench-ocracy', to bring the patriotic discipline and aggression of the front to bear on Italy's stunted democracy. The following year, as the post-war wave of labour militancy receded, squads of Fascists began to build their movement by dishing out ferocious beatings to strikers and socialists across northern and central Italy. They attracted the favour of land-owners and industrialists who were keen to assail the labour movement while it was on the retreat. Local police and other officials often turned a blind eye to the shootings, vandalism, and life-threatening doses of castor oil that the Fascist squads administered to their victims.

In the central-northern city of Bologna, there was one man who was not prepared to tolerate the activities of the black-shirted gangs who believed that their struggle to save the father-land from the red menace set them above the law. In 1921, Cesare Mori, the boy from the foundling hospital, reached the top of the career ladder when he was appointed prefect of Bologna. There he treated the self-styled 'national youth' of Fascism as he had done other subversives. And Mori stuck to his task until blackshirts from nearby towns converged on Bologna and set up camp around his headquarters. They dramatized their protest in Fascist style by urinating in concert against the prefecture walls. The government backed down and Mori was transferred. The episode would leave a legacy of bitterness between Mori and the leaders of the Fascist squads.

Although the Partito Nazionale Fascista did not have great numerical strength in parliament, its tight organization and willingness to take risks gave it the upper hand over divided, vacillating politicians. In October 1922, Mussolini's 'March' on Rome challenged the state to either give him power or put down his movement by force. In response, he was invited to form a coalition government and would remain as his country's leader for the next two decades.

After Fascism took power in 1922, the squad leaders took their revenge and dismissed Mori altogether. His career had run aground for the simple reason that he had backed the wrong political masters. He could hardly be blamed, since few outside the Partito Nazionale Fascista would have predicted a blackshirt seizure of power. In an effort to refloat his ambitions, Mori soon came to terms with Fascism and began to mobilize his network of powerful friends. He made known his admiration for Mussolini, and claimed that he had in fact acted 'fascistically' throughout his career. He inserted flattering references to the Fascist project in his book, *Among the Orange Blossoms Beyond the Mist* – the cloying title betrayed his self-dramatizing side. But before Mori's career could resume, Fascism would have to decide to come to grips with the Sicilian mafia.

In Sicily, as in the rest of the South, Fascism was never a grass-roots movement. Sicilian politics, with its clienteles and cliques, was a less ideological affair than in the North. Nor was there much call for strike breakers since the mafia already did that job efficiently enough. But once Mussolini took power, interest groups all over the island suddenly developed a fondness for black shirts and mock Roman salutes. Mafiosi too jumped on to the Duce's victory chariot: the prefect described the ruling group on Gangi town council as 'Fascist-*mafioso*'; another report described the dominant faction in San Mauro as a 'Fascistized mafia'.

The Duce was personally popular in Sicily, but his move-ment lacked a strong base of support, so initially he needed these new friends. For a time it looked as if Fascism would adopt the traditional method of ruling Sicily by delegating power to the local grandees and pretending not to notice if mafiosi managed their election campaigns. One prince who was generally acknowledged to have mafia ties became a Minister in Mussolini's cabinet.

It proved to be a short honeymoon. In its early days Fascism soon began to attract accusations that it was deaf to Sicily's economic needs, while at the same time militant senior Fascists were causing alarm in certain circles in Sicily by proclaiming the need for a crusade against the mafia as well as the landowners and politicians who protected it. In April 1923, one such militant wrote to Mussolini with a plea:

Fascism aims to sweep away all the corruption poisoning the country's politics and administration. It aims to break the shady factions and maggoty cabals infesting the sacred body of the nation. It cannot neglect this terrible centre of infection. If we want to save Sicily we must destroy the mafia ... Then we will be able to set up our tents on the island; and they will be sounder than the ones that we pitched in the north by doing away with socialism.

The lurid language overlay a simple formula. The mafia – whatever it was – could serve the same purpose in Sicily that socialism had done in the North: it could be a convenient enemy for Fascism. In time, Mussolini was to make this strategy his own. His blackshirt movement styled itself as the antidote to the old world of patronage and devious compromise. Because mafiosi were often linked to politicians, a crusade against organized crime would allow the Fascists to strike simultaneously at some of the VIPs of the liberal system. There could be no better way to accentuate Fascism's no-nonsense image.

In May 1924, Mussolini went to Sicily for the first time, sweeping into Palermo on the battleship *Dante Alighieri* with an escort of planes and submarines. In the province of Trapani, the Duce heard about Cesare Mori's achievements before and during the war, and about how serious the mafia problem was there. A deputation of veterans told him that 216 murders had been committed in Marsala in a year; they explained that the mafia was the main reason for Fascism's failure to take root on the island.

While Mussolini's cortège was moving through Piana dei Greci near Palermo, the mayor, mafioso Don Francesco Cuccia, gestured disparagingly towards the Prime Minister's bodyguards and muttered unctuously in his ear, 'You are with me, you are under my protection. What do you need all these cops for?' The Duce did not reply and fumed for the rest of the day at the insolence. His visit to the island was cut short. Don Francesco Cuccia's lapse in etiquette has passed into legend as the catalyst for Mussolini's war on the mafia. Within a few weeks of Mussolini's return to Rome, all Mori's lobbying paid off when he was sent back to Trapani.

Then, in 1924, events in the Italian capital dramatically deepened the chill between Fascism and Sicily. Shortly after the Duce's trip to the island, some of his thugs kidnapped and murdered the Socialist Party leader. Italian public opinion was horrified, and Fascism's political allies started to drift away. The surest way for a national leader to fall out of favour with a certain kind of Sicilian politician is to lose power. In the summer of 1924 Mussolini looked like doing just that.

But opposition inertia allowed the Duce gradually to stabilize the situation and then to move openly towards putting an end to democracy in Italy. When his thoughts turned again to Sicily, he was ready to implement his strategy.

The local election campaign of August 1925, the last before democracy disappeared, was also the last hurrah for the old political dignitaries of Sicily. Too late, with defeat at the hands of Mussolini now inevitable, they came out in opposition to Fascism and discovered the cause of freedom.

Among them was Vittorio Emanuele Orlando, a former Prime Minister and the most powerful Sicilian politician of the old order, whose power base was in a heavily mafia-infested area. Shortly before the vote he made a speech in Palermo's Teatro Massimo, taking his cue from the government's proclaimed intent to combat the mafia:

If, by 'mafia', they mean having an exaggerated sense of honour; if they mean being furiously intolerant of bullying and injustice, and showing the generosity of spirit needed to stand up to the strong and be understanding towards the weak; if they mean having a loyalty to your friends that is stronger than anything, stronger even than death; if by 'mafia' they mean feelings like these, attitudes like these – even though they may sometimes be exaggerated – then I say to you that what they are talking about are the distinguishing traits of the Sicilian soul. And so I declare myself a *maffioso* and I am proud to be one!

It was a squalid tactic that only played into Mussolini's hands. With the liberal state itself in mortal peril, Orlando could only fall back on the old ploy of deliberately confusing the mafia and Sicilian culture. His blatant winking at the bosses has entered history as one of the lowest moments in the long and shameless cohabitation between killers and the people's elected representatives. Tommaso Buscetta would, much later, claim that Orlando was himself a man of honour.

It was time for Mussolini's assault on the mafia to begin, and it was to Mori that he turned to impose Fascist authority on the unruly island. On 23 October 1925, Mori became prefect of Palermo with full powers to attack the mafia and with it the regime's political enemies. He immediately began preparations for the campaign's curtain-raiser: the siege of Gangi.

Cesare Mori prided himself on many things. Prominent among them were his beliefs about the way Sicilians think and behave, beliefs forged by his years of experience around Trapani. Homespun, dogmatic, and crass, they would be the basis for his campaign against the mafia.

I was able to penetrate the Sicilian mind. I found this mind, beneath the painful scars with which centuries of tyranny and oppression had marked it, often childlike, simple and kindly, apt to colour everything with generous feeling, ever inclined to deceive itself, to hope and to believe, and ready to lay all its knowledge, its affection and its co-operation at the feet of one who showed a desire to realise the people's legitimate dream of justice and redemption.

The key to the mafia's success, he argued, was its ability to strike an attitude designed to prey on this vulnerability and credulity at the core of the Sicilian make-up. The mafia, Mori believed, was not an organization. But, for the sake of maintaining law and order, the police and judicial system could assume that it was. In reality it was best described as 'a peculiar way of looking at things'. Mafiosi were drawn together by a natural affinity rather than by initiation rites or formal bonds of any kind.

Upon these distinctly unpromising foundations Mori built his whole repressive programme. Quite simply, the impressionable mass of Sicilians had to be made to see, in as down-to-earth a way as possible, that the state was tougher than the men of honour. The Fascist state was to out-mafia the mafia. *Theatre* was to be the essence of Mori's drive to establish law and order in Sicily. The Gangi operation was conceived in this spirit, as a way of striking awe into the simple souls still in thrall to the criminals.

Four months after the siege of Gangi, Mori put the same tactics to work against Don Vito Cascio-Ferro, a famous mafioso who had begun his career in 1892 by infiltrating the *Fascio* in Bisacquino not far from Corleone. Since then he had ventured as far as the United States and made his fortune smuggling cattle with a small fleet of boats. It is said that when Don Vito toured his mountain realm at the peak of his career, the officials of the towns he visited would wait for him outside the gates to kiss his hand. On May Day 1926, Cesare Mori came to address a public meeting in Cascio-Ferro's territory. As a scirocco blew fine Saharan sand across the piazza, the 'iron prefect' opened with a pun both startling and corny: 'My name is Mori and I will make people die!' ('Mori' means 'die' in Italian.) 'Crime must vanish just as this dust carried away by the wind vanishes!'

A few days later the 'interprovincial' antimafia police force that Mori had set up began a round-up in the area that included Bisacquino, Corleone, and Contessa Entellina. Over 150 suspects were arrested, among them Don Vito. His godson went to the local landlord to seek support but received a resigned reply: 'Times have changed.' It was the end of Don Vito's reign. Soon afterwards, an old murder charge against him was resurrected. He adopted an acquiescent pose during his trial in 1930 while his lawyer forlornly ran through a familiar argument. Citing his client's honourable behaviour in all circumstances, he maintained that 'We must conclude that either Vito Cascio-Ferro is not a *mafioso*, or that the mafia, as scholars have often pointed out, is a conspicuous individualistic attitude, a form of defiance that has nothing wicked, base or criminal about it.' It seems that the scirocco was blowing again when the judge handed down a life sentence. Don Vito died in prison in 1942.

Mori evidently thought that his dramatic techniques would work, not just on the Sicilians who were in awe of the mafia, but also on the mafiosi themselves. Soon after arresting Don Vito Cascio-Ferro in May 1926, he invited every estate warden in the province of Palermo to a stage-managed ceremony of loyalty. Twelve hundred of them assembled in military formation on a small hill near Roccapalumba. The only two invitees who could not make it sent medical certificates. Mori reviewed the ranks before making his speech: henceforth they were to protect private property on behalf of the state rather than the mafia. A military chaplain said mass on an open-air altar before reminding the wardens that they were about to take an oath of the utmost seriousness. Mori invited anyone present who was not prepared to swear loyalty to leave; he then turned his back to the audience. No one moved. When the 'iron prefect' turned round again, he read out the pledge. The wardens responded as one, 'I swear.' Martial music and Fascist hymns were played as they filed forward to sign their names.

The following year the redoubtable men who guarded the citrus fruit groves of the Conca d'Oro underwent a similar ritual. At the end, to mark their new allegiance, they were given boy scout-style brass badges, bearing crossed rifles on a background of orange blossom.

It should be said that this propaganda offensive was backed up by a hard-headed political strategy designed to win over the landowners to the regime. The masters of some great estates certainly appreciated Fascist efforts to cow overweening *gabelloti* and wardens. Many of Mori's successes, such as the Gangi operation, were obtained by the eminently traditional method of putting pressure on landowners to betray the criminals they had been sheltering. More generally, Mori's goal was to impress the population through strength rather than justice. The result was the kind of undiscriminating repression with which the islanders were all too familiar. Within less than three years of the start of Mori's campaign, some 11,000 people were arrested, 5,000 of them in the province of Palermo alone. It is not possible that all of them were men of honour, or even members of bandit networks. Even one of the prosecuting magistrates involved in the antimafia war believed that honest men were arrested along with criminals.

The huge round-ups were followed by equally huge trials. The most prominent ones were carried out in an intimidatory atmosphere. Mori censored press accounts of proceedings, and endeavoured to create the sense that defending a mafioso was tantamount to being a mafioso. The convictions that Fascism needed often followed. The Duce proudly announced to parliament that the boss who had cheeked him in Piana dei Greci had received a lengthy sentence.

One of Mori's most loudly trumpeted successes was triggered by the theft of a single ass in Mistretta. The case provides a good example of the ambiguities of the Fascist repression of organized crime. The theft of the ass set in motion a long chain of leads for the police, who eventually raided the offices of a wealthy defence lawyer and politician, Antonino Ortoleva. They discovered ninety suspicious letters describing transactions involving 'saddles' and pleas for intervention on behalf of 'young students' from across Sicily. The police thought they were coded references to animal thefts and arrested criminals. In fact the code was by no means clear. The letters may just have referred to the management of day-to-day shady favours – common political sleaze rather than violent organized crime. But Mori's police entertained no such doubts: Antonino Ortoleva, they asserted, was nothing less than the boss of the 'interprovincial mafia'.

Soon afterwards their theory found support when a man claiming to have been a member of the gang sent a letter of confession to the sub-prefect of Mistretta. A mafia court had been held regularly in Ortoleva's office since 1913, he said. There, with Ortoleva presiding, the leaders – a ring comprising other professional men and some twenty toughs – would decide on the fate of anyone who obstructed their business. Soon afterwards the informant was shot down in the open countryside.

In all, 163 members of the 'interprovincial mafia' were put on trial in August 1928. Ortoleva did not turn up to pre-trial hearings, pleading that he was ill. The judge ordered that he be examined by two doctors. Their opinion was unequivocal: 'Ortoleva has a normal constitution; his temperature is normal; there are no irregularities in his respiratory and cardio-vascular system; his nervous and sensory organs are normal, as are his mental state and intelligence.' Two days later he was found dead in his cell.

It is not known whether there was any foul play involved in Ortoleva's death. What is certain is that he never got the chance to put his side of the story, or to implicate anyone else. Ortoleva could have been the capo of the Mistretta-based organization, or simply a client of the criminals, impelled more or less against his will to favour their interests. He may have been murdered to stop him involving people higher up who were close to the regime.

There is much else that remains obscure about the 'interprovincial mafia'. Although many of the defendants in the case were clearly up to no good, it is not known whether they did in fact constitute an organized, exclusive mafia on the model of the *cosche* of western and central Sicily. It may be that they were just the losers in a struggle between local factions. (But in the 1980s, Antonino Calderone, the same *pentito* who had such painful memories of the Fascist era, would name a descendant of one of the main Mistretta defendants as a member of Cosa Nostra.)

Despite all these doubts, there was only ever going to be one verdict to such a case in the ideological climate of the late 1920s. The propaganda value of dismantling a giant, centralized mafia conspiracy was just too high: 150 men were duly convicted of forming a criminal association.

Not all mafiosi fared badly under Fascism. Official American sources estimate that 500 of them escaped Mori's clutches by emigrating to the USA. As will be clear from the following chapters, they found Prohibition America a welcoming refuge. Others discovered that the iron fist of Fascist repression often concealed a greasy palm of corruption. Giuseppe Genco Russo, the boss of Mussomeli in central Sicily, would survive the Mori operation to become one of the most prominent men of honour of the post-war years. Through the Fascist decades of the 1920s and 1930s, he accumulated a criminal record that is a mafioso archetype. He was repeatedly charged with theft, extortion, criminal association, intimidation, violence, and multiple homicide. Again and again charges were dropped or he was acquitted for 'insufficient evidence' – the formula used when witnesses are too scared to come forward. Genco Russo was even snared in one of Mori's round-ups near Agrigento, but he only ever served three years. In short, Fascism's much-vaunted war on the mafia left Giuseppe Genco Russo all but unscathed. The most that can be said is that the increased attention from the law was an annoyance; the 'special surveillance' to which he was subjected between 1934 and 1938 certainly hampered his operations. In 1944, Genco Russo was officially declared 'rehabilitated'. He was, of course, no such thing.

The word 'mafia' was coined both as the description of a criminal organization and as a political weapon, an accusation to be hurled at opponents. Cesare Mori recognized this truth. 'The label of *mafioso* is often applied in complete bad faith,' he wrote. 'It is used everywhere . . . as means to carry out vendettas, to work off grudges, to pull down enemies.' His words were strikingly disingenuous. Mori's 'surgery' on organized crime showed that Fascism pushed this old method of smearing opposition to new extremes.

The final irony of Mori's campaign was that the 'iron prefect' himself was guilty of using the label mafioso in his own interests. In January 1927, as the Fascist Party was purged, Mori brought down his rival for influence in Rome, the Palermo Fascist chief Cucco – the ophthalmologist who had shared a platform with Mori in Gangi. The instrument of Mori's wrath was the accusation that Cucco had helped young men fake eye diseases to avoid the draft. Mori did not stop the smearing there. Cucco was soon accused of fraud and being a member of the mafia. It took him until 1931 to clear his name.

Black shirts, badges, and nationalistic slogans notwithstanding, the 'Mori operation' was ambivalent in the same way that earlier attempts to repress the mafia had been: it combined brutality with hypocrisy. In the long term, the state's reputation in Sicily could only suffer, and the results of Fascism's war on the mafia were destined not to last; the mafia was suppressed, but it was not eradicated.

On 23 June 1929, after more than three and a half years as prefect of Palermo, Cesare Mori received a brief telegram from the Duce to tell him that his job was finished. Changes in the political balance of power within the party and the regime had undermined his backing. In a farewell speech to the Fascist Federation of Palermo, Mori tried his hand at modesty:

[T]here remains the man, the citizen Mori, the Fascist Mori, the fighter Mori, the man Mori, living and vital. Today he takes his path towards the horizon that is open to all men, to all men of good will. I have my star. I watch it faithfully because it shines, and will continue to shine, along the path of work and duty. I will be guided by the light of the Fatherland. There, my friends, we will meet again.

In reality, Mori was bitter about his removal. When he returned to Rome, the regime carefully avoided giving him much of a platform from which to make trouble. The former 'iron prefect' gave himself over to writing a self-glorifying, sententious account of his 'hand-to-hand fight' with the mafia. 'Men of action make things happen, but do not judge them . . . From words I passed immediately to deeds.' It was given a poor reception by the Fascist press. Some blackshirts had clearly not forgotten the day they pissed against the prefecture walls in Bologna.

During the 1930s, the official line was that Mori's task had been completed. Fascism had beaten the mafia; it had solved the problem for good. Mori's successor ordered the press to play down reports of crime. There were to be no more round-ups or show trials. It was much easier and less conspicuous just to send suspects into internal exile without proper legal process; this, after all, was how the authorities had dealt with the mafia problem through most of the pre-Fascist era. Grey Fascist functionaries rapidly followed one another through the corridors of Palermo's public buildings. With the regime's attention switched elsewhere, Sicily sank into a sump of corruption and factionalism.

Mori's death in 1942 went virtually unreported. The following year the Fascist regime collapsed and his work was entirely undone. The mafia's salvation came from the United States. For during the same decades in which it struggled with socialism, Fascism, and war in Sicily, the mafia had become a part of American life.

5

The Mafia Establishes Itself in America
1900–1941

Joe Petrosino

Between 1901 and 1913, some 1.1 million Sicilians emigrated – a little less than a quarter of the island's entire population. Of those, roughly 800,000 made the United States their destination. Inevitably, some were men of honour, smart and ruthless criminals who sought to establish protection regimes and other criminal activities among their fellow migrants and along the trade routes connecting the two shores of the Atlantic.

For most of the nineteenth century, men on the run in Sicily had sought refuge in the USA. The lemon trade, heavily infiltrated by mafiosi, connected Palermo with New York. In the 1880s and 1890s. American police had linked some violent deaths in the Italian community with the mafia. Particularly notable was the murder of New Orleans Police Chief David Hennessy in 1890; the Sicilian suspects were lynched. But it was only from the days of the great migration after 1900 that the traffic between the US and Italy in criminal ideas, resources, and personnel became a vital part of mafia operations.

There are two fables about the mafia's arrival in America. The first was born at the time of the mass Sicilian migration. Following a famous mafia murder in 1903, the *New York Herald* proclaimed in alarm: '"The boot" [i.e. Italy] unloads its criminals upon the United States. Statistics prove that the scum of southern Europe is dumped at the nation's door in rapacious, conscienceless, lawbreaking hordes.' To natives of New York, the mafia seemed like an invasion, an infestation borne in the teeming bellies of steamships. Or, in a variant on the same account, it was an international criminal conspiracy bent on expansion into the virgin territory of the USA.

The second fable is recent; it was fashioned in the 1960s

and 1970s by the descendants of Italian immigrants who were by now completely integrated into American society. They recreated the mafia's arrival in the USA as a tale that almost turned the 'criminal invasion' fable on its head. The Sicilian peasants who crossed the Atlantic were steeped in ancient 'rustic chivalry' traditions. Faced with the grimy savagery of big-city capitalism and machine politics, they adapted the cultural resources that they had brought from their rural homeland. The mafia was born when the old Sicilian values of family and honour met the dark side of the American dream – or so the story went.

In reality, urban America and Sicily were not as wildly different as either of these fables would have us believe. Corleone, for example, was not a country village. It was one of many 'agro-towns' where market economics, patronage politics, and organized violence held sway. Although they were poor, superstitious, and downtrodden, the peasants of Corleone were not the innocents that Italian-American journalist Adolfo Rossi suggested when he went to interview Bernardino Verro and write his sentimental portrait of the Fasci. The working people of Sicily knew how important it could be, in terms of their livelihoods, to be loyal to the right faction in town, the faction able to dole out work, land, and charity. Many had no illusions about what it took to get on in politics and business. Most aimed to accumulate money and contacts in the US and then return to Sicily. The island's emigrants were not like the Jewish refugees who spat on the quay at Riga before setting sail for a wholly new future across the Atlantic.

Neither Sicilian politics, nor the island's sophisticated violence industry, had much that was antiquated about it. Sicilians of all kinds were well equipped for life in the burgeoning cities of the United States. When they crossed the ocean they found a home from home, whether they wanted to or not. Their first access to American society was often through the *padrone* system. To get a job – typically in construction – you had to become a client of a boss. Sometimes, the boss would use intimidation to corner a sector of the jobs market. Bosses would even advance poorer emigrants the price of their steamer ticket and recoup it later, with high interest, from their wages. The world of the new immigrant in North America was, like Sicily, one where power was invested not in institutions, but in tough, well-networked individuals.

Politics in the Italian quarters of New York City would also have had a familiar look to Sicilians. Bosses farmed wards of the city for votes on behalf of the Democratic Party organization – Tammany Hall, 'the Wigwam'. They did so by tapping into every possible source of influence and patronage on their turf, including criminal gangs. In America as in Sicily, organized labour militancy would often be met by a combination of corruption and violence.

Elizabeth Street was the heart of the New York Sicilian community. In 1905, roughly 8,200 Italians – the vast majority of them Sicilians – lived in 'Elisabetta Stretta', as they called it. This concentration of people constituted a territory comparable in size to many of the agro-towns of the Sicilian interior. Cinema has done a fairly good job of recreating the look of places like Elizabeth Street in the early twentieth century, with its cramped tenements, its sweatshops, and its streets lined with laden traders' carts. (Italian export industries prospered on keeping emigrants in the US supplied with the foodstuffs they had grown up on.)

At the time of the great Sicilian influx, Americans observed the development of the immigrant quarters with a mixture of alarm and pity. As one reformer wrote of Elizabeth Street in 1909:

Here were myriads of human beings, stifling in boxes arranged like drawers in a bureau, with holes to look out upon the opposite boxes and the roaring 'elevated'. Those who were at home hung out of the windows in as few garments as were decent; while the long seething bare canons of brick, paving stone and asphalt were swarming with children in quest of air and amusement.

It was the memory of poverty in Sicilian agro-towns and the prospect of a better future that made the conditions tolerable for the recent arrivals in New York.

But neither well-meaning contemporary accounts like these, nor today's cinema images, manage to capture the economic dynamism of Little Italy. When Adolfo Rossi first went to America in 1878, Mulberry Bend was an Irish slum. He remembered the area's 'lurid, dingy hovels, mostly built of wood'. During the years of the great transatlantic exodus, he became an emigration commissioner for the Italian government, reporting on the fortunes of Italians in the US. In 1904 he went back to Manhattan and was pleased to report that, since Little Italy had been created, house prices and rents had risen, the quality of the buildings had improved markedly, and Italians themselves were the major investors in the property market. The new arrivals from the peninsula, especially the women, had also discovered a passion for education. In every way they could, Italians in the United States were grabbing the chance to better themselves.

It was into this dynamic environment – at once very Sicilian and very American – that the mafia transplanted itself. The mafia does not spread nearly as far and as fast as people often assume. When it does travel, it does so in two basic ways. The first is fast, flexible, and is usually related to a specific business initiative, such as the trade in a particular drug. With the approval and assistance of the capos back home, individual mafiosi can take the mafia brand anywhere they choose, setting up more-or-less temporary trading posts as they go.

But men of honour are not just businessmen, they are also the administrators of a shadow state. A great deal has to be in place for the mafia's system of territorial control through *cosche* to spread outside western Sicily: protection rackets; political contacts; the agreement of neighbouring *cosche*; a friendly attitude from elements in the press, police, and local population; and so on. Exporting this privatized form of government is a slow affair at best. Even in western Sicily, the extent of the mafia's domination varies from one place to another. And after some 140 years of history, the mafia still has only isolated outposts on the Italian mainland. The fertile criminal soil of the United States was one of the rare environments into which the mafia's method could be transferred wholesale. The story of two Italian-American men – Joe Petrosino and Giuseppe 'Piddu' Morello – brings the mafia's arrival in America into sharp relief.

Internal letter to the Police Commissioner of New York, 19 October 1908:

> Sir:
>
> In compliance with the provisions of paragraph 3 of Rule 30 of the Rules and Regulations of the Police Department, I respectfully request that I be granted permission to receive a gold watch tendered me by the Italian government.
>
> > Respectfully,
> > Joseph Petrosino,
> > Comm. Italian Branch
> > Detective Bureau

Undated memorandum from the American consul in Palermo to the Police Commissioner of New York:

Petrosino was registered under the name of Guglielmo De Simoni at the Hotel de France in Palermo. On March 12, 1909, he was standing at the base of the Garibaldi statue in the Piazza Marina waiting for a trolley when two men fired four shots at him. Three hit him and he died instantly. He was hit on the right side of the back, through both lungs and in the left temple. Petrosino was unarmed. A Smith and Wesson revolver was found in his valise in the hotel. A heavy Belgian revolver with one barrel discharged was found near the scene.

New York Police Department memorandum dated 11 May 1909:

Received from the Police Commissioner, Lt. Petrosino's gold watch and chain, pair gold cuff links, cane, two dress suit cases containing personal effects, package of letters and a check for $12.40. Signed, Louis Salino.

At 6 a.m. on 14 April 1903, Frances Connors, a plump, middle-aged woman on her way to work, passed the New York Mallet & Handle Works at 743 East 11th Street close to the corner of Avenue D. A coat caught her attention. It had been draped over the top of a weather-beaten sugar barrel placed near the pavement, next to a pile of timber. Lifting the coat, she saw a right foot and a left hand. When she looked into the barrel, she found it contained a man's body, fully clothed and bent double, the head squeezed between the knees, a coarse burlap sack wrapped around the neck. Mrs Connors' screams drew two patrolmen to the scene. The body was still warm.

Analysis would later reveal that the victim had eighteen shallow stab wounds to the neck, and a slash across the throat so deep and wide that the head had nearly been detached. The man was respectably dressed. Both of his ears were pierced. He had eaten heavily just before his death: potatoes, beans, beets, salad, spaghetti. In the bottom of the barrel there was a three-inch layer of sawdust, containing onion skins and the chewed stubs of dark Italian stogies.

The 'body in the barrel' mystery, as the New York papers quickly dubbed it, triggered America's fears of an invasion of criminal hordes from 'the boot'. But behind these scare stories, the case offers intriguing clues about the reality of the mafia presence in the United States in the era of the great Sicilian exodus. It also marked a milestone in the path to fame of an Italian-American policeman named Joseph (Giuseppe) Petrosino. It may also have led directly to his death, six years later, in Piazza Marina, Palermo – one of the most famous murders in the mafia's history.

A day after the discovery of the body in the barrel, the police arrested nine members of a mafia gang of counterfeiters and extortionists. For some time they had been under surveillance by men from the US secret service division. It was suspected that they were importing forged US currency in the false bottoms of olive oil cans. The money was distributed to other east-coast cities through a network of agents.

The evening before the murder, the victim was seen entering and leaving a butcher's shop at 16 Stanton Street – it was one of the gang's haunts. A little later, he went to a saloon with a small restaurant at the rear. When he did not come out again, the surveillance ended for the night. The saloon belonged to a 34-year-old man from Corleone, Giuseppe 'Piddu' Morello, known to be the gang's leader.

When Morello was arrested in the Bowery, he was armed and had cigars in his pockets identical to the ones found in the barrel. His saloon had sawdust on the floor in which were found onion skins and cigar stubs. He was not difficult to pick out: his right hand had only the little finger remaining. When interrogated, he refused to answer, and refused even to tell his interrogators how he lost his other fingers.

The barrel in which the body was found communicated more than Morello. A stencil mark on the underside – W & T 233 – led detectives, via the great sugar refineries on the Long Island side of the East River, to the grocers Wallace & Thompson at 365 Washington Street, Manhattan. They had only one Sicilian customer, Pietro Inzerillo, another member of Morello's *cosca*. Two more barrels with the same markings were found at Inzerillo's pastry shop and café at 226 Elizabeth Street.

The breakthrough in identifying the victim came through Detective Sergeant Petrosino, a short, square, immensely strong man with a badly pitted face and a shapeless nose. (Ernest Borgnine would play him in a disappointing 1960 film, *Pay or Die!*) Born into poverty near Salerno on the southern Italian mainland in 1860, Petrosino had emigrated to the USA as a young boy. Learning to read and write in New York City's public schools was his first step in rising above his parents' station. He became a street-cleaner and then the foreman of a gang of 'scow trimmers' – the men who crewed the flat-bottomed barges that ferried the city's rubbish away. At that time the police supervised refuse collection in New York. Petrosino came to the attention of a local officer who gave him the chance to become a uniformed cop.

Petrosino's slow rise through the ranks of the NYPD accelerated at the turn of the century when the numbers of Italian immigrants, and criminals, increased dramatically. He had already attracted attention to himself by issuing a warning that a gang of mostly Italian anarchists in Paterson, New Jersey, were planning to assassinate President William McKinley. The warning went unheeded. On 6 December 1901, McKinley was shot dead as he inaugurated the Pan-American Exhibition in Buffalo.

A few days after the discovery of the body in the barrel, Petrosino travelled fifty kilometres up the east bank of the Hudson River to the grey blocks of Sing Sing. His contacts in Little Italy had suggested that Giuseppe Di Primo, a man serving a three-year sentence for counterfeiting, might help put a name to the body in the barrel. He interviewed Di Primo in a cell that had been built seventy years before with stone hewn by inmates from the prison quarry; it was damp, cold and tiny: 2.1 metres deep and 197 centimetres from floor to ceiling, and only 97 centimetres wide. Sing Sing deserved its dreadful reputation.

When Di Primo was shown a picture of the dead man, he identified him immediately as his brother-in-law, Benedetto Madonia. Grief-stricken, and made desperate by the conditions in Sing Sing, Di Primo confessed that both he and Madonia were part of the same counterfeiting operation as one-fingered Piddu Morello. Madonia was one of the agents used by the gang to pass the counterfeit dollars into circulation; he had gone to recoup some of Di Primo's property from Morello. That was the last time that Di Primo had seen him before he was murdered.

When Joe Petrosino returned to the city, he arranged for Madonia's widow to identify the corpse. The murdered man had been found with a watch-chain on his waistcoat, but no watch. His widow was able to describe the missing timepiece: it had a locomotive stamped on the base.

One of the arrested gang members, a hulking, bull-necked man of twenty-four called Tommaso Petto, known as the Ox, had a receipt in his pocket from a pawnshop on the Bowery. It bore the same date that the body in the barrel had been discovered. When police returned the ticket, they found the watch with the locomotive design. The Ox was now strongly suspected of being the man who had performed the murder.

The inquest into the case came to court on 1 May 1903. None of the gang members had given in to the NYPD's habitual, impatient interrogation methods. Only eight of sixteen people subpoenaed to serve on the jury turned up. The victim's son was the first to be called to the stand to identify the watch. One detective involved in the case recalled what happened next:

He looked at it and was about to speak when there was a shuffling of feet and hissing in the courtroom, which was filled with swarthy-faced men. One of these jumped up and put his fingers to his lips. Young Madonia was now not sure it was his father's timepiece.

Under identical pressure, Madonia's widow had a comparable lapse of memory.

Di Primo was brought down from Sing Sing to give evidence. The police alleged that there had been bad blood between himself and the Ox for some while. But Di Primo cheerily asserted that they were very good friends. He had evidently decided, on reflection, to serve out his time in Sing Sing in silence. The case fell apart.

What Petrosino and his colleagues discovered about the Morello gang can be set alongside what is now known about the mafia in its country of origin. Some of the men arrested in the aftermath of the barrel killing were described as importers of wine, oil, and other agricultural produce from the island. The trade in citrus fruit, oil, cheese, and wine provided excellent cover for criminals on their journeys back and forth across the Atlantic, and within the United States. These commodities also offered opportunities for mafiosi to extort protection money and create monopolies as they did in Sicily.

Gun licences were clearly a hinge between the gangs and the authorities in New York as they were in Sicily. The members of Morello's gang who were arrested in April 1903 were in possession of perfectly legal permits to carry firearms within the city limits. They had been granted by the Deputy Police Commissioner on the recommendation of the Captain of the local precinct. One such permit holder had only been in the US for twenty-eight days. Criminal relationships *across* the Atlantic were evidently so strong that a mafioso could set off from Palermo confident in the knowledge that he would be carrying a legal weapon soon after being cleared through Ellis Island. In some embarrassment, the Police Commissioner revoked 322 firearms permits shortly after these facts were publicized in the *New York Herald*.

There is strong evidence of close ties between mafiosi in America and Sicily. One associate of the Morello gang, who was wanted for questioning by Petrosino during the 'body in the barrel' investigations, was Don Vito Cascio-Ferro, later to be imprisoned by 'iron prefect' Cesare Mori. Before the body in the barrel murder, he had fled Sicily to avoid the special police surveillance imposed on him following his suspected involvement in a kidnapping, although he later claimed that he went to the US on business – as a lemon importer. He escaped arrest in the 'body in the barrel' round-up by fleeing to New Orleans, home to some 12,000 Sicilians and a strong mafia presence, before returning once more to Sicily. In 1905, Morello's gang was joined by another new emigrant, Giuseppe Fontana – the mafioso recently acquitted of killing Emanuele Notarbartolo.

The composition of the Morello gang may well reveal important information about the level of coordination between men of honour back in Sicily. Morello was from Corleone; Cascio-Ferro from nearby Bisacquino – both in the interior, south of Palermo. Fontana was from Villabate closer to the capital. Other members were from Partinico, further away to the west. In other words, these were men of honour from *different* Sicilian *cosche*. Piddu Morello's gang clearly constituted a trading post for particularly enterprising men of honour from across the province of Palermo and beyond. American business was becoming a matter of interest to the whole Sicilian mafia. Moreover, the sense of a common interest between men of honour was strong enough for criminal credentials acquired in various corners of provincial Sicily to be recognized and appreciated on the other side of the Atlantic.

The Morello gang based its power in New York on the same principles of territorial control as any *cosca* back in Sicily: protection rackets and patronage; relationships with police to ensure immunity from prosecution. Immigrant communities also made for very solid packages of votes; lacking a real interest in or understanding of the politics of their new country, many immigrants were happy to trade their votes for small favours from a patron.

Nevertheless there were some important differences between the environments that mafiosi worked in at home and in New York. The problem faced by the mafia's system of territorial dominance was that America was a more mobile and diverse society, with a long tradition of crime and corruption all of its own. The population of Elizabeth Street, as in the other immigrant quarters, was in constant flux. People came and went from the Old World. Many new arrivals moved on to other parts of the US. Others, as they improved their living standards, moved up and out to more salubrious areas in Harlem, Brooklyn, and beyond.

Mafiosi had to be as mobile in the New World as the Italian population they preyed on. Morello had travelled within the US before settling in New York; his gang also had another base in the Sicilian community of East Harlem. Nicola Gentile, a young Sicilian, who was initiated into the mafia in Philadelphia in 1905, moved between mafia *cosche* in different cities several times in his career. (Gentile is the subject of the next chapter.) He had dealings with men of honour in Manhattan and Brooklyn, Pittsburgh, Cleveland, Chicago, Milwaukee, Kansas City, San Francisco, and Canada. What he describes in the years before the First World War is a criminal network firmly rooted in Sicilian communities across North America, but having very little influence outside those communities.

New York was where this network looked to for leadership; it had by far the largest Sicilian population, and it was the main terminal for goods and people arriving from the island. The same mafioso – as reliable a witness as there can be to such things – affirmed that Piddu Morello was the supreme boss of the whole American branch of the mafia until 1909.

Whatever Morello's status within the Sicilian mafia nationally, it did not make his position much easier in New York. At the time of the 'body in the barrel' murder, the Morello *cosca* found its neighbourhoods bounded by crews who played by different rules, spoke a different Italian dialect, or even hailed from an entirely different country. Instead of the constant consultation that took place between *cosche* affiliated to the same association in Sicily, mafiosi in New York City were faced with the underworld equivalent of international diplomacy.

By the time the Morello *cosca* had set up operations in Little Italy, the New York criminal marketplace had already been an arena of ferocious competition for years. The tenements of Manhattan at the turn of the century were a patchwork of territories for gangs of sharp-dressed young hoodlums like the Gas House Gang, the Gophers, the Hudson Dusters, and the Pearl Buttons. In 1903, Paul Kelly's Five Points gang controlled the area between the Bowery and Broadway that included Little Italy. Kelly had been born Paolo Antonio Vaccarelli in Naples. He took his new Irish-sounding name during a short boxing career. A dapper, soft-spoken man, he reputedly commanded 1,500 toughs, most of them Italian, but including some Jews, Irish, and others. Kelly's organization embraced prostitution, gambling, protection, property, and machine politics.

Although he never stood for office himself, he fed support upwards to Tim 'Dry Dollar' Sullivan, the undisputed Democratic boss of the Lower East Side. American-born politicians, particularly the Irish like Sullivan, were the only ones who seemed capable of building a power base that traversed the different ethnic slums.

If, as the papers suggested at the time, the Sicilian mafia had wanted to conquer New York, it would have needed to have arrived half a century earlier. From their base within the Sicilian communities, mafiosi had the resources and skills to carve out a competitive slot in the New York underworld. But they found it impossible to dominate.

The Sicilian mafia in America also faced the problem of trademark control. It was America that turned 'mafia' into the best-known brand name in organized crime. Celebrated cases like the body in the barrel began to spread 'mafia' far and wide. Yet in the process the logo drifted out of the grasp of the cluster of local Sicilian firms who originally traded under that name. Rather in the way that, in common parlance, a 'Hoover' now means any old vacuum cleaner, the American press applied 'mafia' to all forms of Italian organized crime, and then to any gang activity whatsoever. (This was, in a sense, a notable achievement for the Sicilians, who were latecomers in an already mature market.)

The so-called 'Mano nera' ('Black Hand') offers further illustration of this brand-name inflation in the United States. The 'body in the barrel' case attracted press attention to a spate of extortion demands that were directed at wealthy Italian-Americans. Headlines in the *New York Herald* read: 'New York Italians Kept Silent by Terror of the Far Reaching Arm of the Mafia.' 'Scores of New York Business Men Pay Blackmail to Mafia.' On 3 August 1903 – a few months after the discovery of the body in the barrel – Nicola Cappiello, a successful Brooklyn building contractor, received the following note (in Italian) marked with a skull and crossbones.

If you don't meet us at Seventy-second Street and Thirteenth Avenue, Brooklyn, to-morrow afternoon, your house will be dynamited and you and your family killed. The same fate awaits you in the event of your betraying our purposes to the police.

Mano nera

Across southern Italy, demands like these were called *lettere di scrocco*, 'scrounging letters', because the authors often protested their poverty as well as issuing threats. It was a method employed in the violence industry even before the mafia emerged. Thus Mr Cappiello's story conformed to a well-established pattern from the Old World. When he refused to cooperate, further messages followed. The amount demanded escalated to $10,000. Then three old friends, along with a stranger, came to visit and offered to mediate with the extortionists for $1,000. Cappiello decided to go along with the proposal, but a few days after he handed over the money the same men came back to ask for more. Fearing that he would be bled of his entire wealth, Cappiello went to the police. His 'friends' were arrested and convicted.

The name 'Mano nera' was destined to be more successful than this particular gang. Gradually more and more blackmail letters were signed with a black hand. The excited press coverage patently began putting the idea into criminals' heads. The name spread from New York to Chicago, San Francisco, and New Orleans until it became, for a while, more popular even than 'mafia' as a designation for Italian organized crime.

'Black Hand' became a criminal fashion. Professional gangs apart, jealous neighbours, commercial rivals, hard-up workers, and pranksters also sent 'Black Hand' letters. In Sicily, this kind of abuse of a criminal 'logo' used by the honoured society would have been unthinkable. Mafia *cosche*, with spies in every street, brutally protected their monopoly on intimidation.

Despite the failure to achieve convictions, the 'body in the barrel' case established Joseph Petrosino as a new kind of hero in the eyes of New Yorkers, a sort of frontiersman of Mulberry Bend. His own life story was a parable of America's redemptive power: from poor dago to upstanding detective. Who better to patrol the dark and overcrowded tenements and sweatshops where the swarthy new immigrants from 'the boot' lurked?

Petrosino was responsible for sending hundreds of Italian criminals back to the peninsula, and for imprisoning many others. His rise through the ranks of the NYPD continued. In January 1905, he was appointed head of the force's new Italian branch. Soon afterwards, he became the first Italian-American to make lieutenant. In 1907, he married Adelina Salino in the old St Patrick's Church on Mott Street in the heart of Little Italy.

The following year Petrosino was assigned to police Raffaele Palizzolo's visit to New York. The man absolved of ordering the death of Emanuele Notarbartolo was coming to thank those who had reputedly contributed $20,000 to his cause. Interviewed by a *New York Herald* reporter, Don Raffaele declared that the main purpose of his visit was to 'instil into his Sicilian compatriots the principles of good citizenship'. He laughed when asked whether he had anything to do with the mafia.

By this time Petrosino's reputation had spread. Criminals newly arrived from southern Italy would ask to be taken to police headquarters and have friends point out the cop of whom they had heard so much. In the autumn of 1908, the gritty lieutenant was awarded a gold watch by the Italian government for his part in the arrest of a leading Neapolitan gangster.

Despite the gold watch, Petrosino and his superiors grew tired of the Italian authorities' failure to stop criminals and anarchists leaving Italian shores for America. In February 1909, Petrosino became head of a new secret service arm of the police department. His first mission was to go to Italy to set up an independent information network on gangsters with criminal records in Sicily. Given the difficulties in convicting mafiosi, Petrosino hoped to use the information gathered on the island to expel as many as possible from the USA as illegal immigrants.

On 21 February 1909, Petrosino arrived in the northern Italian port of Genoa. Travelling south, he stopped off to meet officials in Rome and to visit his brother near Salerno. On 28 February the scourge of the Black Hand landed in Palermo ready to take on the mafia in its homeland.

His body arrived back in New York on 9 April aboard the *Slavonia* of the Cunard Line. Nearly four weeks had passed since his murder; the ship had been delayed by bad weather. Petrosino's remains were taken in procession to his apartment at 233 Lafayette Street. Five platoons of mounted police and a guard of honour accompanied the funeral carriage, which was laden with wreaths from official bodies in both Sicily and New York. The plan had been to have an open coffin while he lay in state, but there was only a photograph on the lid because the embalming had failed. The *New York Herald* estimated that 20,000 people came to pay their respects. It also aired the suspicion that the embalming had been botched deliberately – the Sicilian mafia's final insult to its victim. On 12 April, another grand procession took Petrosino through the streets for a funeral service at St Patrick's in Mott Street.

Petrosino died because he badly underestimated the power and ruthlessness of the mafia in Sicily. His street wisdom was attuned to New York, but he had an émigré's condescending attitude to the old country. When he was interviewed about the mafia during the 'body in the barrel' investigation, his comments smacked of prejudice and folklore:

Practically everyone who comes here from Sicily is afflicted with this moral disease. It is inherited and ineradicable. The Mafia is a loosely organized organization, but the same spirit of opposition to all forms of law and all forms of authority is instinctive with everybody at all connected with it. In Sicily the women and children will work hard in the fields and the man will strut around with a gun over his shoulder.

Petrosino's supposedly 'secret' mission to Italy had been pre-announced in the New York press. When he reached Palermo, he refused the offer of an armed escort. The only protection he thought he needed were the dollars he handed out as bribes. He used the methods that had proved so successful at home, boldly seeking to make personal contact with criminals and mafiosi out in the streets. This, of course, was what the Sicilian police did too; but they would never have dreamed of trying to do it in isolation. After Petrosino's death, it was found that he had even left his revolver in his hotel room.

Police in Palermo suspected a link between Petrosino's death and the 'body in the barrel' gang. Two members had travelled back to Sicily at the same time as Petrosino, keeping in touch with Piddu Morello using coded telegrams. The theory was that Morello and Giuseppe Fontana had asked Vito Cascio-Ferro to arrange the killing on their behalf. When Cascio-Ferro was arrested, he was found to have a photo of Petrosino. Yet there was an alibi: Don Vito's political collaborator, an MP, claimed that the mafioso had been at his house when Petrosino was shot. Much to the indignation of the American press, the case never even came to trial.

Many years later, after a life sentence had finally brought his career to an end under Fascism, Cascio-Ferro was interviewed in jail. He claimed to have only ever killed one man in his life, 'and I did that *disinterestedly*'. This cryptic phrase was taken to refer to the most famous murder with which his name had been associated: that of Joe Petrosino. The implication was perhaps that he had carried out the murder as a favour to his American colleagues. This 'confession' does not necessarily mean he committed the crime. It might simply have been an attempt to bask in the stolen glory of another mafioso's work. Like the 'body in the barrel' case, Joe Petrosino's murder is still classified as unsolved.

Along with most Sicilian immigrants to the United States, the members of the Morello gang probably did not intend to make their stay permanent. Like many of those same immigrants, however, the most prominent members remained in the USA for the rest of their lives. For some this was not a very long time. Inzerillo opened another little pastry shop but was shot and killed soon afterwards. Di Primo, a model prisoner in Sing Sing, was released early. Petto the Ox moved to Browntown, Pennsylvania. On the night of 25 October 1905, he was hit by five bullets from a shotgun in his own back yard. Petrosino suspected that Di Primo was the murderer. Giuseppe Fontana disappeared soon after the Petrosino killing.

Other members of the gang played a role in New York's organized crime scene for decades. In the year of Petrosino's death, Piddu Morello was convicted of running a counterfeiting business in East Harlem and given twenty-five years in Atlanta Federal Penitentiary. He lost his role at the head of the organization.

In 1916, the other members of the Morello mafia fought a war against Brooklyn Neapolitans; Piddu's brother was shot dead in an ambush outside a coffee shop in Navy Street, Brooklyn. The Neapolitans failed in their attempt to take over the Morello monopoly on a key component of the Italian diet: artichokes. The trade in this particular vegetable was controlled by Piddu's half-brother Ciro Terranova, who would remain the 'artichoke king' into the 1930s. The Morello gang emerged victorious in the war when the Neapolitan leaders were arrested and, to their great surprise, sent to jail for the killing.

Piddu Morello was released soon afterwards. He was apparently spotted in Sicily in 1919, trying to get support from men of honour in the old country because his successor as supreme boss had condemned him to death. These diplomatic efforts seem to have been successful because he survived to fight three years later alongside the same man who had condemned him. But by that time, the landscape of organized crime in America had altered radically.

Cola Gentile's America

The single most important turning point in the history of organized crime in America was not an execution, a meeting of senior mobsters, or the arrival of some 'superboss' from Sicily. It was the approval of Prohibition. In January 1919, after a boost from a ludicrous wartime outcry against brewers of German origin, the Eighteenth Amendment to the US Constitution was passed; it banned the 'manufacture, sale, or transportation of intoxicating liquors'. Later the same year the Volstead Act provided for the Eighteenth Amendment's enforcement. At a stroke, one of the country's most lucrative industries was handed over to criminals. From raw materials, production, packaging, and transport right down to the table at the speakeasy, gangsters raked in colossal tax-free profits from booze. Prohibition is estimated to have put $2 billion into the illegal economy before it was abolished in 1933.

At the same time, simply because many ordinary Americans liked a drink and could not see why they were not allowed to have one, the gangsters became the consumers' friend. The high mortality rate among bootleggers added glamour to their job. 'They only kill each other,' was the common view. The vast profits that accrued from booze, and the benign public attitude to its illegal manufacture, also lowered the threshold of corruption. Police, politicians, and judiciary took their share of the bonanza.

The criminal free-for-all that was Prohibition made America forget its turn-of-the-century fascination with the mafia and the Mano nera. It was simply not feasible to treat bootlegging as if it were the fruit of a 'dago' invasion. The mass influx of people from Europe was brought to a halt by the First World War. When peace returned, a series of laws closed what Americans liked to call the 'Golden Door' on arrivals – or at least those who did not have the clandestine channels open to mafiosi. The classic gangster years between the two world wars were an era dominated in the public mind by multi-ethnic 'mobsters' and 'hoodlums', not by Italian 'mafiosi' and 'men of honour'.

It was not until the 1950s that American public opinion would again begin to confuse the mafia with organized crime per se. The publication of Mario Puzo's *The Godfather* in 1969 then set in concrete the mistaken public perception that American syndicates were entirely a Sicilian import. The facts about the Prohibition era speak clearly against this perception: in the New York metropolitan area, 50 per cent of bootleggers were Jewish, compared to about 25 per cent who were Italian.

Yet within the Italian communities in cities right across America, a specifically Sicilian mafia association was already well established when Prohibition was introduced. The best witness to their history in the 1920s and 1930s is Nicola Gentile, a man born in Sicily but initiated into the mafia in Philadelphia in 1905. He was known as 'Nick' or 'Cola' depending on which side of the Atlantic he happened to find himself. In 1963, Gentile, now nearing eighty and living in retirement in Rome, made an unprecedented resolution: he decided to write his autobiography. He handed it over, part dictated, to a journalist who helped him fill in gaps in a series of interviews. Gentile was the first Sicilian man of honour ever to tell his own story in this way.

A lingering mystery surrounds the reasons for Gentile's decision. As always in Italy, the political context probably has something to do with it. Yet the simplest motives, the ones proffered by Gentile himself, are as likely to be the most important. He describes himself as an embittered old man. His children were all established in professional careers, but they were ashamed of the criminal origins of their well-being and shunned the man who had paid for their education, their houses.

Cola Gentile's narrative is an ambiguous attempt to justify his life – as much to himself as to anyone else. He strives, not always successfully, to present himself as a 'man of honour' in what he claims is the true sense, someone who had always sought the path of peace and justice within the organization. There is anecdotal evidence to suggest that Gentile had been trying to show himself in this flattering light for quite some time. One man claims to have spent a whole afternoon talking to him in 1949; indeed, he quite fondly remembers being patronized by Gentile, who addressed him half-mockingly as *duttureddu* ('little professor') throughout. The man in question – a young student at the time – says that the veteran man of honour explained his approach to being a mafioso with a hypothetical story:

Duttureddu, if I come in here unarmed, and you pick up a pistol, point it at me and say: 'Cola Gentile, down on your knees.' What do I do? I kneel. That does not mean that you are a *mafioso* because you have forced Cola Gentile to get down on his knees. It means you are a cretin with a pistol in your hand.

Now if I, Nicola Gentile, come in unarmed, and you are unarmed too, and I say to you: '*Duttureddu*, look, I'm in a bit of a situation. I have to ask you to get on your knees.' You ask me 'Why?' I say: '*Duttureddu*, let me explain.' And I manage to convince you that you have to get on your knees. When you kneel down, that makes me a *mafioso*.

If you refuse to get on your knees, then I have to shoot you. But that doesn't mean I have won: I have lost, *duttureddu*.

Gentile apparently had problems sustaining even a hypothetical mental picture of himself without a gun in his hand.

The 'duttureddu' was Andrea Camilleri, now a literary phenomenon in Italy. His crime fiction, written in a mellow, ironic prose richly inflected with Sicilian dialect, dominates the best-seller list. There is no way of independently confirming how reliable Camilleri's memory of this encounter is. But it does capture the way in which the old gangster Cola Gentile, despite his best efforts to seem noble, is honest about the violence that comes with his job. In his autobiography he conceded that 'You cannot become a *capomafia* without being ferocious.'

At the same time that Nick Gentile was quietly recounting

his story in Rome, a similar precedent was being set in the US. Joe Valachi, an American mafioso who feared he was going to be killed in prison by his former associates, was talking to federal agents. It was Valachi who first told the world that mafiosi in the US tend to refer to their organization as 'cosa nostra'. Intense publicity surrounded Valachi when he testified to a Congressional Sub-Committee on organized crime in 1963. Robert Kennedy, appointed attorney general by his brother the President, described Valachi's evidence as 'the biggest single intelligence breakthrough yet in combatting organized crime and racketeering in the United States'. *The Valachi Papers* sold in large numbers.

But as more cautious observers pointed out right from the outset, Valachi did not count in the American mafia. He was a mere foot soldier who would not have been party to discussions at the highest level. By contrast Cola Gentile, the sad and lonely don in the Roman suburbs, moved in elite criminal circles. He worked closely with all the most famous bosses of the 1920s and 1930s: Joe 'the Boss' Masseria, Al Capone, Lucky Luciano, Vincenzo Mangano, Albert Anastasia, Vito Genovese. Surprisingly, Cola Gentile's Italian testimony remains untranslated and unknown to all but a few people outside of the peninsula.

Gentile's story takes place against a background shaped by the transformation of ordinary Sicilian migrants into Americans. At the same time, paradoxically, they were becoming Italian. Italy has a notoriously weak sense of national fellow feeling. The huddled masses from Palermo, Naples, and Parma would arrive at Ellis Island speaking mutually incomprehensible dialects. 'Italy' for many of them was an abstraction. In the encounter with new arrivals from other countries, they began to think of themselves as Italians for the first time. They adapted customs from the old country, or latched on to new ones like Columbus Day, to express this acquired Italian identity.

Italian-American criminals were going through a similar change, but in their case assimilation was a bloodier and more

Machiavellian affair. By 1920, there were 1 million ethnic Italians in New York alone. Only a small proportion of them, needless to say, were criminals. But the community's increasing wealth offered a plethora of illegal economic niches. It also brought into closer contact mobsters originating in different parts of Italy. Street lotteries were as popular in Italian-American neighbourhoods as they had been in the hundred cities of Italy. The southern Italian diet also provided targets. The threat of violence could be used to profit from the traffic in foodstuffs like olive oil that came from Europe – or increasingly from the west coast of the United States, like Ciro Terranova's artichokes.

Italians had also become the most numerous ethnic group in New York's docks. In 1880, 95 per cent of the city's longshoremen were Irish. By 1919, 75 per cent were Italian. They were particularly dominant on the East Side and in Brooklyn. The Red Hook neighbourhood of Brooklyn – Italian through and through – was the seat of a syndicate for the whole inter-war period and beyond. The system operating in the docks was all-embracing, brutal, and highly lucrative. International Longshoremen's Association officials bullied workers to ensure their union's monopoly over recruitment. They bribed shipping and stevedoring company managers to ensure a monopoly over the work that was available. Political protection was assured through the City Democratic Club founded in the late 1920s – it was little more than a mob front. Smuggling, robbery, and extortion were endemic. Many of the ILA officials were from the same small group of blood families. They were backed by a uniquely ruthless protection regime run by men like Albert Anastasia and Vincent Mangano.

Cola Gentile was born in a sulphur town near Agrigento. When he arrived in America in 1903 he was only eighteen years old, a tough youth with a high sense of his own worth – the classic raw material of the mafioso. He moved to Kansas City where he began work as a travelling fabric salesman. His product was based on a confidence trick: the rolls of cloth that he sold as linen were nothing of the sort – apart from a small sample.

Through his work Gentile made contacts in many US cities, gaining a reputation as a sharp kid who could look after himself and his friends. At twenty-one he was initiated into the mafia in Philadelphia. Three years later he returned to his home village in Sicily as a man with money and status. He married and had a child before heading back to America to continue his career within the honoured society. His wife and child remained on the island.

In 1915, he moved to Pittsburgh and recruited a group of ten *picciotti* – young thugs – loyal only himself, independent of the local capo. They were to be the instrument of his rise. Gentile found that the honoured society in the Iron City was subordinated to a large gang of Italians from Calabria and Naples whose power base was the wholesale fruit and vegetable market. Even the mafia capo collected protection money from the Sicilian community on behalf of these Camorristi, as Gentile dismissively called them. (He had in mind the Camorra of Naples – a less-organized criminal fraternity.)

Gentile's reputation in Pittsburgh was made quickly. He and one of his men created a sensation by executing a man in a crowded city-centre bar. Boosted by the success of this operation, Gentile decided to take advantage of the Sicilian capo's submissiveness towards the Camorristi. His *picciotti* set to work: a series of rapid and efficient killings quickly brought the men from the Italian mainland to the negotiating table. The leaders of the two sides met under Gentile's chairmanship. He humiliated the Camorristi by openly threatening them with all-out war if they so much as offended another Sicilian. They meekly submitted to Sicilian leadership. 'From that evening the *camorra* in Pittsburgh and the towns around it was finished,' Gentile concluded. Shortly afterwards he had the Pittsburgh mafia capo shot and sent back to Sicily in a luxury coffin. Cola Gentile had turned himself into the boss of Italian crime in the city. In the process he had made his own early contribution to the Americanization and Italianization of the mafia.

One of the remarkable things about Nick Gentile's career is his geographical mobility. He transferred his membership many times from one *cosca* to another: first Philadelphia and Pittsburgh, then San Francisco, Brooklyn, Kansas City, and back to Brooklyn. Gentile refers to these groups as *borgate*, the Italian term for the kind of suburban townships around Palermo that were the cradle of the honoured society.

Each time he changed *borgata*, Gentile needed a testimonial from a senior boss back home in the province of Agrigento. The letters or telegrams would take the form of a character reference, as if for an ordinary job. Clearly the mafia in the old country was important enough to its wealthy new offshoot in the States for this kind of authentication of membership to be necessary. Italian investigating magistrates have good evidence that this system of references operated until at least the early 1980s.

Gentile provides a fascinating picture of the way men of honour from all over the US coordinated their activities in the years before Prohibition. Death sentences on dissident dons would be issued from one *borgata* to all the others in the area. A select 'council' comprising only senior bosses made the most important decisions. A bigger 'general assembly' would elect capos and debate proposed contracts to kill mafiosi. There could be as many as 150 men at such meetings – bosses and their entourages from all over the USA. Gentile is reluctant to call such meetings courts, and is scathing about the 'judicial procedures' followed in the general assembly: 'It was made up of men who were almost all illiterate. Eloquence was the skill that most impressed the hall. The better someone knew how to talk, the more he was listened to, and the more _____ able to drag that mass of yokels the way he wanted.'

The stresses of the job emerge between the lines of Gentile's autobiography. Occasional bouts of ill-health and nervous exhaustion would see him return to his homeland to recharge his batteries. Not that the trips were always restful; on one occasion in 1919 he had to go into hiding from the law after a man from a rival political faction was shot. During those months in hiding he received some visitors from America. They were Piddu Morello and other remnants of the gang that Lieutenant Joe Petrosino had believed was responsible for the 'body in the barrel' murder back in 1903. They had been sentenced to death by the new boss of New York and were desperate for Gentile's mediation. Gentile had invested considerable effort and courage in developing a reputation as a roving mediator, a man able to smooth out dangerous disputes. Diplomacy was one of the main reasons for his wanderings across the United States. On this occasion, in the end most of the gang was spared, but only because the New York capo was himself killed and supplanted by the pudgy, neckless mafioso Joe Masseria, who would become known simply as 'Joe the Boss'.

Stuck in Sicily, Gentile was unable to take advantage of the whisky he had stockpiled just before the introduction of Prohibition. Nonetheless he was soon able to siphon off his share of the vast cash flows from the drink industry. In Kansas City he ran a company dealing in wholesale supplies for barbers. The business was a front: it gave him access to large quantities of neat alcohol on the pretext that they were destined for after-shave. Gentile also became a dealer in the corn sugar needed to feed illegal stills.

Prohibition meant bootlegging, and bootlegging brought the toughest and brightest of the multi-ethnic youth gang members to the fore. Viewed from a broader perspective, the years until born or brought up in the United States. Their rise coincided with the Italianization and Americanization of the mafia.

Salvatore Lucania hailed from the sulphur town of Lercara Friddi. He left Sicily at the age of nine in 1905. When he grew up he could only speak a few stumbling words of his native dialect. At eighteen he was found guilty of his first serious offence: unlawful possession of narcotics – he was both user and pusher. Prohibition made him into one of the most famous American mobsters of them all. He is better known as Charles 'Lucky' Luciano. Both his nickname and the disconcertingly large scars around his neck date from the occasion when he was slashed and left for dead by some early rivals. From the outset Luciano mixed easily with felons from other backgrounds, working very closely with men like Meyer 'Little Man' Lansky, for example.

Francesco Castiglia, known as Frank Costello – one of Luciano's associates – was another example. He was born near Cosenza in the 'toe' of mainland Italy in 1891; the mafia in Sicily has never recruited from that region. Costello's family brought him to East Harlem when he was four. His first brush with the law – for assault and robbery in 1908 – did not lead to a conviction because it was his first offence. In 1914, he was sentenced to a year in jail for carrying a concealed weapon. On his release he married a non-Italian and embarked on a criminal career based around cosy relations with politicians. With his business partner Henry Horowitz, he started up the Horowitz Novelty Company to produce kewpie dolls, razor blades – and gambling paraphernalia. He would become the king of New York's slot machines.

The most famous gangster of them all, Al Capone, was also a case in point. Born in Williamsburg of Neapolitan parents, he was a member of the Five Points gang – as Luciano had been – before he moved to Chicago as a gunman, rising to the summit of the city's underworld in the mid-1920s. His Chicago syndicate contained Italians but also men like Murray 'the Camel' Humphreys and Sam 'Golf Bag' Hunt. (The American underworld may not be as darkly fascinating as the Sicilian version, but it does produce quirkier nicknames.) Capone's womanizing and greed for publicity would have been anathema to mafiosi back in Sicily.

As a businessman, Capone was more of a networker than the 'managing director' of crime imagined by many feature films about his life. His method was to make case-by-case 50/50 deals with men like truck dealer Louis Lipschultz, for liquor distribution. Or with Frankie Pope to manage the Hawthorne Smoke Shop gambling den. Or with Louis Consentino to run the Harlem Inn, a two-storey whorehouse in Stickney.

Capone is perhaps best known for ordering the St Valentine's Day massacre of 1929, although his involvement was never proved. Seven members of a rival gang were slaughtered in their garage headquarters at 2122 North Clark Street, Chicago. Capone hoodlums, dressed as policemen, faked a raid and made them line up against a wall. Four more men with machine-guns then arrived to perform the execution. Of the seven victims (one was a dentist who just got a thrill from the company of gangsters) and six presumed trigger men, none was Italian.

It was men like Luciano, Costello, and Capone, with strong ties outside the Sicilian and Italian communities, who would accelerate the Americanization process within the mafia organization as Prohibition drew to an end. Cola Gentile, once more, provides a perceptive explanation of how it happened.

But like all autobiographies by men of honour, Gentile's needs to be treated cautiously. Most of a mafioso's life is spent trying to make sense of the fragments of information that come his way from within the association. Bosses often exercise control simply by being inscrutable, by the careful way they control who gets to know what. For that reason, no mafioso ever has a completely reliable map of any given situation. Gentile's memoir is bound to suffer at points from this play of silence and second-guessing. Gentile was also deliberately selective about some aspects of his story – he gives very little information about Sicilian-based men of honour and their contacts with the US, for example.

For all his travelling, Gentile continued to move in a very Sicilian world. For that reason he was not always able to guess the power of mafiosi in the bigger world of organized crime. For example, Anthony D'Andrea was Chicago mafia capo at the time Prohibition came in. Nick Gentile knew him and describes him as being feared across America. Yet D'Andrea lost a tussle with an Irish machine boss for control of the city's Nineteenth Ward. By the end of the First World War the ward had become 70 per cent Italian, having previously been dominated by Germans and Irish. Despite this numerical dominance, in an election campaign punctuated by beatings and bombings in 1921, the Irish boss emerged victorious by 3,984 votes to 3,603. D'Andrea was shot dead three months later by one of his own men. Gentile's only measure of power was internal to the mafia, yet Sicilian bosses like D'Andrea were by no means guaranteed to come out on top in struggles between gangs.

Gentile also suffers from a slightly distorted perspective when looking back at Sicily. Palermo, which dominated the Sicilian mafia, is less important to him than Agrigento or the tiny coastal town of Castellammare del Golfo. Mafiosi who travelled to make their fortune in North America tended to come from minor, poorer centres like these; the powerful Palermitani would have had less incentive to move.

Despite all of these limitations, and the fact that many of the details of his narrative cannot be independently confirmed, it is Gentile's general line of interpretation of a crucial period in mafia history that is significant. He understands the laws of motion of the mafia in America because his survival and success depended on that understanding. Above all, more than many historians, Gentile has a sophisticated grasp of the way the mafia is constantly drawing and redrawing a simple but important boundary. As an institution, the mafia depends on a line separating 'us' the men of honour from 'them' the ordinary, lesser folk.

Gentile's perspective is particularly telling when it comes to a moment in the history of the mafia that has now entered American folklore, the Castellammarese war of 1930–1 – so called because one side was dominated by mafiosi who originated from Castellammare del Golfo. Much of what is known about the leadership of the mafia in the last years of Prohibition comes from accounts of this war by Valachi and other American gangsters, but many aspects of it still remain obscure.

Gentile's account, where it has not been ignored, has been seriously undervalued. He sensed that the key to the devious machinations of the Castellammarese war was the way in which the line separating the mafia from the world outside was manipulated. Just like the other articles in the mafia rule-book, the crucial boundary between 'us' and 'them' is never absolute, and always tactical. The same principles applied in Sicily, but one important reason why things were different in America is that outside the boundary were other gangsters, men from different ethnic backgrounds but with comparably powerful organizations behind them. What follows is Gentile's particularly Sicilian view of how the Castellammarese war unfolded.

The military leader of the Castellammaresi was Salvatore Maranzano who had arrived in New York only in 1927, a mafia refugee from the Fascist crackdown. The other side was led by Joe 'the Boss' Masseria, thought at that time to have been boss of bosses. One of the early victims of the war between the two was a mafioso of the previous generation, Piddu Morello – the one-fingered leader of the 'body in the barrel' gang; he was shot dead in August 1930 in his East Harlem office. Gentile, who arrived back from one of his more prolonged visits to Sicily only the following month, is unable or unwilling to shed any light on the reasons for Morello's murder. Its motives remain unknown.

Cola Gentile relates that, on his return to the States, he was chosen by a mafia general assembly held in Boston to lead a deputation to Castellammarese leader Maranzano. The same general assembly deposed Joe 'the Boss' Masseria, Maranzano's opponent, and put in his place an interim leader as boss of bosses. The aim was to stop the conflict destabilizing the whole association.

In mafia wars, in the short term, superior military power

often wins out against political protection and status within the honoured society. But syndicates based on force alone do not last. Maranzano's campaign was based on the gamble that he would be able to stabilize his authority after achieving military victory. He refused to see Gentile's deputation, probably for the simple reason that he was winning not only the war but perhaps even the political battle too. As the killings continued, and civilians were caught in the crossfire, great political pressure was brought down on Joe 'the Boss'. According to Gentile, the Chief of Police explicitly told him to stop the bloodshed or face losing support.

Eventually Maranzano agreed to meet Gentile's peace delegation and ordered the group to be brought to a villa 135 kilometres from New York. When Maranzano greeted them, he was surrounded by heavily armed men and had two pistols tucked in his belt – a sign that he considered himself a military leader rather than a businessman. Gentile thought he looked like Pancho Villa and referred to the Castellammaresi as the 'exiles' or 'bandits', but not because they had come from Sicily or resembled Mexican guerrillas. It was because they were an alliance of mafiosi who were recruited from across the structure of the different *borgate* of New York. Maranzano's tactics were to make allies out of Joe 'the Boss' Masseria's enemies wherever he could.

The peace delegation was kept at Maranzano's retreat for four days and nights. Gentile was not even sure whether he would be allowed to leave alive. But while under guard he became convinced that other members of his negotiating team had gone over to the Castellammarese camp. It was a sign that the mafia as a whole was moving from a position of neutrality to one of support for Maranzano. All that the Castellammarese leader had to do was delay. The peace delegation was eventually allowed to leave without resolving the conflict.

Maranzano's military offensive was accompanied all the way by a propaganda campaign. He protested that Joe 'the Boss' was a dictator who had condemned all the Castellammaresi to death. As in Sicily, mafiosi often strenuously claim that their actions are compatible with the mafia's own customs. The honoured society has its own laws, but everyone in it is a barrack-room lawyer, eager to interpret the rules in his own favour. Maranzano also berated Masseria for admitting Al Capone – a non-Sicilian stained by pimping – to the mafia.

The role played by Capone in the climax of the Castellamma-rese war is crucial in Gentile's version. 'Scarface Al' was not actually a member of the mafia until the mid-1920s, claims Gentile. Joe 'the Boss' admitted him as part of an attempt to de-stabilize the authority of the then capo of the Chicago honoured society. Capone, loyal to Masseria in New York rather than to the Chicago boss, was authorized to use his own crew to make a bid for leadership in the city. Gentile does not speculate about the exact extent of Al Capone's power in Chicago relative to the rest of the city's extensive, multi-ethnic underworld. What concerns Gentile, as always, is the map of power *within* the honoured society. Once Scarface Al's status in Chicago was secure, he started to exercise influence within the mafia back in New York. Gradually, during the course of the Castellammarese war, it became apparent to Capone that Joe 'the Boss' had been so decisively outfought and outmanoeuvred in New York that even his own lieutenants were becoming restless.

The first phase of the Castellammarese war came to an end at Scarpato's restaurant on Coney Island on 15 April 1931. There Joe 'the Boss' ate a full lunch with one of his lieutenants, Lucky Luciano, and began to play cards. When Luciano went to the men's room, a team of killers he had instructed came in and shot Masseria dead. Later a press photographer placed an ace of spades in the victim's hand to add a wry touch to the scene. Cola Gentile suspected that Capone and Luciano had together decided that Masseria was too weak to bring about the peace that was necessary for business to continue.

Having removed his own capo, Luciano sought peace terms with Maranzano and the Castellammaresi. A meeting to discuss the implications of Maranzano's victory was hosted by Al

Capone. Gentile says little about the meeting other than that there was 'indescribable confusion'. Maranzano eventually obtained what he wanted: the position of *capo dei capi*. He held a banquet in Chicago to celebrate his election and had tickets printed priced at $6 each. A thousand of them were dispatched to Capone who showed his deference by sending back a cheque for $6,000. Similar gestures were made by other bosses. Further tributes were expected. In the centre of the gaudily decorated table in the banquet room was a large dish in which guests placed bundles of banknotes. Gentile estimated that Maranzano gathered $100,000 from his benefit evening.

A short time later, on 10 September, the newly crowned boss Maranzano was stabbed and shot to death in his Park Avenue office by non-Italian mobsters pretending to be from the Inland Revenue Service. They had been employed by Luciano. The Castellammarese war was over, ended by the murder of both of its leading combatants.

Underworld legend portrays the murder of Maranzano as the moment when Lucky Luciano 'modernized' the mafia. Luciano has gone down in some versions of the story as a kind of criminal management consultant, the business brain behind a top-down restructuring of the mafia on new, corporate lines. Some testimonies claim that after Joe 'the Boss' was murdered, Maranzano tried to impose himself as a dictator. Luciano's response was to kill him and institute a more 'democratic' form of leadership. He established a governing commission comprising the capos of the New York Families plus one outsider. (Gentile suggests that the five Families already existed by this time.)

Most of the mobsters who later recalled the Castellammarese war also said that within two days of Maranzano's death, twenty, forty or even ninety Sicilian mafiosi were eliminated across America on Luciano's orders. This was the famous purge of the 'greaseballs' or 'Moustache Petes'; the modernization of the mafia apparently involved exterminating these superannuated Sicilians. The problem with this theory is that there is no documentary evidence whatsoever of a grand transnational extermination of mafiosi at the time of Maranzano's murder. The junior mobsters who were told of twenty, forty or ninety Sicilians being killed clearly did not read the newspapers. The oft-repeated tale of the purge of the 'Moustache Petes' is mythical.

The idea that the Sicilian mafia was 'old-fashioned' is another diehard misconception. Whatever criminal aptitudes Joe 'the Boss' had brought with him to New York from Palermo had been modern enough to enable him to build a career lasting more than two decades. Maranzano, the short-term victor in the Castellammarese war, had arrived much more recently. But his astonishingly rapid rise to power in the US is testimony both to the influence that Sicilian affairs still had on the American branch of the mafia, and to the ease with which some 'Moustache Petes' were able to adapt to the challenges of the Big Apple. In other words, the template that sets modernizing American gangsters against conservative greaseballs does not fit neatly over the events of 1930–1.

Gentile's interpretation of the ending of the Castellammarese war is different and more convincing. The idea for a Commission was not Luciano's; it had already been floated during the 'indescribable confusion' of the meeting following Joe 'the Boss' Masseria's murder. Gentile does not seem to regard the Commission as a particularly radical innovation; there were clearly consultative meetings of senior mafiosi in the United States before the First World War. Men of honour are forever tinkering with the rules and structures of the association. It is likely that the invention of the Commission was another instance of constitutional tinkering.

In Gentile's eyes, Masseria and Maranzano were neither more nor less dictatorial or old-fashioned than previous senior bosses. In Sicily, mafia capos are usually smeared before and after they are eliminated; they die because they are variously too greedy, too authoritarian, too weak, too old-fashioned. Or so their killers say. Some justification has to be fabricated for executions that are, in reality, almost always driven by the same old motives of power and fear. The victors in mafia warfare also love to present their rise to power as the coming of a new era. It seems that this was also the case in New York in 1931.

Nick Gentile was too astute to believe this kind of internal propaganda. He claims that it was only after murdering Maranzano that Luciano actually entered the mafia hierarchy as such, becoming one of the members of the Commission. Luciano was obviously already a powerful man long before this, and a key element in Joe 'the Boss' Masseria's power base. Thus, as Capone had been earlier, Luciano was an external force enlisted to tip the balance in a struggle for power within the relatively narrow confines of the honoured society. Lucky's contacts with the much larger universe of Jewish and Irish organized crime were the key resource that he brought to bear *within* the mafia.

Maranzano's death can be taken, all the same, as marking the point when the mafia in the United States became an Italian-American organization rather than a Sicilian one. And for that reason, the American mafia will appear henceforth in these pages only when its affairs impinge upon events in Sicily. But, for all that, the Americanization of the mafia was not a dramatic transformation, a once-and-for-all break with the traditional ways of the Old World. The mafia's ethnic make-up became slightly more mixed as Neapolitans and other southern Italians were absorbed. The two organizations gradually separated, although the Americans always recognized the prestige due to the original mafia, and there continued to be strong family and business links across the Atlantic. The core of the American honoured society's membership remained ethnically Sicilian after 1931. In some places there was no challenge to Sicilian dominance. In Buffalo, for example, Stefano Magaddino from Castellammare del Golfo had an astonishingly long reign; he was capo from the 1920s until his death in 1974. Sicilian methods would characterize the American mafia long after the young guns of the Prohibition era – Luciano, Capone, and their like – were gone.

Above all, mafiosi in both Sicily and the US continued to think of themselves as a breed apart from other human beings and even other criminals. American or Sicilian, to be a man of honour means to operate beyond society's measures of right and wrong.

When Prohibition was finally abolished, America was four years into the great Depression. Organized crime survived these changes thanks in no small measure to the gaming industry. Nick Gentile entered the new boom: he became a partner in a gambling house in Manhattan's Little Italy.

But the end of Prohibition also saw the national mood harden against organized crime. Whether in America or in Sicily, the mafia would not exist without links to the political domain. At the Democratic Party national convention in Chicago in 1932, Frank Costello shared a suite at the plush Drake Hotel with the leader of the 11th assembly district in Manhattan. Lucky Luciano shared another with the Democratic leader of New York's 2nd assembly district. But unlike Italy before the Second World War, the United States was a democracy. The competition for power in America was more open, making it almost as easy to build political careers out of crusades *against* crime as it was to use the vote-gathering powers of mobsters. The Hollywood movies of the early 1930s accurately track a switch in public attitudes and political tactics as Prohibition ended. Instead of the gangster movies of the early 1930s, like *Little Caesar* (1931) and *Scarface* (1932), Hollywood began to make films lauding the deeds of law enforcement officers. James Cagney, who had played a hood in *Public Enemy* (1931), was recruited to the FBI for *'G' Men* (1935). In New York, Fiorello La Guardia was elected mayor in 1933. He proceeded to drive Frank Costello's illegal fruit machines from the city. (Costello was not unduly perturbed; he moved them to New Orleans where Senator Huey Long invited him to come and share his gambling income around.)

The appointment in 1935 of Thomas E. Dewey as New York special prosecutor was a still more worrying development for organized crime in the city. Dewey would run twice (unsuccessfully) as Republican candidate for the Presidency on the strength of his much-hyped successes against the hoodlums. In 1941 he did manage to become Governor of New York.

There were some eminent victims of the new anti-gangster campaign. Arthur 'Dutch Schultz' Flegenheimer, one of Luciano's lieutenants and the king of numbers rackets in Harlem, came under pressure from all sides. He faced increased legal bills, defending himself from Dewey's tax-dodging charges. His political protectors needed more money to respond to the challenge from reforming candidates. He was steadily losing his grip on the people who ran the numbers games on the street when he was shot dead in the Palace Chop House in Newark in October 1935. Dewey then cornered Lucky Luciano himself; he was sentenced to thirty to fifty years on prostitution charges (on which more in the next chapter). Brooklyn district attorney – and future mayor of New York City – William O'Dwyer even sent Louis 'Lepke' Buchalter, the garment industry extortionist, to the electric chair; he was the first eminent gangster to be executed by the state.

A new drive to combat the narcotics business put an end to Cola Gentile's career in America. In 1937, he was arrested by federal agents in New Orleans for his part in organizing a drug-dealing syndicate that stretched from Texas to New York. His version is that, after consulting his capo in Brooklyn, he jumped bail and fled back to Sicily, never to return. But there may well be a great deal more to the story. A mafioso who turned state's evidence in the 1980s claimed that the Palermo bosses asked his own Catania Family to assassinate Gentile as a favour to the Americans, and added in passing that Gentile had fled from America after talking to the police. Nobody acted on the request. 'They left the poor old man alone. He had fallen so low at the end of his life that he only survived because of charity from neighbours who gave him the odd plate of pasta.' Whether it really was pity that saved Cola Gentile's life will probably never be known.

The Second World War brought respite for American mobsters after the troubles of the mid to late 1930s. It drew press attention away from crime and created profiteering opportunities; Americans were particularly resistant to petrol rationing. In a much more dramatic way, the war also proved to be the salvation of the mafia back in Sicily.

6

War and Rebirth
1943–1950

Don Calò and the Rebirth of the Honoured Society

It is said that on the morning of 14 July 1943, an American fighter plane flew low over Villalba. It naturally drew the people out into the streets. When it roared down to rooftop level they could see, attached to its fuselage, a golden-yellow flag with a large L in the centre. As it passed over the house belonging to the parish priest, Monsignor Giovanni Vizzini, the pilot dropped a small package. But it was intercepted by an Italian soldier and passed on to the commander of the local *carabinieri*.

Four days earlier 'Operation Husky' had been launched when 160,000 Allied troops landed along a broad section of the south-eastern coast of Sicily; 300,000 more American and British fighting men followed. This huge force was now fanning out across the island. The British headed north-east towards Catania, Messina, and the mainland. The Americans advanced north and west. It was the first time the Allies had invaded the territory of an Axis power.

Villalba, in the very centre of Sicily, was hardly a major strategic objective. It was not much more than a collection of peasant hovels known principally for its lentils – an important component of the diet of the poor. The town's sloping grid of narrow, dirt-track streets had grown in the eighteenth century to provide farmhands for the giant Miccichè estate that stretched out in all directions below. Life in Villalba revolved around the tiny Piazza Madrice where there were two bars, a branch of the Bank of Sicily, and a church.

Yet the fighter plane returned the following day, still bearing its unusual banner. Another package was dropped, and this time it found its way to the right person. Its nylon wrapping bore the Sicilian words 'zu Calò' – 'Uncle Calò' – who was mafia boss Don Calogero Vizzini, the priest's older brother. It was picked up by the Vizzinis' butler who took it to his master. It was found to contain a golden-yellow silk handkerchief with a large black L in the centre.

That very evening, the story goes, a rider left Villalba with a message for a certain 'zu Peppi' in Mussomeli. The message read as follows: 'On Tuesday 20th Turi will leave for the fair at Cerda with the calves. I will set off the same day with the cows, the oxen, and the bull. Prepare the kindling for the fruit and organize pens for the animals. Tell the other overseers to get ready.'

The letter was in a code that had an Old-World simplicity. The addressee, 'zu Peppi', was 'uncle' Giuseppe Genco Russo, boss of Mussomeli. He was being informed that Turi (another mafioso) would lead the American motorized divisions (calves) as far as Cerda. Don Calogero Vizzini meanwhile would set off the same day with the bulk of the troops (the cows), the tanks (oxen), and the commander-in-chief (the bull). The mafiosi under Genco Russo's command were to prepare the battleground (kindling) and provide cover for the infantry (pens).

On the afternoon of 20 July, three tanks duly rumbled up to the gates of Villalba. The turret of the first bore the same yellow flag with the large L in the middle. An American officer appeared from the hatch. In a Sicilian accent slurred by years in the States, he respectfully asked for Don Calò. Word reached the old *capomafioso* at home. He was four days away from his sixty-sixth birthday. On hearing of the Americans' arrival, he shambled slowly across town in shirtsleeves and tortoiseshell sunglasses, his braces straining to keep a pair of crumpled trousers tethered high over the improbable protrusion of his gut. When he reached the Americans, he wordlessly proffered the silk hankerchief his butler had picked up. Along with his nephew – who spoke English because he had not long returned from the States – he then climbed up on to the tank and was driven away.

Meanwhile, back in Villalba, mafiosi began to intimate the meaning of these marvels to the townspeople. It was explained that Don Calò had contacts high up in the American government who had reached him through Charles 'Lucky' Luciano – hence the L on the flag. Luciano had been released from prison early in return for arranging the mafia's help with the invasion. Not only that, some said, but the famous Sicilian-American gangster was himself inside the tank that carried Don Calò away. Because of his great authority, Villalba's own man of respect had been chosen, on Lucky Luciano's advice, to lead the American advance.

Six days later Don Calò returned to Villalba in a big American car, his mission accomplished. A perfectly executed pincer move-ment had brought the calves, cows, and oxen together at Cerda, thus completing the Allied conquest of central Sicily. Now Don Calò, with his American backers, was ready to return the mafia to its rightful place in Sicilian society after the dark days of Fascism.

Most Sicilians know the tale of Don Calò and the yellow hand-kerchief, and many still believe it. The endless retellings of the episode have painted a thick crust of apocryphal conviction over it, blurring its detail in some places, building up hardened swirls of pure invention in others. Most historians now dismiss it as fable.

The events of Lucky Luciano's life, intriguing though they are, certainly do not support the legend. Back in the autumn of 1933, Luciano led a combined Italian-Jewish syndicate in a move to establish centralized control of bordellos in New York City. The move was a commercial failure. When the madams com-plained that the burden of kickbacks was too heavy and that their margins were non-existent, they were met with a wall of dumb muscle from Luciano's enforcers. The result was wide-spread 'tax dodging' throughout the industry. Isolated acts of intimidation could do nothing to stop the fall in the extortion syndicate's income.

This misfired business venture had catastrophic legal conse-quences for Luciano too. In February 1936, he and the other members of his gang were arrested by agents working for special prosecutor Thomas E. Dewey. The testimonies of a number of sex industry workers were crucial in securing a conviction. In June of the same year Luciano began a thirty- to fifty-year term in New York State's maximum-security penitentiary at Dannemora. It was the harshest sentence ever handed down for compulsory prostitution.

Luciano's luck began to turn when the USA entered the Second World War. In February 1942, the SS *Normandie*, a luxury liner that had once held the Blue Riband for the fastest Atlantic crossing, caught fire and rolled over at her moorings on the Hudson River. It was probably an accident but at the time nobody was sure. To avoid further acts of sabotage, naval intelligence began to seek the help of the mobsters who controlled the waterfront. Their first contacts were with Joseph 'Socks' Lanza, the boss of the huge Fulton fish market. He organized false union cards for navy agents so that they could carry out investigations on the waterfront. On Lanza's recommendation, Luciano was also recruited to help extend the navy's anti-espionage operation. Lucky was brought from Dannemora to a more convenient (and comfortable) prison to be interviewed by intelligence officers. The rumours on the waterfront were that American mobsters had eliminated suspected German spies on the orders of naval intelligence.

That is almost certainly the full extent of Lucky Luciano's collaboration with the Federal government. There is no evidence that Luciano was in Sicily during the war. Nor is there evidence of a deal to free him in exchange for enlisting Sicilian mafia support for the Allied invasion. Luciano was released and expelled from the USA to Italy only in 1946. There was nothing necessarily suspicious about Luciano's release even then; ten years was still the longest anyone had served for his particular vice offence. The man who gave final approval for the decision was the Governor of New York State, Luciano's nemesis, Thomas E. Dewey.

So there was no American plot to enlist the mafia as an ally in the invasion of Sicily. Quite simply, it is hardly likely that the Allies would entrust the secret of Operation Husky, then the largest amphibious assault in history, to hoodlums.

Yet the legend of Don Calò and the yellow handkerchief persists. In June 2000, a journalist from the Rome newspaper *La Repubblica* interviewed the original source of the story, Michele Pantaleone, a well-known left-wing writer and politician who was now ninety. It was put to Pantaleone that a leading historian had expressed scepticism about his tale. 'Why doesn't he go and say these things in Villalba?' he replied. 'They'll spit in his face. An American jeep came, took Calogero Vizzini away from the town, and brought him back after eleven days.' Despite his haziness about certain particulars, Pantaleone's words do at least carry the authority of experience. The Pantaleone family home stands on the downhill side of Piazza Madrice in Villalba. Michele had tangled with Don Calò in person, and he was there when the Americans arrived.

The lasting uncertainties over what happened that day in Villalba are significant in their own right; they are just one small example of the doubts over many aspects of the history of the mafia since the Second World War. To many Italians the powers that be are enveloped in a mist of suspicion. Looming somewhere in the mist, people claim to make out the outlines of corrupt politicians and judges, businessmen, Masonic lodges, the intelligence services, right-wing subversives, the police and military, the CIA and, of course, the mafia. Mistrust has contaminated Italian democracy since its birth in the aftermath of the Second World War. Many Sicilians, indeed many Italians, either do not know whom to believe, or choose to believe whom they like. Peddling conspiracy theories is a national sport; the Italians call it *dietrologia*, literally 'behindology'. The legend of Don Calò and the yellow handkerchief is perhaps the earliest instance of *dietrologia*. It tries to convince us that the US government was 'behind' the Sicilian mafia's resurgence after the fall of Fascism. In other words, it tries to shift the blame.

The strongest argument against the Villalba legend is simply that the Sicilian mafia is too complex a creature to be resurrected by a mere plot. The real story of the mafia's return to power spreads the blame for its revival more evenly than the fable of the yellow handkerchief. It is a story about Don Calogero Vizzini, the American secret services, and political violence. But it is primarily about how the mafia used its traditional strengths – networking and brutality – to engineer a place for itself within the Italian democratic system as it slowly took shape after the war. Given the opportunities that history offers, the Sicilian mafia is quite capable of determining its own fate.

Another Villalba historian provides an account of that famous day in 1943 that is almost certainly closer to the truth. He says simply that Don Calò led a celebratory delegation of local people to meet an Allied patrol whose commander had asked to speak to whoever was in charge. A few days later the old capo was proclaimed mayor. In this respect Don Calò's story is typical. In Villalba, as in every village, people gave the invaders a joyous welcome because they were tired of the hardship that Fascism and war had brought. They also loved America; many Sicilian emigrants – they called them *americani* – had returned from the New World with savings, an education, and newfangled consumer tastes to show for their travels. And a good number of the GIs were themselves from Sicilian families that had emigrated to 'la Merica'.

As they advanced across Sicily, Allied troops summarily dismissed the Fascist mayors of the towns like Villalba that they liberated. They replaced them with men who sometimes owed their positions to nothing more than the say-so of a Sicilian-American interpreter. To fill the power vacuum, rural centres that had spent two decades without politics often turned, or were forced to turn, to the local men of honour; after all, many men of respect could present themselves as victims of Fascist repression.

Don Calò owed his nomination as mayor to the good offices of the Catholic Church as well as the American army. In the chaos that followed the collapse of Fascism in Sicily, the Americans often looked to senior churchmen for advice on whom to trust. Don Calò was one of the people they recommended. He had a long record of involvement with a Catholic social fund and there were clergymen in his family: two of his brothers were priests; one of his uncles was an archpriest, and another was Bishop of Muro Lucano.

According to Don Calò's own account of the day he took office as mayor of Villalba, he was carried shoulder high through the town. He claims to have acted as a peacemaker; only his intervention saved his Fascist predecessor from being lynched. What is known for certain is that the official appointment ceremony was attended by both an American lieutenant and a priest representing the bishopric of Caltanissetta. According to some sources, the old mafioso was embarrassed to hear his friends outside shouting, 'Long live the mafia! Long live crime! Long live Don Calò!' It is thought that his first act as the town's foremost citizen was to expunge from the court archives in Caltanissetta, and from the police and *carabinieri* headquarters, records of previous charges against him (robbery, criminal association, cattle rustling, corruption, fraudulent bankruptcy, extortion, aggravated fraud, ordering murders). Don Calò had erased his past, but there was still much to do before his, and the mafia's, future would be secure.

On 17 August 1943, thirty-eight days after the first landings, General Sir Harold Alexander telegraphed Churchill to say that Sicily was entirely in Allied hands. (By then the invasion of Italian soil had already precipitated the fall of Fascist dictator Benito Mussolini, deposed and arrested on 25 July.) For the next six months the island would be under AMGOT – Allied Military Government of Occupied Territory. It was under AMGOT that the mafia made its first attempts to determine the political shape of Sicily as it emerged from the war.

AMGOT had its hands full. The island was in a dreadful state in the late summer of 1943. Even before Operation Husky, many of its 4 million inhabitants lived in penury. Now food supplies were low and the railway infrastructure had been shattered by bombing. The crime rate soared. A number of prisoners had escaped in the confusion of the invasion, and the black market, which was already widespread during the last years of Fascism, became the only means of survival for many. In October it was discovered that the reserve of ration books had been looted in Palermo; at least 25,000 illegitimate books were in circulation. The Allies ordered the compulsory purchase of all grain. Small farmers and great landowners alike preferred to avoid this obligation, so that black marketeers enjoyed considerable popular support. Just as it had done after the First World War, banditry returned once again to the Sicilian countryside.

Soon after American troops passed through, police began to pick up clear signs of mafia involvement in the crime wave. One report to police headquarters in Palermo listed a series of towns in which mafiosi had seized power:

In Villabate the mafia has taken control of the town hall; the mayor is the butcher Cottone – a man with a criminal record . . . It is rumoured that, after the American troops came, *maffiosi* in Marineo, Misilmeri, Cefala, Diana, Villafrate and Bolognetta ransacked the farm buildings on the Stallone estate . . . they got hold of the weapons and munitions left by the German troops that had camped there . . . Yesterday criminals attacked Gangi town hall. It is thought that there has been violence against Baron Sgadari, Baron Marciano and Baron Lidestri who cooperated with the discovery of a vast criminal association that operated in the Madonie back in 1927.

Mafiosi were evidently seeking revenge for the defeats inflicted by the 'iron prefect'.

The Allied authorities could hardly be blamed for these episodes. But they were far from innocent in the mafia's resurgence as a political force. Even before the invasion of Sicily, the British and Americans certainly knew about the mafia, and envisaged gleaning information from local men of honour for the purposes of governing the island after its liberation. A secret British War Office document from before the invasion listed prominent residents who might be useful. It demonstrates a relaxed attitude to relations with mafiosi. One Vito La Mantia is described as 'the head of a mafia *cosca* ... An antifascist who, if still alive, could provide important information. Not educated but influential.'

Over the six months of AMGOT rule, all party political activity in Sicily was prohibited. British and American officials found that creating a compliant interim government in the towns and villages was a messy task. Sicilian anti-Fascist groups were an unknown quantity and did not always offer an obvious new governing elite. The Allied view was that left-wing influence had to be avoided at all costs. As ever, the mafia and its politicians were ready to act as a reliable 'instrument of local government'. So it was that during the AMGOT period there were regular contacts between the Office of Strategic Services (the OSS, forerunner of the CIA) and senior mafiosi. Joseph Russo, the Corleone-born head of the OSS's Palermo desk, has recently said of the bosses: 'I got to know them all. It did not take them long to re-cement their solidarity.'

Naivety also played its part in the mafia's re-emergence as a political force under AMGOT. The British thought that their empire offered a formula for finding reliable natives. In Sicily, as in the pink-shaded portions of the globe, landowners and aristocrats would exercise authority on behalf of London (and Washington). But Sicily was not the Raj. At the end of September 1943, the Allies nominated Lucio Tasca Bordonaro mayor of Palermo. He was a landed gentleman of just the kind that the British thought they could trust. But he lived 'in the odour of mafia'; Nick Gentile later claimed that Tasca Bordonaro was actually a member of the honoured society. Other similar men were appointed across Sicily. Like his peers, Tasca Bordonaro sensed that the end of the war would bring a new struggle to control the land. His response was to lead the first political organization to become active in occupied Sicily: the Sicilian separatist movement. The separatists wanted Sicily to become a free country under the wing of the American eagle. That way, men like Tasca Bordonaro hoped, the authority of the old elite could be preserved and the dreaded leftists kept at bay. The separatist landowners had a natural ally in their cause: the mafiosi who guarded and managed their estates and found political protection in return.

In January 1944, political freedoms were restored in preparation for Sicily's return to Italian rule, and the island sprang into tumultuous political life. It was then that one of the separatist movement's leaders gave a revealing speech in the mafia stronghold of Bagheria. Andrea Finocchiaro Aprile was a frenzied, thin-lipped orator who had the habit of talking about 'Winnie' Churchill and 'Delano' Roosevelt as if he chatted with them on the telephone every day. In Bagheria he made it clear who else he included in his circle of close acquaintances: 'If the mafia did not exist, it would need to be invented. I'm a friend of the *mafiosi*, even though I am personally against crime and violence.' (Mafia defector Tommaso Buscetta would later claim that Finocchiaro Aprile was a member of his own mafia Family.)

In February 1944, AMGOT control ended and Sicily came under the authority of a new government, based on the liberated southern portion of the Italian mainland. By then both mafiosi and the separatists had managed to create the widespread impression that they were Uncle Sam's favourite Mediterranean nephews. It looked to many as if Sicily's future would be as an autonomous American protectorate and mafia fiefdom.

With the mafia's political wing lined up overwhelmingly behind the separatist cause, its military wing was called on to oppose a new threat from the Left. In the autumn of 1944, the Communist Minister of Agriculture in the new Italian coalition government piloted some radical reforms that were to open a new and bloody chapter in the story of the mafia's renaissance. The reforms aimed at nothing less than a final resolution of the land question that had caused turmoil in the southern countryside for more than a century. The measures showed the influence of Bernardino Verro and the Fasci: peasants were to get a better share of the produce of land they worked and rented, and they were given permission to form cooperatives and take over badly cultivated land. The Minister of Agriculture even tried to ban middlemen from operating between the landowners and the peasants – a direct attack on the *gabelloti*.

The weak Italian state was in no position to enforce these new rules quickly, but the peasants took them as a signal that those in power were finally ready to back their yearning for land and justice. The landowners sensed that their fears of the red peril were soon to be realized. So, just as they had done after the First World War, the men of property turned to mafiosi to confront the peasants with force.

Once again it was a famous episode in Don Calò's Villalba – a true one this time – that inaugurated this new phase in the mafia's resurgence. Like many other mafiosi, Don Calogero Vizzini's prime concern in 1944 was land – in his case the Miccichè estate round Villalba. To gain control of it, he had to see off a particularly bothersome enemy: Michele Pantaleone – the man who would later set down the story of the American fighter plane and the yellow handkerchief. Pantaleone was from a local family of professionals whose republican traditions placed them in the opposing faction to the Catholic Vizzinis. Don Calò had tried hard to persuade Michele Pantaleone to marry his niece Raimonda, but this small-town dynastic romance failed to blossom. (Pantaleone knew what dangerous obligations such a union with the Vizzinis would bring.) For Don Calò this failure of marriage diplomacy was bad enough. Worse still was the fact that Pantaleone became a Socialist. The young rebel drew attention to the Miccichè land issue in the burgeoning leftist press and was trying to use his leverage with the left-wing parties in Villalba. In return Don Calò arranged for crops on the Pantaleone family's land to be vandalized, and there was even a failed attempt on Pantaleone's life.

The attempt may just have been a warning, because the *capo-mafioso* was also mobilizing his contacts. Ever the peacemaker, he had offered a deal to the Communist Party in the provincial capital, Caltanissetta: he would help them set up a branch in Villalba – as long as one of his own estate wardens was installed as secretary. The Communists wisely turned down the offer.

With the equanimity that befitted his calling, Don Calò also continued to draw on his long-established links with conservative landowners. Lucio Tasca Bordonaro, the separatist leader appointed as mayor of Palermo under AMGOT, was a close ally (they both owned land nearby). On 2 September 1944, on Don Calò's invitation, Andrea Finocchiaro Aprile – 'friend' of Winnie, Delano, and the mafia – gave a typically incendiary speech in Villalba, promising riches for all if Sicily became independent.

The temperature in the town was rising. Michele Pantaleone increased it further by inviting regional Communist leader Girolamo Li Causi to speak. The Partito Comunista in Caltanissetta, perhaps worried that Pantaleone was leading their man into trouble, contacted Vizzini. The old boss gave them reassurances; he was offering them his personal hospitality, after all. There would be no trouble as long as they did not touch on local issues. On 16 September 1944, a truck carrying Li Causi and his comrades arrived in Villalba.

Don Calò began by politely addressing the new arrivals: 'May I have the honour of offering you coffee?' Sensing the menace in the welcome, the left-wing militants followed the old man as he shuffled across the square towards a bar. As they walked, they noticed that thick black crosses had been painted across the posters advertising their public meeting. Don Calò tried to reason with the visitors while they drank his coffee and smoked his cigarettes. Villalba was like a monastery, he said; it would not do to disturb its tranquillity. But if they insisted on speaking, then they should be polite. When Don Calò finished his little speech, the activists turned back towards the piazza, prepared for confrontation.

Apart from some local Communists and Socialists, most of the inhabitants of Villalba had thought it wiser to listen to the speeches from behind closed shutters. When the militants emerged from the bar, a pack of Don Calò's men stood staring, with arms folded and smirks on their faces. Among them was Don Calò's nephew; he had recently taken over as mayor from his uncle. Don Calò himself emerged from the bar to join the group.

Pantaleone got up on a table and introduced the main speaker. Communist leader Girolamo Li Causi was not a man to be intimidated. Only a few weeks earlier, he had returned to his native island for the first time in twenty years, most of them spent as a political prisoner under Mussolini and as a leader of the resistance against the Nazis in Milan. He was a calm and charismatic orator; mixing dialect into his Italian, he spoke of the abuse of workers and peasants by industrialists and landlords. The militants who were there with him later reported hearing assenting voices from behind the shutters: 'He's right! What he says is Gospel.'

Don Calò became agitated. Undeterred, Li Causi began to talk about the way the peasants in Villalba were being deceived by 'a powerful leaseholder' – a scarcely disguised reference to Don Calò. 'It's a lie,' bellowed the *capomafioso*. People immediately started to leave the piazza. An old man told Don Calò to let the speaker be heard; after all, this was a time of political freedom, he said. He was cudgelled to the ground as the first shots were fired. Pandemonium ensued.

Astonishingly, with bullets fizzing past him, Li Causi stayed on the platform and tried to calm the situation, offering to engage in an open debate with anyone who disagreed. Don Calò's nephew lobbed a grenade. When it exploded, Li Causi fell, wounded in the leg. Pantaleone took charge, dragging the Communist chief to safety and firing his pistol in the air to cover his withdrawal. More than a dozen bullet holes were found in the wall behind the spot where Li Causi made his speech. Fourteen people were wounded.

Don Calò ordered his men to calm down, and offered to help repair the leftists' truck, which had been damaged by a grenade. A few days later, he sent an emissary to offer apologies to Li Causi as he lay in hospital. These were empty gestures; the gunfight in Villalba had already served its intimidatory purpose. Six months later Don Calò's local power base was secured when he became manager of the Miccichè estate.

The Villalba incident created headlines across liberated Italy. More than his other misdeeds it made Don Calogero Vizzini famous. He would not have been particularly concerned. Indeed, the way he avoided paying the judicial consequences of his actions only bolstered his reputation. By pulling strings, he engineered long periods of conditional freedom while the case ground slowly on. It was not until November 1949 that Don Calò, along with his nephew, was found guilty of wounding Li Causi and was sentenced to five years in prison. He simply went on the run until granted more conditional freedom during an appeal. In 1954 the sentence was confirmed, but he was given an amnesty. The judge admitted that 'he was indicated as being the head of the mafia', but decided to absolve him of any punishment on the grounds of his age and his lack of previous convictions.

The events in Villalba inaugurated a long season of mafia attacks on political activists, trade unionists, and ordinary peasants that lasted into the early 1950s. Dozens were not as lucky as Li Causi and Pantaleone. Each killing was followed by the familiar judicial outcome: the suspected murderers being released for lack of evidence. In some towns and villages, the peasant movement was simply terrorized into submission.

The great question about Don Calogero Vizzini is whether he was as dominant within the mafia as he was famous outside it.

Could the lentil-capital of Villalba really be the headquarters of the honoured society as well?

American secret agents certainly seem to have treated Don Calò as the mafia's overall ruler. When the American consulate in Palermo was set up in February 1944, it relied on the OSS for its intelligence. The OSS in turn relied partly on the mafia, and particularly on Don Calò. At one period, the chief of the OSS Palermo office, Joseph Russo, met him and other bosses 'at least once a month'. Vizzini was known by the codename of 'Bull Frog' in secret communications. Russo says the mafiosi came for 'moral support' and truck tyres, which they needed to do 'their good work, their beneficence. Whatever that was.'

Even if these exchanges were as trivial as Russo maintains, and even if Don Calò was bluffing the OSS about his power on the island, we should not assume that events in little Villalba were a sideshow. Way back in 1922, the semi-literate Don Calò, who had extensive sulphur mining interests, went to London for high-level talks on setting up an Anglo-Italian sulphur cartel to respond to American competition. The small Sicilian delegation included a future magnate of the Italian chemical industry.

Don Calò's Church and political contacts also gave him a formidable power base. In the few years following Operation Husky, one Angelo Cammarata occupied the jobs of prefect of Caltanissetta, administrator of property belonging to the diocese of Caltanissetta, superintendent of provisions in Sicily, and commissioner for agrarian reform. He was close to both the bishop and Don Calò.

Economic changes beyond the mafia's control also played in Don Calò's favour. War and Fascism had made cattle and grain more important to the Sicilian economy during the first half of the twentieth century. The inland province of Caltanissetta produced the most corn of any western Sicilian province in the harsh year of 1944. The cash-crop lemon business – so fundamental to the *cosche* of Palermo – had been paralysed by an export crisis. Don Calò's status within the mafia probably reflects a temporary shift in the balance of power within the criminal economy: from the capital and its environs to the countryside.

Not that Don Calò was always stuck out in the hills. He kept a base in the Hotel Sole in Palermo's Corso Vittorio Emanuele where, to the end of his life, he could be seen being watched over by two young corduroy-clad minders.

But it was Don Calò's political influence that was his most significant contribution to the mafia's resurgence; he was intimately involved with the creation of a mafia-friendly settlement in post-war Sicily. That settlement would see the fading of separatism and the emergence of a new pan-Italian party prepared to use the mafia in the traditional way: as an instrument of local government.

In September 1945 – a year after the gun battle in Villalba – Don Calò was the only mafioso present at a secret meeting of separatist leaders at which it was decided to mount an armed insurrection. It was a move born of desperation. The separatists' American support had evaporated after the end of AMGOT. Now they had a strong new national party to compete with: Christian Democracy (Democrazia Cristiana, or the DC). By successfully proposing a regional assembly for Sicily rather than full independence, the DC had taken much of the steam out of separatism. Don Calò was at the meeting because through him the separatists could arrange the help of the large bandit gangs that still roamed the countryside. But the insurrectionary forces were easily defeated.

In the wake of the separatist debacle, Don Calò became increasingly convinced that the DC – and not the separatists – represented the best vehicle for his interests. It would be a gradual but decisive shift in his, and the mafia's, allegiances. Some DC politicians were destined to become Sicilian organized crime's favourite mediators with Rome for over four decades.

The DC was far from being a mafia front. At the birth of the Italian republic it stood for family values, private property, and social peace; and in Sicily it appealed particularly to peasants with small plots of land who were afraid of Communism. The

DC also had the huge advantage of Vatican support. Once the Cold War began in 1947, the DC could also count on American backing against the Partito Comunista Italiano – the most powerful Communist Party in Western Europe. In the same year the DC leader excluded the leftist parties from the Italian national coalition government. In the spring of 1948, Italy held its first parliamentary election since Mussolini established his regime. The result was a DC triumph. Christian Democracy would hold power in Italy for the next forty-five years without interruption.

It was the traditional arts of favour-based politics that were at the heart of the DC's appeal to the mafia. The Sicilian DC came to comprise a myriad of local factions based on patronage. The faction leaders could offer exactly the kind of personal relationships that mafiosi preferred. The exchanges between politicians and criminals that had become so difficult under Fascism could at last be restored: one hand washes the other, as the Sicilian saying goes.

The alliance between men of honour and DC politicians was hardly a secret. In the lead-up to the momentous polling day of 1948, Don Calò and his *compare*, the boss of Mussomeli, Giuseppe Genco Russo, attended a sumptuous DC electoral lunch in Villa Igea, a Palermo hotel that had been one of the Florio family's old palaces. The two mafiosi sat at the same table as some of the party's leading lights. In 1950, when Genco Russo's oldest son married, Don Calò was a witness at the ceremony, as was the DC president of the Sicilian regional assembly. Encounters like these were not shamefaced and secret. When politicians and bosses met in this period, they often intended to be seen together because their encounters advertised the solidity of the alliance between the informal power of the mafia and the official power of the new political grandees.

It was the DC that finally, in 1950, brought the land issue in Sicily to a conclusion. The way they did it was typical of their methods. The redistribution of the remaining estates was entrusted to a quango that became a patronage engine for local

DC politicians. Corruption was endemic; one third of its budget went on administrative costs. In the meantime many landowners gave in to the inevitable and began disposing of their land. They often sold it to mafiosi, including Don Calò, who then made a huge profit reselling plots to individual peasants.

In 1950, the government also announced a massive programme of investment for the backward economy of southern Italy. It was to be a major turning point in the history of the mafia. From now on, if the organization wanted access to Sicily's major sources of wealth, it would have to turn to professional politicians and not landowners. The restoration of Italy's democratic system – and of the mafia's role as the island's informal state – was nearing completion.

Still, despite all this evidence, the exact extent of Don Calò's power within the honoured society is not known. Some later mafia turncoats denied that he was ever boss of the whole of Sicily. Indeed, it is said that Don Calò and his successor, Giuseppe Genco Russo, irritated other mafia leaders because of their high media profile. 'Did you see Gina Lollobrigida in the newspaper today?' one mafioso used to say, referring to the notoriously coarse and ugly Genco Russo.

We do not know how centralized the mafia was after liberation. A conservative guess is that during the pangs of its rebirth after Fascism, the mafia bosses first re-established communications between themselves. They then sought information direct from the places where political decisions were taken, and a leader or leaders with diplomatic skill to balance their own competing interests. Don Calò was in a very good position to fulfil that transitional role.

He would never have admitted as much, of course. In a newspaper interview given just before his death, the wily old capo put about a modest account of his job. 'The fact is that every society needs a category of person whose task it is to sort out situations when they get complicated. Generally these people are representatives of the state. But in places where the state doesn't exist, or is not strong enough, there are private individuals who . . .'

Intrigued, the interviewer let slip the word 'mafia'.

'The mafia!' Don Calò murmured with a smile. 'Does the mafia really exist?'

Don Calò died peacefully in the arms of his nephew on 10 July 1954. The press recorded his last words as being, 'How beautiful life is.' He is said to have left a fortune of 1 billion lire, although there is no way of confirming this report; the true extent of mafia wealth for most of its history is destined to remain mysterious. At Don Calò's lavish funeral, a slew of political and criminal dignitaries followed a hearse drawn by four black-plumed horses. Villalba town hall and the DC headquarters were closed for a week; an elegy was pinned to the church door:

> Humble with the humble,
> Great with the great,
> He showed with words and deeds
> That *his* mafia was not criminal.
> It stood for respect for the law,
> Defence of all rights,
> Greatness of character:
> It was love.

During Don Calò's life, the peasants of Villalba had often cited a more down-to-earth couplet about him: 'Cu avi dinari e amicizia, teni 'nculu la giustizia' – 'He who has friends and cash, can take justice up the ass.'

Meet the Grecos

The long-term future of the mafia lay not in little Villalba, but in the traditional mafia strongholds around Palermo. The mafia's recovery from the battering it was given by 'iron prefect' Cesare Mori was due in large part to the fact that its methods worked at the grass roots in these areas. And those methods worked in good measure because, in an unstable society, they enabled men of honour to bring wealth and status to their families.

The years 1946–7 saw a particularly savage mafia war in the citrus fruit village of Ciaculli, set on the sea-facing slope of a high ridge just to Palermo's east. As a later parliamentary inquiry into the mafia discovered, the war set two related blood families against each other. From their struggle would emerge some of the most powerful mafiosi of the coming decades. At first glance the Ciaculli war of 1946–7 seems to come right out of Sicilian folklore. It is what outsiders often expect the mafia to be about: debts of honour that lock families into spiralling pagan feuds. It sounds like a case of 'blood washes blood', to quote an overused Sicilian saying. But some of the facts shed a different light on the story, and on what 'family' means to the mafia.

One surname had commanded unconditional respect in the Ciaculli area for generations: Greco. In 1946, men bearing that name ruled both Ciaculli and a neighbouring village, Croce Verde Giardini. The two Greco clans probably had a common ancestor in Salvatore Greco, named in the Sangiorgi report as *capomafia* in Ciaculli at the turn of the century. As if to show the close ties that bound them, both branches of the family chose their children's first names from the same narrow range of options; between them there numbered three Francescos, three Rosas, three Girolamas, four Salvatores and four Giuseppes.

Nicknames were essential. The good relations between the two families had been cemented when the Ciaculli boss had married the Giardini boss's sister.

The war that set the Giardini and Ciaculli Grecos against each other began in earnest on 26 August 1946. The victims were the two patriarchs of the Ciaculli branch of the family, two brothers aged fifty-nine and seventy-seven. The ferocity of the attack on the two old mafiosi – machine-guns and grenades were used – left no doubt as to its importance.

Yet again, no one was ever convicted of the double murder. But in Ciaculli everyone suspected that the boss of Giardini, another Greco, had masterminded the assault; he was known because of his war record as 'Piddu the lieutenant'. The Ciaculli Grecos acted on their suspicions a few months later. Two of Piddu the lieutenant's men fell victim to the short-barrelled Sicilian shotgun they call a *lupara*. In revenge for this act of revenge, the Giardini *cosca* kidnapped two of their enemies. Only their clothes were ever found. (Sicilians refer to such disappearances as *lupara bianca* – 'white shotgun' – killings.)

The struggle between the two Greco clans came to a climax with a full-scale gunfight in the piazza in Ciaculli on 17 September 1947. First an important member of the Giardini *cosca* was cut down by a blast of machine-gun fire. Watching from a balcony were two Greco women: Antonina (fifty-one) and Rosalia (nineteen), the widow and daughter of one of the Ciaculli bosses killed the previous year. When they noticed that the man below them had not died of his wounds, they went down into the street and finished him off with kitchen knives. (It is exceptionally rare for women to take part in the military aspects of mafia activity in this way.) Antonina and Rosalia were fired on in their turn by the brother and sister of their victim; Antonina was wounded and her daughter killed. Their attacker was then himself shot and killed by Antonina's eighteen-year-old son.

Palermo bosses began to put pressure on Piddu the lieutenant to bring an end to the carnage. Clamorous incidents like the battle in Ciaculli drew unwanted public attention towards the whole mafia system. What is more, with the deaths of the two old Greco brothers from Ciaculli, Piddu the lieutenant was expected to take on responsibility for the welfare of *both* branches of the feuding family. His status among bosses would depend in part on how he faced up to that responsibility.

Piddu sought the help of the boss of nearby Villabate, a capo who was feared and particularly respected because of his family ties to some important US mafiosi. This was a period when the comparatively extravagant wealth of many US men of honour gave them great prestige back in Sicily. One sign of this influence was that at around this time the term 'Family' was imported from America as a name for mafia organizations (*cosche*) whose members are by no means all related to each other. Joe Profaci, born in Villalba, was a Brooklyn waterfront gangster, later named by Joe 'Bananas' Bonanno as being the head of one of the five New York Families. At the time of the Greco war Profaci was resident in Sicily and it seems that he played a key role in bringing peace to Ciaculli.

Piddu the lieutenant followed the advice he was offered by Profaci. Two of his orphaned nephews were given posts on the fruit farm he managed; it produced the tangerines for which Ciaculli is famous. The Greco cousins who had been at war were soon co-owners of a citrus fruit export business, and also partners in a bus company. Peace brought prestige to Piddu the lieutenant. His relationship with the Villabate mafia was formalized when his son married the Villabate boss's daughter.

The police had little idea what had caused all the bloodletting between the Grecos. Since the initial double murder, a wall of *omertà* had blocked their investigations. Police contacts in Ciaculli said that the mayhem was triggered by a desire for vendetta following a dispute seven years earlier between cousins at the Festival of the Crucifix. The festival took place every year in Ciaculli on 1 October. On that day in 1939, six young men from Giardini came to Ciaculli to watch the crucifix being exposed to the adoration of the faithful. Two of them were the sons of Piddu the lieutenant. Following the example of the locals, they went into the church and brought out a pew to sit on. An argument over the pew developed with boys from Ciaculli of a similar age, among them a cousin of the two Giardini Greco boys. On the way home later that evening, the Giardini party suddenly found themselves faced by a group of Ciaculli Grecos armed with revolvers and knives. Piddu the lieutenant's son Giuseppe, seventeen years old, was shot dead. His Ciaculli cousin was wounded; four years later he died in prison of natural causes while awaiting trial.

So a family feud, according to the rumours in Ciaculli, was the origin of the war that would explode in 1946. But historians are now rather sceptical about this theory. What actually happened is not in question. The issue is whether this adolescent spat would really have been allowed to become the catalyst for a hecatomb that put at risk mafia interests in the whole area east of Palermo. It is also striking that six of the victims in the war did not bear the Greco name. At stake was the control of the fruit business at a time when the mafia was emerging from under the thumb of Mussolini. In other words, this was probably a war between *cosche* – or factions within a *cosca* – which was motivated by power and money, and not between blood families motivated by honour and vengeance.

The implication is that Piddu the lieutenant stored up his son's death in 1939 and used it after the event to justify his calculated bid to control the whole Ciaculli–Giardini area in 1946–7. Once he had killed the Ciaculli bosses, he then set the mafia rumour machine to work to retell the story of the war as if it all began with the teenage cousins fighting over a church pew, as if it was all a matter of blood. When a boss is seen to look after his kin, his mafia honour and his status in the community are bolstered; he becomes known as someone whose friendship is worth cultivating. By making out that he was aggressively defending his own family, Piddu the lieutenant was simultaneously boosting his business reputation.

In other words, the likelihood is that a version of the 'rustic chivalry' myth was once more being used as a tool of mafia interests. There is a precedent for this kind of deception in Ciaculli itself. Back in 1916, the village priest was shot dead. The Grecos, as leading members of Ciaculli's religious confraternity, arranged the funeral and took a prominent role in it. At the same time they put about the rumour that the priest was a philanderer who had been killed by a husband he had cuckolded – a 'typically Sicilian' crime of passion and family honour, it would seem. In reality the priest, an honest and courageous man, had been trying to bring to light the Grecos' crooked management of Church property and charity funds.

Because of this manipulation of the truth, when the Giardini Grecos emerged victorious from the war of 1946–7, they would have been able to look back on their role in it with greater tranquillity. Piddu the lieutenant could tell himself that he had reconciled his duties as a father with his duties as a capo. He is just one example of the care that mafiosi devote to managing the delicate entanglement of business and family. Much of that care is made manifest in rules. Regulations about the place of family members within the mafia organization are constantly made, bent, broken, and made again: no more than two sons of the same father may be allowed membership of any given Family; sons whose mafiosi fathers have been killed in a power struggle are barred from becoming members for fear that they will seek revenge.

By playing the rules carefully, men of honour can turn their blood families into mafia dynasties. The Grecos are the leading case in point. One of Piddu the lieutenant's sons, Michele, was in his early twenties at the time of the war of 1946–7. Thirty years later, Michele Greco became boss of bosses. He was the very archetype of a mafia capo: unsmiling, taciturn, given to speaking only in maxims and allusive parables. VIPs, ranging from bankers to aristocrats, were invited to hunt and dine at his estate. There was also a heroin refinery in the grounds and, on one notable occasion during the mafia war in 1982, tens of mafiosi – virtually the entire Partanna Mondello Family of Cosa Nostra – were murdered there following a barbecue. Michele

Greco dressed expensively and conservatively, deporting himself with an almost ecclesiastical dignity; his nickname was 'the Pope'. His manner was not due to reticence or affectation; it was part of a professional skill-set that had been handed down by his forebears through the best part of a century.

The Greco war of 1946–7 pacified Ciaculli. But calm would not return to the rest of the island until Salvatore Giuliano, the last bandit, was shot down.

The Last Bandit

From its beginnings in the 1860s and 1870s, the mafia always had an intimate and duplicitous relationship with bandits; the honoured society used and protected bandits when it needed to, and then betrayed them to the police the moment they became an inconvenience. The pattern was repeated for the last time in the 1940s with Salvatore Giuliano, the most famous and murderous bandit of them all. But the Giuliano story is more than the grisly coda to the history of Sicilian brigandage. It set the seal on the mafia's re-emergence from under the Fascist iron fist, and it may also have marked the beginning of the democratic Italian state's collusion with terrorist acts against its own people.

At the peak of his notoriety, Salvatore Giuliano made himself as accessible for photojournalists as he was elusive for the authorities. Consequently his features are still instantly recognizable in Italy. In one of the most familiar photographs he looks straight into the camera, his thumbs hooked inside the belt from which his holster hangs, his jacket pushed behind his hips to reveal a loose shirt unbuttoned at the neck. Giuliano had what is called an open countenance. By a recent calculation forty-one biographies of him have been written since his death – more than of any other person in post-war Italian history. Each book has promised finally to reveal the secrets hidden behind that broad, handsome face.

Despite all these books, it took cinema properly to grasp the fundamental truth that, in the Giuliano story, seeing and understanding are not the same thing. Francesco Rosi's masterpiece *Salvatore Giuliano* was made in 1961 – a decade after the bandit's death. It was shot on the mountains around Montelepre that were Giuliano's stronghold; the extras were peasants from the same area; a woman who had recently lost her son played Giuliano's mother in the scene where she identifies his body; Rosi even used the real bandit's rifle. All this care to ensure the film's authenticity makes it even more striking that the protagonist himself is only ever shown from behind or from an oblique angle; his famous face is hidden behind binoculars or masked by his mother's shawl. He appears most frequently in the distance, dressed in a white overcoat, as if he were a blank in the centre of the picture, an empty screen on to which the other characters each project their own version of the story. The truth about Giuliano lies not in the figure of the bandit himself, Rosi is suggesting, but somewhere in a tangle of relationships between the bandits, the peasants, the police, the army, the politicians, and the media. At the centre of that tangle was the mafia.

Salvatore Giuliano was the youngest of four children from a peasant family in Montelepre in the mountains some fifteen kilometres west of Palermo. As a boy he worshipped all things American; this love of America was also one of the few constant features of his romantic and muddled political beliefs.

Giuliano's career in banditry began in the autumn following the Allied invasion. He was twenty-one years old and working as an errand boy for an electricity company when the *carabinieri* caught him with a sack of black-market grain. He shot his way out of trouble and took to the hills, leaving a *carabiniere* dead on the ground behind him.

He machine-gunned the second of his many victims among the forces of order three months later. A dozen members of his family were arrested on suspicion of sheltering him. Early in 1944, with his help, they staged a breakout from Monreale jail that gave a huge boost to his prestige as well as providing the nucleus of his gang.

For the next year Giuliano ran his band in the classic fashion; most of its members came together for black-market operations, robberies, or kidnappings, and then melted back into the community when the job was done. Their leader had a rough-edged charm and a gift for publicity; he made a point of cultivating a 'Robin Hood' fable around himself. But intimidation and bribery were more effective than corny myths in ensuring the silence and collaboration of those around him. His pitiless execution of anyone suspected of betrayal gives the lie to the 'robber prince' image; the number of his victims has been estimated at a staggering 430.

Giuliano's relationship with the mafia also fits a classic pattern; he would not have been able to survive these early years and build his band into the most successful in Sicily without protection from men of honour. When he kidnapped someone, the captive's relatives knew that they had to turn to the local boss who would ensure a safe return in exchange for a portion of the ransom. In other words, the mafia 'taxed' both the bandit leader and the people he persecuted.

It was later revealed by one of Giuliano's closest collaborators that he had been through a mafia initiation ritual. Mafia supergrass Tommaso Buscetta said that he was presented to Giuliano as 'the same thing'. If true, this does not necessarily mean that the bandit was an integral part of the association; initiating him was more likely to have been a way of reinforcing his loyalty and keeping watch on his activities.

What distinguishes the last bandit from his predecessors is the fact that he became involved in political ideology. The separatists were the first to try to recruit him to their cause. In the spring of 1945, Giuliano met with separatist leaders including the son of Tasca Bordonaro, the former mayor of Palermo under AMGOT. The bandit demanded 10 million lire in return for joining the proposed separatist army. He was beaten down to 1 million, plus the rank of colonel, and the promise of arms and uniforms. Like some other bandit leaders, Giuliano did his part in the failed separatist uprising by attacking five *carabinieri* barracks. Nor did the workaday criminal activity cease; the band also held up the Palermo–Trapani train. Despite Giuliano's efforts, elsewhere the main thrust of the separatist revolt was crushed.

The decline of separatism looked as if it might leave Giuliano politically orphaned. Things seemed bleak for him in 1946 because the state was finally organizing an effective military response to the bands, while at the same time the mafia was beginning to abandon the outlaws it had protected. One after another, bandits were either killed or captured. It was often contacts between the police and mafiosi that led to the arrests. As so often in the past, an expedient line was being drawn between bandits who could be sacrificed and mafiosi who kept close to political power. The police found some of the bandit leaders dead – dispatched by hands unknown. In the communities of western Sicily, the mafia, once again, was posing as a force for 'order'.

Giuliano responded publicly to the crisis with his habitual panache, by announcing that he had put a price on the Minister of the Interior's head. Yet he would also have to win new political friends if he were to achieve his aim of being pardoned when Sicily reached a definitive political settlement. He decided to offer his guns in the struggle against Communism. Through an American journalist, he sent a letter to President Truman in which he complained of the 'intolerable baying of the Communist hounds' and announced his commitment to fighting the red menace. The results of the elections in April 1947 for the new Sicilian regional assembly came as a shock to Giuliano, as they did to many others. The leftist parties, united in a People's Bloc, made huge gains; they took nearly 30 per cent of the vote and became the biggest single grouping. It was the cue for the so-called 'King of Montelepre' to commit his most infamous crime.

Salvatore Giuliano's name will be associated for ever in Italian memories with a place – Portella della Ginestra. Today, nowhere in Sicily seems more bleak and haunted by violence than this piece of open ground at one end of a valley between Piana degli Albanesi and San Giuseppe Jato. It was here that peasants came together to celebrate May Day in 1947. Families assembled in their best clothes for a picnic, a song, and a dance; their donkeys and painted carts were decorated with banners and ribbons. It was to be a celebration of the freedoms that had returned after the fall of Fascism.

At 10.15 a.m. the secretary of the People's Bloc from Piana degli Albanesi stood up amid the red flags to open proceedings. He was interrupted by loud bangs. At first many people thought they were fireworks, part of the celebration. Then the bullets fired by Giuliano's men began to find their mark. Ten minutes of machine-gun fire from the surrounding slopes left eleven dead, among them Serafino Lascari, aged fifteen; Giovanni Grifò, aged twelve; and Giuseppe Di Maggio and Vincenzo La Fata, both seven years old. Thirty-three people were wounded, including a little girl of thirteen who had her jaw shot off.

The impact of the massacre on the local communities was profound and lasting. When Francesco Rosi came to film the Portella della Ginestra sequence for *Salvatore Giuliano*, he asked 1,000 peasants to go back and enact exactly what they, their friends and relatives had been through fourteen years earlier. Events nearly slipped out of the director's control. When the gunfire sound effects started, the crowd panicked and knocked over one of the cameras in the rush to escape; women wept and knelt in prayer; men threw themselves to the ground in agony. One old woman, dressed entirely in black, planted herself before the camera and repeated in an anguished wail, 'Where are my children?' Two of her sons had died at the hands of Giuliano and his band.

Despite public outrage at the horrors of Portella della Ginestra, the 'King of Montelepre' remained at large for a further three years. Following the massacre, the molten lava of social conflict in post-war Sicily slowly hardened into a new political landscape dominated by the Christian Democrats. It was these political changes, rather than the fury and sorrow aroused by Giuliano's actions, that began to make him look like a wild anachronism. The electoral victories secured by the DC slowly removed the need for his clamorous brand of anti-Communist terror.

Giuliano continued his attacks on peasant activists and institutions, but the members of his band gradually fell into the hands of the authorities – often with the help of information from the mafia. At the same time, Giuliano's actions became more difficult to read. In the summer of 1948, he killed five mafiosi including the boss of Partinico. It is not known exactly why. Not surprisingly, many people identify this as the moment when Giuliano's fate was sealed. Nevertheless a year later he was still powerful enough to murder six more *carabinieri* in an ambush at Bellolampo just outside Palermo.

All this time investigations into the Portella della Ginestra massacre plodded on amid growing speculation that someone – possibly the Minister of the Interior – might have ordered Giuliano to carry it out. The bandit himself wrote a public letter, taking sole responsibility for the murders and denying that there was anyone behind him. He claimed that he had only intended his men to fire above the heads of the crowd; the deaths had been a mistake. He cited the fact that children had died as evidence that it was an accident: 'Do you think I have a stone in place of a heart?' The 800 spent rounds of ammunition found at the scene are enough in themselves to make this denial ring dreadfully hollow.

Speaking at Portella della Ginestra on the second anniversary of the massacre, Sicilian Communist leader Girolamo Li Causi, who had become a Senator since surviving Don Calò's grenade attack in Villalba, publicly called on Giuliano to name names. The appeal led to an extraordinary public exchange. Li Causi received a written reply from the bandit leader: 'It is only men with no shame who give out names. Not a man who tends to take justice into his own hands; who aims to keep his reputation in society high, and who values this aim more than his own life.'

Li Causi responded by reminding Giuliano that he would

almost certainly be betrayed: 'Don't you understand that Scelba [the Minister of the Interior, a Sicilian] will have you killed?'

Giuliano again replied, hinting at the powerful secrets that he possessed: 'I know that Scelba wants to have me killed; he wants to have me killed because I keep a nightmare hanging over him. I can make sure he is brought to account for actions that, if revealed, would destroy his political career and end his life.' No one was sure how much of this to believe.

In the summer of 1950, Giuliano's captured associates were finally arraigned in Viterbo near Rome for the trial that was supposed to answer all the questions. But no sooner had the hearing got under way than the mysteries deepened when Giuliano's body was found in the courtyard of a house in Castelvetrano – outside his mountain realm.

The film *Salvatore Giuliano* opens with images – meticulously based on reality – of the bandit's dead body lying face down in the small courtyard in Castelvetrano. He is dressed in socks, sandals, and a blood-soaked vest; there is also a small stream of blood dried into the beaten earth beneath him. His right hand, on which a diamond ring is visible, is stretched out towards a Beretta sub-machine-gun. In fact the sequence is shot through with irony; as Rosi knew very well, the 'real' scene of Giuliano's death was as much a fake as this cinematic version. When the press came to photograph the bandit's body, the *carabinieri* claimed that they had killed him in a furious gunfight. But a courageous investigative reporter soon exposed the official account as a fiction; the headline read: 'The only thing certain is that he is dead.' Once the official version of his death had been discredited, a more likely account emerged: Giuliano was shot in his bed, probably by his cousin and lieutenant Gaspare Pisciotta – an agent of the *carabinieri*; the *carabinieri* themselves moved his body into the courtyard to be photographed as the basis for a cover-up. Quite *what* they were covering up was to remain obscure. But the fact remains that Giuliano was killed when he very probably could have been captured, and there were certainly politicians, policemen, *carabinieri*, and mafiosi for whom he was less dangerous dead.

In the Viterbo courtroom, the members of Giuliano's band fed the frenzy of public suspicion. The Minister of the Interior, Mario Scelba, was again said to have been involved in the plot to carry out the Portella della Ginestra slaughter. The accusations were often contradictory or vague – passing the responsibility upwards to politicians and policemen evidently served the bandits' interests – but it was nonetheless an alarming and disconcerting spectacle. In the end the judge concluded that no higher authority had ordered the massacre, and that the Giuliano band had acted autonomously. Their aim had been to punish local leftists for the recent election results.

The verdict left few people satisfied simply because there were too many pieces of the puzzle that did not fit. Although it would be futile now to try to solve the mysteries surrounding Portella della Ginestra and Salvatore Giuliano, it is certainly worth listing some of the evidence. Ever since Giuliano's death, 'behindologists' have been trying to assemble a coherent picture out of these and other facts:

- Several witnesses recalled that Giuliano received a letter just before he carried out the Portella della Ginestra atrocity. When he read it, he destroyed it carefully and told the members of his band, 'Boys, the hour of our liberation is at hand'; he then announced the plan to attack the peasant celebration. No one has ever discovered who sent the letter.
- After the massacre at Portella della Ginestra, the Chief of Police in Sicily met senior Monreale mafiosi at his house in Rome. There they handed him a written testimony by Giuliano which he in turn seems to have sent to the home address of the chief prosecutor at the Palermo Court of Appeal, a man who may also have had contacts with Giuliano. The testimony has never been found.
- The same Chief of Police had a regular correspondence with Giuliano through the same mafia channels. On at least one

occasion he actually met the bandit leader – they shared *panettone* and two different kinds of liqueur.

The one man able and possibly willing to reveal the truth about Portella della Ginestra was Gaspare Pisciotta, Giuliano's dapper cousin who betrayed and probably killed him on behalf of the *carabinieri*. While he was with the band he had a pass, signed by a colonel in the *carabinieri*, that allowed him to move about the island freely. He had even visited a doctor under the supervision of another officer – he suffered from tuberculosis. During the Viterbo trial, Pisciotta had proclaimed, 'We are one body: bandits, police and mafia – like the Father, the Son and the Holy Spirit.'

At the conclusion of the Viterbo trial, Pisciotta was given a life sentence for his part in the events at Portella della Ginestra. While he was in prison – he spent his time writing an auto-biography and doing silk embroidery – it became clear that the authorities were starting to give more credit to some of his evidence. There was to be a new trial at which he would be charged with Giuliano's murder. Perjury and other charges were to be made against police and *carabinieri*. Pisciotta contacted an investigating magistrate and said that he was intending to reveal much more than he had done before.

On the morning of 9 February 1954, Pisciotta made himself a cup of coffee. Into it he stirred what he thought was his tuberculosis medicine. He took an hour to die, his body tormented by the violent head-to-toe convulsions that are the characteristic symptom of strychnine poisoning. His auto-biography vanished.

Pisciotta was poisoned in the Ucciardone prison in Palermo – the mafia's university of crime since the middle of the nineteenth century. It is inconceivable that he was killed without at least the honoured society's approval. Whatever the mafia's involve-ment in the intrigues behind Portella della Ginestra and the Giuliano band, it was they who made sure that the whole truth would never come out.

7

God, Concrete, Heroin, and Cosa Nostra
1950–1963

The Early Life of Tommaso Buscetta

It was in the years following the Second World War that the Sicilian mafia probably began to refer to itself as Cosa Nostra – 'our thing'. It may be that the most recent of the mafia's many names is an American import. The theory has been put forward that the term originated in Sicilian immigrant communities in the United States; it was 'our thing' because it was not open to criminals from other ethnic groups. But because the mafia does not leave written minutes of its dense, cryptic internal conversation, there is no way of proving where 'Cosa Nostra' came from. In fact there would be little to be gained even if there was, because names are not very important to the Sicilian mafia. Most mafiosi would probably prefer it if 'their thing' did not need a name at all, if its existence could be intimated solely by the raising of an eyebrow or a stony glare. As was the case with the other titles that have come and gone over the years – the Brotherhood, the honoured society, and so on – the arrival of 'Cosa Nostra' does not signal any real change in the organization's structure or methods.

Tommaso Buscetta himself believed that Cosa Nostra was an ancient name. There is no evidence that he is right, and this theory probably carries no more authority than his belief that the Sicilian mafia had medieval origins. Buscetta may have been a bad historian, but he was a good witness, and the testimonies and memoirs that he left stretch back over half a century. It is after the Second World War that Buscetta enters the mafia's story. Between 1945 and 1963 – the dramatic year in which he, like many other important mafiosi, fled abroad – he saw first-hand some profound developments in Cosa Nostra. It was between 1950 and 1963 that it established a new governing body

– the Commission or Cupola – and remade ties with the American Cosa Nostra that drew it deep into the transatlantic heroin trade. It was in these years that Cosa Nostra found what was both a new source of income and a bond in its relationship with the political system: concrete.

Buscetta's opinions are not always entirely reliable. For one thing, he remembered the 1950s as the 'good old days' of Cosa Nostra, when respect and honour reigned rather than greed and violence. As will become clear, he was far from right about that. For another thing, Buscetta spent a good deal of his career away from Sicily. So the history of the Sicilian mafia is not the same as either the story Buscetta told or the story he lived. But because Buscetta will appear and reappear in these pages from this point onwards, it is important to get a sense of both the man and the mafioso.

There is a reason why so much is known about Tommaso Buscetta's sex life. The first man of honour to explain Cosa Nostra's rules to Judge Giovanni Falcone was also the first on whom Italian journalists could test a cherished theory: that mafiosi were prime examples of the archetypal macho, sensual, Mediterranean male. Buscetta's famous features – the thick, generous lips, the round, sad eyes – made him look as if he had been cast for the role.

On one occasion in 1986, Italy's best-known journalist and TV presenter, the genial raconteur Enzo Biagi, went to New York to interview Sicily's most famous mafia boss. To do so he had to brave an elaborate Drug Enforcement Administration (DEA) witness protection operation: a rendezvous at the Hotel St Moritz on Central Park with a security chief known only as 'Hubert', a long drive upstate, a change of car, and a thorough frisking. Biagi's reward was to spend several days with Buscetta in an isolated, temporary safe house. After winning the mafioso's trust by chatting about family and football (Buscetta was a Juventus fan), Biagi blurted out the question he had been burning to ask the legendary 'boss of two worlds', self-confessed multiple murderer, and keeper of some of the darkest secrets in Italian history: 'Do you remember when you made love for the first time?'

Buscetta was happy to play up to what the chirpy Biagi called 'gallismo meridionale' – 'southern cockerel-ism'. After all, not long before, Buscetta had been recalling altogether more stressful memories in the vast, bombproof courthouse at the Ucciardone prison in Palermo. The questions he had had to field then were about international drug-dealing and bloodshed, and the audience were the mafiosi who had killed six members of his family in the space of three months. Talking about his sexual conquests with Biagi was a stroll on the Marina by comparison. It also got him on to one of his favourite subjects, his own magnetism: 'Mother Nature gave me charisma, I've got something extra.' It was his (less than entirely convincing) explanation for the fact that other men of honour so revered him.

For the record, Tommaso Buscetta lost his virginity at the age of eight. It was the first and only time he ever had sex with a prostitute; the woman in question also ran a roadside stall selling olives, cheese, and anchovies, and requested only a bottle of olive oil in return for her favours. Thereafter romance played a big part in Buscetta's life. Of his three marriages – punctuated by countless infidelities – the first was contracted when he was sixteen, the second overlapped with the first, and the third was to a prominent Brazilian lawyer's daughter who was twenty-two years his junior. In all, Buscetta had six children. He was also that very rare thing, a groovy don – at least as far as his dress-sense is concerned. One picture, taken in Brazil in 1971 or 1972 soon after he met his third wife, shows a smiling Buscetta in cream shoes, cream slacks, and a frilly shirt unbuttoned down to the solar plexus to reveal a delicate pendant. He even experimented with plastic surgery on his nose – this long before the US authorities asked surgeons to alter his appearance for his own protection.

Even if Buscetta was happy to present himself as a typical specimen of Mediterranean male, he was certainly not a representative *Homo mafiosus* in this respect. Discreet sleeping around is no crime for men of honour, but mistreating a wife certainly is. Buscetta's marital record brought him trouble within Cosa Nostra. In the 1950s, he was suspended from the association for six months because of his infidelities. In 1972, he was extradited from Brazil and incarcerated in the Ucciardone prison in Palermo where he learned that the head of his Family had wanted to expel him altogether from Cosa Nostra for disrespecting his first two wives.

Buscetta was born on the eastern outskirts of Palermo in 1928 into a family without mafia connections. Although he was the seventeenth of seventeen children, he was not an urchin drawn to crime by dint of having no other chance in life. His father ran a workshop and employed fifteen people making and selling decorative mirrors. Like many Sicilian families, however, the Buscettas fell on hard times during the war, and the teenage Tommaso became a black marketeer. He also began stealing petrol, jam, butter, bread, and salame from the Germans, building up in the process an extensive network of contacts in the Palermo underworld. Once the Allies had liberated Sicily, Buscetta joined a group of about fifty young tearaways who went to Naples to fight the Nazis – partly out of a sense of adventure, and partly in the hope of booty. After two or three months of sabotage and ambushes on the Italian mainland, he returned to Sicily with his reputation greatly enhanced. It was then that he began to be approached by 'cautious, mysterious men who expressed themselves in allusions, nuances, and hints'; he felt they were watching him, assessing him. One in particular – a furniture polisher – probed him about his attitudes to the police and magistrates, to family morality, and loyalty to friends.

The furniture polisher, one Giovanni Andronico, eventually proposed him for membership of the Porta Nuova Family of Cosa Nostra in 1945. Once the proposal was made to the capo, a note of Buscetta's name was circulated to all the Families in the Palermo area so that they could undertake their own investigations into his reliability and check that neither he nor any of his family had any relations with the police. Once the investigations were complete, it was Andronico himself who pricked Buscetta's finger with a pin during the initiation ceremony.

The Porta Nuova Family that Buscetta joined was comparatively small – there were about twenty-five men of honour in it – but very select. Among its members he discovered that there were four notables: the holder of the Sicilian franchise for a famous beer brand, a monarchist MP, a consultant psychiatrist, and Andrea Finocchiaro Aprile – the 'friend' of the mafia who was exercising his fiery rhetorical skills in the cause of Sicilian separatism. (This story, like some of the others that Buscetta relates about this period, has not been corroborated from other sources and must therefore be treated sceptically. They do, nonetheless, give a sense of the man's style.)

In 1947, another famous figure was introduced to Buscetta: Salvatore Giuliano, the last bandit. The young Buscetta was awed by Giuliano's presence, by the 'special light' that seemed to emanate from him. It seems that Buscetta was considerably less impressed by another man of honour he met early in his career, Giuseppe Genco Russo, the boss of Mussomeli, sidekick of Don Calò Vizzini, and the man whom other mafiosi referred to as 'Gina Lollobrigida' for his love of the media spotlight. For an urban sophisticate like Buscetta, Genco Russo embodied the coarse life of the Sicilian interior. He was by then a wealthy landowner and a DC politician, but he still kept his mule inside the house and the toilet outside (it was little more than a hole in the ground with a stone for a seat and no walls or door). This detail particularly struck Buscetta because, as he later recalled with horror, Genco Russo actually sat down and used the 'toilet' in front of him during their discussion.

Buscetta soon began to travel. He spent his first years abroad, from 1949 to 1952, in Argentina and Brazil. In 1956 he returned from another stay in Argentina with plans to resume the cigarette smuggling at which he had already proved to be adept. The

Palermo he found on his homecoming was just beginning to be buried in concrete – and its burial would seal a new kind of pact between organized crime and political power.

The Sack of Palermo

The 'sack of Palermo' – the building boom of the late 1950s and early 1960s – still inspires a certain melancholy in Palermo residents. To get a sense of that melancholy it is enough to head north-west along Palermo's main artery from the Quattro Canti, the crossroads where the four quarters of the baroque city meet. To walk along the via Maqueda, past the giant bronze lions guarding the Teatro Massimo, and carry straight on into via Ruggero Settimo, is to follow the path of Palermo's expansion during the late nineteenth century. Via Ruggero Settimo in its turn becomes the broad avenue of via Libertà, where the fashion-conscious bourgeois of the Florio era promenaded in their carriages and built splendid Liberty-style homes. On the eastern side of via Libertà, just before the Giardino Inglese, the road opens out into Piazza Francesco Crispi, its centre now dominated by giant advertising hoardings. Almost lost below the hoardings are the rusting scrolls and spikes of an elegant wrought-iron railing – an oddly grand surround for the shabby open-air car park that lies behind. The railing is, in fact, all that remains of one of the jewels of Florio-era Palermo.

The Villa Deliella once stood here, surrounded by palm trees. Its watchtower, slim windows, grand balcony, and gently sloping roofs were designed in lush homage to the architectural idiom of the Tuscan Renaissance. On 28 November 1959 – a Saturday – plans to knock down the Villa Deliella were submitted to the city council. They were approved in time for demolition to begin that very afternoon, and by the end of the weekend one of the most beautiful houses of the Liberty era was rubble. A month later the Villa Deliella would have reached fifty years of age, and therefore become protected by law. The loss of the Villa

Deliella is only one minor tragedy of the many that together make up the story of the sack of Palermo.

When the Second World War ended, Palermo was still, in essence, the same city it had been in the Florio era. Beyond via Libertà, the Conca d'Oro with its villas and its lemon groves began. Palermo as a whole was ringed with countryside. But despite its beauty, it was a city in desperate need of renewal. Allied bombing was partly responsible; it had rendered homeless an estimated 14,000 people, many of whom lived in shacks amid the rubble of the old centre where the bomb damage was concentrated. The pressure to build more homes only increased in the 1950s when there was an influx of provincials seeking the public sector jobs available now that Palermo was, once again, a capital city, the headquarters of the new regional government. Between 1951 and 1961, the population increased by 20 per cent to 600,000.

A post-war building boom was inevitable – as it was in much of Europe. It was also inevitable that the often giddily high expectations for planned urban development would meet with disappointment. But the results of Palermo's expansion in the 1950s and 1960s were far worse than anyone could have foreseen. When the building boom ended, a good portion of the city centre still lay in ruins; much of the rest was a half-abandoned slum; and some of its finest private homes – baroque and Liberty alike – had been demolished. The verdant periphery had disappeared under concrete; most of the lemon groves of the Conca d'Oro had fallen to the bulldozer. Before this transformation, it was hard to detect the signs of the city's underworld in its fabric of buildings and streets. The sack of Palermo turned every crumbling baroque palace, every jerry-built council estate, every aspirational apartment stack, into a monument to corruption and crime.

But the story of the sack of Palermo is in essence political rather than architectural, and as such it begins in another city. When Italians complained that the mafia was 'run from Rome', they were expressing a simplistic version of an undoubted truth.

The politicians, contractors, and mafiosi responsible for the sack of Palermo were at one end of a chain that led directly to the headquarters of the Democrazia Cristiana in Piazza del Gesù, Rome. It was there that a whole new structure of patronage government for the democratic era was invented.

The first link in the chain was Amintore Fanfani, a tiny, proud-chested university professor from Arezzo in Tuscany. When he became leader of the DC in 1954, he proposed a wholesale modernization of the party that aimed to put more power in his own hands. The DC dominated government, but was itself susceptible to the influence of outside powers: above it, the Vatican and the titans of Italian industry; below it, the conservative grandees who supplied packets of votes in the towns and villages. There was little to guarantee the DC's claim on the support of these outside powers. To deal with them on at least equal terms, Fanfani believed that the party had to become a modern mass organization and a power in its own right.

In Sicily, as in much of southern Italy, the Fanfani revolution meant two things. First a new breed of political manager – the 'young Turks' – emerged within the party. Second, the same men colonized every post they could in local or national government, in quangos and nationalized companies. Thus, in the new DC, the charismatic old notables had to come to terms with dynamic young bureaucrats of sleaze who set about 'occupying the state' on behalf of their party and themselves. The young Turks turned public resources into DC resources.

The young Turk principally responsible for implementing Fanfani's programme on the island, and the next link in the corrupt chain linking Rome and the pillaging of Palermo, was Giovanni Gioia. Gioia did not have a high public profile – Tommaso Buscetta describes him merely as having a 'glacial character' – and he never held any office in the municipality, but he was nonetheless fundamental to the history of the city in these years. Insiders called him 'the Viceroy' and regarded him as having sole power to choose who became mayor of the city. At twenty-eight, in 1954, Gioia became secretary of the DC in the province of Palermo and, just as importantly, the head of the party's Organization Office, which supervised membership. Gioia, or one of his followers, controlled the Organization Office for nearly a quarter of a century thereafter. It was from this key position that the glacial Gioia would reinvent Sicilian machine politics.

Under the Fanfani reforms, local DC Party branches were set up across Italy for the first time; there were fifty-nine in Palermo, for example. The aim, ostensibly, was for Christian Democracy to reach out into the community, recruiting new members as it did so. Fanfani's followers issued new party slogans proclaiming an end to '*maccheroni* politics' – votes exchanged for favours. The mechanics of this political modernization were simple: the DC's new structure meant that card-carrying members elected party leaders; the members also voted for delegates who in turn selected election candidates. Or, at least, that was the theory. In practice, in Palermo, the power lay not in the hands of the members, but in Gioia's. With Gioia in the DC Organization Office, party memberships were given out to friends, relatives, dead people, and names plucked from the phone book. The more members a local party section had, the more delegates it could send to conferences. In other words, the more members a local party chief like Gioia could boast, the more power he was able to offer upwards to the head of a national DC faction like Fanfani. The prodigious rise in membership on the island subsequently gave the Sicilian DC, and Fanfani, a disproportionate influence within the DC nationally. (The little university professor from Tuscany served as Prime Minister six times.)

All this power that 'Viceroy' Gioia won *within* the new Democrazia Cristiana in Sicily counted for nothing in itself; it only paid off if the party could distribute the jobs, licences, grants, and other valuable assets that came from control over local and regional government. The scene was set for the sack of Palermo, and for the emergence of its two principal villains: Vito Ciancimino and Salvo Lima, both elected to Palermo city council for the first time in 1956, and both supporters of Gioia. It was they who would turn *maccheroni* politics into concrete politics.

As characters, Ciancimino and Lima were almost diametrically opposed. Ciancimino was born the son of a Corleone barber. He was arrogant, loutish, bright, and ambitious. Photos of him from the sack of Palermo era show a weaselly man in a sharp three-piece suit, a garish tie, slicked-back hair, and a dark pencil moustache. Lima, the son of a municipal archivist, had a law degree and began his working life in the Bank of Sicily. With eyes bulging beneath neatly curling hair, he was as chubby, polished, and slippery as Ciancimino was thin, coarse, and abrasive.

Despite both being in Fanfani's faction of the DC, Ciancimino and Lima had different mafia connections. Hence the fact that Tommaso Buscetta had a contrasting view of the two. He recalled Ciancimino as 'a pushy Corleonese embezzler' who only looked after his own interests and those of the men of honour from his home town. Buscetta – a long-standing opponent of the Corleonesi – channelled the votes under his own control towards Lima. The two were never on first-name terms, and they were both men of few words, but their business relationship was based on what Buscetta called 'reciprocal respect and sincere cordiality'. Knowing Buscetta's passion for opera, Lima would make sure he always had tickets for the Teatro Massimo.

Between them Ciancimino and Lima turned the seemingly humble municipal post of Officer of Public Works into Italy's most shameless and lucrative patronage engine. Between 1959 and 1963 – the hottest years of the construction fever, and the years when first Lima and then Ciancimino were at the Office of Public Works – the city council granted 80 per cent of 4,205 building permits to just five men. The bulk of Palermo's economy depended on publicly funded construction at this time. So a huge proportion of the city's wealth was routed through those same five names.

But they were not, as one might expect, construction magnates of national stature. In fact they were nobodies. The Office of

Public Works was supposed to award licences only to civil engineers qualified to carry out the work. Yet someone had spotted a regulation dating back to 1889 – before modern civil engineering qualifications existed. According to this regulation, companies that were granted a licence to build needed to have a 'master mason' or a 'capable contractor' on their books. The council kept lists of such approved persons. All five of the major licensees in the Lima–Ciancimino system were on a list that dated back to before 1924. Even then, it looked very much as if the qualifications they cited were false; one of the five men seemed to be nothing more than a coal merchant. Another turned out to be a former bricklayer; he subsequently took a job as a doorkeeper and janitor in one of the apartment blocks whose construction he had supposedly supervised. When interviewed, he said merely that he was a guy who did what he had to do to get along; he had signed the licences as a favour to some 'friends'.

Seen from the point of view of the 'friends' rather than that of the politicians, the sack of Palermo began on the ground, with the mafiosi who now kept watch over the building sites just as they had once kept watch over the lemon groves. Vandalism and theft could bring any construction project to a halt if the local boss chose. The second storey of mafia influence was a dense tier of small subcontractors who supplied workers and materials. Even if Lima and Ciancimino had not existed, politicians and construction companies would have had to come to terms with mafia power at this level. On the level above them were the great building entrepreneurs, men tied into corrupt webs of friends, relatives, clients, and cohorts. Those networks become thicker and thicker the more one probes, connecting local politicians, municipal functionaries, lawyers, policemen, building contractors, bankers, businessmen, and mafiosi.

At the centre of these networks were Gioia, Lima, and Ciancimino. The young Turks' method was a form of carefully engineered chaos, as the story of the Palermo town plan shows.

It began its life back in 1954. Each time it looked close to being finalized, in 1956 and 1959, hundreds of amendments were made in response to applications from private citizens, many of whom turned out to be DC politicians, mafiosi, or their relatives and associates. The plan gained definitive approval in 1962. Yet by then the Office of Public Works had granted many building licences on the basis of the 1959 version; blocks of flats already stood on many areas that the plan was supposed to regulate. Even after 1962, people with access to Gioia, Lima, and Ciancimino could get the plan altered in their favour, or have breaches of planning law retrospectively condoned. Only in one case was the demolition ordered of an illegally built structure. No company dared come forward to take on the contract to knock it down.

There is, it must be said, a certain genius in these methods. The town plan, like the regulations setting out who could be awarded planning permission, was meant to prevent illegal building. Under Lima and Ciancimino, these measures only served to place firmly in the politicians' hands the power to build illegally. It is a bitter paradox with which Italians are all too familiar: the more severe a rule is, the higher the price a politician is able to command for finding a way round it.

Then there is the fear factor. A glimpse into the fear that the 'pushy Corleonese embezzler' Ciancimino was able to marshal is provided by the Pecoraro case. In August 1963, Lorenzo Pecoraro, a partner in a construction firm, sent a letter to Palermo's chief prosecuting magistrate, accusing Ciancimino of corruption. The case derived from an incident in which Ciancimino had illegally denied a building licence to Pecoraro's company. At the same time, a licence to build on an adjacent plot was granted to another company, Sicilcasa, despite the fact that this successful proposal broke planning regulations in a number of respects.

Pecoraro's company responded to the block on their project by approaching Ciancimino through an intermediary, the mafia boss of the area in which it was hoped to build. The approach seemed to bring results; Ciancimino promised to release the licence. But then there was a delay caused by a council workers' strike. By the time it ended, Pecoraro had, for reasons that remain unknown, lost the mafioso's support. Ciancimino had also adopted a new tactic: the executives in Pecoraro's company were told that they could only have their licence if they deposited a large bribe with Sicilcasa.

In his letter to the investigating magistrate, Pecoraro named a witness who had stated that Ciancimino was secretly a partner in Sicilcasa. Pecoraro also said he had a tape recording of Ciancimino boasting that Sicilcasa had given him an apartment for nothing. On another recording in his possession, Pecoraro claimed, a notary could be heard confessing that he was the channel through which huge backhanders paid for planning licences were passed to Ciancimino's Office of Public Works. Between the events of the Sicilcasa case and Pecoraro's report to the prosecutor, the mafia boss and three partners in Sicilcasa were arrested and charged with murder.

Despite all this evidence, the magistrate to whom Pecoraro had addressed his original report found no grounds for a prosecution. It was only the following year that the case came under the scrutiny of a parliamentary commission of inquiry. But when it did, Lorenzo Pecoraro submitted a letter to the inquiry, stating that his earlier accusations against Ciancimino were the 'result of mistaken information'. Furthermore, he said, the rumours that Ciancimino was corrupt had originated with people who had a personal and political grudge against him. Ciancimino, Pecoraro concluded, had 'always been exemplary for his decency and honesty'. The matter ended there.

Ciancimino and Lima were the most infamous DC politicians of their day, the fastest travellers on a new and serpentine road to wealth and influence. For decades, a horde of favour-broking politicians turned the Sicilian DC into a maze of clienteles, cliques, factions, counter-factions, covert alliances, and open feuds. Even experienced journalists despaired of ever making any sense of it all. At the end of the 1960s, one such journalist went to report on what he called a leading DC 'personage'. On entering the politician's new Palermo apartment, the journalist found a marble interior, old master paintings, furniture of every style, splendid ancient gold artefacts in perfect condition; displays of jewels, coins, archaeological relics; priceless ivory crucifixes keeping promiscuous company with pot-bellied jade Buddhas. I was stunned, as if I had stumbled across a corsair's swollen heaps of booty. The personage in question was there, dressed in a long dressing gown, smooching with his election chiefs who had come in from the area. This was the same man I had met at the beginning of his political career when he had been as poor as Job. I could not help wondering what witchcraft had caused that river of gold to spring from the ground around him.

The power that, along with others, Ciancimino and Lima first created for themselves in the 1950s would last for decades. Ciancimino was only arrested in 1984 and was not finally convicted until 1992 – the first politician ever to be successfully prosecuted on charges of working for the mafia. On 12 March of that same year, Salvo Lima – at that time a member of the European parliament – fell victim to a less ponderous judicial system: he was shot dead near his home in Palermo's beach-resort suburb of Mondello. Whether Lima was actually a man of honour, as some mafia 'penitents' claim, is not known for certain. Buscetta thought it unlikely, but said that Lima's father had been a member of the central Palermo Family. What nobody doubts is that it was Lima's former friends who brought his political career to its sudden end.

As always, mafia stories raise questions about Italy as a whole; in this case about why Italian public opinion was not so outraged about what was going on in Sicily – and in large parts of southern Italy – that people tried to do something about it. The reasons, it need hardly be said, are related to both power and money.

The most frenetic years of the sack of Palermo coincided with Italy's economic 'miracle'. In the late 1950s and early 1960s, the country's economy launched itself into the era of mass industrial production. The vast funds channelled into the hands of the young Turks of the South derived from the surging profits made by the factories of Genoa, Turin, and Milan in the North. Yet big business was not inclined to protest about the waste. Many of the larger construction companies were northern owned. Northern industry also needed the consumer market of southern Italy to be primed by public spending. Much of the cash scattered with such abandon in Palermo and Naples found its way back up the peninsula to buy radios, fridges, scooters, and cars. As a political bonus, the Christian Democrat electorate of the South also helped keep the Communists out. For decades, many Italians preferred to follow a principle made explicit by a leading right-wing journalist in the 1970s: 'Hold your nose and vote DC.'

And then, of course, through all the changes of the 1950s and 1960s, the DC could always count on the support of the Church. The Cardinal Archbishop of Palermo between 1946 and his death in 1967 was Ernesto Ruffini, a man who brought the Church in Sicily to the nadir of its culpable blindness towards the reality of organized crime and political collusion. Ruffini was from Mantua in northern Italy, but he was more Sicilian than the Sicilians when it came to his obstinate love for the island. Here, Ruffini imagined, faith went deeper than individual belief; it had sturdy roots in peasant customs whence it reached up into political life. Sicily was the closest thing the world had to the ideal of a wholly Christian society. Being Sicilian and being a believer were inseparable. If the Italians had a mission to bring the Church's message to the globe, then the Sicilian people had a special mission in Italy: when the industrial North looked like succumbing to materialism, the happy island of faith would set an example and be a fortress against Mammon, Marx, and the Masons. In short, Ruffini's was an entirely fabulous picture of the world.

The Cardinal Archbishop had a righteous terror of Communism and dismissed the mafia as the invention of Communist scare tactics. Back in 1947, after Salvatore Giuliano's band machine-gunned peasant families at Portella della Ginestra, the Cardinal had written to the Pope to explain that, while he 'certainly could not approve of violence' from any side, 'resistance and rebellion were inevitable in the face of the Communists and their bullying, lies and deceitful scheming, their anti-Italian and anti-Christian theories'. Before the 1953 general election he announced that it was a 'grave obligation' for believers to put their cross against the DC symbol on the ballot paper. More than that, to fail to vote against the 'impending threat posed by the enemies of Jesus Christ' was nothing less than a mortal sin. Despite this admonition, and despite five years of DC government in Rome, the percentage of the vote won by the DC in Sicily dropped dramatically, from just under 48 per cent to just over 36 per cent. There were clearly a great many mortal sinners on the island.

It was the beginning of a period of rapid social change that could only seem like a long wave of catastrophes to a man with Ruffini's views. The 'rampant apostasy' of Communism spread through some regions of Italy in a dense network of cooperatives and housing associations. Then the economic boom of the late 1950s and early 1960s tore great numbers of southern peasants from the local fabric of their religion, and sent them to work in the building sites and factories of Genoa, Turin, and Milan. Even government and Church censorship could not stop Hollywood from schooling young people in the ways of immorality and consumerism.

Worse still, the Christian Democrat party, the Holy Church's chosen vanguard in the crusade against the atheist Left, did not seem to be living up to its lofty mission. The DC's disorganization, its vicious factional infighting, and its casual handling of public money were even becoming the subject of guarded criticism by senior churchmen. What is more, after its setback at the 1953 election, the DC was forced to rely on lay allies to its right or left in order to stay in power. Some of the party's factions were trying to lure the Socialist Party away from its alliance with the Communists; the Socialists went on to form a government with the DC for the first time in 1963. At the same time, what the Church called free-market 'liberaloids' and 'agnostics' were gaining strength within the DC as it grappled with the reality of managing a modern capitalist economy.

None of these developments altered Ruffini's support for the DC, or his lifelong struggle to keep the contemporary world at bay. But he could not dodge the mafia issue for ever. On Palm Sunday 1964, Cardinal Ruffini issued a pastoral epistle, entitled 'The true face of Sicily', which was the ecclesiastical hierarchy's first ever official, explicit public statement about the mafia – ninety-nine years after the word was first used. 'The true face of Sicily' denounced a fiendish media conspiracy to slander the island; it was a conspiracy with three prongs. The first two were the most celebrated figures to be associated with Sicily in the 1950s and 1960s: Danilo Dolci, known as the 'Sicilian Gandhi', whose non-violent campaigning drew attention to the hardships endured by the fishing and peasant communities of western Sicily; and aristocratic novelist Giuseppe Tomasi di Lampedusa, author of *The Leopard* (1958) with its sensuous, disconsolate portrayal of the island's history. The third prong of the media offensive against Sicily was the mafia, which, Ruffini asserted, was nothing more serious than the same kind of crime that could be found elsewhere in Italy and around the world.

Joe Bananas Goes on Holiday

Giuseppe 'Joe Bananas' Bonanno had the longest reign of any of the bosses of the five New York mafia Families. Born in the tiny seaside town of Castellammare del Golfo in 1905, he fled Mussolini's Italy in the 1920s, fought with Salvatore Maranzano, his fellow Castellammarese, against Joe 'the Boss' Masseria, and was then installed as capo of his Family following Lucky Luciano's pacification of the New York mafia in 1931. For over three decades thereafter, Joe Bananas led the Brooklyn-based Bonanno clan. While he was in charge, it remained the most Sicilian of the New York Families. The island's dialect was the language of choice; Bonanno himself always struggled with his English. Along with the Magaddinos in Buffalo, to whom Joe Bananas was related by blood, the Bonanno Family maintained close links with the mafia back in Castellammare del Golfo.

In 1983, Joe Bananas published *A Man of Honour*, a ghosted narrative of his life, that is shot through with absurdly self-justifying references to 'my Tradition' – by which he means the mafia. One of the most interesting chapters in *A Man of Honour* tells of how, for several weeks in October 1957, the Brooklyn boss returned in style to where his 'tradition' originated. His account of what he calls his holiday in Sicily is replete with the usual old cant about a time-honoured Sicilian culture of family and self-respect. This was Bonanno going back to his roots, to a little world that he had forsaken in his search for freedom and success. On arrival, he expressed admiration for the Italians' 'art of living' and 'exuberance of warmth'. More perceptively, he called the Italian government machinery 'appalling'. He exemplified this particular point by recounting that, when he first landed at Rome airport, he was pleasantly surprised to be given a red-carpet welcome by the DC Foreign Trade Minister – another native of Castellammare. 'Wouldn't my friends in the FBI have been astonished at this princely welcome?' was Bonanno's comment. There is no evidence to support this highly improbable story. But the fact that it has been repeated many times ever since perhaps demonstrates the low esteem enjoyed by the Sicilian DC. Once in Palermo, the visiting don was taken in hand by a deputation of dignitaries and men of honour who proudly showed him the splendid new motorways and office buildings that were mushrooming around the city. Perhaps not surprisingly, this early view of the sack of Palermo did not count among the highlights of his holiday.

Although one would never guess it from the humbug in Bonanno's book, his holiday in Sicily was in fact a turning point for Cosa Nostra on both sides of the Atlantic. For it was then that the US mafiosi franchised out heroin-trafficking operations to their Sicilian cousins. Just as importantly, during the same trip the Sicilian mafia created a Commission on the model of the one instituted in New York at the end of the Castellammarese war. These two, intimately related developments set the stage for all the drama of mafia history over the next four decades. Everything that happened up to and beyond the staggering violence of the 1980s and early 1990s can be traced back to the time when Joe Bananas came to visit.

The surviving information about what actually went on during that trip is partial but highly suggestive. Making sense of the evidence, understanding not just the 'what' but the 'why', is a delicate matter. This is one of those occasions when Italian historians of the mafia have found it imperative to stretch a tissue of informed supposition across the nervure of available fact. What follows here is therefore a mixture of knowledge and supposition, a mixture created with one central aim: to get inside the *politics* of Cosa Nostra. The word 'politics' is important and it is not used loosely. For if the gearing-up of Cosa Nostra's involvement in heroin was a matter of business, then the creation of the Commission was the mafia equivalent of constitutional

politics. To non-Italians there is no longer any scandal in referring to mafiosi as businessmen; the mafia boss, seen as the sinister
double of the company CEO, is now a cinematic cliché. However, outside Italy, writers are still reluctant to dignify the machinations of murderers and thieves with the word 'politics'. But
as those who strive to understand the Sicilian mafia in its homeland have learned over the decades, to use any other word is
gravely to underestimate Cosa Nostra. For the Sicilian mafia
has a politics in a very literal sense. As today's investigating
magistrates continually emphasize, Cosa Nostra will never be
beaten unless it is understood that it is a shadow state, a political body that sometimes opposes, sometimes subverts, and
sometimes dwells within the body of the legal government.

During the Palermo leg of his Sicilian jaunt, at a lavish five-
hour luncheon at Spanò's sea-front restaurant, Joe Bananas met
Tommaso Buscetta – or at least he did according to Buscetta's
own version of events. At that time Buscetta – the future 'boss
of two worlds' and history-making mafia defector – was only
an up-and-coming Palermo soldier. So the meeting at Spanò's
understandably made a much bigger impression on him than
it did on Joe Bananas, who did not bother to record it among
his holiday memories. Buscetta, by contrast, effusively expressed
the 'enchantment' he felt as he talked intimately with a man
he described as 'distinguished, elegant, endowed with a special
intelligence'. Buscetta had evidently found a role model.

Apart from the then gap in status between Buscetta and
Bonanno, there are many other differences between their two
accounts. By the time Buscetta came to tell his story, he was a
pentito living under a witness protection programme; when Joe
Bananas told his in 1983 he was, at most, in semi-retirement. For
that simple reason Buscetta is by far the more credible of the two.
(Although it should be said that the US authorities took *A Man
of Honour* seriously enough to call its author before a grand jury.)

It is striking, but hardly surprising, that both mafiosi left
exactly the same highly significant hole in their stories: narcotics.

Joe Bananas maintained that he never had anything to do with drugs, which were, he protested, completely alien to his Tradition. Buscetta scoffed at the very idea that Bonanno's visit to Sicily had anything to do with heroin. Both men were lying outright, but both were also lying in a more interesting way than might at first appear to be the case. This was not just a question of two criminals trying to protect themselves.

Buscetta was undoubtedly a more interesting liar than his Italian-American role model. Until his death, he continued to deny that he had ever made any money from drugs. Rather contradicting himself, Buscetta also maintained that 'There is no one in Cosa Nostra who is unconnected with narcotics trafficking.' These statements bear all the hallmarks of the kind of tactical lie at which Sicilian men of honour are particularly adept. In fact, the signs are *so* clear that they are probably deliberate. Buscetta was making sure that anyone who knew how to decode him – Judge Falcone, for one – would understand perfectly well *both* that he was lying *and* that he was not prepared to say any more on what was evidently an important subject. It was such a big lie that he had to throw a cordon sanitaire around it to stop it infecting the credibility of the other things he had to say.

All this lying became necessary because, by the time Joe Bananas stepped off the plane in Palermo, Cosa Nostra was at a crossroads in the United States. In a sense it had to decide just how illegal it wanted to be. The American mafia has always worked most freely in those markets – like liquor under Prohibition or numbers rackets – which are 'only just' illegal and therefore not a source of embarrassment to its political friends. Gambling was another case in point; the 1940s and 1950s were years when organized crime invested heavily in the rapidly expanding, desert betting Mecca of Las Vegas. The same principles of semi-illegality apply to the mafia's intervention in labour relations. It offered its services to employers to break strikes; or it worked with trade unions to extort money from workers and employers alike. Either way, Cosa Nostra did not move too far from the protective shadow of legal institutions and powerful interest groups in the upper world.

Drugs were a different kind of business. In 1950, Tennessee Democrat Senator Estes Kefauver picked up on alarming warnings from the Federal Bureau of Narcotics about the mafia's international drugs network. The hearings of Kefauver's 'Senate Special Committee to Investigate Crime in Interstate Commerce' were televised in 1951. Americans watched dozens of mafiosi taking the Fifth Amendment in the face of Kefauver's questioning. Frank Costello, the former bootlegger and king of New York City's slot machines, did not allow the camera to show anything above his shoulders; but the 'hand ballet' that accompanied his shifty explanation of his business interests became the emblematic memory of the hearings for many viewers.

In the wake of the Kefauver hearings, the United States rediscovered its fear of the mafia – a fear that had last gripped the nation nearly half a century earlier, in the days of the 'body in the barrel' murder and Lieutenant Joe Petrosino. This time round, the dread and fascination aroused by the mafia was also fuelled by a drugs scare. Politically motivated hype and a minor publishing boom followed; one writer, inspired by Kefauver, called the mafia 'history's greatest threat to morality' and 'the principal fount of all crime in the world'. America's long postwar love affair with the mafia had begun.

For all the exaggeration and plain fantasy in the new American mafia scare, and despite the fact that J. Edgar Hoover, director of the FBI, still refused to believe that the mafia existed, the effects of the Kefauver hearings for men of honour were severe. They led the Federal government to introduce the Narcotics Control Act in 1956; it stipulated a forty-year maximum prison sentence for drug-related offences. According to one US police estimate, by the time Joe Bananas came to Sicily to 'unwind', as he put it, one in every three members of the Bonanno Family had been arrested on narcotics charges. The other New York mafia Families were faring even worse; the Lucchese clan had lost a reported 60 per cent of its personnel.

As both Buscetta and Bonanno later explained, the leadership of the American mafia introduced a ban on drug-dealing in response to the crackdown. (Both of them also claim, wholly improbably, that only other mafiosi broke it.) There are many other sources that confirm that there was indeed such a policy, and each of those sources also points out that the rule was routinely transgressed. It was, in fact, a façade intended to create the impression that the organization had distanced itself from 'junk'. But it could only be a stopgap measure.

To make matters worse, in 1956–7, Cosa Nostra's most important offshore base for its narcotics smuggling – the Caribbean island of Cuba – was also slipping from its grasp. Fulgencio Batista y Zaldìvar's corrupt and brutal dictatorship was already crumbling in the face of Fidel Castro and Ernesto 'Che' Guevara's much-publicized guerrilla war in the Sierra Maestra. The Americans finally withdrew military aid from Batista in 1958 and Castro entered Havana in January the following year.

So it does not take a very 'special intelligence' to work out why Joe Bananas came to unwind back in Sicily in 1957. His organization needed three things for its narcotics interests: a trustworthy source of manpower; a partner to which it could franchise out a business that had become too damaging to run hands-on; and a new transhipment base.

In Sicily, Cosa Nostra's control of territory was far more thorough in the 1950s than it was in the United States – hence Bonanno's delight at his red-carpet reception. But Italy's attractions did not end with its gratifyingly 'appalling' government machinery; it also had a negligible rate of drug consumption, and therefore no political interest in addressing the problem. Moreover, because Sicilian men of honour moved around the Mediterranean in the course of their cigarette smuggling, it would not be much trouble for them to pick up refined heroin from the South of France while they were at it. A new wave of Sicilian emigrants was now heading west across the Atlantic too, taking their belongings in trunks that were the perfect vehicle for drug transportation. The only reason that Joe Bananas did not take his holiday any earlier is that the Kefauver hearings had caused high-level transatlantic contacts between the two mafias to be broken off.

Over four days in October 1957, Joe Bananas chaired a series of meetings between Sicilian and American mafiosi in Palermo's Grand Hotel des Palmes. The hotel – the most splendid in the city at the time – was one of the Whitaker family's town houses before it was converted, and Richard Wagner famously orchestrated his last opera, *Parsifal*, there in the winter of 1881–2. The Hotel des Palmes is now where most Italian journalists stay when they go down to Palermo to cover the latest mafia outrage or trial.

Although there are no first-hand accounts of those meetings, and although the police took little interest in goings-on at the hotel, the list of guests makes for instructive reading. Among those seen coming and going from Bonanno's suite were his *consigliere*, Camillo 'Carmine' Galante, and other leading members of the Brooklyn-based Bonanno Family, including Giovanni 'John' Bonventre and the capo's immediate deputy, Frank Garofalo, who had been in Castellammare del Golfo since the summer. The US delegation also numbered senior members of the Magaddino-run Family from Buffalo, as well as Lucky Luciano, who was living in exile in Naples after being expelled from the US in 1946. The most important Sicilian presence was the head of the Family in Castellammare del Golfo, a Magaddino like Joe Bananas' relatives in Buffalo. The others also had strong transatlantic ties.

Some have suggested that Buscetta was there too. He flatly – and therefore suspiciously – denied that the meeting ever took place. Whether or not he was there, the names of those who certainly did attend give a pretty clear idea of what kind of meeting it was: the gathering in the Hotel des Palmes reforged a link between the most American of the Sicilian *cosche* with the most Sicilian of the American Families. In other words, this was not a conference between *the* American mafia and *the* Sicilian mafia as such. It was a business convention rather than a diplomatic summit. And drugs were the business on the agenda.

The Sicilian mafia's involvement in the US drug trade was not a novelty in 1957. Morphine was already being smuggled through Palermo, in cases of oranges and lemons, back in the 1920s. Nick Gentile mentions how drugs would be hidden in shipments of cheese, oil, anchovies, and other Sicilian products. New York boss Joe Profaci's Mamma Mia Importing Company was one of many commercial fronts for narcotics trafficking. But the pattern of arrests and drug seizures in the years after Joe Bananas' holiday in Sicily show a marked increase in Sicilian involvement, and much closer cooperation between the two shores of the criminal Atlantic; the effects of the decisions taken among the red carpets and gilt-framed mirrors of the Hotel des Palmes are measurable. As a US attorney would later remark, everyone at the meeting was a 'narcotics track star'. Heroin was to be the new transatlantic sport for men of honour.

There was one invitee at the Hotel des Palmes who stuck out like a toad in a tutu. It was Giuseppe Genco Russo – the 'Gina Lollobrigida' who had once voided his bowels in front of a young and incredulous Tommaso Buscetta. By the time of the Hotel des Palmes meeting, Genco Russo had succeded Don Calò Vizzini as the authority in central Sicily and now enjoyed the undeserved reputation of being the 'boss of bosses' of the whole Sicilian mafia. At the time, as Buscetta makes clear, there was no such post – and even if there had been, it would not have been occupied by a man of honour from isolated Mussomeli. Genco Russo was probably at the Hotel des Palmes only because one of the American mafiosi present was a relative. Genco Russo did not have the power in Palermo, let alone in New York, to contribute much to the discussion at the Hotel des Palmes. But from this semi-detached perspective he did manage to pinpoint the political problem that came in a package with Joe Bananas' business propositions. He was overheard in the lobby croaking, 'Quannu ci sunu troppi cani sopra un ossu, beato chiddu chi pò stari arrassu' – 'When there are too many dogs going after one bone, it's best to stay out of the way.' In layman's terms, access to the North American heroin market on the scale envisaged by Joe Bananas was bound to trigger rivalries.

It was in order to manage these business rivalries that the Commission was created. Although Tommaso Buscetta keeps an implausible silence on the matter of narcotics, he goes into detail about how the idea for a Commission evolved. He explains that, after the fall of Fascism and before 1957, communications within Cosa Nostra in Sicily were intense but compartmentalized. Small groups of particularly influential men of honour from different Families would meet to discuss things in their usual telegraphic, allusive way; decisions would only evolve slowly, after long rounds of consultation.

The decision to create the Commission evolved in just this roundabout fashion. It was at the lunch at the Spanò restaurant that Buscetta first heard Joe Bananas suggest the creation of a Commission to the three or four Sicilian men of honour sitting immediately around him; he probably aired the idea to many others during his stay. Everyone seemed to like it. Once a consensus was reached in the habitual way, Buscetta himself undertook to turn Bonanno's suggestion into a working reality. Helping him were two young mafiosi who would play a crucial role in the coming history of Cosa Nostra: Gaetano 'Tano' Badalamenti, the underboss of Cinisi – where the *cosca* was closely linked to the Detroit Family; and Salvatore 'Little Bird' Greco – so called because of his small, delicate frame. 'Little Bird' was one of the Ciaculli Grecos who had survived the war of 1946–7. All three were to become major narcotics dealers.

This three-man constitutional working party – Buscetta, Badalamenti, and 'Little Bird' Greco – set the new ground rules for Cosa Nostra. Each province of Sicily was to have its own Commission. (It was not until 1975 that a Region or Inter-provincial Commission would be created for the whole island.) In the province of Palermo, there were too many Families – around fifty – to make it feasible to have a consultative body in which all of them were represented. Thus there would be an intermediate level, the *mandamento* (district), combining three neighbouring families; together the three families would choose a single representative from their *mandamento* who would take a seat on the Commission. To avoid too much power being concentrated in the hands of a few people, it was forbidden for anyone to combine the roles of capo of their Family and representative on the Commission. And the Commission's crucial function would be to make rulings on the murders of men of honour.

So the Palermo Commission was not a board of directors of the international heroin trade. It was actually a very carefully constructed representative mechanism – a creature of politics rather than of business. As such, there is nothing inherently new about it. It is now known from the Sangiorgi report that already in the late nineteenth century the *cosche* of the Palermo area had formal rounds of consultation and a unified system of trials. So – despite what both Buscetta and Bonanno themselves believed – the Commission was not a complete novelty in mafia history; it was a new solution to a problem as old as the mafia itself: how to combine territorial control with illegal commerce. That said, the creation of the Commission undoubtedly had epoch-making political implications; in effect, the power of life and death over other mafiosi was being taken out of the hands of the Family bosses.

The question is: 'Why now?' Why exactly did the gearing-up of Sicilian involvement in the narcotics business lead to the creation of such an elaborate constitutional apparatus? The answer that Italian historians have come up with leads to the heart of the relationship between business and politics within Cosa Nostra. And the best way to explain it is, once again, through the eyes of Tommaso Buscetta. For on this issue, as on so many others, Buscetta is a crucial but not entirely objective witness – crucial, in fact, for the very reason that he is not objective.

Buscetta sunnily describes the Commission as 'an instrument of moderation and internal peace', 'a good way of reducing the fear and risks that all *mafiosi* run'. This description is very much in tune with how he likes to visualize life in the mafia as a whole. Buscetta thinks of Cosa Nostra as a noble brotherhood rather than as a hierarchy; in his mind, men of honour are all peers, and the bond holding them together is mutual respect rather than obedience to a capo. 'We all felt we were part of a very special elite,' he says. It is a nostalgic vision that fits with the image Buscetta is trying to portray of himself – as a kind of roving emissary of the underworld. As such it is as captivating, and as implausible, as a party political broadcast. In reality Buscetta had very hard-headed strategic reasons for wanting the Commission to take the shape that it did, reasons that are best explained by looking at his career path.

There are essentially two types of career in Cosa Nostra; politics and business. A man of honour can climb the shadow state's internal ladder of promotion, becoming a *capodecina*, a *consigliere*, a capo, and so on upwards. Or he can develop his own commercial interests outside of his particular Family's territory, travelling the world to exploit the mafia's unrivalled criminal networking opportunities. Buscetta, despite the huge respect he commanded within Cosa Nostra, never rose above the rank of soldier, and he travelled very widely throughout his life of crime; thus he was a prime example of a mafioso who followed the second career path. As, for that matter, was Cola Gentile, the Sicilian-American man of honour of the early twentieth century.

Lucky Luciano is an interesting case in that he followed both routes at different stages in his life. Before he was imprisoned on pimping charges in 1936, his authority was territorial; he was at the head of what is sometimes called a power syndicate, a criminal gang that exacts an extortion tax from legal and illegal businesses in a given area. After being expelled from the US in 1946, Luciano did not settle in Palermo as might seem the natural thing to do for a Sicilian-born mafioso. He went instead to Naples on the Italian mainland whence he organized all sorts of illegal trafficking, including in narcotics. For the rest of his life he was therefore what is called an enterprise syndicate criminal, one who engages in illegal trade but does not have the power to control territory. A low-level Neapolitan crook once demonstrated this point in dramatic style by publicly slapping Luciano, who could do nothing to avenge this *sfregio*.

The point is that, as a man of honour who was more of an enterprise syndicate type than a power syndicate type, more of a narcotics businessman than an extortion-racket statesman, Buscetta had every interest in weakening the power of the heads of Families, in gaining more commercial autonomy for individual men of honour. With the surge in heroin trafficking between Europe and America, the high-flying young drug-dealers like Buscetta, Badalamenti, and 'Little Bird' Greco did not want their commercial wings clipped by the power syndicate bosses. The Commission was created – with Joe Bananas' support – as a new mechanism of mafia government. But the aim of its founding fathers was not to centralize control over the mafia; it was to apply overall rules that gave more freedom to individual mafiosi. The Commission was supposed to make the mafia more like the association of autonomous men of honour that Buscetta thought it should be.

As it happened, in the early 1980s the Commission metamorphosed into exactly the reverse of what Buscetta hoped. It would ultimately become, in the hands of the Corleonesi, the instrument of a dictatorship. And yet before that historical irony could unfold, another would be visited on Joe Bananas' plans to use the Sicilian mafia as tame manpower for the US Cosa Nostra's heroin operation. Even Buscetta, a man with great sympathies for the American mafia, felt that US mafiosi in the 1950s and 1960s often patronized their Old World colleagues, treating them like 'poor cousins', calling them 'zips' because they spoke Sicilian so fast. But once the zips were allowed into the traffic in heroin in North America, they did not prove as obedient as had been hoped. By the 1970s, the zips would be running the once-mighty Bonanno Family's drug operation.

When the Commission was founded in 1957 all of this still

lay far in the future. When Joe Bananas got on the plane to return to New York, the constant struggle to reconcile business and politics within the Sicilian Cosa Nostra entered a new and turbulent phase. Only six years after being set up, the Commission was temporarily dissolved in dramatic circumstances.

8

The 'First' Mafia War and its Consequences
1962–1969

The Ciaculli Bomb

Set alongside a road that climbs through the tangerine groves of Ciaculli, there is a monument commemorating one of the worst of the many horrors perpetrated by Cosa Nostra. Perhaps fittingly, the monument is not particularly attractive: a tall wedge of pink marble crowned with seven metal stars that perch in wisps of wire. On it are chiselled the names of four *carabinieri*, two military engineers, and a policeman. A glance at the list reveals that the mason made a small mistake as he began his work. Beneath the first name – Lieutenant Mario Malausa of the *carabinieri* – one can see signs that the name of another man with a lower rank has been chipped gently away. Absurdly, but somehow touchingly, someone must have pointed out that the hierarchies of military life must be preserved even in death.

The monument is set in a tiny garden from which the view is both stunning and disquieting. Here in Ciaculli, perhaps more than anywhere in western Sicily, the power of the mafia is made visible in the landscape. With one's back to the sea, one can see lines of tangerine trees rising towards the curved ridge of Monte Grifone. Turning to look at the ground below the monument's base, one discovers small square wells feeding into narrow channels – the arteries of the citrus groves, the pressure points that the mafia once squeezed to exert its territorial control. From this point, rows of trees run down through Ciaculli and Croceverde Giardini, the fiefdoms of the two branches of the Greco dynasty that fought out their war in 1946–7. Villabate, where a *cosca* has been rooted for as long as the mafia has existed, lies at the foot of the hill. To Villabate's west is Brancaccio, a new industrial quarter and a virtual no-go area for the authorities; the *carabinieri* station here is a villa confiscated from the local mafia.

So heavily fortified was it that the military police scarcely needed to do more than put a new sign over the door when they took over. Beyond Brancaccio and Villabate the sea stretches across the middle distance, an expanse wider than can be taken in with a single glance. Palermo lies further along the coastline to the west; its concrete arms stretch out eastwards to embrace what were once independent towns and villages of the hinterland. When a journalist asked a mafia defector from Brancaccio how he would tackle Cosa Nostra, his answer was simple: send troops along the two roads that lead up to Ciaculli and start shooting. 'They are all there,' he said.

As well as offering a panorama of a landscape that the mafia has helped shape, the monument at Ciaculli also marks a turning point in the mafia's history. It bears the date 30 June 1963. Mid-morning on that day, a man phoned Palermo police headquarters to say that a car had been left on his land where the monument now stands. The car, an Alfa Romeo Giulietta, had a flat tyre and its doors were still open. It was immediately clear what this might mean: in the early hours of the same morning, a car bomb – another Giulietta – had exploded in Villabate, killing a baker and a motor mechanic. Responding rapidly to the call, the police and *carabinieri* coaxed their vehicles up what was then a potholed track to find the abandoned car. On the back seat, clearly visible, was a tank of butane with the burned end of a fuse attached to the top. On seeing it, they secured the surrounding area and called in the army engineers. Two hours later, two bomb disposal experts arrived, cut the fuse, and pronounced the vehicle safe to approach. But when Lieutenant Mario Malausa made to inspect the contents of the boot, he detonated the huge quantity of TNT it contained. He and six other men were blown to pieces by an explosion that scorched and stripped the tangerine trees for hundreds of metres around.

There had been bloodshed on the streets of Palermo before 30 June 1963, of course. In 1955–6, two mafia Families fought out a brutal conflict when the city's wholesale market was moved from one territory to another. But most onlookers were relatively unconcerned. As one Rome conservative newspaper commented at the time: 'When it comes down to it, reciprocal elimination is a method that brings benefits for public order in Palermo . . . These last remnants of Sicilian crime are destroying themselves on their own initiative.'

After the Ciaculli bomb, no one could shrug their shoulders and argue that 'they only kill each other' or that the mafia was in its death throes. The papers rightly called it the worst crime since the days of the 'last bandit', Salvatore Giuliano. The police response was immediate: Villabate and Ciaculli were surrounded on the night of 2 July, their streets illuminated by rocket flares; forty people were arrested and a large quantity of arms confiscated. It was only the beginning of what would become the biggest round-up of suspects since the days of the 'iron prefect'. Three days after the tragedy at Ciaculli, under an enervatingly hot sun, an estimated 100,000 people, including the Minister of the Interior, followed the virtually empty coffins of the seven victims to Palermo Cathedral. The political pressure to take the mafia problem seriously became irresistible.

The Ciaculli car bomb marked a historical point of no return. Until then, every generation of Italians seemed doomed to 'discover' the mafia as if no one had ever heard of it before. Tajani's speech to parliament in 1875, the Notarbartolo murder in 1893, the iron prefect's Fascist 'surgery': with each outrageous killing or political crisis, an understanding of the problem had to be reconstructed from the ground up. Every time, as apathy, cynical politicking, and criminal complicity reasserted themselves, that knowledge crumbled once again into incoherent ruins. After the Ciaculli bomb, Italy began to remember and – slowly, painfully, confusedly – to learn.

The outrage of 30 June 1963 was a turning point for Cosa Nostra itself. It brought to an end what has become known as the 'first mafia war' – the title itself betrays how short is Italy's historical memory. The crackdown that followed scattered men of honour across not only Italy but the globe. Yet to this day, no one knows for certain who it was who left the Giulietta that morning in 1963. To this day, no one has ever been brought to justice for the murder of the seven servants of the state whose names are carved in pink marble above Ciaculli. However, one man is still strongly suspected of the crime: Tommaso Buscetta.

Like Chicago in the Twenties? The First Mafia War

In late 1962 and early 1963, explosions, car chases, and shoot-outs suddenly became regular events in Palermo. The papers said – with unconscious irony – that the Sicilian capital had become like Chicago in the 1920s. At first glance, the war of 1962–3 does indeed seem like a Chicago-style cliché; it could come from one of the tiresome gangster yarns that fill the true-crime sections of British and American bookstores. The first mafia war looks, in other words, like the usual cycle of tit-for-tat killings. But internal conflict in the mafia is never that predictable. For within Cosa Nostra, deceit and politics are as important as guns and bombs. The first mafia war may in fact have been the most cunningly fought of them all.

One 'Chicago' cliché can be dispatched straightaway. It was often thought that because of who the leading combatants were, the first mafia war was a struggle between the 'old' mafia and the 'new' mafia, between venerable landed bosses and audacious young hoods grown precociously rich on drugs and concrete. On one side, it was pointed out, was Salvatore 'Little Bird' Greco, the son of the Ciaculli boss murdered by Piddu the lieutenant Greco in 1946. In other words, 'Little Bird' was a scion of Cosa Nostra's most revered dynasty. Pitted against this mafia blue blood was Angelo La Barbera, the capo of Palermo-Centre. Angelo and his brother Salvatore came from nowhere; their father sold firewood for a living. From being street criminals they rose within the organization and took a major role in the sack of Palermo. Angelo La Barbera's territory took in much of the area around via Libertà where the sack was initially concentrated; he also had a good working relationship with DC young Turk, Salvo Lima.

It is worth taking a closer look at the figure of Angelo La Barbera to see whether he was really as 'new' a mafioso as he seems. In fact he is unusual in that, while he was being held on a prison island some years after the events of the early 1960s, he allowed himself to be the subject of a series of fascinating interviews by a British-based Italian journalist, Gaia Servadio.

Servadio was struck immediately by La Barbera's shrewd features, slick elegance, and 'lupine teeth'. But the man beneath these physical traits remained elusive. Servadio is as engaging and astute as she is brave, so it is certainly not her fault if her portrait of La Barbera could hardly be tagged 'intimate'. No gangster on trial for murder, as La Barbera was at the time of the interviews, was ever likely to give a great deal away; that much is understandable. But there is, one suspects, a more profound reason why Angelo La Barbera's individual identity is not captured by Servadio's pen: he probably did not have much of an individual identity to capture.

The mafioso was as rigidly stylised in his behaviour as an imperial Chinese courtier. Everything about La Barbera that Servadio observed was mannered: he had a slow, measured gait and openly disdained physical effort; he had a kind of poker-faced generosity; and he habitually referred to himself in the third person. La Barbera was also what his interviewer called an 'accomplished hypochondriac' – medical conditions make a good delaying tactic in court hearings. There is no way of knowing with any certainty, but it seems that all of his mannerisms had been learned from a time-honoured repertoire. One can only wonder how closely the way La Barbera carried himself would have aped the bearing of the 'taciturn, puffed up, and wary' Antonino Giammona back in the 1870s. 'New' mafioso he may have been, but Angelo La Barbera probably made sure he conformed to an old mafia style.

There is definitely nothing novel about the way Cosa Nostra acts as a ladder of social promotion for hard young men from poor backgrounds like Angelo La Barbera. The mafia has always been a meritocracy of violence. In fact there were blue bloods and barrow boys on either side in the first mafia war. An ally of 'Little Bird' Greco's was Luciano Leggio, the child of a humble peasant family who rose through the ranks and took over the Corleone Family in the late 1950s. On the La Barberas' side in the war was Pietro Torretta, a former member of Salvatore Giuliano's brigand band, and now boss of Uditore – the same territory ruled by Antonino Giammona a century earlier. A Torretta is even mentioned in Chief of Police Sangiorgi's report back in 1898. So neither side in the first mafia war had a better mafia pedigree than the other. The story about a 'new' mafia challenging an 'old' mafia – that staple of the true-crime genre – provides a misleading map of the battle lines.

And so to the war dispatches. The first mafia war was triggered when someone cheated on a drug deal. In February 1962, the La Barbera brothers and the Grecos were all members of a consortium that financed a consignment of heroin from Egypt, delivered to the southern Sicilian coast. A man of honour, Calcedonio Di Pisa, was sent to make sure it was safely forwarded to New York on the liner *Saturnia*. But the mafiosi in Brooklyn who collected the drugs found that the packages they received did not contain as much heroin as expected. The waiter on the *Saturnia* to whom Di Pisa had handed the drugs was tortured but did not reveal anything. Suspicions began to fall on Di Pisa himself. At a meeting of the Commission called to decide on the case, Di Pisa was acquitted of having stolen any of the drug shipment. But the La Barberas made plain their displeasure about the decision.

On 26 December 1962, Di Pisa was shot dead in Piazza Principe di Camporeale on the western edge of Palermo. He had just parked his car and was heading for the tobacconist's when two men fired at him with a .38 and a sawn-off shotgun. Other members of Di Pisa's Family were soon attacked. Then, in January 1963, the retaliation began when Salvatore La Barbera became the victim of a 'white shotgun' killing: his Alfa Romeo Giulietta was all that was found, burned out. His brother and capo Angelo also vanished, only to pop up in Rome to give a press conference; it was a way simultaneously of telling his friends that he was still alive, and making himself too public a target for his enemies to kill easily.

Angelo La Barbera was determined to continue the war after his brother's death. On 12 February, a huge car bomb – a Giulietta – destroyed 'Little Bird' Greco's house in Ciaculli. Despite being unharmed, 'Little Bird' responded in equally spectacular fashion. At 10.25 a.m. on 19 April, a cream-coloured Fiat 600 pulled up outside the Impero fishmonger's in via Empedocle Restivo. Some of the many housewives on the street at the time remembered thinking it odd that, in a drizzle, the car's soft top was open. Before they had time to reflect further, two men stood up on the seats and showered the fishmonger's with machine-gun fire. Two men were killed, including the fishmonger himself who was thought to be a La Barbera hit man; two people were wounded, one of whom was a passer-by. Whoever was in the shop at the time – probably Angelo La Barbera – was clearly expecting trouble because the occupants returned fire with a revolver and a shotgun. Later, as police recovered an arsenal of small arms from the shattered shop, Communist activists with megaphones toured the area in cars to demand action.

A Greco ally was the next to fall. The Cinisi boss was killed near the iron gate of his lemon grove by a bomb placed, inevitably, in an Alfa Romeo Giulietta. This dainty four-door family saloon was one of the symbols of Italy's economic miracle – 'svelte, practical, comfortable, safe and convenient', as the adverts proclaimed. But as the car bombs detonated in Palermo, the Giulietta was quickly coming to symbolize something rather more dangerous and, apparently, atavistic.

Investigators later surmised that this most recent Giulietta attack in Cinisi was a last desperate attempt by Angelo La Barbera to show that he could still reach his enemies. If it was, it did not work. La Barbera was finally put out of action in the early hours of 25 May 1963. What struck Italian public opinion about his shooting was not its ferocity – two cars pulled up beside him and their occupants fired repeated volleys of shots; nor was it the remarkable fact that La Barbera survived, despite being hit in his left eye, neck, chest, back, leg, and groin; nor was it even that doctors found another bullet lodged in his head from an earlier attack (perhaps he had some basis for his 'accomplished hypochondria' after all). What was surprising about the incident was rather where it happened. La Barbera was shot in viale Regina Giovanna, a residential street in Milan – the booming northern city where the Giuliettas were built. The headlines in the *Corriere della Sera* spelled out the city's surprise, and hinted at its attitude to 'typically Sicilian' behaviour: 'War between mafia *cosche* shifts to Milan. Sicilian, riddled with six bullets, tells police: "I don't know anything."' When the mafia spread beyond Sicily, the issue moved up the whole nation's political agenda.

If the first mafia war had really been no more than the usual chain of retaliatory killings set in a 'Chicago' built from true-crime stereotypes, it would have come to an end when Angelo La Barbera was arrested in a Milanese hospital; all the publicity that the war generated would have died down, and the Ciaculli bomb – which went off only just over a month after the La Barbera shooting in Milan – would never have happened. The war's brutal coda betrays the fact that it was a subtler affair. Most of the subtleties involve Tommaso Buscetta.

There are two accounts of Buscetta's role in the first mafia war. The first is the product of police work at the time and probably draws on anonymous mafia informers; the second is Buscetta's own, written more than two decades after the event. The official version is, broadly speaking, more credible. Buscetta's account needs to be treated with as much circumspection as the other parts of his testimony that have not been verified in court. He airbrushes drugs out of the picture and underplays his own cunning and aggressive role in the unfolding of hostilities. But as ever, 'the boss of two worlds' also adds both insight and intrigue to the story.

The official sources on the first mafia war place Buscetta on the La Barberas' side at the outbreak of hostilities. Buscetta may well have been in the fishmonger's that was machine-gunned by Greco men – he was certainly a frequent visitor. But it seems that when the Grecos began to look as if they would prove victorious, both Buscetta and Uditore boss Pietro Torretta decided to change their allegiances; losing mafiosi are rarely too proud to try and get a foot on the victor's rostrum.

Nevertheless, according to the official version, when Angelo La Barbera was shot and arrested in Milan, the result was a power vacuum in the Family that he had ruled, Palermo-Centre. Both Tommaso Buscetta and Pietro Torretta considered them-selves jointly to be Angelo La Barbera's natural successors; Torretta proposed himself as capo of Palermo-Centre and Buscetta as his deputy. But the Grecos thought Buscetta in particular a dangerous man to promote. The protracted dis-pute gradually reignited hostilities between Buscetta, Torretta, and the Grecos. Buscetta and Torretta acted first by ambush-ing two of their enemies in Torretta's house. A new spate of violence was just getting under way when, on 30 June 1963, the umpteenth Giulietta stuffed with TNT accidentally killed the seven members of the forces of order whose names are inscribed on the Ciaculli monument. The intended targets were once again the Grecos, but a puncture stopped the killers carrying through the attack. Whether those killers were Buscetta and Torretta in person, or merely men of honour acting on their orders, is not known.

By predictable contrast, in his own account of the first mafia war Buscetta presents himself as an impartial mediator and a good friend to both 'Little Bird' Greco and Salvatore La Barbera. He is much less kind about Salvatore's younger brother and capo, Angelo La Barbera, whom he blames for escalating the conflict – he calls him 'haughty and arrogant'. Buscetta admits to having accepted a contract to kill Angelo La Barbera, but claims that someone else carried out the shooting in Milan before he could. It is still not known for certain whether he was, in fact, involved.

The main thrust of Buscetta's story is to blame another man altogether for starting the trouble: Michele 'the Cobra' Cavataio, the new capo of the Family that had lost out to the Grecos in the war over the wholesale market back in the mid-1950s. It was Cavataio, Buscetta tells us, who carried out the murder that set off the war in the first place – the shooting of drug trafficker Calcedonio Di Pisa outside the tobacconist's. Buscetta's theory is that 'the Cobra' killed Di Pisa in the knowledge that the La Barberas would be blamed and that a war with the Grecos would be the result. Cavataio it was, according to Buscetta, who was also responsible for the Ciaculli bomb. The first mafia war, in essence, was all the result of a trick designed to play the La Barberas and Grecos off against each other.

Reading through these conflicting accounts, one begins to get a sense of why mafia wars so often failed to end in successful prosecutions. But what also becomes clear is that it is slightly beside the point to try to sort out who murdered whom or, in the language of 'Chicago' schlock, to 'finally reveal the shocking truth' about the extravagant shootings and bombings of 1962–3. It is more important to realize that even the mafiosi involved did not really know what was going on. Both Buscetta and the official account make it apparent that one of the reasons that mafia bosses reflected for so long before approving a new capo for Palermo-Centre was simply that they were trying to work out what on earth had happened. The first mafia war – like many mafia wars – was a giant game of murder in the dark.

It was also politics in the dark. Buscetta disingenuously claims that the Commission was invented to be a parliament of felons; he presents it as an impartial institution designed to bring light and equity into the gloom and treachery of Cosa Nostra's affairs. But in its own way the Commission was as much an instrument of struggle within Cosa Nostra as were the Giuliettas loaded with TNT. It was designed to impose rules across Cosa Nostra that would make life easier for the 'enterprise syndicate' mafiosi operating in the transatlantic heroin trade. But the Commission soon became a power in its own right. It was, for example, beginning to act like a joint stock company for the heroin traffickers; or at least that is the implication of the fact that both the La Barberas and the Grecos – mafiosi from opposite sides of the city – were jointly funding a heroin shipment in 1962. So the Commission's growing influence was running into conflict with the long-established power of the individual Families.

Buscetta believed that behind both 'the Cobra' Cavataio and La Barbera was an alliance of bosses from the north-west of Palermo who resented the Commission's growing power, and the influence thereby enjoyed by south-eastern Palermo men of honour like 'Little Bird' Greco. Amid the intrigue and confusion, the root cause of the first mafia war was a problem as old as the mafia itself, the same problem it had had to manage when its main interests were lemon groves and cattle rather than construction sites and heroin: that is, the conflict between its role as a shadow government and the business interests of its members – between the territorial structure of the *cosche* and the highly lucrative smuggling networks that cut across the map of Family domains.

Truth, territory, and business are always at stake in mafia wars. And by the 1960s, whatever happened within Cosa Nostra in Sicily also had diplomatic ramifications. At about the time that the first mafia war started, the American Cosa Nostra was coming under unprecedented pressure from the Kennedy administration. Robert Kennedy had built his political profile through his scrupulous work on the Senate Labor Rackets Committee. As attorney general, part of his brief was to tackle the mob. Under Kennedy, convictions of racketeers by the Organized Crime Section and the Tax Division trebled between 1961 and 1963; they nearly doubled again in 1964. Tax law, famously the instrument used to catch Al Capone three decades earlier, was still the main weapon against organized crime.

In 1962, faced with the electric chair, imprisoned Gambino soldier Joseph Valachi started to talk. He did not make a particularly compelling witness when he appeared before the Rackets Committee, and many people were very sceptical about what he said. But Valachi did at least succeed in getting J. Edgar Hoover's FBI to take the syndicate crime issue seriously for the first time. In 1959, the New York office of the FBI had 400 agents investigating American Communism, and only four working on organized crime. Valachi led to a change in priorities: by 1963, the New York office had 140 people in its rackets team. In 1964, FBI hidden microphones recorded Teamsters union boss Jimmy Hoffa in a series of business exchanges with the Detriot mafia.

Inevitably, the Kennedy anti-racketeering campaign lessened the influence of the American mafia in Sicily. As a result, the Sicilian bosses whose interests were centred on the territorial dimension of Cosa Nostra's operations probably calculated that it was a good time to settle accounts with the drug traffickers on the Commission now that their American protection had weakened.

It is probably also highly significant that the first mafia war followed only a few months after Lucky Luciano died of a heart attack while waiting to meet his biographer's plane at Naples airport. Lucky was known to be close to the La Barberas, and it is strongly suspected that the relationship was based on narcotics. When Lucky Luciano died, it left Angelo La Barbera having to prove to both the Families and the Commission that his power within Cosa Nostra was based on more than his American friends. Despite all the Giuliettas filled with TNT, he failed.

Angelo La Barbera was sentenced to twenty-two years for his part in the first mafia war in 1968. In 1975, the representative of the 'new' mafia died the most traditional of 'old' mafia deaths when he was stabbed in a prison yard.

Whatever the truth behind the intrigues of the first mafia war, the results of the Ciaculli bomb that brought it to a close were dramatic. There were close to 2,000 arrests; 'The police seemed to have gone mad,' was Buscetta's comment. Faced with this backlash, the mafia adopted the simplest self-defence method of all: it went into hiding. In the summer of 1963, the Commission met and decided to dissolve itself. The Families disbanded; according to one *pentito* not even protection money was collected in Palermo. Mafia crimes dropped to almost zero over the next few years. A number of leading bosses fled abroad. 'Little Bird' Greco went first to Switzerland and then to Venezuela. Tommaso Buscetta's wanderings took him to Switzerland, Mexico, Canada, and then the United States.

As Lucky Luciano had done when he was expelled from the United States in 1946, many Sicilian men of honour simply changed the direction of their careers within the organization: from becoming power syndicate criminals – statesmen of the mafia's shadow government – they evolved into enterprise syndicate leaders, international paramilitary businessmen. As they did, the Italian political system once again became the chief player in the mafia's history.

The Antimafia

The years before the Ciaculli bomb were a depressing time for anyone prepared to speak out against the mafia. With both the Church and the DC intent on denying not only the seriousness of the problem but even its very existence, only marginal voices broke the silence. The most important of those voices was a collective one; the fight to expose the truth about the mafia during the 1950s was led by the independent left-wing newspaper *L'Ora*. The title had begun life as the organ of Florio interests in Sicily at the turn of the century. In the 1950s, 1960s, and early 1970s, it created an astute blend of incandescent sports coverage and girls in bikinis with sophisticated writing on literature, music, and art. But for all these attractions, it was *L'Ora*'s courageous investigative reports on organized crime and corruption that were often its main selling point. When it published the names, interests, and political contacts of leading mafia bosses in 1958, there was a devastating dynamite attack on its offices. *L'Ora* refused to bend and carried on its campaign. (In the early 1970s, two *L'Ora* journalists, Mauro De Mauro and Giovanni Spampinato, would pay with their lives for their work.)

Inspired by the example provided by the Kefauver hearings on organized crime in the United States, in the 1950s the Italian Communist Party began to call for a parliamentary inquiry into the Sicilian mafia. Impetus to those calls was added by the bombing of *L'Ora*'s offices, but the impetus would never be sufficient as long as the mafia issue remained solely the political property of the Left. As late as 1959, a DC junior Minister of the Interior dismissed the need for a parliamentary inquiry, and blamed mafia crimes on the islanders' tendency to 'take justice into their own hands out of a misplaced sense of honour'.

Yet by then the political map of Italy was already changing; the DC was divided, and some of its factions were beginning to look to the Socialist Party as a potential coalition partner. The Socialists were the mafia's historical enemies; they had not forgotten the slaughter of trade unionists and other militants in the post-war years. This new political environment was one in which the calls for a parliamentary inquiry into the mafia could find a sympathetic hearing even within the ranks of the DC. In September 1961, the Sicilian Regional Assembly got its first 'Centre-Left' government which included both the DC and the Socialists, and was given issue-by-issue support by the Communists. Early the following year, the Assembly voted unanimously to ask the Italian parliament to set up a commission of inquiry into the mafia. Even the mafia's own politicians voted in favour because they now considered an inquiry so inevitable that opposition at this stage would be both useless and conspicuous.

As the country's centre of political gravity shifted gently to the left, the voices that had spoken out about the mafia became louder. One of them belonged to Leonardo Sciascia, a schoolteacher from the unremarkable little town of Racalmuto in the sulphur region near Agrigento. Leonardo Sciascia's *The Day of the Owl*, an elegant, bleak novella about a detective's failed investigation into a mafia killing, was published in 1961. *The Day of the Owl* – a work of fiction, it should be stressed – was the first book to put a face on the mafia and words in its mouth, in the unforgettable figure of Don Mariano Arena.

It is now known that, in the same year that Sciascia's novel came out, there was a meeting of the Cosa Nostra Commission in the province of Palermo to discuss the organization's response to the Italian state's awakening interest in the mafia issue. It was decided to keep killings to an absolute minimum until the politicians lost interest. But the truce held only for a year before the latent tensions over business and territory led to the outbreak of the first mafia war in December 1962. The renewed killing spree cranked further political momentum into the plans for a parliamentary inquiry.

Less than a week after the Ciaculli car bomb, the parliamentary commission of inquiry finally began its work. It was the first official inquiry into the mafia since 1875, but the political conditions were now much more favourable to a serious investigation than they had been in the year of Tajani's revelations in parliament about police collusion with criminals in Palermo. The Socialist Party was moving into government with the DC, pulling it in the direction of reform and transparency, as the cross-party support for the parliamentary inquiry seemed to show. Expectations in society were high: public opinion seemed ready to hold the politicians to account for the way they responded to the crisis. Thus the Antimafia – as the new inquiry became known – began at a brisk pace. Within a month it had made strong recommendations including, for the first time in Italian history, criminal legislation specifically targeted at the mafia. Italian democracy seemed finally ready to confront organised crime in Sicily.

It is, alas, all too easy to tell the story of the Antimafia as one giant anticlimax. The indignation that followed the Ciaculli bomb of 1963 faded rapidly. With the mafia all but silenced, there were few outrages to fuel the Antimafia's work. The commission of inquiry's opening sprint rapidly slowed to a gentle amble that would continue for no less than thirteen years. The Antimafia dragged on until it became the longest parliamentary inquiry in Italian history. It came to seem less like a response to an emergency than a permanent and dreary part of Italian political life.

Interest in the Antimafia's work revived periodically following some particularly sensational revelation, but sensation repeatedly failed to translate into effective political measures or judicial action. Even the criminal law passed in 1965 as a result of the Antimafia's recommendations proved to be partially counterproductive. The law stipulated that mafia suspects could be forced to live far from their homes. It was an effort to break contacts between mafiosi and the society around them – as if the mafia was caused by an unhealthy exhalation of the soil in western Sicily. Dozens of men of honour were posted all over the peninsula under these 'obligatory residence' measures, with the unintended result that the mafia gained new bases for its operations right across Italy.

Each leak or scandal emerging from the Antimafia about a politician with connections seemed to be blunted by denials and libel suits. It is also, quite simply, extremely difficult for evidence of discreet, face-to-face collusion between politicians and the mafia to reach the standards of proof required by criminal law. Vito Ciancimino – the DC young Turk in the hands of the Corleone mafia – was forced to resign following revelations made by the Antimafia in 1964. He surfaced again in 1970 when, incredibly, he became mayor of Palermo. The national scandal that followed ended in his resignation. In 1975, he submitted a lengthy self-defence to the Antimafia. Its breathless, page-long opening sentence complained about the 'denigratory publicity', 'corrupting sophisms', 'personal rancour', 'servile demagoguery', and 'affront to Latin legal traditions' to which he, as a man who had 'sacrificed himself for society', had been subjected. He remained a power behind the scenes of Palermo politics until he was finally arrested in 1984.

Part of the problem with the Antimafia was a turnover in personnel. When a new president of the Antimafia was appointed in 1972, he confessed that everything he knew about the mafia came from reading Mario Puzo's *The Godfather*. But this lack of continuity in the Antimafia's membership was only a symptom of its main handicap: the deep-seated factionalism of Italian political life. Apart from the legacy of Fascism and the fact that Italy was on the front line of the Cold War, there were also other fissures, notably between Catholic and lay world-views and between different regions of the country. Rather than being a 'ship of state', Italy often seems more like a flotilla of boats, each piloted according to a different chart, each competing for access to the most favourable winds, yet each afraid of being isolated from the other craft. Like all government institutions, the parliamentary commission of inquiry became the subject of factional tussles, with each group trying to put its own members into the chairs around the Antimafia table. The reason for this was that the word 'mafia' remained the same political weapon that it had always been ever since it entered the Italian language back in 1865. It was a weapon that no party or faction, least of all the DC, was prepared to leave in other hands.

Among the members of the Antimafia commission were some outstanding figures like Franco Cattanei of the DC and Girolamo Li Causi of the Communist Party (he was the Resistance veteran who survived a grenade attack by Don Calò Vizzini in Villalba town square back in 1944). It was politicians like these who tried to make the Antimafia into an impartial expression of the national interest. Their task was not an easy one. In 1972, a new government was formed in which two Palermo 'young Turks', with links to the mafia that had been revealed by the Antimafia, were given ministerial office: Salvo Lima was undersecretary at the Ministry of Finance, and Giovanni 'the Viceroy' Gioia was Minister for the Mail and Telecommunications. One of Gioia's supporters was even placed on the Antimafia commission; the man in question was not only on record as stating that the mafia did not exist but had himself been investigated by the commission at an earlier stage. The result was a five-month bout of political squabbling during which the Antimafia's work came to a complete stop. It is only one example of the way in which the vitriolic factionalism of the Italian system undermined the unity and authority of the country's response to the mafia.

When the Antimafia finally concluded its work in 1976, its most substantial legacy was a mountain of paper. Between the 'tomes' and 'parts' of the documentation it gathered, the interim reports, concluding report, and minority reports (for there was no political consensus on the lessons to be learned), the Antimafia bequeathed nearly forty fat volumes to the few libraries that had enough shelf-space to stock them. Anyone with the patience to read, for example, the turgid prose of the interim report of 1972 – all 1,262 pages of it – will get a pretty good picture of the mafia. The report talks of the association's systematic use of an 'unparalleled, bloodthirsty violence', its parasitical relationship to business, its links to local and national government; it explains that the *cosche* ruling different areas have a 'tacit accord' that is not broken even when there is pitiless fighting between them. The papers of the Antimafia are a vast and rich source of material for historians. So vast and rich, in fact, that the thousands of pages smothered the 'powder keg' of revelations about political collusion that one early president of the inquiry promised would emerge. It was during the long years of the Antimafia that post-war Italy became acquainted for the first time with mafia fatigue.

The Antimafia's results were undoubtedly a huge disappointment when compared with the expectations of 1963. But the commission did at least bring a substantial increase in Italy's awareness of the issue. Some of the stories that surfaced from the investigations lodged themselves in the public memory, like the town of Caccamo where, next to the mayor's seat in the council chamber, a special chair for the mafia boss was permanently set. In the wake of the commission of inquiry, through well-informed authors like Michele Pantaleone (the left-wing activist who had tangled with Don Calò in his native Villalba), studies of the mafia came to command a small but solid readership in Italy, as they still do to this day. Partly as a result fewer politicians had the brass neck – or the 'bronze face' as the Italian idiom has it – to deny completely that the mafia existed. The mafia was now no longer an issue that was restricted to the Left. All told, the Antimafia slightly increased the price (in terms of a loss of credibility and national influence) that politicians who colluded with the mafia risked paying. It was not much to show for thirteen years of work. But it was something, and that something had been achieved democratically.

'A Phenomenon of Collective Criminality'

One hundred and seventeen of the combatants in the first mafia war were sent to trial in Catanzaro, in Calabria, in 1968. When the verdict was issued in December of that year it proved as big a judicial anticlimax as the Antimafia was a political anticlimax. At Catanzaro a small handful of leading mafiosi received long sentences: Uditore boss Pietro Torretta was given the longest term – twenty-seven years – for the murder of the two men in his home; Angelo La Barbera was sentenced to twenty-two and a half years; 'Little Bird' Greco and Tommaso Buscetta, both tried *in absentia*, were sentenced to ten and fourteen years respectively. But most of the rest of the defendants were either acquitted or received short sentences for membership of a criminal association. Given the time they had already spent in captivity while awaiting trial, the vast majority were freed immediately.

The Catanzaro verdict is often viewed as a prime example of how toothless the Italian legal system has been when dealing with mafia crime. It seems in many respects like a dispiriting replay of the 1901 trial based on the Sangiorgi report. But there is a difference: in this case there are no suspicions of collusion between the judiciary and the mafia. In fact Catanzaro is an example of just how objectively difficult it was to construct a legally convincing picture of Cosa Nostra in the days before Tommaso Buscetta decided to collaborate with justice. In Italy judges prepare public documents to explain their decisions. The Catanzaro ruling, 461 pages long, provides a fascinating glimpse into the thinking behind a big mafia court case, and explains just how judicially slippery Cosa Nostra was even when the Italian legal system was working well.

Much of the work that the members of Cosa Nostra carried out to avoid conviction in Catanzaro went on well before the case ever came to court. As happened in Sangiorgi's day, the police found that witnesses emerged from deep within the mafia environment to give evidence during the early stages of investigations. But their evidence was then retracted at a later stage as fear took its toll.

A striking case is that of Giuseppe Ricciardi who suffered a long sequence of injustices at the hand of the La Barbera brothers. First they murdered his father, a man of honour. Then they intimidated him into selling them his father's trucking business at a knock-down price. Subsequently they used him – without his knowledge – to bring two of their enemies to Brancaccio station on Greco territory; Ricciardi watched as Tommaso Buscetta led the two away at gunpoint never to be seen again. Not long after recounting these events to magistrates, Ricciardi made a complete retraction, proffering a forlorn stream of explanations for his turnaround: he did not know anyone, he was ill, he had lost his well-paid job just because he was his father's son, he was afraid of everything and everyone and just wanted to live a quiet life. He protested that the police had beaten his story out of him, but then withdrew even that accusation – which the judge took to be baseless. It is little compensation to investigators to prosecute such sorry individuals for withholding evidence.

Like Sangiorgi more than sixty years before, the prosecutors at Catanzaro were forced to rely on anonymous sources to provide a map of the battle lines in the mafia war; such sources were vital in providing a framework that made sense of what would otherwise seem like a random sequence of crimes. When it came to the trial, there was no disguising the fact that the evidence was thin in proportion to the number of defendants and the seriousness of the charges. So the prosecutors made an explicit plea for the bigger picture to be taken into consideration. The defendants' criminal records, their fearsome reputations, the signs of a deliberate plan to contaminate evidence and intimidate witnesses: it all pointed to a pattern, and that pattern was the organization known as the mafia.

Defence lawyers can hardly be blamed for arguing that there was not enough concrete evidence to make this pattern into anything more than a legal hypothesis. They claimed that the pattern was actually invented by prosecution lawyers as a way of making up for glaring gaps in the evidence. What if the mafia were not an organization but a widespread Sicilian attitude of hostility towards the law?

Corruption, collusion, and intimidation explain a great many of the acquittals for insufficient evidence that mafiosi listed on their CVs. But the Catanzaro verdict on the first mafia war shows that at the centre of the problems faced by the judicial system was simply the enigma of the mafia itself. The pre-trial judge, who made a preliminary evaluation of the prosecution's evidence, and the trial judge both discounted the theory that the mafia was a centralized pyramidal organization. But in doing so they were unable to grasp the fact that Cosa Nostra can be organized without being a rigid bureaucracy of crime. The judges also discounted any suggestion that the mafia had 'norms' and 'criteria' common to all its members. The trial judge's final ruling wordily conceded that the mafia could indeed be considered 'a psychological attitude or the typical expression of an exaggerated individualism'. But it did point out that these social factors were only the background to what was in reality a 'phenomenon of collective criminality'. The picture he had in mind was not of one criminal association but of many independent ones, whether they be local *cosche* or networks of traffickers. In short, the Italian judicial system was moving towards an acceptance of the fact that the mafia was a thing and not an idea, but it was still too indistinct a thing to be caught in the legal net.

At a quarter to seven on the evening of 10 December 1969, five men in stolen police uniforms burst into a single-storey office building in viale Lazio in Palermo and began to machine-gun the occupants. There followed a furious gunfight during which one of the attackers was killed; his companions dumped him in the boot of one of the getaway cars before making their escape. In their wake they left four of their enemies dead, two more wounded, and over 200 shell cases. As soon as police arrived they realized which of the dead men was the primary target of the attack; he was found with his trademark Colt Cobra by his side. It was Michele Cavataio, the mafioso blamed by Buscetta for starting the first mafia war.

With its machine-guns and its getaway cars, the massacre in viale Lazio was the work of eminently modern gangsters. It took place in a new construction company office in a swanky residential quarter that had mushroomed during the sack of Palermo. Yet the murder of 'the Cobra' was a collective execution of exactly the kind performed in the same area by the men of honour cited in Chief of Police Sangiorgi's report seventy years earlier. *Pentiti* have since revealed that the assassins disguised as policemen were representatives of different mafia Families from Palermo and beyond.

In fact, it is now clear that the attack in viale Lazio at the end of 1969 was the last act of the war of 1962–3, and it added credibility to Buscetta's version of events. According to *pentiti*, the murder of Cavataio was instigated by 'Little Bird' Greco, who had come to subscribe to Buscetta's theory about how the first mafia war began. His proposal to kill 'the Cobra' was accepted by an impromptu panel of leading bosses (the Commission was not reconstituted until soon afterwards). Thus it was that, with the Catanzaro verdict safely behind it, the 'phenomenon of collective criminality', which the judges had struggled so hard to define, decided to put the troubles of the mid-1960s behind it and go back to work.

The Origins of the
Second Mafia War
1970–1982

Rise of the Corleonesi:
1 – Luciano Leggio (1943–1970)

As most American mafia films do, Francis Ford Coppola's *The Godfather* received a poor critical reception when it was released in Italy in 1972. One critic branded it a 'distillation of all the commonplaces about Italian-American gangsters'. It is an opinion that may owe something to a certain Italian resentment at the way that, through Hollywood, the US has claimed the mafia as its own. The same critic also thought the Sicilian episode of *The Godfather* 'offensively stupid', and on this count he was right: the Sicilian sequences of the god-daddy of all American mafia films are undeniably crass. In one scene Al Pacino's Michael Corleone wanders through the streets of the town whose name he bears. Struck by the black-clad widows and the funeral announcements pasted to the walls, he wonders aloud where all the men have gone. 'They are all dead,' one of his local body-guards replies, 'from *vendetta*.' He speaks the word as if it meant some unholy force of nature, a variant of the Black Death that mows down only Sicilian men.

At the time when Michael Corleone paid his fictional visit to his father's home town, typhus was a bigger danger to the population than mafia crime; some forty people succumbed to it in the summer of 1947. Corleone, with its roads and drainage system damaged by the passage of American tanks, was still an extremely poor place. But if the murder rate in those years did not reach the apocalyptic levels suggested by *The Godfather*, it was nonetheless strikingly high. There were eleven murders in 1944, sixteen in 1945, seventeen in 1946, eight in 1947, and five in 1948. As elsewhere in western Sicily, these were the years of the mafia's resurgence and of its brutal response to renewed peasant militancy. But in Corleone, in retrospect, the murder statistics have acquired a particularly baleful significance because among them are the first crimes committed by Luciano Leggio, a mafioso who would come to exert a dominant influence within Cosa Nostra. Following Leggio's example, his favourite pupil and fellow Corleonese, Totò 'Shorty' Riina, would orchestrate an unparalleled slaughter of men of honour – a slaughter known as the second mafia war of 1981–3. Under Riina, the Corleonesi would establish a dictatorship over the organization and, in so doing, almost bring its history to an end. Even today, Riina's successor as boss of bosses is a man born in Corleone and tutored by Luciano Leggio. Thus, by nothing more than luck, when *Godfather* author Mario Puzo chose a birthplace for Don Vito Corleone (né Andolini), he picked on the town that gave the world the most feared and powerful men of honour of them all.

The best-known photographs of Luciano Leggio date from a court appearance in Palermo in 1974. It is difficult to avoid concluding from them that he decided for the occasion to adopt a look based on Brando's Don Corleone. And with his cigar, his long, heavy jaw, and his arrogant bearing, he actually managed to pull it off; there is a more than passing resemblance between the two. In fact Leggio's face was already infamous before *The Godfather* was released. The Antimafia commission's analysis of Leggio, published in the same year that the movie came out, is not a document that tends to dwell on anything as frivolous as appearances. Yet it was transfixed by Leggio's 'big, round, cold face', his 'ironic and scornful' glower. If the cinematic Don Vito was the face of the mafia as it likes to think of itself – judicious and family-centred – then Luciano Leggio's features, by contrast, were an emblem of capricious terror. Whereas Brando's heavy lids gave his character an almost noble reserve, Leggio's staring eyeballs suggested that he was as volatile as he was malevolent. One *pentito* said that Leggio 'had a look that struck fear even in us *mafiosi*. It only took the slightest thing to get him worked up, and then there would be a strange light in his eyes that silenced everyone around . . . You could sense death hovering in the air.' This was a man who, on one occasion, according to the same *pentito*, killed a mafioso and his lover, and then raped and killed her fifteen-year-old daughter.

But like so many real mafia biographies, Luciano Leggio's story only withers into gangster cliché if it is told in a psychological vein. Although Leggio inspired acute dread, the reason he and his followers became so powerful in Cosa Nostra was not because they were made of more fearsome stuff than the rest. Rather it was because they reinvented mafia tactics by creating a new combination of old methods. The Corleonesi developed a system for dominating the Sicilian mafia that suited the new climate emerging in the years of the Antimafia, when the state and public opinion became more alert to the problem, and the drug business put new strains on the traditional structure of the Families. In a sense, the Corleonesi became within the body of Cosa Nostra what Cosa Nostra was within the body of Sicily: a secret and deadly parasite. To understand how these tactics evolved, it pays to trace the rise of the Corleonesi from Leggio's first murders in the 1940s.

Luciano Leggio was born into poverty in 1925. When the honoured society resurfaced after the Allied invasion of 1943, the petty thief Leggio was drafted by Michele Navarra, a round-headed physician, who was also the Corleone capo. (There is a long tradition of mafia medics like Navarra, who was a general practitioner in Corleone; in 1946, he became the director of the hospital after his predecessor was murdered by hands unknown.) Through Navarra's sponsorship, at the age of only twenty, Leggio obtained a job as a guard on an estate near Corleone. Since before the time of murdered Fasci leader Bernardino Verro, positions like this had been dominated by the Corleone mafia and used to smuggle, steal, intimidate labourers, and extort protection money from landowners.

In 1948, probably on Navarra's orders, Leggio performed one of the most notorious political murders of the post-war years; Corleone's peasants were given another socialist martyr to mourn. On the evening of 10 March – not by coincidence, the Italian Republic's first parliamentary elections were imminent – Leggio marched trade unionist and Resistance veteran Placido Rizzotto out of town at gunpoint; he then forced him to kneel down before shooting him in the head three times at point-blank range. Rizzotto's remains, along with two other human skeletons, were found in a sixty-metre-deep cave eighteen months later. Only a few fragments of clothes and a pair of rubber-soled American shoes allowed his mother to identify him. Leggio was never convicted for the crime, despite the fact that two men who had helped him perform the kidnapping gave evidence and told the authorities where to find the victim's body. Placido Rizzotto has never had a tomb, but a bust of him, inaugurated only in 1996, now stands outside Corleone town hall.

Leggio absconded soon after the Rizzotto murder. He was only recaptured in 1964, but disappeared again in 1970 before being locked up for the final time in 1974. He remained a fugitive from justice for so long that he acquired the nickname of the 'Scarlet Pimpernel' of Corleone. But he was far from the dashing figure that this literary parallel would suggest; he suffered from chronic prostate problems and spondylosis, an inflammation of the spine that forced him to wear a leather brace. His poor health meant that much of his time 'on the run' was actually spent in expensive clinics and spas. It should be said that there was nothing unusual about a mafioso going underground for a while in this way. Even a fat old don like Calò Vizzini had done it. But Leggio's almost permanent life of concealment was to set a pattern. The Corleonesi have all been 'Scarlet Pimpernels', invisible not just to the forces of law and order, but also to rival mafiosi. This invisibility was to be part of a new model of mafia power; no longer would the boss hold court at a café table in the local piazza. The only manifest trace of the power of the Corleonesi would be their savagery.

In 1956, Leggio, still officially in hiding, started up a livestock-breeding business as a cover for his cattle-rustling operation. It was to be the base for his challenge to the authority of his own boss, Michele Navarra. First Leggio bullied one of Navarra's men into renouncing his share of the livestock company. Then, when one of Navarra's senior lieutenants bought some adjoining land, Leggio made him the target for a campaign of vandalism. Predictably, in June 1958, Leggio was ambushed in his own farm buildings by Navarra killers. But it seems that they were so wary of his reputation as a flawless shot that they opened fire from too far away, allowing Leggio to fight them off at the cost only of a graze to his hand.

It was the doctor's last chance. Two months later, Navarra was returning by car to Corleone from Lercara Friddi with another doctor – an entirely innocent man. As they rounded a bend, they were confronted by Leggio's Alfa Romeo 1900 blocking the road. When police and reporters reached the scene some time later, they found that the victims' car had been rolled down the verge; the dozens of bullet holes in it made for a telling 'Chicago' photograph. It was the first mafia killing in Corleone to grab the headlines since the disappearance of Placido Rizzotto a decade before. Leggio's notoriety now stretched well beyond Corleone.

The move against Navarra was an act of extraordinary daring. The evil doctor of Corleone represented a kind of stability and political protection that Cosa Nostra values. In addition to his medical responsibilities, he was the president of the Corleone peasants' federation, a trustee of the farmers' union, and an inspector for the region's health insurance scheme; he placed his friends on a host of influential quangos; and one of his brothers ran the Sicilian regional bus company that Navarra himself had started up with abandoned military vehicles in 1943. The Corleone doctor controlled a significant packet of votes for the DC, he had support from the other mafia bosses of the region, and he could count among his clan men of honour with considerable experience as well as contacts in the United States. He had even been awarded the Italian equivalent of a knighthood just before he was shot dead, this despite a period of internal exile for his suspected involvement in the Rizzotto murder. No wonder the peasants of the town called him 'U patri nostru' – 'Our Father'. Mafiosi rarely have an interest in allowing a rank-and-file killer like Leggio to disturb such patiently accumulated and profitable prestige.

After murdering Navarra, Leggio's band had no alternative but to keep up the momentum of their offensive; by now, survival and victory were one and the same thing. A month after Navarra's death, three of the doctor's most feared soldiers were shot dead in a battle involving tens of gunmen in the very centre of Corleone; several bystanders, including children, were wounded. Corleone acquired the nickname 'Tombstone'. In October of the same year, 1958, *L'Ora* ran a full-page exposé of Leggio's activities under the single-word headline 'Dangerous'. Three days later the newspaper's offices were bombed.

Leggio's spectacular coup against the established Corleone bosses was unusual, but far from unprecedented. In one sense it represented a confirmation of what has probably been true all through the mafia's history. Although political influence is important, ultimate power in the honoured society lies with its military rather than its political wing. A readiness to pay the short-term political price for using overwhelming violence, shown by Leggio in 1958, was to be a characteristic of the tactics adopted by the Corleonesi thereafter.

The shooting and kidnapping in Corleone continued for five years. Leggio's upstarts were on the verge of total victory over the Navarra establishment when, on 30 June 1963, the Ciaculli car bomb led to mass arrests and brought almost all mafia activity to a temporary halt across western Sicily. The 'Scarlet Pimpernel' himself was finally arrested in Corleone in 1964 in a house belonging to a middle-aged spinster who had been completely above suspicion for the reason that she was the former fiancée of murdered trade unionist Placido Rizzotto.

When sixty-four of the participants in the war between the

Leggiani and the Navarriani finally came to trial in 1969, they were all acquitted. Astonishingly, despite nearly a quarter of a century as a mafia killer, Leggio still only had one conviction on his criminal record: for stealing a few sheaves of corn. The final report of the Antimafia parliamentary commission of inquiry later criticized the verdicts, blaming them on the way Leggio and his men intimidated witnesses, and on the judge's 'unconscious' tendency to be unusually rigorous when he evaluated prosecution evidence. It seems that Leggio also found a way to destroy material proof at some time between the investigations and the trial. Fragments of a car's rear light had been found at the scene of the Navarra murder; they had been identified at the time as coming from an Alfa Romeo of a kind owned by Leggio. When the evidence bag was opened for reinspection many months later, it was discovered that the fragments had been replaced by others from a different make of car. The prosecution appealed against the acquittals, but by the time Leggio was given a life sentence at a second trial he had gone underground once more.

Mafia activity started up again in earnest following the 1969 acquittal of Leggio and his men. And when it did, a new map of mafia power became visible. Among the firing party disguised as policemen who executed Michele 'the Cobra' Cavataio in viale Lazio were two of Leggio's top killers: Calogero Bagarella (the man who was killed in the assault and thrown into the boot of the getaway car), and Bernardo 'the Tractor' Provenzano (the man who at the time of writing is the reigning boss of bosses). The status that Leggio now had within Cosa Nostra was confirmed when the Commission was reconstituted shortly afterwards. As a provisional measure there were initially only three members. The first was Gaetano 'Tano' Badalamenti, a major drug-dealer with solid links across the Atlantic and one of the three men on the 'constitutional working party' that had drafted the rules for the Commission. The second was Stefano Bontate, known as the 'Prince of Villagrazia', capo of the largest Family in Palermo, and scion of a prestigious mafia dynasty – his father had been one of the pallbearers at Don Calò Vizzini's funeral. The third was Luciano Leggio himself, although he was often represented in meetings by his trusted deputy Totò Riina, known as 'u curtu' – 'Shorty'.

The composition of this triumvirate was a sign that the new Commission was to be a different kind of body from the one first established following Joe Bananas' visit to Sicily in 1957. The rule that prevented heads of Families from having a seat on the Commission had gone. The three members of the triumvirate were now, without doubt, the most powerful men of honour in the province of Palermo, and therefore in the whole of the Sicilian mafia. The Commission now no longer acted merely as a counterweight to the authority that local Family bosses had over individual men of honour, as Buscetta had hoped it might back in 1957. Indeed, it now actually reactivated and reorganized the Families from the top down. When the full Commission became operative in 1974, Cosa Nostra assumed the more hierarchical command structure that Tommaso Buscetta would describe to Giovanni Falcone, and that it still has today.

The question is how Luciano Leggio, hailing from backward Corleone as he did, came to take a place among the Palermo elite. The truth is that, despite the notoriety that both Leggio and Marlon Brando have conferred on it, Corleone is not the 'capital' of the mafia. Long before he was first arrested in 1964, Leggio was more than the boss of the Corleone Family; he had extended his influence where it really counted – into Palermo.

Palermo was where Leggio spent most of his time in hiding; the city's wholesale meat market was where his own small trucking firm took his illegally butchered cattle; it was in Palermo that 'pushy Corleonese embezzler' Vito Ciancimino was elbowing his way to power on the town council; Palermo was where Leggio had a company that rented out lucky dip machines full of contraband cigarettes; Leggio had close relationships with mafiosi who became the leading combatants in the first mafia war – La Barbera, Buscetta, Greco, Cavataio, Torretta. Palermo was where the mafia had its roots; it was where power in the honoured society was still concentrated. Palermo was to be the prize in the second mafia war.

Leonardo Vitale's Spiritual Crisis

The history of the Sicilian mafia is not composed only of high politics, big business, and war. The 1970s were also the setting for two tragedies – related in this chapter and the next – that speak of the acute anxieties of daily life as they affected the men, women, and children living deep within the mafia system.

At around eleven o'clock in the evening on 29 March 1973, Leonardo Vitale walked into the local headquarters of the Palermo flying squad, to declare that he was undergoing a religious crisis and intended to begin a new life. He was thirty-two and a man of honour from the Altarello di Baida Family of Cosa Nostra in which he held the rank of *capodecina* (head of ten). In the presence of dumbfounded officers, Vitale admitted to two murders, an attempted murder, a kidnapping, and a host of lesser crimes. He named the culprits in other homicides. He explained how a mafia Family is organized, who the members of his own Family were, and revealed the existence of the mafia Commission. Although he was at too low a level in the organization to know who exactly was on the Commission, he did explain that on one occasion the Corleonese triumvirate member Totò 'Shorty' Riina had come to give a ruling on a dispute between his Family and its neighbour. When news reached the press, he was dubbed 'the Valachi of the Palermo suburbs'. Once again, long before Tommaso Buscetta, a *pentito* had exposed mafia secrets to anyone prepared to listen.

Three weeks after Vitale had first given himself up, an investigating magistrate invited a team of forensic psychiatrists to the Ucciardone prison and instructed them to ascertain whether the *pentito* was sane enough to be a credible trial witness. Some signs that his state of mind was fragile were already evident. Earlier that year, while being held for a week on the island of Asinara on suspicion of taking part in a kidnapping, he had covered himself in his own excrement. To the psychiatrists, he explained why:

Doing something like that helped me to understand in some way – to understand that something like that is not bad, but other things *are* bad. Something like that cannot hurt people, but other things *are* bad – the things I did before.

Vitale's gesture of smearing himself with faeces was far more eloquent than his words – he was a poorly educated man. Yet for all his verbal stumbling, the story he went on to tell the forensic psychiatrists constitutes one of the most revealing insights into the emotional cost of belonging to an association that operates in a realm of silence and death.

The most influential man in Vitale's life, the man from whom he sought the affection he missed after his father's death, was his uncle who also became his capo. 'He was everything to me,' Vitale said. The most influential anxiety in his life revolved around his uncertain masculinity: 'I believed I was a pederast, and I've always carried this thought with me.' At the age of fourteen he stopped going to mass because he blamed God for the 'ugly thoughts' that went through his mind. He became a mafioso, he said, 'as a protest against my own nature, because God had given me these complexes. A protest against God, for the complex of not being a man.'

But it was not because of any 'complex' that Leonardo Vitale's destiny was already fixed when he was a boy. The mafia value system had been transmitted down the generations of the Vitale family; he was probably a descendant of a killer cleared of working for Don Raffaele Palizzolo back in the 1890s. Following the family tradition, when Leonardo's uncle sensed young Leonardo's admiration for him, he began to put his mettle to the test, asking him on one occasion, 'Do you see my hands? They are stained with blood, and your father's hands were even more stained than mine.' His uncle asked him to demonstrate his 'valour', first by killing a horse, and then, at the age of nineteen, by killing a man; he was driven past the victim in a tiny Fiat 500 and stood up on the back seat to fire at him with a shotgun. Leonardo's reward was to be taken skylark hunting by his uncle and then to be initiated into the Altarello di Baida Family. In what we now know was a historically resonant variant on the usual initiation ritual, his finger was pricked with the thorn from a Seville orange tree; its bitter fruit has been valued for its essence since Arab times.

Poisoning guard dogs, burning cars, vandalizing citrus fruit trees, killing a lemon thief, sending threatening letters with skulls drawn on them, placing bombs in offices, damaging machinery on building sites, and a great deal of hanging around: for the next thirteen years, Leonardo Vitale was engaged in the day-to-day business of extortion, of 'taxing' his Family's territory on his uncle's orders. In 1969, Vitale acquired more honour when he killed another mafioso. As a consequence, his uncle began to reveal more of the organization's secrets to him, telling him of the existence of the Commission that had ordered this most recent killing, and also the murder of *L'Ora* journalist Mauro De Mauro who disappeared in 1970. Vitale was promoted and became a *capodecina*, which did not mean a great deal to him other than a higher share of the loot.

To the psychiatrists Vitale explained that he had left behind his earlier self and its anxieties by revealing the mafia's secrets. It was, he said, as if someone else had committed his crimes. He had refound God, his inner peace, and with it the final reassurance that he was not, in fact, a pederast. But as he filled in more details of his story to the psychiatrists, it was noted that his mood became more depressed and unpredictable. He appeared one day with self-inflicted cuts on his arms; he then went around with no shoes and a long beard, declaring, 'Madman, I was a madman.' Magistrates began to wonder whether he was still going through the spiritual crisis that had led him to defect from the mafia, or whether he had been pressurized into playing up his insanity in order to undermine his testimony.

When the psychiatric examination was concluded, Vitale was pronounced 'mentally semi-infirm'; but the experts also decided that his condition did not impair his memory and thus the credibility of his testimony. Vitale's own written reaction to how the psychiatrists classified him is harrowing in its strained lucidity:

Mental semi-infirmity = psychic sickness. Mafia = social sickness. Political mafia = social sickness. Corrupt authorities = social sickness. Prostitution = social sickness, syphilis, condyloma, etc. = physical sickness that influences the ailing psyche right from childhood. Religious crises = psychic sickness that derives from these other sicknesses. These are the evils to which I, Leonardo Vitale, resurrected in the faith of the true God, have fallen victim.

The case came to trial in 1977. Of the twenty-eight defendants, only Vitale and his uncle were convicted. His 'mental semi-infirmity' and his erratic behaviour had been enough for the prosecution argument to be fatally weakened. If these acquittals were understandable, the same cannot be said for the way Vitale's profoundly important insights into the nature of the mafia were subsequently completely ignored by the authorities. Vitale was sentenced to twenty-five years. He spent most of his term in mental institutions before being released in June 1984. Soon afterwards much of what he had said back in 1973 was confirmed when Tommaso Buscetta turned state's evidence. On Sunday, 2 December 1984, Vitale was coming back from mass with his mother and sister when an unidentified man shot him twice in the head. Late the following year Giovanni Falcone and Paolo Borsellino presented their evidence in support of the 'Buscetta theorem' in preparation for the maxi-trial. They began the document by telling the story of Leonardo Vitale, a story they brought to a conclusion as follows: 'It is to be hoped that at least after his death Vitale will get the credence he deserved.'

Death of a 'Leftist Fanatic': Peppino Impastato

In the 1970s – known as the 'years of lead' – Italian democracy faced its darkest days since the fall of Fascism. Once again, understanding and fighting the mafia was not high on the nation's list of priorities. On 12 December 1969, two days after the attack on Michele 'the Cobra' Cavataio, which signalled a renewal of Cosa Nostra activity after the quiet years of the mid-1960s, a bomb exploded in a bank in Piazza Fontana in the centre of Milan; sixteen people were killed and dozens more wounded. Three days later an innocent anarchist pulled in for questioning about the Piazza Fontana bombing fell to his death from a fourth-floor window at Milan police headquarters. Soon afterwards evidence began to emerge linking neo-Fascist groups with the Piazza Fontana massacre, and also connecting elements in the Italian secret services with those same neo-Fascists. Militant left-wing groups adopted the slogan: 'It was a state massacre.' They were far from the only ones who believed that a plot to undermine democracy was afoot. There is little doubt that there was such plotting; the only question – still an open one – is how far into the institutions it extended. This was the 'strategy of tension': a programme of terrorist outrages intended to prepare the ground for a right-wing *coup d'état*.

The strategy of tension was a direct response to a perceived threat from the Left. The years 1967–8 saw a wave of student protest that was only radicalized by an often heavy-handed police response. More serious still was the season of strikes and demonstrations that began in the 'hot autumn' of 1969; for a while it looked as if the workers' movement was about to outflank the Italian Communist Party to the left.

The Piazza Fontana bomb outrage heralded a new season of

political instability and violence. Further right-wing terrorist acts were to follow throughout the decade and beyond. The worst atrocity was the murder of eighty-five people by a bomb placed in the second-class waiting room of Bologna station in August 1980. But political violence was by no means confined to the extreme Right. In the mid-1970s, as a world economic crisis helped tame labour militancy, the cluster of highly motivated but intensely quarrelsome parties to the left of the Communist Party began to realize that the revolution was not just around the corner, as they had hoped in the late 1960s. For a small minority of such militants of the Left, armed action, aimed at exacerbating social conflict and preparing the ground for a working-class insurrection, was the appropriate response to the decrease in strike action and the 'state massacres'. The Red Brigades proclaimed 'an attack on the heart of the state', and in the late 1970s and early 1980s staged prominent murders of policemen, magistrates, entrepreneurs, journalists, and even Communist Party members suspected of collaborating with the 'state of the multinationals'.

The mafia's involvement in the strategy of tension and in right-wing plotting since 1969 is one of the favourite subjects of 'behindologists'. There are one or two unequivocal links. In December 1970, a neo-Fascist prince occupied the Ministry of the Interior in an attempt to trigger a *coup d'état*; he withdrew peaceably a few hours later and the public were not made aware of the incident for several months. Subsequently Tommaso Buscetta and other *pentiti* would reveal that the mafia's leadership had been asked to participate in the coup in return for the revision of certain important trial verdicts. Buscetta and 'Little Bird' Greco even crossed the Atlantic to discuss the matter with Leggio and the others in a series of meetings in Catania, Rome, Milan, and Zurich during the summer of 1970. It seems that many of the senior bosses were diffident about the proposal. One *pentito* drily observed that the football World Cup was on at the time and, as Italy progressed through the tournament to meet Brazil in the final, many men of honour were more

interested in watching the matches on television than in meeting
to discuss a Fascist revolution. The mafia agreed to participate
in the revolt, but it seems that this was out of a desire to keep
a close eye on developments rather than because of any commitment to the cause. The repression of the mafia by 'iron prefect'
Cesare Mori had left a legacy of mistrust between the extreme
right and Cosa Nostra.

Apart from the abortive *coup d'état* of 1970, it is also known
that the mafia helped right-wing terrorists plant a bomb on a
train running between Milan and Naples on 23 December 1984
– it killed sixteen. Such episodes have helped fuel speculation
that Cosa Nostra itself was merely a tool of shadowy figures
in the corridors of Roman ministries, that above the highest
echelons of Cosa Nostra was the guiding hand of a mysterious
puppet-master. This is almost certainly fanciful. Cosa Nostra's
history suggests that when it did collaborate with violent right-
wing subversives, it probably did so only on its own terms, in
the hope of exacting precise concessions. The revision of trial
verdicts is probably an archetype of what the mafia wanted to
gain out of any such deal.

Behind the bloodshed and plotting of the late 1960s and early
1970s, much less conspicuous changes were taking place within
the judicial system that would have a profound influence on the
future history of the mafia. In Sicily, as in many other parts of
Italy, the old guard of magistrates and judges were instinctively
conservative and some of them were closely tied to the political
class through Masonic societies and family ties. Even if there
had not been any individuals who deliberately colluded with
Cosa Nostra, such a body of men – and they were all men –
was never likely to have the animus required to tackle organized
crime at its highest levels.

Then in the 1960s, recruitment was widened by the spread of
higher education; at the same time the magistrature finally
acquired its own governing body and with it a degree of independence from government that compared favourably with other
European countries. Towards the end of the decade an organiz-

ation called Magistratura Democratica spearheaded a drive by younger magistrates to reform the sclerotic legal system. Some of the new generation of magistrates sought to bring more white-collar criminals – polluters, building speculators, corrupt politicians – to book.

As the magistrates grew more powerful, they also became highly politicized and organized into politically aligned factions. Partly as a result, the suspicion that investigations were launched, and even verdicts reached, for partisan political motives became a growing complaint. Nevertheless the great successes in the battle against the mafia in future years would have been unthinkable without this slow transformation in Italy's legal system. But these were changes that would take years to have their effects on the struggle against Cosa Nostra.

There were times in the 1970s when it seemed that Italian democracy might not survive the twin assaults from the strategy of tension and left-wing terrorism. The most worrying moment of all came on 16 March 1978 when the Red Brigades kidnapped the most influential figure in the Christian Democrat party, former Prime Minister Aldo Moro; his entire escort and his driver were murdered in the assault. For fifty-five days Italy held its breath as politicians of all parties debated whether to stand firm against the kidnappers' demands, or negotiate to try to save Moro's life. On 9 May, Moro was killed and his body left curled up in the boot of a red Renault in a Rome side street just a few dozen metres from the headquarters of both the DC and the PCI.

Understandably these terrorist emergencies helped to drown out concerns about the mafia's re-emergence, and about its day-to-day regime of terror in western Sicily. There is no clearer illustration of this than a story that appeared on the same day that Moro's body was found in Rome. The conservative Milanese newspaper *Corriere della Sera* briefly reported an incident in Cinisi, a small town on the western coast of Sicily, far from 'the heart of the state'. The headline was: 'Leftist fanatic blown apart by own bomb on railway track.'

The 'leftist fanatic' was Giuseppe 'Peppino' Impastato. But his death, at the age of thirty, was not the result of either a terrorist attack that went wrong, or even suicide, as was later claimed. Peppino Impastato was murdered by the Cinisi mafia, although it would take nearly a quarter of a century and a dogged campaign by friends and relatives for justice to be done in his case. To begin to get a sense of why his story is historically significant, it is enough to look at the photograph of a group of 'men of respect' from Cinisi in the picture section of this book; the photo was taken in the early 1950s. Peppino is the smaller of the two little boys in short trousers, the one with his left hand tucked under his father's right arm.

The little boy in the picture did indeed grow up to be a left-wing militant; he was an intelligent and occasionally tortured rebel who devoted half his life to the cause of fighting capitalism and oppression. Like many young Italians at the time, he participated passionately in what now seem arcane sectarian disputes conducted in an arid Marxist jargon; he argued through his ideological stance on everything from the Vietnam war to nudism; he moved from one tiny revolutionary party or initiative to another, oscillating all the time between euphoria and despair (he found personal and romantic relationships difficult). But if Peppino's politics are an essential ingredient of his story, then even more important to it is the fact that Peppino's rebellion was lived out within one of the most mafia-saturated family environments it is possible to imagine. Peppino's father was a mafioso, a low-ranking member of the Cinisi Family. There were several other men of honour in the extended family, as there had been for decades. Peppino's rebellion against this background was unprecedented.

The surviving members of the Impastato family would later look back on one moment in 1963 as the first sign of Peppino's revolt against the mafia culture that had surrounded him all his young life. When Peppino was fifteen, Cesare Manzella, the then boss of Cinisi who was also his uncle by marriage, was killed by a TNT-laden Alfa Romeo Giulietta during the first mafia war. The teenage Peppino was horrified. As the whole town knew, pieces of his uncle were found stuck to lemon trees hundreds of metres from the crater where the car had been. He asked another uncle, 'What must he have felt?' The reply – 'It was all over in an instant' – did little to quell the young man's anxiety.

By the time he was seventeen, Peppino was already an activist, addressing rallies and co-editing a news-sheet, *The Socialist Idea*. His confrontation with the mafia was immediate, direct, and astonishingly brave in a town where the murderous suppression of the left-wing peasant movement in the post-war years was still a recent memory. In 1966, he wrote an article entitled 'Mafia: a mountain of shit'. After reading it, one of his many mafioso relatives warned his father, 'If he were my son, I'd dig a ditch and bury him.' Peppino was banned from the parental home.

Peppino Impastato's home town of Cinisi was no minor outpost of Cosa Nostra's empire. By the 1960s it was one of the most important centres of mafia activity in western Sicily. Palermo's new airport – obviously a prime target for racketeering and contraband operations – was built there in the late 1950s. Of Cinisi's population of 8,000, 80 per cent had relatives in the United States. It is no coincidence that the town was one of the major entrepôts of the transatlantic heroin business. Cinisi boss Don Tano Badalamenti had strong family ties to the Detroit mob, bases for his drug-dealing operations in Rome and Milan, and a whole string of construction companies under his control. He was massively influential within Cosa Nostra too. He had helped Tommaso Buscetta draw up the rules of the first Commission in 1957, and he was a member of the triumvirate established in 1970. Upon assuming his place in the triumvirate, according to one *pentito*, his first act was to have a small-time Neapolitan criminal shot. This was the man who, years earlier, had slapped Lucky Luciano at Naples racecourse. Thus, eight years after Luciano's death, Badalamenti was able to inform his contacts in the American Cosa Nostra that the insult had been avenged. When the full Commission was reconstituted in 1974, it was Badalamenti who sat at the head of the table.

Peppino's revolt tore at fissures that already existed in the Impastato household. His mother, Felicia Bartolotta Impastato, took to giving him food surreptitiously. She had married into the mafia, but did not have blood relatives who were men of honour. Peppino's father was an inarticulate, domineering man who would only allow his wife out to meet other mafia wives. He vented on her the 'dishonour' and anxiety that his inability to control his son brought down on him. 'It was a dictatorship. Desperation . . . fear. When I heard him come home I used to piss myself,' she would later recount. Although Felicia was too afraid to attend Peppino's rallies, she tried to persuade her son to moderate the tone of his campaigning. 'Giuseppe, look, I'm against the mafia as well. But can't you see what your father is like? Be careful, my son.'

Despite the mafia's threats and his mother's fears, Peppino pressed on. In his mother's words he fought for 'just and precise things', things that almost always clashed with mafia interests. He was heavily involved in a campaign in support of the peasants whose land was to be expropriated so that a third runway for the airport could be built. He also struggled alongside building workers who were exploited by mafia-protected employers. Much of his time in the mid-1970s was taken up with the fight against what the Italian Communist Party (the PCI) called its 'historic compromise' – its decision to support Christian Democrat governments where it felt they were moving in a progressive direction. Leftists cried out at this betrayal, although there is some justification in the claim that the 'historic compromise' saved Italy from the fate of Chile, where Pinochet's bloody military coup overthrew a democratic government in 1973. Whatever the rights and wrongs of the PCI's moderate strategy in the rest of Italy, in western Sicily compromise with the DC meant collaboration with the mafia in the eyes of Peppino and his network of comrades.

Peppino was also harsh in his ideological critique of the hippies who had set up Italy's first commune in an abandoned Florio villa near by; he thought it demoralizing that they had forsaken politics in favour of nudism and cannabis. In 1977, he founded a tiny local radio station, Radio Aut. Its highlight was an evening show of music and satire directed at 'Mafiopolis' and its 'Mafia-cipality' – in other words Cinisi and its DC-dominated town council. The show's sketches lampooned the local Family and its shady affairs by setting them in grotesque versions of Dante's *Divine Comedy* or the Wild West; ruling boss Tano Badalamenti was transparently mocked as 'Tano Seduto' ('Sitting Bully'). In a newspaper article, Peppino also referred to Badalamenti as 'a paleface adept in drug trafficking and the use of the sawn-off shotgun'. In the spring of 1978, Peppino helped set up a photographic exhibition in the town on 'The mafia and the landscape', demonstrating the damage done by cowboy road building; at the same time he was selected as a candidate in the local elections. There is a chilling photo of several men of respect closely examining one of the panels of the 'mafia and the landscape' exhibition; it was taken on the day before Peppino was murdered.

Peppino Impastato knew the risks he was taking. His mother warned him that the mafia were 'animals', for whom 'snuffing out a candle was nothing'. He probably calculated that he would be protected to some extent by the fact that his father was a man of honour. His father is now known to have taken considerable risks to protect his son from Badalamenti's vengeance. Then, in September 1977, he was knocked down and killed by a passing car. For many years the family thought his death was an accident, although they have now come to believe he was murdered. Whatever the truth, Peppino was left unprotected by his father's death. At the funeral, Peppino refused to shake hands with the mafiosi who came to pay their respects – a resounding insult; nor did his campaigning decline in intensity in the following months. He almost certainly knew he was going to be killed.

On the night of 8–9 May 1978, Peppino was kidnapped on his way back from Radio Aut and taken in his own car to a tumbledown stone shack a few yards from the Palermo–Trapani railway line near the boundary fence of the airport. There he was beaten and tortured before being dumped on the track with several sticks of dynamite strapped to his torso.

Early the following morning railway workers reported that a fifty-centimetre section of track had been damaged. When the *carabinieri* arrived at the scene, they found Peppino's car, his white Scholl clogs and his glasses near the hole blown by the explosion. Fragments of his body and clothes were scattered over a 300-metre radius around it; only his legs, parts of his face, and a few fingers were recognizable. Peppino's death was a horrific echo of the way his uncle the mafioso had died back in 1963 – the very murder that had provoked him to ask, 'What must he have felt?' and begin his rebellion against the mafia.

On 6 December 2000, twenty-two years later, a parliamentary commission of inquiry published a report into the way the authorities dealt with Peppino Impastato's death. It concluded that the investigation had been handled in an insensitive and slapdash way that in effect supported the killers' own efforts to make Peppino's death look like a suicidal terrorist attack. Peppino's friends and family had proclaimed all along that there was a cover-up.

Incredibly, despite Peppino's well-known campaign against the mafia, despite the fact that Cinisi was a notorious mafia stronghold, despite the threats that activists had received, and despite the fact that even the *carabinieri* themselves had earlier reported that Peppino and his comrades were 'incapable' of committing terrorist acts, investigators in the immediate aftermath of Peppino's death did not even entertain the possibility that he could have been murdered, let alone by men of honour. Witnesses who participated in the initial inspection of the scene, including the mortician brought in to collect what could be found of the victim's body, are certain that there were clear traces of blood inside the shack where Peppino was tortured. Because the shack had no openings facing the railway track, those traces of blood could not have got there as a result of the explosion. Yet the initial report into the case by the *carabinieri* fails even to mention the stone shack, although Peppino's car was found right next to it.

The morning after Peppino's death, the *carabinieri* raided Radio Aut and the houses of his friends and relatives. His mother's house was searched before she was even told of her son's death. At his aunt's house they found a letter in Peppino's hand dating from several months previously; in it he alluded to his 'failure as a man and as a revolutionary' and hinted that he might take his own life. This was to be the slender basis for the 'terrorist suicide' conclusion reached by the initial report into the incident. The same story was immediately leaked to the press. In the following few days, as evidence of the bloodstains in the shack emerged, there were further misleading leaks to the newspapers. An anonymous article in the *Giornale di Sicilia* reported that the blood was menstrual and that it came from sanitary towels found near by. No such towels had, in fact, been discovered. Peppino's friends visited the site and spent a day of inconceivable anguish filling several plastic bags with bits of Peppino's body that the authorities had neglected to recover. In the shack, they also found a stone covered in more blood; when they showed it to an independent forensic scientist, the blood turned out to be from the same rare group as Peppino's.

In the days following, Peppino's friends' houses were subject to mysterious break-ins. There were rumours in Cinisi that Peppino had a dossier on the local mafia and its political and business links – Peppino himself had hinted as much – but no such dossier was ever located. Tensions ran high; at Peppino's funeral procession, 1,000 activists and friends carried banners:

'Peppino was murdered by the mafia', 'With Peppino's ideas and courage we will carry on'. Some later gathered in front of Don Tano Badalamenti's house shouting, 'Butcher.'

The parliamentary inquiry of 2000 is a sorry catalogue of omissions and suspicions. Peppino's brother testified to the parliamentary commissioners that relations between the local mafia and the *carabinieri* appeared to be good before the murder. 'I often saw them [the *carabinieri*] walking arm-in-arm with Tano Badalamenti and his deputies. You can't have faith in the institutions when you see *mafiosi* arm-in-arm with *carabinieri*.' The commission of inquiry concluded that this was a symptom of the way that the authorities had traditionally sought to live side by side with the informal power of the mafia in places like Cinisi.

Whatever the reasons for the way the investigation was handled in its early stages, the trail had gone cold by the time more competent investigating magistrates took over the case. They could only conclude, in 1984, that Peppino had indeed been murdered by the mafia but that it was not possible to identify the individual culprits.

The case was reopened eight years later as the result of campaigning by those close to Peppino, notably his mother, his brother, and the historian Umberto Santino. But even in 1992, investigators had to conclude that there was not enough evidence for a prosecution. New testimonies from *pentiti* finally resulted in Don Tano Badalamenti's being committed for trial in 1999; by then he was already serving a long sentence in a New Jersey penitentiary for drug trafficking. While the trial was still continuing, and while the parliamentary inquiry was looking into the case, a powerful film of Peppino Impastato's story won the Leone d'oro for the best screenplay at the Venice Film Festival; it was called *I cento passi* – 'One Hundred Steps' – because that was the precise distance between Peppino's home and Tano Badalamenti's.

At last, in April 2002, Don Tano was given a life sentence for ordering the murder. Felicia Bartolotta Impastato's reaction to the verdict was profoundly dignified:

I have never had any feelings of *vendetta*. All I have done is call for justice for my son's death. I have to confess that, after so many years of waiting, I had lost faith – I never thought we would reach this point. Now I feel a great deal of contentment, of satisfaction. I always knew what happened. Badalamenti used to call my husband Luigi to complain about Peppino, and my husband begged him not to kill the boy.

These words demonstrate the astral distance that there now is between Peppino's mother and the deathly domestic environment of honour and *omertà* in which she had been confined for so long. Her experience has provided crucial insights into the role of women in Cosa Nostra. For it is through the women of families close to Cosa Nostra that the mafia's values – the code of honour, the contempt for the law, the tolerance of violence – are taught to the very young and handed down through the generations. Interviewed in 2001, Peppino's mother made it clear how important women were to the mafia, how proud some Cinisi women were to call themselves *mafiose*; as she heard one such woman say, 'My brothers were born mafiosi. Some are born stupid, and some are born mafiosi; my brothers were born mafiosi!'

Antimafia campaigners are now no longer as isolated and as alienated from the authorities as Peppino Impastato. Sicily has a varied constellation of antimafia associations. Felicia Bartolotta Impastato, like her son, has become one of the symbols of this broad-based movement. All the same, it is a sign of Sicily's misfortunes that it still needs symbols like them. And it is difficult to conclude that the justice they have finally won after a quarter of a century is really justice at all.

Heroin: The Pizza Connection

The bosses who began to be released from jail following the trial verdicts of 1968–9 had lost a great deal of money. Legal fees and the expense of supporting prisoners had emptied their coffers. Catania man of honour Antonino Calderone, who later turned state's evidence and talked to Judge Falcone in 1987, had a particularly vivid memory of those hard times. He recalled that Totò 'Shorty' Riina had wept because he was unable to pay for his mother to come and visit him while he was awaiting trial. Calderone also remembered how rapidly the situation changed once the mafia became active again. 'They all became millionaires. Suddenly, in a couple of years. Because of drugs.' The history of Cosa Nostra in the 1970s rides on a flood tide of heroin profits. And it was that flood that ultimately led to the bloodiest conflict in the mafia's history.

Not that all Palermo mafiosi were poor in 1970. The Grecos, Cosa Nostra's royal family, were still more than comfortable. In Cinisi, Don Tano Badalamenti's transatlantic business had not been hampered by the aftermath of the first mafia war. But many of the other capos needed money quickly, the Corleonesi more than any of them. Thus it was that they turned to kidnapping as a way of meeting their basic needs and accumulating capital. The principal targets were the offspring of leading Palermo businessmen; the profits earned were then turned into seed capital for illegal business. The 1970s saw a boom in tobacco smuggling, centred on Naples. Whereas Tommaso Buscetta had been trafficking in hundreds of cases of cigarettes between Sicily and the mainland back in the 1950s, Neapolitan smugglers and their Sicilian partners were now dealing in shiploads. Camorra chief Michele 'Mad Mike' Zaza later admitted dealing in 50,000 cases of cigarettes per month. More and more mafiosi were drawn towards Naples to partake of the profits.

Even the immense profits of tobacco were soon to be outstripped in importance by heroin. US President Richard Nixon announced a 'war on drugs' soon after his inauguration in 1969. Like most such wars, it ultimately proved counter-productive. By causing the closure of Corsican-run refineries in Marseilles, the Nixon administration created the opportunity for Sicily to become the new base for this crucial phase of heroin's long journey from the poppy fields of the Near and Far East to the streets of American cities. In 1975, a Turkish drugs and arms dealer who had been the main supplier of morphine base to the Marseilles refineries approached Cosa Nostra directly. Soon afterwards heroin laboratories began to appear across western Sicily, staffed initially by chemists who were refugees from Marseilles. The figures for heroin addiction across Western Europe and North America registered a huge leap in 1977 as the Sicilian refineries came on stream. The amount of heroin seized across the world increased by nearly six and a half times between 1974 and 1982, the years when the Sicilian mafia established its dominance of the market.

But mafiosi from Sicily were not content to be refiners and importers of heroin; with the collaboration of their US peers they also aimed to control their own distribution network. Tommaso Buscetta started up his first pizzeria as long ago as 1966 with a loan from New York's Gambino family. By the late 1970s, nine out of every ten Sicilian illegal aliens deported from the US were found working in pizzerias. The importation and production of Italian foodstuffs had been important to the American mafia since the beginning of the century. So it is no surprise that the supply of ingredients to the network of restaurants springing up across the USA was monopolized by mafia-protected firms. The Pizza Connection case in the USA in 1986 would prove that many of these outlets were dealing in much more than the odd *margherita* or *quattro formaggi*. Pizza parlours were the mafia's transnational heroin distribution network.

By 1982, Sicilian mafiosi were estimated to control the refining, shipping, and much of the distribution of 80 per cent of the heroin consumed in the north-eastern United States. The profits that funnelled back to Sicily, of which no definitive calculation will ever be reached for obvious reasons, were certainly of the order of hundreds of millions of dollars per year. In the late 1970s, Cosa Nostra became wealthier and more powerful than it had ever been before.

The Pizza Connection also involved a new balance of power between the two arms of Cosa Nostra. The Sicilians – the 'zips' as lower-ranking US men of honour enviously called them – were no longer just cheap labour for the American bosses. Senior American mobsters could no longer afford to adopt the patronizing attitudes towards the Sicilians that Joe 'Bananas' Bonanno had done on his holiday back in 1957. With their numbers, their organization, and their access to seemingly limitless supplies of heroin, the Sicilians now had considerable autonomy in the United States.

Knickerbocker Avenue, in the Bonanno Family's Brooklyn territory, became a Sicilian colony and heroin terminal. One DEA agent who infiltrated the Philadelphia Family of Cosa Nostra learned that

Brooklyn meant the Sicilian mafia, as distinguished from the Italian-American La Cosa Nostra in the United States. There was a distinct difference . . . Brooklyn controlled all the heroin in the United States . . . The Sicilians used the Italo-Americans to distribute the heroin.

But the zips had not only established an enterprise syndicate in the United States; they were also making serious inroads into the American Cosa Nostra power syndicate. Special Agent Joseph D. Pistone (a.k.a. Donnie Brasco) infiltrated the Bonanno Family in New York on behalf of the FBI from 1975 until 1981. He recorded the following anxious conversation between two American men of honour who had heard that some of the Sicilians were going to be made into captains:

– those guys [the zips] are looking to take over everything. There's no way we can make them captains. We'd lose all our strength.

– . . . them fucking zips ain't going to back up to nobody. You give them the fucking power, if you don't get hurt now, you get hurt three years from now. They'll bury you. You cannot give them the power. They don't give a fuck. They don't care who's boss. They got no respect.

In 1979, a Sicilian man of honour actually took over the whole Bonanno Family of the New York mafia for two years. He is said to have stepped down only because he found it difficult doing business in English.

But Sicilian and American mafiosi were by no means always rivals in the heroin industry. In fact many of them were relatives. A mafioso looking for trustworthy partners and workers for his drug business will turn first to his blood family, preferably family members who provide the extra guarantee of being mafia initiates. When heroin commerce moved into overdrive in the 1970s, many men of honour were in the fortunate position of already having transatlantic family businesses that could adapt easily to trading in whatever illicit commodity they needed to. This is particularly true of those coastal towns that tended to have the closest links with the United States. An obvious case in point is Cinisi, home of Don Tano Badalamenti. Another is the nearby Castellammare del Golfo, place of origin of Sicilian-American criminal bloodlines like the Magaddinos and the Bonannos. Palermo too had such links; Salvatore Inzerillo, the capo of the venerable Passo di Rigano Family and a major heroin dealer, was the cousin of Carlo Gambino who headed the most powerful of the five New York Families until his death in 1976. Clans like the Inzerillos, the Badalamentis, and the Magaddinos kept on travelling back and forth across the Atlantic; cousins from the US and Sicily kept on marrying each other down through the generations. The Inzerillos' transoceanic family tree caused Judge Falcone to scratch his head at the 'incredible kinship tangle'.

Drug trafficking is all about contacts, about bringing together a gallery of specialists: from investors, to the suppliers of morphine base, to technicians able to refine the drug, to transporters, to small-time dealers who put it on the streets, to financiers with the expertise required to launder the profits and keep them out of the grasp of the Guardia di Finanza (the Italian tax police). These networks are international and they spread from the top to the bottom of society. And they are *not* the same thing as the mafia.

Mafiosi have dealt in drugs for as long as drugs have been dealt. But the mafia *as such* has never been a heroin conglomerate. As Buscetta said, 'In narcotics trafficking everyone was autonomous. The people who had the most economic opportunities did the most work.' 'Having economic opportunities' means weaving webs of contacts with specialists outside the organization.

Of course there are limits to the principle of autonomy, and everything that a man of honour does can have political implications within Cosa Nostra. A Family has the right to tax any economic activity carried out on its turf, or to exact tribute from any of its men of honour who are involved in enterprises not directly under its control. The easiest way for a mafia boss to profit from drugs is to 'protect' the dealers. This method has the added advantage of keeping the narcotics trade at one remove from the Family; because the specialists that the trade requires are not bound by *omertà*, they bring higher risks because they are likely to tell the police too much when they are arrested.

But when the profits are so large that they generate rivalries between Families, then the Commission is likely to become involved. And when the Commission is involved, it absorbs the business in question into Cosa Nostra's structure; it is the criminal equivalent of taking a company into public ownership. Getting a panel of senior bosses to manage a business is a way of making sure that they all know what is going on, and that they all get a share of the profits.

A typical instance is the tobacco smuggling through Naples

in the mid-1970s. The Commission began to act as a consortium or joint stock company to buy tobacco shipments through Michele 'Mad Mike' Zaza – in exactly the way that it had done for heroin deals before the first mafia war. In 1974, Zaza and several other prominent Camorristi were even initiated into Cosa Nostra as a way of flattering them and keeping them under control. All the same, the Commission did not and could not monopolize either the mafia's cigarette smuggling or its heroin trade. For one thing, it represented the province of Palermo rather than the whole island. Much of the heroin business remained off the Commission's radar and outside its control. The result was the same volatile admixture of business, politics, and suspicion that had led to the first mafia war.

Bankers, Masons, Tax Collectors, Mafiosi

The drug revenue flowing back from the United States put gold taps in tiny peasant houses, built apartment blocks and seaside villas, emptied the shelves of Palermo's burgeoning luxury boutiques, and was reinvested in legal and illegal ventures across Italy and Europe. The heroin dollars also leaked into the grass roots of the financial sector (in the 1970s, an archipelago of local private and cooperative banks doubled its share of the Sicilian investment market) and were sucked towards the commanding heights of the Italian banking system where they mingled with the profits of political corruption. Following the money, mafiosi reached further than ever into the topmost echelons of society.

Giovanni Falcone arrived in the Palace of Justice in Palermo in 1978. Within two years the 'Falcone method' produced a breakthrough in a case that went to the heart of Cosa Nostra's transatlantic drug business: it linked Passo di Rigano boss Salvatore Inzerillo; the so-called 'Cherry Hill Gambinos' in Brooklyn; the building magnate and largest taxpayer in Sicily, Rosario Spatola; and former triumvirate member Stefano Bontate – each of them part of a sprawling web of marriage alliances. Falcone was also working with magistrates in Milan on a fraud and murder case that threatened to expose the very worst of Italian society in the form of corruption, mafia influence, and anti-democratic conspiracy at the highest levels of the political and financial institutions.

The case centred on banker Michele Sindona. In the early 1970s, Sindona was the most influential financial figure in Italy. He was in charge of one of the biggest banks in the USA, had control over the Vatican's foreign investments, and was a major funder of Christian Democrat politicians. In addition, he was

19. 'Pushy Corleonese embezzler' Vito Ciancimino (with the cigarette) who was linked to Cosa Nostra's 'sack of Palermo'.

20. Cardinal Ernesto Ruffini lends legitimacy to a mafia-backed politician, Salvo Lima. Palermo, 1957.

21. The remains of the stolen Alfa Romeo Giulietta that exploded killing seven officers and men at Ciaculli, June 1963.

22. The monument to the victims of the Ciaculli bomb. Its inscription now has a hollow ring: 'Placed by the Sicilian regional government in memory of the men cut down by the mafia in Ciaculli. Their sacrifice transformed public abhorrence into a movement for civic redemption'.

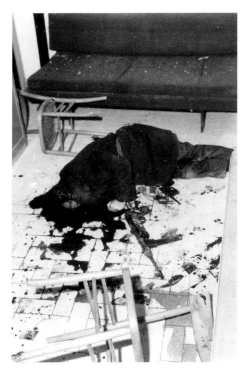

23. The massacre in Viale Lazio, 10 December 1969. It signalled the mafia's return to action following the Ciaculli outrage.

24. Women from within the mafia environment can pose a threat to the organization: Serafina Battaglia pictured during the trial of the two mafiosi who were suspected (but later acquitted) of killing her son. She had earlier encouraged her son to avenge the murder of her husband who was himself killed in a mafia feud. 1960s.

25. Funeral in 'Tombstone'. Followers of Michele 'Our Father' Navarra are taken for burial after a gun battle with Luciano Leggio's men in the centre of the town. Corleone, 1958.

26. Luciano Leggio, in court in the 1970s, adopts a pose that seems to owe much to Marlon Brando in the guise of the fictional Don Corleone.

The two killings that inaugurated the second mafia war, the *mattanza*, in April and May 1981.

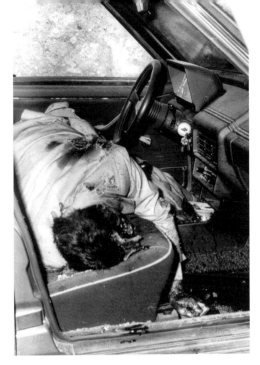

27. Stefano Bontate, 'Prince of Villagrazia'.

28. Salvatore Inzerillo, capo of Palermo's Passo di Rigano Family and cousin of New York boss Carlo Gambino.

29. Cinisi, 1952. Peppino Impastato, later to become a martyr of the struggle against Cosa Nostra, is the little boy to the left of the picture, holding his father's hand.

30. Seven-times Prime Minister of Italy Giulio Andreotti (with the glasses) pictured alongside his friend Salvo Lima, who was for decades the hinge between the mafia and politics.

31. Another day in court for the defendants at the maxi-trial, 1986.

32 & 33. The last-known picture, taken in 1959, of the man who now leads Cosa Nostra, Bernardo 'the Tractor' Provenzano. Alongside it is a police photofit of what he may look like today.

34. September 1989: Giovanni Falcone (with hand in jacket pocket) arrives at the scene of a so-called 'transversal vendetta' (in which the family of a mafioso are killed in retaliation). In this case the victims were the mother, sister and aunt of Francesco Marino Mannoia, a mafia defector.

strongly suspected of laundering money for Cosa Nostra. But in 1974 his financial empire collapsed amid fraud charges and he fled to the United States. From there, in 1979, he commissioned a mafioso to shoot dead the lawyer in charge of liquidating his Italian affairs. As the authorities on both sides of the Atlantic closed in on him, Sindona then enlisted the help of the same mafiosi who were involved in the Inzerillo–Gambino–Spatola–Bontate heroin smuggling ring to stage his own hoax kidnapping by the 'Subversive Proletarian Committee for a Better Life' (a non-existent left-wing terrorist group). He spent nearly three months in Sicily in the hands of the 'terrorists', and even arranged to be anaesthetized and shot in the left thigh as evidence of their deadly intent. The real goal of the kidnapping was to issue thinly disguised blackmail notes to Sindona's former political allies in the hope that they could still engineer the salvation of his banks – and therefore of Cosa Nostra's money. The plot failed; Sindona was 'released' by his captors and gave himself up to the FBI; he died in prison in 1986 after drinking coffee laced with cyanide.

In the summer of 1982, another disgraced Italian banker, Roberto Calvi, was found hanging under Blackfriars Bridge in London. Calvi's career reads like an echo of Sindona's: a rapid rise, close ties to the Vatican, funds channelled to governing political parties, and a financial collapse followed by desperate attempts to save himself by blackmailing politicians. It took until April 2002 for it to be confirmed – in the minds of the Italian authorities, at least – that Calvi had not taken his own life as was first believed, but was in fact 'suicided'; the Italian language twists 'suicide' into a transitive verb to describe such cases. At the time of writing, a mafia boss close to the Corleonesi seems likely to go on trial for allegedly ordering his death. The prosecution's thesis, based on the evidence of a mafia *pentito*, is that Calvi was recycling drug money for the Corleonesi in the same way that Sindona did for the Inzerillo–Gambino–Spatola–Bontate group, and that he was murdered because he too had proved unreliable. It is anticipated that the man of honour in question will deny the charges.

Both of 'God's bankers' were members of a Masonic lodge known as Propaganda 2 or P2. In March 1981, magistrates from Milan investigating Sindona's fake kidnapping discovered a list of 962 members of P2 at the office of its Grand Master, Licio Gelli. Among the men who had taken its oath were the entire leadership of the secret services, forty-four members of parliament, and a slew of senior businessmen, military figures, policemen, civil servants, and journalists. The parliamentary inquiry into P2 concluded that its aim had been to pollute public life and undermine democracy, although not all of the Lodge's members were aware of its underlying aims; its Grand Master had almost certainly been keeping secret papers on members for blackmail purposes. The exact extent of P2's influence is still unclear.

The relationship between the mafia and other Masonic groups is easier to define. Starting in the 1970s, some senior men of honour joined lodges as a way of making contact with businessmen, bureaucrats, and politicians. As one *pentito* explained, 'Through the Freemasons you can make comprehensive contact with businessmen, with the institutions, with the men who wield a different kind of power to the punitive power that Cosa Nostra has.'

One example demonstrates how insidious an influence these networks can be: the parliamentary inquiry into the Sindona affair found that the plastic surgeon who anaesthetized and wounded Michele Sindona during his fake kidnapping was, by his own definition, 'a sentimental international Mason' with close links both to mafiosi and to the Grand Master of P2. For nineteen years he was also the resident doctor at Palermo police headquarters and may have had friends in the US government.

It would be a mistake to assume that the 'white-collar' Masons were the dominant partners in this venal tango with the thugs of Cosa Nostra. For one thing, there was no question of a conflict of loyalties for anyone who was a member of both secret societies. Cosa Nostra's interests always come first, as one *pentito* explained: 'The [Masonic] oath is a fiction because we've only got one oath that we respect – the one we take in Cosa Nostra.'

It is now known that the two richest men in Sicily in the 1960s and 1970s took both oaths, Masonic and mafioso. They were the Salvo cousins, Nino and Ignazio. Nino Salvo was an abrasive, outgoing man of honour from the Salemi Family in the province of Trapani. In 1955, he married a woman whose father ran one of the small companies that held tax-collecting contracts. In Sicily both direct and indirect taxes were paid through private firms in a system that the leading historian of Palermo has called 'an infernal money-eating machine'. Together with his father-in-law and his more urbane cousin Ignazio, Nino would go on to form a cartel that in 1959 secured the right to collect 40 per cent of Sicily's taxes. In 1962, with the help of 'young Turk' Salvo Lima, the Salvo cousins' company won the contract to collect taxes in Palermo – a business that alone generated over $2 million (1960s values) per year in profit. Their control over the tax-collection system grew still further in the mid-1960s, and would last until the early 1980s. Where similar businesses elsewhere in Italy generally took around 3 per cent of what they gathered as profit, the Salvos raked off a constant 10 per cent. The cousins supplemented their income by cornering huge European Union and Italian government subsidies for the agribusiness concerns that they set up with their tax-collecting booty.

Naturally this level of robbery could not have been maintained without solid and extensive political support, particularly in the Sicilian Regional Assembly. In fact a corrupt short circuit between the Salvos, the mafia, and sections of the DC deformed the whole Sicilian political system. It was bad enough that Salvo funds were kicked back to politicians in return for support when it came to renewing tax-collecting contracts or fending off the periodic attempts to bring this valuable service under public control. But there was more to it than that. In the Regional Assembly, as in town councils across the island, many politicians were actually recruited and chosen by the mafia in consultation with senior DC bosses.

In 1982 Judge Falcone subjected the Salvo cousins' affairs to an audit – an unheard-of gesture of *lèse-majesté*. His head-on confrontation with Cosa Nostra was only just getting under way. But by then the narcotics boom had begun to immerse the Sicilian mafia deeper in blood than it had ever been.

Rise of the Corleonesi:
2 – Towards the *Mattanza* (1970–1983)

The second mafia war of 1981–3 is known in Italian as *la mattanza*, a term that comes from the fishing industry. Short of travelling to watch a *mattanza* at the old Florio fishery on Favignana, the best way to get a sense of the power of this metaphor is to see how Roberto Rossellini registered the impact of a real *mattanza* on the face of his lover and leading actress, Ingrid Bergman, in the most famous sequence from his 1950 film *Stromboli*. Bergman plays a Lithuanian refugee who marries a poor Sicilian fisherman to escape an internment camp. The harsh reality of his life is played out before her eyes when the tuna fishermen tow their catch into a calm bay, circle their boats and wail a rhythmic dirge as they haul nets full of huge, thrashing fish to the surface. Then Bergman looks on in shock as the tuna are battered and hauled aboard with fearsome hooked harpoons, turning the water to gore and spume.

The savage mafia cull of 1981–3 did not come unannounced. A full three years before the slaughter began, the *carabinieri* were given an accurate map of the battle lines and a briefing on the tactics of the winners – the Corleonesi. In April 1978, Giuseppe Di Cristina, a man of honour, secretly arranged to talk to a captain of the *carabinieri* in an isolated cottage. Di Cristina was a far higher-ranking informer than poor Leonardo Vitale. For one thing, he was the boss of Riesi in central-southern Sicily. For another, he was probably one of the men of honour who dressed up as a policeman to take part in the viale Lazio massacre of 1969; his presence at that symbolically important collective execution was meant to demonstrate that it was willed by the whole of Cosa Nostra, not just Palermo. Di Cristina, in short, was at the heart of the mafia system. Yet the *carabinieri* present at the meeting said he looked like a hunted animal.

The man who inspired Di Cristina's fear was Luciano Leggio. As Di Cristina explained, Leggio was now a multi-millionaire. The former 'Scarlet Pimpernel' of Corleone had been in jail for four years, but was still running his affairs from behind bars through his avatars 'Shorty' Riina and 'Tractor' Provenzano; Di Cristina estimated that these two, known as 'the beasts', were each guilty of at least forty murders. Leggio's sources of income included kidnappings carried out on the Italian mainland. In 1973, Eugene Paul Getty III, seventeen-year-old grandson of one of the richest men in the world, was abducted in Rome. He was only freed five months later when a ransom in the region of $2.5 million was handed over; the boy's ear and a lock of his hair had earlier been sent to a newspaper as proof of the kidnappers' strength of mind. It was all Leggio's work, according to Di Cristina.

But more significant even than Di Cristina's revelations about Luciano Leggio was the picture he drew of the political divisions within Cosa Nostra. The organization was splitting between two factions. The undisputed leader of the first was Leggio. Set against him was a faction led by Don Tano Badalamenti, the 'Sitting Bully' of Cinisi (and, incidentally, Leggio's *compare*).

What Di Cristina had realized is that the Corleonesi were engaged in a long-term strategy aimed at encircling the opposing faction. They were enlisting supporters one by one from the Families that presided over the small towns in the province of Palermo and the rest of Sicily. As a loyal follower of former triumvirate member Stefano Bontate – a key component of the Badalamenti faction – Di Cristina was one of the last provincial obstacles the Corleonesi had to remove before they could complete their plan of attack with an assault on Palermo itself. (Because he was so close to Bontate, Di Cristina was much less forthcoming about Badalamenti's faction and did not mention that it also included two of the most important heroin dealers in Cosa Nostra: Passo di Rigano boss Salvatore

'Totuccio' Inzerillo and, still lurking in prison, Tommaso Buscetta.)

Like almost all mafiosi who have talked to the police at different times through the association's history, Di Cristina had few options left. Leggio commanded an elite death squad of fourteen men with bases not only in Sicily, but also in Naples, Rome, and other Italian cities. The Corleonesi had infiltrated the Families of their enemies. (It later emerged that they were also building a secret army by initiating men of honour without informing the other leaders.) Di Cristina's only hope was that the *carabinieri* could act against the Corleonesi first, perhaps by capturing Provenzano who had been a fugitive from justice for fifteen years. Di Cristina told the *carabinieri* that 'the Tractor' had been seen very recently near Bagheria, in a white Mercedes driven by the young Giovanni 'lo scannacristiani' Brusca. The Bruscas of San Giuseppe Jato were among Leggio's oldest allies – they constituted the keystone of the Corleonese faction in the province of Palermo. It is not by chance that Totò 'Shorty' Riina was godfather to 'lo scannacristiani' when he was initiated in 1976.

Di Cristina concluded his chat with the *carabinieri* in a reflective mood: 'By the end of next week I'll be taking delivery of a bullet-proof car . . . You know, I've got a few venial sins on my conscience. And some mortal ones too.' A few weeks later his sins caught up with him when he was shot dead in Passo di Rigano on the outskirts of Palermo. Had they known how to interpret it, the *carabinieri* would have derived further confirmation of how the coming war would evolve from the manner of Di Cristina's death, because Passo di Rigano was the fief of Salvatore 'Totuccio' Inzerillo, a leading member of the anti-Corleonese faction. There could hardly be a more blatant *sfregio* than this: the killing of a boss carried out on someone else's territory without permission.

Thousands of people attended Di Cristina's funeral – virtually the whole town of Riesi. At around the same time the *carabinieri* produced a lucid report on just how important was his testimony:

The information provided by Di Cristina reveals a hidden and truly paradoxical truth; it reveals the chilling reality that, parallel to the authority of the state, there is a more incisive and efficient power that acts, moves, makes money, kills, and even makes judgements – all behind the back of the authorities.

No judicial action followed.

Since Di Cristina, and since the *mattanza*, more mafia defectors have helped the political build-up to the second mafia war to be reconstructed. The Corleonesi began manoeuvring to establish their domination over Cosa Nostra very soon after the organization started operating again under the Bontate–Badalamenti–Leggio triumvirate in 1970. Militarily strong but financially weak at this stage, Leggio and his 'beasts' turned kidnapping into a gesture aimed at redistributing wealth and demonstrating their power. One victim was the son of Don Ciccio Vassallo who was the leading construction magnate during the sack of Palermo. Both Badalamenti and Bontate were close to Vassallo, but neither could do anything to free the hostage. When after five months the negotiations bore fruit and the ransom was paid, 'Shorty' Riina distributed it to the neediest Families in the Palermo area; the Corleonesi were already thinking for the long term, investing in their allies within Cosa Nostra's state structure rather than in new business ventures.

In 1975, Riina inflicted an even more smarting humiliation on Stefano Bontate by kidnapping and killing the father-in-law of Nino Salvo – one of the cousins who ran Sicily's private tax collection empire. For all their political connections, wealth, and pedigree as men of honour, neither Bontate nor Salvo could even recover the old man's body. Riina simply denied having anything to do with the abduction, but as Buscetta later said, 'Shorty' was sending a signal 'as big as a house'. Other mafiosi, observing not only his power and arrogance, but also Badalamenti's and

Bontate's impotence and blindness to the signals, drew the appropriate conclusions about which way to jump if fighting broke out.

In 1977, the Corleonesi expelled Don Tano Badalamenti from Cosa Nostra. The charge was that he had been getting rich on drug money behind the backs of the other bosses – or at least that was the explanation that radiated out from the Commission. It was an extraordinary demonstration of the control that the Corleonesi now had within the Commission, over which Cinisi's 'Sitting Bully' had presided after it was re-established in 1974. Despite being expelled, Badalamenti still retained a formidable power base in Cinisi and its environs, even though he now lived thousands of miles away in the US, but the humiliation that the Corleonesi inflicted showed that his power within Cosa Nostra's institutions was at an end. Badalamenti's replacement as titular head of the Commission was Michele 'the Pope' Greco, the son of Piddu 'the lieutenant'. It was the sign of a firm alliance between the most powerful mafia dynasty of the Palermo out-skirts, the Grecos, and the upstarts from the provincial town of Corleone – with the upstarts easily the more powerful partner. This was the alliance that would go to war in 1981.

Giuseppe Di Cristina's murder saw the Corleonesi establish their authority over the central Sicilian province of Caltanissetta. A few months later they killed Pippo Calderone who in 1975 had set up the Region, the mafia's governing body for the whole of Sicily. Calderone's Catania Family was placed in the hands of a Corleonese ally and one of their major suppliers of drugs and arms – Nitto 'the Hunter' Santapaola. With 'the Hunter' in place, most of Cosa Nostra's structure outside of Palermo was now in the grip of the Corleonesi.

At some point around this time, the leadership of Leggio's faction passed into the hands of his disciple 'Shorty' Riina, closely assisted by 'Tractor' Provenzano. One later mafia defector who knew Riina well described how his docile and humble manner contrasted with that of the volatile Leggio: 'I've never seen him angry.' It was a practice of deceit that he tried to pass on to his followers: 'They always had a smile on their lips. Riina chose people like that and taught them that they had to smile – even if there was an earthquake.'

From one perspective, Bontate, Inzerillo, and Badalamenti still held a great deal more power than the smiling Corleonesi. They were all the capos of Families, well connected in the United States and spectacularly wealthy drug traffickers, able to call on political protection at the highest levels; Bontate was also the most important conduit between the mafia and the world of secret Masonic societies. But much of their power now lay *outside* Cosa Nostra. The Corleonesi, by contrast, were cut out of the major flows of the transatlantic narcotics trade. Yet as their strategy evolved over the years, they patiently cultivated power *within* Cosa Nostra. Secretly they invested money and honour in winning control of the Families and the Commission, in dominating the power syndicate rather than making huge short-term profits through enterprise syndicate activities. In taking over the Commission, the Corleonesi had also taken over Cosa Nostra's collective decision-making apparatus, its judicial system, its office of propaganda and, most importantly, its military machine. If Cosa Nostra is a kind of state, then the Corleonesi were now ready to mount a military *coup d'état*.

Tommaso Buscetta was released from jail in 1980. Before joining his young wife in South America, he spent several months in Palermo, touring a world of pharaonic luxury and power that was about to sink in gore. He stayed for a while in a hotel complex belonging to the Salvo cousins; Nino asked him to act as a counterweight to Riina, but Buscetta sensed what was just over the horizon and stuck to his plans to go abroad. He also lived with both Bontate and Inzerillo, finding them impervious to the impending carnage and completely absorbed in the heroin industry, which was now at its very peak. Every day between fifty and a hundred cars were parked outside Inzerillo's villa as the worker ants of the drug trade – mafia soldiers, heroin refiners and carriers – came and went. '[Bontate and Inzerillo] talked about villas by the sea and in the mountains, about billions of lire, yachts and banks – all as if they were talking about a morning's food shopping.' Buscetta resisted their appeals to stay and join the bonanza; they were even able to give him $500,000 as a goodbye present – so he claims. In January 1981, the 'boss of two worlds' took a plane to Brazil, intending never to return.

The *mattanza* that Giuseppe Di Cristina had predicted, and for which the Corleonesi had so long prepared, finally started on 23 April 1981. The first victim was Stefano Bontate, the 'Prince of Villagrazia'. He was driving his brand-new, limited-edition red Alfa Romeo back from his own birthday party when he was rendered unrecognizable by machine-gun fire at a traffic light. Two and a half weeks later the same fate befell Salvatore Inzerillo. He had also recently taken delivery of an Alfa Romeo, an armoured version. But his killers shot him as he left his lover's house and before he reached the car.

With Tommaso Buscetta and Tano Badalamenti now in Brazil and the United States respectively, the Corleonesi had simply decapitated the opposing faction by killing Bontate and Inzerillo. The daring of the attack seemed breathtaking. Most mafia-watchers expected a ferocious reaction from the Bontate–Inzerillo group. But what ensued was simply a mass execution of their followers. The losing side was totally disorientated. What Judge Falcone called a 'ghost army' of Corleonese assassins, recruited in the small towns of the province of Palermo, would appear in the city, kill, and vanish again. A month after Inzerillo's death, Tommaso Buscetta telephoned Palermo from Brazil to speak to a construction entrepreneur close to both Bontate and Inzerillo. The man begged Buscetta to come back and organize the resistance to the Corleonesi. But 'the boss of two worlds' knew better than to give his life in a hopeless cause. Just as they had done in Corleone back in 1958 with the murder of Dr Michele Navarra, the Corleonesi were pitting overwhelming military force against wealth and political influence. It was no contest.

In the weeks and months that followed, 200 men belonging to the Bontate–Inzerillo faction were killed in the province of Palermo – to count only the bodies that were actually found. More disappeared, the victims of 'white shotgun' murders. On 30 November 1982 alone, twelve men of honour were shot dead at different times and in different parts of the city. Most of the enemies of the Corleonesi were killed before they even knew they were in danger, betrayed by men within their own Family who had secretly joined the Corleonesi; some were even eliminated by their own men and presented as sacrificial offerings to the victors. The Families and *mandamenti* of murdered leaders were immediately handed over to Corleonese loyalists.

The *mattanza* even extended to the United States. John Gambino was reportedly sent over from New York to Palermo to find out what was happening. He returned with a clear instruction: all possible efforts were to be made to find and eliminate Tommaso Buscetta; all Sicilian mafiosi from the losing faction who attempted to escape death by fleeing across the Atlantic were to be killed. Shortly afterwards Inzerillo's brother was found dead in Mont Laurel, New Jersey, with five one-dollar bills stuffed in his mouth and another in his genitals.

The Corleonesi were not just exterminating their enemies, they were killing any man of honour whose absolute loyalty was even remotely in doubt. They also enforced a scorched earth policy of stunning brutality around any member of the Bontate–Inzerillo faction who went into hiding. Any friends, relatives, or business associates who might plausibly offer shelter were cut down.

The emblematic case is that of faithful Bontate soldier Salvatore Contorno, who escaped in dramatic fashion from a carefully coordinated machine-gun ambush in the main street of Brancaccio, a township to the east of Palermo. An incredible thirty-five of his relatives were then murdered. Contorno began to give information to the police off the record. When he heard that Buscetta had turned state's evidence in the summer of 1984, he would not believe it until he was brought face to face with 'the boss of two worlds'. At their meeting Contorno knelt down before Buscetta and received his blessing before taking the decision to give evidence to Judge Falcone. His testimony would be almost as important to the maxi-trial as Buscetta's.

The *mattanza* dragged on and on; in fact there never was a clear ending because when 'Shorty' Riina had done with his enemies and with the fence-sitters, he turned on any of his own allies who had begun to show signs of independent thinking. The most prominent victim of this new phase of the killing was Pino 'the Shoe' Greco, underboss of the Ciaculli Family, the leading Corleonese assassin in the early stages of the *mattanza*. 'The Shoe' was a member of the firing party that had murdered both Bontate and Inzerillo. He had then murdered Inzerillo's teenage son after the boy swore to avenge his father's death. The rumours inside Cosa Nostra were that 'the Shoe' had cut off the boy's arm before killing him so as to demonstrate the futility of rebellion against the power of the Corleonesi. In the autumn of 1985, 'the Shoe' was shot dead by his own men on the orders of Riina.

The tactics that the Corleonesi had evolved over more than three decades had come to fruition: they had established a dictatorship over Cosa Nostra based on a rolling programme of executions. In doing so they had not betrayed Cosa Nostra's value system, as many defectors later claimed; they had instead revealed its very essence.

10

Terra Infidelium
1983–1992

The Virtuous Minority

A British historian has spoken of the 'virtuous minorities' within the Italian state. A few countries are lucky enough to take certain things almost for granted, like the notion that everyone is equal before the law, or that the state should serve the interests of all its citizens rather than the friends and family of whoever happens to wield power, whether it be in a national ministry or in a local hospital. All too often in Italy – and not just in Italy – such values have to be fought for, day to day, by a virtuous minority of people from all walks of life and of all political persuasions. It is not, of course, that the majority of Italians are corrupt, or that Italian public life is entirely rotten. As is doubtless true of most societies around the world, the majority just adapt to survive in the environment in which they find themselves.

Italy's virtuous minorities have rarely seemed so beleaguered as during the 1980s. The terrorist emergency slowly subsided, the labour movement went into retreat, support for the PCI declined, and a new economic boom began to gather pace. But at the same time sleaze sank deeper than ever into the fabric of society. The Socialist Party, now a permanent partner in governing coalitions, all but abandoned its reforming goals and strove to 'occupy the state' in the same way that the DC had done since the 1950s. These were the years of what Italians called the 'party-ocracy', when all state employees from the board members of nationalized banks down to school janitors seemed to have been chosen on the basis of party affiliation. For businesses in some towns and cities, winning a government contract of any kind inevitably involved paying kickbacks to party bag carriers.

Amid the constant horse-trading between factions in parliament, and with public opinion increasingly resigned and disillusioned, the Italian political class of the 1980s was hardly likely to slough its century-old habit of treating Sicilian society as if it amounted to no more than a squabbling band of politicians to buy off. Tragically, this same political class was called on to confront Cosa Nostra at a time when it became wealthier and more bloodthirsty than ever before.

The Sicilian mafia has always brought out the worst and the best in the Italian state, both its most duplicitous villains, and the most virtuous of the virtuous minorities. In the year before his death, Giovanni Falcone gave a series of interviews to a French journalist in which he famously explained that he was not some suicidal Robin Hood: 'I am simply a servant of the state in *terra infidelium*' – in the land of the infidels. In a country that now had a respectable claim to be the fifth largest industrial economy on earth, Sicily was still a frontier zone for the rule of law.

Falcone was in many ways the figurehead of Italy's virtuous minorities, and it is not hagiographic to say that he demonstrated their virtues in a pure form: courage, of course, but also devotion to his job and a legendary capacity for hard work. Falcone was also rigorously honest and correct in his dealings with people; it was a trait that could at times make him seem stiff and unfriendly. But more than a facet of his character, it was a calculated defence mechanism both for himself and for those around him. Anyone who had regular access to him, even the most upright of his friends, was a potential channel through which Cosa Nostra could make an approach.

Francesco La Licata, one journalist who often interviewed Falcone, experienced just such an approach at first hand. His bizarre encounter with the mafia began one morning over coffee in a bar when someone asked him, 'Do you remember me?' It was Gregorio, a man from the quarter of the city where La Licata had grown up; Gregorio lived on the margins of organized crime. 'Let's go for a ride, and we can talk about how things were when we were kids,' he suggested. Warily, La Licata agreed to get in Gregorio's red VW, but no sooner had he sat down than he noticed the handle of a pistol protruding from the seat pocket. 'There are some people who want to talk to you, but don't worry. Everything's OK,' Gregorio said with a smile.

During the journey La Licata tried to calculate how likely he was to be murdered. After a change of car, he was taken deep into a lemon grove in what remained of the Conca d'Oro. There he was brought face to face with a *capofamiglia* whom he recognized from a police mugshot. The boss began, 'Please excuse us for the way we invited you here. But as you know I'm on the run from the law. We have found out about you. We know you are a reliable type and you do your job honestly.' The mafioso then began to deliver a circuitous, maudlin speech in his own defence. All the while, La Licata struggled to follow what he was hearing while casting nervous glances at the deep water of a cistern near where they stood.

Finally the boss got to the point: 'We know that you can talk to Judge Falcone. You have to tell him how things stand, that we are just family men who are the victims of a shameful smear. All you need to tell him is what I've just finished telling you.' It was a classic opening gambit. Establishing even a vaguely compromising connection of this kind with a judge could open the way for an exchange of favours, blackmail, or intimidation.

La Licata knew that a blank refusal to act as go-between could easily be fatal. Thinking frantically and speaking with measured politeness, he explained that anyone making contact with Falcone on a mafioso's behalf was likely to be put under investigation; he suggested that the boss could make his point through a newspaper interview instead. 'I'm not authorized,' came the reply. 'We don't do that kind of thing.' La Licata's second suggestion – a memorandum sent to Falcone and the press through his lawyers – met with a better reception. 'Well done! Good idea! That way Falcone won't take offence. He's a nasty character.'

In the space of a brief exchange, La Licata had successfully staked his life on Falcone's reputation for rigorous honesty and procedural correctness – what the mafioso called his 'nasty character'. Feeling as if he had survived an air disaster, the journalist was taken back unharmed to the bar he had left a few hours before. He did not tell Falcone the story of his abduction until several years later. By way of reply, Falcone matter-of-factly confirmed that he would indeed have placed him under investigation. The two men became friends.

Eminent Corpses

Emanuele Notarbartolo, the banker and former mayor of Palermo stabbed to death on a train in 1893; and Joe Petrosino, the New York policeman shot dead in Sicily in 1909: in the first century of its existence, the Sicilian mafia killed only two establishment figures, two men whose status in the world of business, politics, administration, journalism, justice, or law enforcement qualified them as *cadaveri eccellenti*. Since the late 1970s, as the power of the Corleonesi has grown, there have been dozens of these 'eminent corpses'. A few of them were friends who failed to respect their pact with the bosses, but the vast majority have been Cosa Nostra's enemies. After 1979, violence became the dominant note in the mafia's duet with the upper world of the institutions. And the violence reached a crescendo as Falcone and other members of the virtuous minority made unprecedented advances in the struggle to defeat Cosa Nostra.

Looking back, the first sign of the new aggression came in 1970 with the disappearance of *L'Ora* investigative reporter Mauro De Mauro. It is still not clear what he had discovered, perhaps evidence of the heroin trade or of the neo-Fascist putsch that year in which Cosa Nostra was asked to take part. In 1971, the Palermo prosecutor Pietro Scaglione was shot dead after visiting his wife's tomb. Considerable suspicion surrounded Scaglione at the time. But it is now known that the doubts about his reputation were the result of the smear tactics the mafia frequently uses against its innocent victims. That is why his death was easily dismissed in some circles as an internal mafia affair. Even the 1977 murder of a colonel in the *carabinieri* near Corleone could still be treated as an anomaly. But in 1979, the new pattern of mafia tactics became unmistakable. In that year, as if to demonstrate how comprehensive was its assault on the institutions, Cosa Nostra killed a journalist (the *Giornale di Sicilia*'s crime correspondent), a politician (the leader of the Palermo DC), a policeman (the chief of the Palermo flying squad), and a magistrate (Cesare Terranova, the man who had led investigations into the first mafia war). The mafia's message was now clear: no matter how prominent, any public figure who stood in the way of Sicily's state within a state was going to be killed.

The demonstrative recklessness and brutality with which many of these murders were performed by the Corleonesi bore its own message too. Terranova died in the street outside his Palermo home; despite the risk of being seen, the three killers fired more than thirty pistol and rifle shots, and even took the time to walk up to the old magistrate and administer a *coup de grâce*. Again and again, around the eminent cadavers were strewn the corpses of guards, drivers, family members, friends, and passers-by. Cosa Nostra was flourishing its savage might. The following year, 1980, saw three eminent corpses: the captain of the *carabinieri* in Monreale, the president of the Sicilian Region, and the chief prosecutor in Palermo. The latter was gunned down in the very centre of the city, within sight of the Teatro Massimo; it was the Sicilian equivalent of carrying out an execution in Piccadilly Circus or Times Square. (This murder was actually ordered by Bontate and Inzerillo to show that they could leave eminent corpses with the same abandon as the Corleonesi.)

Nineteen-eighty-one saw the beginning of the *mattanza*, with its almost daily spectacle of murder; bodies were left near police headquarters or simply burned in the street. One of the most prominent of the mafia's victims fell at the height of the slaughter. Pio La Torre was a straight-talking peasant activist who had risen to become a Communist MP, the leader of the PCI in Sicily, and one of the most dynamic members of the Antimafia commission of inquiry. In April 1982, he was the victim of a carefuly planned ambush, again in a busy Palermo street.

The Italian state's response was to send General Carlo Alberto

Dalla Chiesa to be the new prefect of the Sicilian capital. Dalla Chiesa had a long track record of fighting the mafia, even serving in Corleone when Luciano Leggio began his rise. More importantly, the general had just made himself a national hero by bringing home great successes in the fight against left-wing terrorism. Before setting off, he made it clear to his political masters in Rome that he had no intention of being soft on the mafia's political wing. A few short months after his arrival in Palermo, a firing party of about a dozen mafiosi blocked the road in front of his car in via Carini and machine-gunned him, his young wife, and their escort to death. The day afterwards, someone scrawled on the wall at the scene, 'Here died the hope of all honest Sicilians.' The funeral was televised live across Italy, and the nation saw the angry crowd throwing coins at the government ministers who attended.

The politicians had failed to give Dalla Chiesa the powers he wanted, and a campaign of journalistic sniping created the distinct impression that he was isolated, as his son explained five days after the murder:

During the fight against terrorism my father was used to having his back covered, to having all the constitutional political parties behind him – first among them the DC. This time, as soon as he arrived in Palermo, he understood that a part of the DC was not prepared to cover him. More than that it was actively hostile.

With General Dalla Chiesa given such lukewarm backing, Cosa Nostra felt entitled to treat his appointment as yet another empty gesture, and to calculate that the political price of killing him would be correspondingly low. It would be tempting to label the mafia's tactics in the early 1980s as terroristic, except that terrorists usually see themselves as representatives of the oppressed, as lone fighters taking on a powerful state with the only weapons available to the weak and desperate. Cosa Nostra, by contrast, with its new heroin wealth and its old record of impunity, simply did not take the Italian state seriously. More than a campaign of terror, it was a campaign of scorn.

Further names were soon added to the roster of eminent corpses. Looking back through that catalogue of atrocity, one begins to sense how increasing numbers of Sicilians felt at the time, their exasperated hope that, finally, one of these murders would become a turning point, marking the moment when the Italian state found the resolve to stand up to the mafia threat. There were times when the government did respond. Following the death of General Dalla Chiesa, a law pioneered by the murdered Communist Pio La Torre was finally passed; for the first time it became a crime to belong to a 'mafia-type association', defined as a criminal organization that relied on systematic intimidation, *omertà*, and the infiltration of the economy through extortion rackets carried out on a territorial basis. It was the Italian equivalent of America's RICO measures (Racketeer Influenced and Corrupt Organizations), passed in 1970. The law also allowed the state to confiscate a mafioso's ill-gotten gains. These were hugely important new weapons in the fight to bring Cosa Nostra to justice. But the signals from the politicians remained ambivalent. It was never 'the Italian state' as such that took on Cosa Nostra. The turning point never came. The battle against the mafia continued to be fought by a heroic minority of magistrates and police, supported by a minority of politicians, administrators, journalists, and members of the public.

On 29 July 1983, Cosa Nostra deployed a car bomb in central Palermo to kill Falcone's boss, the chief investigating magistrate, Rocco Chinnici; his two bodyguards and the concierge of the apartment block where he lived also died in the explosion. The first mafia war had seen journalists reach for parallels between Palermo and Prohibition-era Chicago; now Beirut seemed the only possible twin town for the Sicilian capital. One anonymous policeman described the desperate mood among investigators to *L'Ora*:

We are at war, but for the state and the authorities in this city, on this island, it is as if nothing is happening . . . The *mafiosi* are firing with machine guns and TNT. We can only hit back with words.

There are thousands of them and only a few hundred of us. We set up spectacular road blocks in the city centre, while they stroll calmly about in Corso dei Mille, Brancaccio and Uditore.

Chinnici's death did lead to a quiet act of extraordinary heroism, typical of the way in which a heroic minority was fighting the battle against the mafia. The news of Chinnici's death had a profound effect on Antonino Caponnetto, a pale, timid magistrate whose hobby was keeping canaries. Caponnetto, a Sicilian with a safe and prestigious job in Florence, was nearing retirement. Yet within days of Chinnici's assassination, he sent in an application to take the murdered magistrate's place. As he later explained, 'It was an impulse that partly came from the spirit of service that has always motivated my work. In part, it also came out of my Sicilian identity.' When he entered his new office in Palermo's Palace of Justice, he found a telegram of congratulations on his desk. It was supposed to say, 'I wish you success,' but it had been doctored to read, 'I wish you dead.' Caponnetto spent the next four and a half years living in a tiny room in the *carabinieri* barracks for his own protection.

No sooner had Caponnetto arrived than he brought together a small team of magistrates who would come to inflict colossal blows on the Sicilian mafia. His idea, borrowed from the campaign against left-wing terrorism, was to form a 'pool' of specialized antimafia magistrates to share information, and therefore reduce the risk of reprisals. Caponnetto chose his team to create an 'organic and complete' picture of the mafia problem; the pool comprised Giovanni Falcone, Paolo Borsellino, Giuseppe Di Lello, and Leonardo Guarnotta. In the atmosphere of quiet determination created under Caponnetto's leadership, they set about their work.

The public only became aware of just how stunningly successful the pool had been when Caponnetto gave a press conference at the Palace of Justice on 29 September 1984. The veteran magistrate announced the news that Tommaso Buscetta, 'the boss of two worlds', was collaborating with justice – 366 arrest warrants had been issued as a result. Even 'pushy embezzler' Vito Ciancimino had been served with notification that he was under investigation; Buscetta revealed that he was in the hands of the Corleonesi. (Later, Ciancimino and both Salvo cousins, the barons of Italy's privatized tax collection system, were arrested.) Many of the indicted men were already fugitives from justice, but the Palermo police still ran out of handcuffs when they came to capture all the defendants. With a broad smile on his thin face, Caponnetto spelled out the significance of the evidence that had been accumulated:

What we have here is not just a variety of mafia cases. The mafia *as such* is going on trial. So it would not be rash to say that this is a historic operation. At last we have succeeded in penetrating right into the heart of the mafia's structure.

The huge trial that Caponnetto was referring to would aim to prove that the mafia was a single, unified structure – the 'Buscetta theorem', as the newspapers came to call it. It was to be a Copernican revolution in thinking about the honoured society.

The Corleonesi responded to the news of Buscetta's defection with attacks on *pentiti* and their relatives: Leonardo Vitale, the *capodecina* who had turned to the police during his spiritual crisis, was shot dead in December, as was Buscetta's brother-in-law. (Italy still had nothing resembling a proper witness protection programme.) And when the police got close to hunting down the bosses who were still in hiding, Cosa Nostra retaliated immediately. At the end of July 1985, Beppe Montana, the flying squad officer in charge of the hunt for mafia fugitives, was shot and killed at the seaside suburb of Porticello. Despite being off duty, Montana was using his little motor launch to spy on the summer homes of mafiosi. Word had gone round that the police had decided that two leading mafia killers were not to be taken alive. In killing Montana, Cosa Nostra issued its vicious response to this challenge: the assassins used dum-dum bullets. Montana's girlfriend, only a few metres away when he was shot, was left alive to run from house to house, trying frantically to find a telephone as the streets of the town emptied and shutters closed. There could be no clearer image of the fear and *omertà* that gripped western Sicily.

Montana was the third man from his unit to die. The police union protested that in Sicily the state only made itself visible at the funerals of policemen killed by the mafia. But the problems for the police only increased when they caught a young semi-professional footballer and sea-urchin fisherman believed to be the killers' lookout; he was tortured and beaten while in custody, and by the time he was taken to hospital it was too late. After attempts at a cover-up ended in a squalid fiasco, the suspect's death was greeted with fury. The Minister of the Interior reacted with unaccustomed alacrity, and dismantled the group of police and *carabinieri* that had been responsible for most of the successes against Cosa Nostra in the previous few years.

Less than twenty-four hours after the Minister's decision was announced, another senior flying squad officer, Ninni Cassarà, was ambushed and killed. The violence of his death was shocking even by the terrible standards of Palermo in the 1980s. A platoon of between twelve and fifteen killers occupied the building opposite Cassarà's home and opened fire as he stepped from his bulletproof car. His wife could only watch from the balcony as more than 200 rounds were sprayed at her husband. Killed with him was twenty-three-year-old policeman Roberto Antiochia who, knowing how vulnerable his superior was, had returned early from his holidays to offer protection. Only a few days previously Cassarà had given an interview in which he said, 'Anyone who takes their job seriously ends up getting killed sooner or later.'

The sense of isolation felt by the police exploded into rage. Members of the flying squad threatened to apply en masse for a transfer. They protested about the lack of witnesses coming forward, and turned away from police headquarters people seeking to renew their passports; one citizen who telephoned with a routine inquiry was simply told to 'fuck off'. At Antiochia's funeral, the presence of the Minister of the Interior and the

President of the Republic nearly provoked a police riot outside Palermo's 800-year-old cathedral. The dead officer's colleagues spat at the two statesmen, shouting insults: 'Bastards! Murderers! Clowns!' Fighting broke out between the flying squad and the *carabinieri*. One officer vented his fury to a journalist:

We are sick of this. We don't need these state funerals. It's always the same faces, the same words, the same condolences. After two days public opinion calms down ... and everything carries on as before. With us dickheads getting ourselves killed because we're hit both by the mafia and by our leaders.

There has never been any suggestion that the two statesmen against whom the police chose to vent their rage were guilty of complicity with Cosa Nostra. But the message was nonetheless clear: it was not Italy that was fighting the mafia; it was an embattled minority bound together by fierce team spirit and a sense of duty.

Watching the Bullfight

Giovanni Falcone and Paolo Borsellino were old friends by the time they prepared the prosecution case in the maxi-trial (their job did not include being advocates in court). They were almost the same age, and had been brought up in the same small quarter of central Palermo by parents from the same kind of middle-class background; Falcone's father was a chemist and Borsellino's a pharmacist. The two men shared the same devotion to duty and the same unshakeable faith in justice. But they were very different, with different political leanings. Without ever associating with any political party, Falcone had left-wing sympathies. Borsellino joined a neo-Fascist group as a young man, and he retained a much stronger Catholic faith than his colleague. Both magistrates always meticulously resisted any overtures from political parties who sought to capitalize on their reputations.

Falcone and Borsellino also had different attitudes to the city in which they lived and worked. Falcone, perhaps in keeping with his more diffident personality, was more pessimistic about the degree to which Palermo supported his work. Every day he went to work in a speeding convoy of four bulletproof cars full of agents with machine-guns and bulletproof vests; a helicopter watched over their route. To judge by the contemporary letters pages of the *Giornale di Sicilia*, some Palermo residents thought that the traffic congestion created by these convoys was a far more serious problem than the mafia. Falcone was particularly upset when one of his neighbours wrote to suggest that he should be forced to move to the suburbs. Borsellino, a more outgoing man with a healthy streak of hedonism, was more sanguine: 'They are cheering us on.'

Both men drew strength from the growing voice of Sicily's

antimafia movement. Students were staging demonstrations against the mafia in the streets of the city. Campaigners had set up a study centre named after Peppino Impastato. In Salvatore Pappalardo, Sicily now had a Cardinal Primate who was not afraid to use the word 'mafia' or to denounce the state's inaction in the face of the slaughter. As a consequence, in 1983, the Cardinal's Easter mass in the Ucciardone prison was boycotted by inmates. Some grass-roots clergymen were much more forthright in their opposition to the mafia.

Forces for change were even gathering within the Democrazia Cristiana. Leoluca Orlando, Palermo's DC mayor elected in July 1985, was a vocal opponent of the mafia who ensured that the city council was represented as a 'civil complainant' in the maxi-trial. He presided over what became known as the 'Palermo spring' – an exhilarating contrast to the grim winter of collusion that had held much of Palermo city council in its grip since the Second World War. Yet the attitude of most Palermitani to the magistrates' battle remained one of nervous neutrality; as Falcone said, 'It seems to me as if the city is watching from the window, waiting to see how the bullfight ends.'

The maxi-trial opened on 10 February 1986; it would last for the best part of two years. As proceedings began, a tense calm descended on Palermo. Cosa Nostra's killers were under orders to lie low while the drama switched from the streets to a massive floodlit concrete bunker abutting the Ucciardone prison where the specially built courtroom was housed. The bunker showed that the public revulsion at all the eminent corpses had at last forced the Italian state into giving a tangible demonstration of its commitment to tackling Cosa Nostra. But it was a far from reassuring sight: one journalist said it looked as if a giant judicial spaceship had landed in Palermo. The main hall was green and octagonal, with thirty cages placed around the outside for the 208 most dangerous defendants. Of the total of 474 men who faced charges, 119 were still on the run, the most important being Luciano Leggio's 'beasts', 'Shorty' Riina and 'Tractor'

Provenzano. Leggio himself, dressed in a blue tracksuit and white tennis shoes, was the first to speak from Cage 23; he announced that he would be conducting his own defence against the charge that he had been running the Corleonese faction from prison.

As the trial opened, journalists sounded out the public mood. Many people in the streets of Palermo were reluctant to talk. Some were openly against the trial, saying that there was more unemployment now that the mafia was on the defensive. Most were sceptical: 'It's a farce. It will only get the ones who have stuck their necks out too far. The big politicians will decide how the trial ends.' Buscetta had made it clear that he did not think Italy was ready to hear all his secrets yet; he was keeping to himself what he knew about the mafia's links to top statesmen. Many people thought that the mafiosi who had fought out the *mattanza* were merely thugs, and that the real mafia were the string-pullers much higher up.

But doubts about the maxi-trial were not confined to vox pop interviews. Some of the most thoughtful opinion-leaders in Sicily simply could not grasp the trial's real significance. For one thing, the sheer dimensions of the case were unnerving – Cardinal Pappalardo called it 'an oppressive show'. In a much-discussed interview given just before the maxi-trial began, the Cardinal seemed to row back from his earlier firm stance on the mafia. He said that abortion killed more people than the mafia, and worried about the effect that all the media attention on the trial would have on Palermo's image. Asked whether he would define himself as an antimafia prelate, he equivocated significantly: 'You can't build anything with a purely negative attitude. It is not enough just to be anti-something.'

Many people shared a fear that the maxi-trial was an attempt to deliver justice in bulk, and that it would be impossible carefully to measure each individual defendant's guilt or innocence. Some suspected that the scale of the trial reflected only the scale of the magistrates' egos.

The evidence of *pentiti* also raised doubts. Many onlookers had grave concerns about how reliable their testimonies would prove. In 1985, a prominent television personality had been the victim of a grave miscarriage of justice after false evidence supplied by a *pentito* from the Neapolitan Camorra. To many observers, using the testimony of Tommaso Buscetta presented the same risks on an even bigger scale.

There was precious little room for neutrality during the months of the maxi-trial. The Buscetta theorem flew in the face of profoundly rooted assumptions about the mafia, and about what it meant to be Sicilian. To grasp its implications would take a giant leap in understanding. It was a leap that even some of the mafia's most outspoken enemies simply could not make. One famous and surprising name came to symbolize how hard it was for many Sicilians to accept what Falcone and Borsellino were doing, to see them as the solution rather than as part of the problem: Leonardo Sciascia.

Sciascia was the novelist who had done so much to bring the mafia to the public's attention back in the late 1950s and early 1960s. Even today it is to novels like *The Day of the Owl* that most non-Italians turn when they want to find out about the mafia. Everything about Sciascia's background, his writing, his sense of his own Sicilian identity, had pitted him against the mafia for over three decades. Tragically, in January 1987, the same forces also brought him down on the wrong side of a city divided and perplexed by the maxi-trial.

Eleven months into proceedings, Sciascia wrote an article in the *Corriere della Sera* that would fatally undermine his reputation as an opponent of the mafia. The article took its cue from two recent events: the publication of a book about the iron prefect's crusade against organized crime during the Fascist years; and Paolo Borsellino's promotion. (Borsellino had just been put in charge of the office of investigation in Marsala on Sicily's westernmost tip where the Corleonesi had close allies.) Sciascia argued passionately that the maxi-trial threatened to trample on civil liberties in the same way that Fascism had done. He fulminated against a climate – we would now call it 'politically correct' – in which any criticism of the antimafia magistrates was treated as if it were a sign of complicity with the bosses. He concluded his polemic by accusing Borsellino of careerism: 'There is nothing better for getting ahead in the magistracy than taking part in mafia trials.'

Sciascia's outburst caused profound shock in Italy where the public tends to look to writers and intellectuals for the kind of moral leadership that politicians too often fail to provide. It was a role that Sciascia took very seriously; in his own way he viewed himself as a voice of reason in *terra infidelium*, as solitary and rational as the detectives in his novels who tried and failed to breach the wall of *omertà*. All the more reason for Borsellino to be deeply hurt by the *Corriere della Sera* article; he said that Sciascia had been an intellectual father figure for him. Some of the mafia's politicians subsequently took a sneering delight in quoting the novelist against the magistrates he had inspired.

By the time he penned his attack on the antimafia magistrates, the author of *The Day of the Owl* was terminally ill. For many solitary years he had devoted all the subtleties of his art to understanding the mafia's thought-patterns, and he resented the antimafia sloganeering that now abounded. But Sciascia's polemic was more than the outburst of a balky, moribund old man. It was the voice of the distrust that generations of Sicilians seemed to feel towards both the mafia and the Italian state.

Sciascia was the self-taught son of a man who worked in the sulphur mines of Agrigento province. He had witnessed as a boy the hypocritical brutalities of the Fascist regime, and he had seen the mafia kill union leaders in the sulphur mines after the war. For him the mafia was an informal branch of the Italian police; both the state and the mafia had the same repressive reflexes. The lesson of both his life and Sicily's history was that the island could expect nothing but trouble from the authorities. Sciascia's pessimism about the Italian state was matched by his fatalism about Sicily. He had long believed that the mafia at its root was not a self-conscious organization but a mental condition that made a prison house for even the most rational of Sicilian minds:

When I speak out against the mafia it also makes me suffer because within me, as within every Sicilian, the residue of *mafioso* feeling is still alive. So when I struggle against the mafia I'm also struggling against myself; it is like a split, a laceration.

Thankfully for the island, Caponnetto, Borsellino, Falcone, and many like them were untroubled by Sciascia's 'laceration' and had a very different idea of what it means to be Sicilian.

The Fate of the Maxi-Trial

The verdict of the maxi-trial was announced on 16 December 1987. Of the 474 accused, 114 were acquitted; 2,665 years of jail were shared out between the guilty. The message in the numbers was clear: the court had upheld the 'Buscetta theorem', but it had demonstrably not dished out the kind of justice in bulk that many civil libertarians had feared. Even Luciano Leggio was acquitted for lack of evidence; it had not been possible to prove that he had still been giving orders from behind bars.

In the days following the verdict, the newspapers that supported the magistrates proclaimed an end to the myth that the mafia was an invincible and inseparable part of Sicilian culture. It was a premature reaction, uttered more in hope than conviction. The maxi-trial verdict would be subject to a long appeals process before it became an established truth, and confirmation of the verdict was far from a foregone conclusion. Leonardo Sciascia, for one, stuck to his sceptical guns, still unable to accept the 'Buscetta theorem': 'My opinion has always been that the mafia is actually a confederation of mafias.' Two years later Sciascia would go to his grave, to the end refusing to admit the hope that either he or Sicily could ever leave the mafia behind.

Falcone took the verdict as proof that 'by respecting the rules of democracy we can achieve important results against organized crime'. He knew that notable progress was already being made against the mafia. Before the maxi-trial had even finished, investigations into Cosa Nostra had produced two further large-scale cases; all three maxi-trials were handled together by Caponnetto's pool. An important new *pentito*, Antonino Calderone, was giving evidence that was due to lead to a fourth maxi-trial; 160 arrests were made in March 1988. Magistrates from other

Sicilian cities were building a series of related prosecutions. But Falcone was at pains to emphasize that the maxi-trial was no more than a good starting point in the battle against Cosa Nostra.

He would have perhaps been even more downbeat had he known what *pentiti* later revealed. 'We were sure that the maxi-trial would turn out to be a bluff. The final verdicts would not accept the "Buscetta theorem".' The word inside Cosa Nostra was that the maxi-trial was a political showpiece created as a response to the bloody years since the *mattanza*. There would have to be convictions in the first trial, but they would gradually and quietly be reversed on appeal; normality would be re-established in the end.

For a while it looked as if that was exactly what was going to happen. Because Italy's legal system took so long to produce definitive verdicts, legislation had been introduced to prevent prisoners spending too long in custody awaiting the final outcome of their cases. And because of their complexity, mafia cases were particularly slow. Thus it was that mafia defendants were among the main beneficiaries of the legislation: by the beginning of 1989, only 60 of the 342 men convicted in December 1987 were still behind bars.

Then, in 1990, the Palermo Court of Appeal reversed some of the maxi-trial convictions and – crucially – failed to uphold the central plank of the Buscetta theorem: that the members of the Commission, by virtue of their position, were guilty of ordering the important murders that Cosa Nostra carried out. The case was then referred to the first section of the Court of Cassation presided over by Judge Corrado Carnevale, who was acquiring the nickname of the 'verdict slayer' because of his habit of acquitting mafiosi on technicalities. (In October 2002, the Court of Cassation quashed Judge Carnevale's conviction for 'external cooperation in the crime of mafia association'. One must conclude that he was merely, as he maintained all along, applying the law with particular punctiliousness.)

There was insidious opposition to Falcone from within the

judicial system. After the maxi-trial verdict, the founder of the antimafia pool, Antonino Caponnetto, decided to return to Florence. Falcone, who wept at Caponnetto's leaving party, was the obvious candidate to take his place at the head of the investigative office. But at the end of a sordid story of politicking, corridor intrigue, and professional jealousy, thinly veiled by attacks on a 'cult of personality' that was supposedly building up around Falcone, the post went to Antonino Meli, a man two years from retirement who had never even investigated any mafia cases. Falcone was not just humiliated and devastated, he was afraid. 'I am a dead man,' he said to friends. He was all too aware that Cosa Nostra would read any sign that the state was not backing him as an indication that he was vulnerable.

Unknown to the public, Meli then proceeded to share out mafia investigations among magistrates seemingly at random, to load the pool members with non-mafia cases, to add new members to the pool without consulting anyone as to their suitability, and to divide up mafia cases and distribute the pieces among investigators from different Sicilian cities. No doubts have ever been raised about Meli's integrity, it was just that his was a method that went against the fundamental principle of Falcone's work: that Cosa Nostra was a single organization that required a coordinated judicial response.

Viewing these developments with alarm from his new post in Marsala, Borsellino eventually felt the need to make his worries public. 'I have the nasty feeling that somebody wants to turn the clock back,' he said. There was an immediate political flare-up, and the national governing body of the magistracy, known as the CSM, met in special session and decided to investigate Borsellino's claims. Falcone wrote to explain that under Meli's leadership, antimafia investigations had ground to a halt. As the supposedly confidential CSM hearings into the affair were leaked by both pro-Falcone and anti-Falcone camps, and as the usual accusations of political bias and 'cult of personality' flew, all sense of the real issues was lost. Falcone offered and then withdrew his resignation. At the end of a time-consuming and demoralizing row, the CSM lamely ordered both sides to patch up their differences, leaving Falcone's position even weaker. Palermo's Palace of Justice became known as the 'Poison Palace'.

The tale of Falcone's troubles at the hands of some of his fellow magistrates in the wake of the maxi-trial is a depressing demonstration of how solipsistic Italy's public institutions can be. In the eyes of many politicians and their allies in the magistracy, the antimafia pool was not seen as a more or less useful instrument for doing what the judicial system is supposed to do: protect the innocent and punish the guilty out there in the real world. Rather it was seen as just one more 'power centre' from which to exercise influence over rivals within the state. In trying to uphold the rule of law, Falcone and Borsellino sometimes gave the impression of three-dimensional beings who were forced to explain their thinking to the inhabitants of a two-dimensional world. The two magistrates could struggle all they might to point to the third dimension of legality, but the very notion that such a dimension existed was all but incomprehensible to men whose only coordinates were petty politics and procedural quibbling.

In June 1989, Falcone's renewed fears about his vulnerability were confirmed when an Adidas sports bag packed with explosives was found on the rocks beside a beach house that he and his wife had rented just outside Palermo. Uncharacteristically, he said openly that he thought unknown politicians close to Cosa Nostra were involved in planning the attempt on his life. The following months saw affairs in the Poison Palace brought before the CSM once again, after Falcone was the victim of a campaign of anonymous defamatory letters probably written by one of his colleagues. The main accusation was that he had used a mafia defector to fight a dirty war against the Corleonesi. The following January, Leoluca Orlando, the antimafia mayor of Palermo who had gone as far as to ally himself with the Communists in an effort to change the climate of city government, was finally brought down by the DC leadership in Rome, who saw him as a political maverick. The prospects for Falcone, and for the antimafia movement, looked bleak indeed.

But in February 1991, Falcone – so often the victim of political opportunism – became its beneficiary. It was a moment when the fate of the antimafia movement was dramatically reversed. Following the fall of the Berlin Wall in 1989, the post-war pack-ice of Italian politics began to break up. The PCI dissolved and reconstituted itself as a social-democratic party; now Italians had much less reason to 'hold their noses and vote DC'. The DC also looked vulnerable in its stronghold in north-eastern Italy; here the raucous Northern League was eating away at the Catholic party's support by decrying corruption in Rome and the South. Reform was in the air. A crime wave, and the outrage in some sections of public opinion at the aftermath of the maxi-trial, gave an ambitious new Socialist Minister of Justice – pre-viously a critic of the antimafia magistrates – the opportunity he wanted to increase his prestige as a defender of law and order. He invited Falcone to become Director of Penal Affairs in the Ministry with the responsibility for coordinating the fight against organized crime at a national level.

Despite the serious misgivings of some of his peers, Falcone took the job. And, in a little over a year, he used the unexpected change in the political climate to completely turn around the fortunes of the fight against the mafia. His main goal was to set up two national bodies that are still today the pillars of Italy's response to organized crime: the DIA (Direzione Investigativa Antimafia), uniting the efforts of *carabinieri*, police, and other law enforcement agencies involved in fighting mafia-style organ-izations – it is a kind of Italian FBI; and the DNA (Direzione Nazionale Antimafia), a national antimafia prosecutors' office, which coordinates twenty-six district antimafia prosecutors' offices in various major cities across the country; each is obliged by law to keep a computer database on organized crime. Thus from the centre, in Rome, Falcone managed to do what he had been prevented from doing in Palermo: create a unified vision not just of Cosa Nostra, but of the whole Italian underworld.

Then there was still the fate of the maxi-trial to be decided. Totò 'Shorty' Riina took measures to ensure that the trial did not have a bloodless journey through the protracted appeals process. Palermo Appeal Court judge Antonio Saetta and his mentally handicapped son were shot dead in September 1988. Court of Cassation prosecutor Antonio Scopelliti was murdered in August 1991 by the Calabrian mafia (the 'Ndrangheta) on Cosa Nostra's behalf. (Three weeks later, mafiosi also shot dead Libero Grassi, a Palermo businessman who led a public campaign against extortion rackets, then estimated to provide an income of $25 billion for criminal organizations across Italy.)

These murders helped put further political weight behind Falcone's reforms. In a way, they were a sign of failure, a sign that the Corleonesi's scorn for the Italian state had finally begun to rebound. They also helped ensure that, as Falcone wished, the so-called 'verdict slayer' Judge Corrado Carnevale did not get to preside over the Court of Cassation's crucial hearing on the maxi-trial. Thus it was that, on 31 January 1992, after proceedings lasting two months, the Court of Cassation overturned the Appeal Court verdict on the maxi-trial and confirmed the three central contentions of Falcone's and Borsellino's original prosecution case: that Cosa Nostra existed and was a single, unified organization; that the members of the Commission were all jointly responsible for murders carried out in the organization's name; and that the evidence of mafia defectors was valid. The 'Buscetta theorem' was now fact, and the leaders of Cosa Nostra faced definitive life sentences.

After 130 years, the Italian state had finally declared the Sicilian mafia to be an organized and deadly challenge to its own right to rule; it was the worst defeat in the entire history of the world's most famous criminal association. And with Falcone widely expected to take over the new national prosecutors' office with the power to drive home the advantage in Sicily, across the country, and even internationally, it looked very much as if further defeats for the mafia would follow. Falcone seemed to have all the powers he needed for the definitive redemption of the *terra infidelium* to begin.

11

Bombs and Submersion
1992–2003

Totò Riina's Villa

Corleone Agricultural College is a curious building, hardly what one would expect of a state educational institution. Brand new, standing three storeys high on a residential road, it has underground parking, lifts, integral air-conditioning and heating, and a neat paved garden. At the front it is overloaded with showy metalwork, with balconies, decorative railings, an imposing gate, and coach lamps. Inside, the desks, blackboards, and computers sit incongruously among black and red marble floors, heavy hardwood doors, and stuccoed walls. In fact the Corleone Istituto Professionale di Stato per l'Agricoltura did not begin life as a college but as exactly what it seems to be: a luxury villa built by a local self-made man, one Totò 'Shorty' Riina.

Nobody has ever asked Riina quite what he intended to do with a home he never got to occupy. But it is likely that this is where he planned to gather his extended family around him when his long career came to an end. This was the retirement home Riina constructed on the assumption that he could arrange to have the verdict of the maxi-trial reversed and return home to enjoy the fruits of his labours. So although it is easy to poke fun at the gaudy taste of the Riina villa, it is difficult not to be impressed by the confidence that it displays, by Riina's sheer inability to comprehend that the state might actually have any right to object to a fortune made from decades of murder.

Thankfully, Riina's confidence has turned out to be misplaced. By the end of 1995, around £125 million, mostly in property, had been confiscated from the boss of bosses. This extraordinary figure almost certainly does not represent the full extent of 'Shorty' Riina's fortune. His Corleone villa was confiscated in 1992 and then, in 1997, given to the town following a civil suit against the family mounted by a brave young antimafia mayor. The people of Corleone knew what they were doing when they made the Riina villa into something so ordinary – a public, educational institution. Cosa Nostra treats all public wealth, no matter how essential – water sources, roads, hospitals, schools – as potential plunder. As a result, for generations it has denied to all the Sicilian families who do not fall within its orbit these banal but crucial paths to progress. And when the state makes good, ordinary things from mafia property in this way, it does not just hurt men of honour financially; it strikes at the heart of their justification for what they do. With treachery and death all around them, they can at least hold on to the belief that they are doing it all for their loved ones.

Since Buscetta turned state's evidence back in 1984, Riina had been promising his men that if intimidation and corruption failed to stop the judicial opposition to Cosa Nostra in Palermo, then his political contacts would stop it in Rome. The problem he faced in making good these promises was that Cosa Nostra's relationship with the DC was in a slowly accelerating tailspin. The outrages carried out in the 1980s led directly to antimafia legislation that Cosa Nostra badly wanted to reverse. Riina now needed to influence headline government policy and not just win piecemeal favours behind the scenes. But the more 'eminent corpses' there were, the more reluctant politicians were to expose themselves in the mafia's defence.

The problem came to a head when Falcone went to Rome in 1991. Mafiosi interpreted his move to the capital as a sign that he would soon be safely sucked into the quagmire of Italian politics, discredited, and rendered powerless. Falcone's achievements in the Ministry of Justice were a startling reversal of these expectations. It was a hair-raising spectacle for mafiosi who were used to regarding the governing parties as their passive partners in misrule: here was Cosa Nostra's mortal enemy shaping the crime policies of a Socialist Minister of Justice under a Christian Democrat Prime Minister. Among many other changes, 1991 saw new laws to prevent money laundering, allow the use of phone taps on mafiosi, and give the government powers to dissolve town councils infiltrated by organized crime.

Worrying though these developments were for Cosa Nostra, the organization's grass roots were led to believe that 'verdict slayer' Judge Carnevale was the ultimate guarantee that things would turn out right in the end. So the Court of Cassation's verdict in January 1992 was a shocking blow to Riina's plans for his family's future and to his prestige within Cosa Nostra. Here was the final proof that the most powerful boss in the mafia's history had made the organization into a political orphan.

Riina's very survival was now at stake. As investigating magistrate Guido Lo Forte explains, 'In the mafia you can't hand in your resignation. You simply get eliminated. It was a case [for Riina and his men] either of accepting their own elimination or of trying to reaffirm their own power in the eyes of the whole membership.' Riina chose to reaffirm his power through a stunning escalation of Cosa Nostra's conflict with the Italian state. The mafia needed to influence the political process more than ever, but had only one means of influence left: violence. The state was to be bombed into backing down over the things that mattered most to Riina and his cohorts: the maxi-trial verdict, and the 1982 law that allowed the authorities to confiscate mafia wealth. 'We must make war in order to be able to mould the peace,' Riina was heard to say. The Commission's death sentences against Falcone and Borsellino – long outstanding – were reactivated within days of the Court of Cassation's pronouncement.

These years, 1992 and 1993 – the aftermath of the Court of Cassation's historic decision – were the most dramatic in the whole history of the Sicilian mafia. Riina's confrontation with the state grew into a full-scale terrorist bombing campaign on the Italian mainland. This unprecedented military action was to end in a defeat so serious as to bring the organization's very survival into doubt for the first time since Mussolini. Both Cosa Nostra and Italy are still living with the consequences of Riina's failed retirement plans.

After Capaci

'Vito, my Vito. My angel. They've taken you away. I'll never be able to kiss you again. I'll never be able to hold you again. I'll never be able to caress you again. You are mine alone.'

At the state funeral of the victims of the Capaci bomb, it was Vito Schifani's tiny, pale widow Rosaria who gave a harrowing voice to her own desolation and to a city's rage. Her husband, with fellow officers Antonio Montinaro and Rocco Di Cillo, was in the car that took the full force of the blast that killed Judge Falcone. Standing at the lectern and looking out into the congregation, before the cameras of several national television stations, she cried out, 'To the men of the mafia – who are here in this church too – I want to say something. Become Christians again. I ask you, for Palermo, a city you've turned into a city of blood.' Before the Cardinal had even finished saying mass, the families and colleagues of the dead policemen moved to prevent any dignitaries getting near the five coffins – 'They are our dead, not theirs,' one was heard to say. Rosaria Schifani, still weeping uncontrollably, let a bottle of water she had been given slip through her fingers and smash on the floor; without seeming to notice, she implored the congregation once more: 'Men of the mafia, I will forgive you, but you will have to get down on your knees.' Her words were repeated again and again on news bulletins.

The moral pressure on Italy's politicians to prove that they were not complicit in the murder of Giovanni Falcone at Capaci was irresistible. In the days following the funeral, some of the people who had endured the dense waves of rain to crowd the streets outside the church of San Domenico, who had looked into the weeping eyes of unknown fellow citizens and seen the same desperate resolve reflected back, began doing their bit to try to turn grief into change. Across the centre of the city, slogans sprayed on bedsheets were hung out of windows: 'Falcone lives.' 'Palermo wants justice.' 'Get the mafia out of government.' 'Stop killing this city.' A 'Sheets Committee' became one of many new grass-roots antimafia organizations. Rosaria Schifani's words – 'Mafiosi: on your knees' – were printed on T-shirts worn during a human chain that ran through the city a month after the attack. A tree outside Falcone's house – by a sad irony he lived in a street named after Emanuele Notarbartolo – was turned into a shrine adorned in flowers, photographs, and messages.

Inconceivably, on 19 July 1992, Cosa Nostra showed that the state could not even protect the man who had stepped into Falcone's shoes, Paolo Borsellino. The explosion that killed him and five members of his escort could be heard halfway across the city. Three days after Borsellino died, Rita Atria, a teenage girl from a mafia family who had started to give evidence to the magistrate after her father and brother were murdered, jumped to her death from the balcony of her safe house in Rome. Her suicide note said simply that there was no one left to protect her. It was a summer in which, as one campaigner wrote, Palermo seemed like a bloody, badly written tragedy: 'We want to get out of the theatre, but we're locked in.'

Despite their stunned dismay, many Palermitani still found the will to protest. Among the countless unforgettable images created by the many sit-ins and processions at the time was of a little boy who took part in a demonstration that marched from the centre of the city to the site of Borsellino's death; he wore a tiny sandwich board with 'I want to be worthy of Falcone' written on the front, and 'I want to be worthy of Borsellino' on the back. For a few extraordinary months, the virtuous minority made Palermo its own and convinced a large part of the population of the urgency of the antimafia cause.

The situation in Sicily was a national emergency. Seven thousand troops were sent to the island to relieve the police of more mundane duties so that they could participate in a gigantic manhunt for Riina and his teams of killers. The law enforcement officials who had not managed to protect the two magistrates were removed. The head of the Palermo prosecutors' office, a man who had repeated run-ins with Falcone, asked to be transferred. In yet another act of exceptional personal courage, a magistrate from the northern city of Turin, Gian Carlo Caselli, volunteered to take up the vacant Palermo job and inject new drive into the fight against Cosa Nostra. Dozens of arrests followed. A law to protect *pentiti* was passed, and they were subsequently given the chance to change their identities. The DIA and the DNA, the new national antimafia institutions designed by Falcone, were brought on stream. The police were given the power to infiltrate the mafia, using simulated drug deals or money laundering operations. Most importantly of all, new, tougher prison conditions were stipulated for mafiosi so that they could not continue to run their empires from behind bars as had been the pattern in the past.

But, as so often in the history of Cosa Nostra, these were paradoxical successes. The political system that seemed finally to have found the resolve to address the mafia problem in 1992–3 was actually liquefying in the heat of a raging corruption scandal. It began in February 1992 when a Socialist politician in Milan was caught as he tried to flush 30 million lire in bribe money down the toilet. 'Operation Clean Hands', as it was called, rapidly spread to other parties and other cities as investigators revealed an ingrained system of spoils-taking that linked business, administration, and politics. The 'party-ocracy' was being overthrown. By the end of 1993, one third of all members of the Italian parliament were under investigation for corruption, and both of the major governing parties – the DC and the Socialists – had ceased to exist. Disbelieving and often amused, the Italian people watched a revolution unfold on their television sets.

The climate inside parts of Cosa Nostra, if nothing like revolutionary, was also undergoing a profound change. Sensing what lay ahead after the Court of Cassation's final verdict on the maxi-trial, men of honour had begun handing themselves in to the police even before the Capaci outrage. Nothing like this had ever happened before. When Riina showed no signs of a switch in tactics after the murders of Falcone and Borsellino, many more mafiosi began to turn state's evidence. Gaspare Mutolo had been initiated by Riina himself in 1973 and became a major heroin dealer. It was he who, in October 1992, explained to magistrates that Cosa Nostra had completely underestimated the damage that Falcone could do to them from his position inside the Ministry of Justice, and that it was the Court of Cassation's verdict in January that had triggered the murders of Falcone and Borsellino. Magistrates now had a very clear picture of what was driving Riina's thinking.

It was information from a mafioso on the run from Riina's vengeance that led directly to the capture of the boss of bosses himself in January 1993. Identifying Riina was the primary problem: the last photo that anyone had of him dated from 1969. But captured man of honour Balduccio Di Maggio picked out Riina's gardener, his son, and his wife in a video of a villa that the *carabinieri* had under observation because it was frequented by a member of the Commission. Early the following morning a snatch squad was ready when Riina was driven from the villa in an inconspicuous family saloon. Four men pounced on him and his driver at a traffic light at Piazza Einstein; he offered no resistance, and showed clear signs of fear that only dissipated when he was told that he was a prisoner of the *carabinieri* and not of his mafia enemies. The following day his mentor and godfather, Luciano Leggio, died of a heart attack in a Sardinian prison.

At last Italy could put a face to the dread name of Totò Riina. One magazine put his blunt, baggy-eyed features on its front cover under the headline 'The Devil'. 'Shorty' himself feigned disbelief at this satanic public image. When brought face to face with Tommaso Buscetta in court, Riina refused to speak to his accuser because of his marital infidelities: 'In my town, Corleone, we live in a morally correct way.'

But more disconcerting even than the Riina freak show were the questions that his capture left unanswered. He had been a fugitive from justice since the late 1960s. In that time he had married, had children, obtained medical care for his diabetes, sent his kids to school, and exercised iron control over a vast criminal organization. The villa where Riina spent the last five years of his life in hiding was even in Uditore – the same *mafiosissima borgata* that had been the base for Antonino Giammona's *cosca* back in the 1870s. How was it possible for Riina to have avoided capture for so long? A worrying shadow was cast over the operation that finally netted him by the fact that his Palermo villa was then left unguarded long enough for a team of mafiosi to clean it out – removing cash, documents, accounts, his wife's fur coats. The magistrates who finally arrived to inspect the property found that it had even been redecorated. An inquiry is currently trying to establish how this was allowed to happen.

After Riina's arrest, the leadership of Cosa Nostra passed into the hands of his brother-in-law and long-term associate, Leoluca Bagarella. After nearly twenty years of domination by 'Shorty' Riina, Cosa Nostra did not respond well to Bagarella's control. Even Corleonese diehards like Giovanni 'lo scannacristiani' Brusca, by now a *capomandamento* in his own right, found the change unsettling:

After Riina's arrest, there wasn't the same calm as before ... All the various bosses started to manage their own *mandamenti* as they saw fit, for their own sake. There wasn't the same homogeneity as before when there had been, well, you could call him the father of the family, everybody's *capo*.

What did not change was the core Corleonese group's thoroughgoing support for what has been termed the massacre strategy. 'Tractor' Provenzano was heard to say at one meeting, 'Everything that Uncle Totò [Riina] did goes ahead; we're not stopping.' A month after Riina's arrest, invoking the rule in Cosa Nostra that stipulates that mafiosi have the freedom to organize any off-island activities they like, irrespective of the will of the rest of the organization, Bagarella, Brusca, and other senior bosses from Palermo and Trapani met to air various proposals for how to continue the war on the state. According to Brusca's account, it was rapidly agreed to mount an attack on Maurizio Costanzo, a prominent chat-show host who had expressed a wish that a mafioso in hospital with a fake illness would subsequently contract a real tumour. They discussed placing a bomb under the Leaning Tower of Pisa, poisoning children's snacks in supermarkets, and littering the beaches at Rimini with HIV-infected syringes. In each case there was to be a warning given in time for deaths to be avoided. The point was to create public alarm and bring the state to the negotiating table.

In the end it was decided not to bother with the niceties of these 'dummy' attacks. On 14 May 1993 in Rome, a bomb went off as TV presenter Maurizio Costanzo's car was approaching; by extraordinary good fortune, he was unhurt. On 27 May, a car bomb exploded in via dei Georgofili in the heart of Florence; five passers-by were killed and forty wounded. There were five more bomb victims in via Palestro in Milan on 27 July. On 31 October, a bomb was planted in via dei Gladiatori near the Olympic Stadium in Rome; it was timed to go off at the end of the Lazio versus Udinese football match, with the purpose of killing as many *carabinieri* as possible. It failed to detonate.

It was during that same year of 1993 that it became clear that Cosa Nostra, in directly confronting the state, had also made an enemy of the Church. In November 1982, in the middle of the *mattanza*, John Paul II had visited Sicily and not once mentioned the word 'mafia'. In May 1993, he made his first visit to the island since the deaths of Falcone and Borsellino. On the eve of his three-day tour, the Vatican paper – the *Osservatore Romano* – invited Borsellino's widow Agnese to write a letter. She recalled her husband's 'simple and profound' Christianity, and appealed for prayers so that the Church 'would not compromise the genuine teachings of Christ with any kind of collusion'. A group of Catholic intellectuals followed up with a letter to the *Giornale di Sicilia* that was even less equivocal, denouncing 'the scandalous links between representatives of the Catholic Church and exponents of mafia power'.

Two days later the pontiff chose the dramatic setting of Agrigento's Valley of the Temples, where priceless ancient Greek monuments are set in a landscape ruined by mafia-backed illegal building, to throw away his prepared sermon and launch into a thundering extemporized condemnation of 'mafia culture . . . a culture of death, profoundly inhuman, anti-evangelical'. Visibly moved, he called on mafiosi to convert: 'One day the judgement of God will come!' Cosa Nostra's response came on 27 July when bombs exploded at the churches of San Giovanni in Laterano and San Giorgio in Rome; there were no casualties. On 15 September, in the eastern Palermo suburb of Brancaccio, Father Pino Puglisi, the finest representative of the embattled tradition of local anti-mafia priests, was murdered at his front door. One of his killers would later confess that Father Puglisi had smiled at them just before being shot: 'I was expecting this,' he said.

In its wild reaction to the Court of Cassation's verdict of January 1992, Cosa Nostra was clearly no longer concerned to perpetuate any doubts over whether it existed or not. Yet it was also cutting away at its own life-support system, at its political ties, at the pseudo-religion that many of its members professed, at the very notion that it could not be separated from Sicilian culture. As a direct consequence, the organization haemorrhaged defectors in hundreds; in 1996 the number of *pentiti* peaked at 424. Caught between the abominable regime of the Corleonesi within Cosa Nostra and a life in isolation under the new, tougher prison conditions, even senior men of honour, members of the core group of Corleonesi, began to collaborate with justice.

One example must serve for many: Salvatore Cancemi was a *capomandamento* who was on the Commission when it approved the decision to murder Falcone and Borsellino. He had been a lookout for the team that placed and detonated the Capaci bomb. Something finally began to change in him the day he heard Riina explaining his plans to deal with the snowballing number of defectors: 'The problem is these *pentiti*, because if it wasn't for them not even the whole world united could touch us. That's why we've got to kill them, and their relatives to the twentieth remove, starting with children of six and over.' But it was not until the following summer, in the middle of the bombing campaign of 1993, that Cancemi walked up to the gate of a *carabinieri* barracks and turned himself in. He subsequently also surrendered his fortune, which he estimates at around £33 million. When he was reunited with Tommaso Buscetta at a trial (the two were in the same Family and had become friends while in prison in the 1970s), he confessed that he had personally carried out Riina's order to strangle two of Buscetta's sons. The history-making mafia defector embraced Cancemi and said, 'You could not refuse the order. I forgive you because I know what it means to be in Cosa Nostra.'

Armed with the evidence of these new *pentiti*, investigators rapidly ascertained who had carried out the Falcone and Borsellino assassinations, the bomb attacks on the mainland, the murder of Father Puglisi, and many other crimes. The Corleonesi were still sowing terror within Cosa Nostra to discourage any opposition to their massacre strategy. But one by one they fell to the ultimate weapon in a mafioso's armoury: betrayal to the state. Leoluca Bagarella was captured in June 1995 in an apartment in the centre of Palermo, the second boss of bosses to be arrested in less than three years. And then, in May the following year, four months after little Giuseppe Di Matteo was strangled and dissolved in acid on his orders, the *carabinieri* burst into the house near Agrigento where Giovanni 'lo scannacristiani' Brusca was hiding with his family. By the time of Brusca's arrest, the massacre strategy had been abandoned and the Sicilian mafia was in the throes of the worst crisis in its history. Cosa Nostra was at last on the verge of defeat.

'Uncle Giulio'

Through its savage response to the Court of Cassation's final verdict on the maxi-trial, Cosa Nostra endangered its very future. But for several years in the late 1990s, the Italian public was more absorbed by the mafia's past. For the dramas of 1992–3 threatened to expose the sinister legacy of collusion between politicians and mafiosi. It looked to some as if the dark truth about Italian history was finally to emerge under the strip lights of the Palermo bunker courthouse. There, in September 1995, the man who had been the country's most powerful politician for a quarter of a century went on trial for working for the mafia: DC magus Giulio Andreotti, seven times Prime Minister of Italy. The press habitually referred to it as the trial of the century.

Andreotti's drama began on 12 March 1992 with the murder of Salvo Lima. It is highly significant that the very first person to fall in Riina's war on the Italian state, weeks before Falcone and Borsellino were killed, was not a magistrate or a member of the police force but a Christian Democrat politician. Lima – the former DC young Turk who had presided over the sack of Palermo and who used to get Tommaso Buscetta his opera tickets – was the victim of an execution of terrifying efficiency. He was being driven into Palermo from his home in Mondello, Palermo's seaside satellite town, when the windscreen and one of the tyres of his car were shot out by the pillion passenger on a passing motorbike. Lima's last words were, 'They're coming back! *Madonna santa!* They're coming back!' He ran from the car but only covered thirty metres before the killer, now on foot, caught up with him, shot him in the back, and then administered a *coup de grâce* to the nape of his neck.

A *pentito* later explained why he thought the Sicilian DC's *éminence grise* had been murdered.

Lima gave a guarantee that everything would be sorted out in Rome ... The reasons for the murder of Salvo Lima were because he did not keep the promises made in Palermo, or someone did not allow him to keep them. For a while Salvo Lima, at least according to what I heard, was actually urging people not to worry.

The 'everything' that Lima assured would be sorted out in Rome was the maxi-trial verdict. Quite whether he had explicitly made such rash promises is not known for certain. The important thing is that Riina had led his people to believe that guarantees had been given. Many of the *pentiti* who emerged during the terror campaign of 1992–3 would confirm the extent of Lima's involvement with the mafia. Since the days of the La Barbera brothers in the late 1950s, he had been the intermediary between the Sicilian underworld and local and national government. Thus, in the minds of the men of honour, Lima's funeral was also the funeral of the pact between Cosa Nostra and the DC that was formed back in the days of Don Calò Vizzini and the bandit Salvatore Giuliano.

On the day after Lima was buried, there was a cartoon on the front page of Italy's biggest-selling daily, *La Repubblica*, that implied that the sensational murder had a clear political meaning. It showed a dark-suited man spreadeagled, face down, with a rasp file protruding from the pronounced hump on his back. Any doubt about the man's identity was removed by the unmistakable, low-slung, bat-like ear drawn in just above his left shoulder: it was Giulio Andreotti, who was just coming to the end of what was to be his last term as Prime Minister. The pun in the cartoon was scarcely more difficult to decode than the figure of Andreotti. The Italian word for a file is 'una lima'. The suggestion was that the real target of the attack on Salvo Lima was Prime Minister Giulio Andreotti. In other words, the cartoon was saying, Cosa Nostra had stabbed a friend in the back.

When he died, Lima was on his way to the Hotel Palace where he was due to finalize the details of a grand reception in honour of Andreotti. Since 1968, when Lima became an MP and fell out with 'Viceroy' Giovanni Gioia, his huge Sicilian following had marched under the banner of Andreotti's DC faction. Before 1968, Andreotti had occupied government posts continually from the late 1940s onwards, but winning Lima's support in Sicily was the decisive moment in his political fortunes. Without Lima behind him, Andreotti would probably never have become Prime Minister at all. With Lima on his side, Andreotti became the most influential politician in the country. No government could be formed without his approval.

Large numbers of DC notables stayed away from Palermo on the day of the Lima funeral, as did the other party leaders, the incumbent President of the Republic, and the Speakers of both houses of parliament. Some newspapers interpreted this as a sign that the public institutions were making a point of not claiming the controversial Lima as one of their own. In fact the murder could not have come at a politically more delicate moment. A general election was due to be held on 5 April, a vote that everyone knew was likely to be decisive in shaping post-Cold War Italy. Andreotti was widely touted to become the next head of state, the President of the Republic. So it was understandable Andreotti was the focus of media attention when he turned up to see his Sicilian friend buried. Normally unflappable and ironic, he was pale and visibly shaken. Before the television cameras, he resoundingly defended Sicily's reputation: 'The island is not the mafia.' In interviews he offered a tangled explanation for the Lima assassination, a mixture of 'behind-ology' and a strain of the *Cavalleria rusticana* myth. Like Sicily, Lima was the victim of a smear campaign, he argued. 'Slanderers are worse than murderers. Or at least they are just as bad. My friend Salvo Lima was slandered for decades.' The attacks on Lima's reputation were the prelude to a politically motivated murder, he claimed; its aim may have been to prepare the ground for a totalitarian takeover. Asked whether he thought the murder could have been a warning aimed at him, Andreotti said he did not know: 'Often the things that happen in Sicily are all but incomprehensible.'

Just how 'incomprehensible' Andreotti actually found what went on in Sicily would soon become the subject of a sensational trial in the Palermo bunker courthouse. Within a year of Lima's death, and with the country in ferment following the murders of Falcone and Borsellino and the explosion of the 'Clean Hands' corruption scandal, the Palermo prosecutors' office asked the Italian Senate for authorization to begin criminal proceedings against Giulio Andreotti 'for having contributed in a non-occasional manner to protecting the interests and reaching the aims of the criminal association known as Cosa Nostra'. Moved by the deaths of Falcone and Borsellino, Tommaso Buscetta joined more recent *pentiti* in starting to talk about the mafia's political links. Two names kept recurring in their testimonies: Salvo Lima and Giulio Andreotti.

The accusations against Andreotti were grave. It was alleged that Italy's most powerful politician of the 1970s and 1980s had had face-to-face business meetings with mafiosi of the calibre of Stefano Bontate, Tano 'Sitting Bully' Badalamenti, and Michele 'the Pope' Greco; Stefano Bontate, it was alleged, had given him a painting as a present. Most media attention centred on the charge that Andreotti had actually kissed Totò 'Shorty' Riina during one secret encounter. Andreotti was said to have been habitually referred to inside Cosa Nostra as 'Uncle Giulio'. More importantly, it was claimed that he had sought to arrange for the 'verdict-slaying' Judge Carnevale to preside over the final hearing in the maxi-trial. The prosecution concluded its case by arguing that Andreotti, 'in a dark delirium of power, made a pact with the mafia', but that his failure to maintain promises made to the men of violence led them to turn first on his ally, Salvo Lima, and then on him; some *pentiti* said that Riina was planning to kill Andreotti or one of his children.

In October 1999, Andreotti was found innocent. The mafia de-fectors' statements were found to be too vague and contradictory to support a secure conviction. But the explanation that the original trial judges issued for their decision hardly constitutes a clarion vindication of Andreotti's morals. More than that, it raises troubling questions about Italy's past.

The seven-times Prime Minister's defence was, in essence, that he did not take any direct interest in Sicilian affairs, that he let his 'slandered' lieutenant Lima get on with the business of local politics while he moved on the national and international stage, innocent of the dangerous criminal environment in which Lima and his ilk were moving. In other words, one of Italy's cleverest and most powerful statesmen found Sicily 'incomprehensible'.

The judges ruled this defence implausible and even, in some limited respects, mendacious. Lima had clocked up dozens of mentions in the papers of the Antimafia commission of inquiry. The judges' ruling determined that, both before and after he entered Andreotti's faction in 1968, Lima boasted to a close member of Andreotti's circle about his relationship with none other than Tommaso Buscetta. In 1973, Andreotti bent over backwards to help God's banker Michele Sindona rescue his banks and escape from the criminal charges hanging over him in Italy and the US. There was further evidence of Andreotti's lack of scruple when 'pushy Corleonese embezzler' Vito Ciancimino joined Andreotti's faction in 1976. The judges ruled that Andreotti 'repeatedly showed himself to be indifferent to the ties that notoriously linked [Ciancimino] to the criminal structure'.

The court found further evidence of dishonesty on Andreotti's part related to the tax-collecting Salvo cousins, Ignazio and Nino – both 'organically inserted into Cosa Nostra', as the judges stated. (Nino died of natural causes during the maxi-trial; Ignazio was given a light sentence at the trial but was then shot dead on Riina's orders in September 1992 for failing to protect Cosa Nostra from Judge Falcone.) Andreotti's claim that he did not know the Salvo cousins was 'unequivocally contradicted' by the evidence; photos of them together turned up during the case, for example. The judges suggested that the most favourable interpretation of Andreotti's reluctance to own up to his regular dealings with the Salvos was that he was trying to protect his image. But the slipperiness of some aspects of Andreotti's defence was not taken to be evidence that justified the prosecution's charge that he was systematically and deliberately working to further the interests of Cosa Nostra.

Following an appeal by the prosecution, the not guilty verdict was confirmed in May 2003. In late July the judges' explanation of this second acquittal was deposited in the Palermo chancellery. The judges ruled that Andreotti had 'made himself available to mafiosi in an authentic, stable and friendly way until the spring of 1980'. Prior to that date he had 'friendly and direct relations [with men of honour] propitiated by his link with Salvo Lima and the Salvo cousins'. There was a relationship 'based on exchange and general electoral support for the Andreotti faction [of the DC]'. After 1980, Andreotti demonstrated 'ever more incisive commitment to the antimafia cause', to the extent that he even put his own and his family's lives in danger. (As Andreotti has frequently pointed out, for example, he was Prime Minister when Falcone was working at the Ministry of Justice in 1991 and 1992.)

The turning point in Andreotti's relationship with Cosa Nostra, in the view of the appeal court judges, came at the outset of the season of 'eminent corpses', and specifically with the murder of the DC President of the Sicilian Region, Piersanti Mattarella, in January 1980. Defined by the judges as 'heroic', Mattarella was seeking to bring a new transparency to the workings of his party and to public life in Sicily. From Cosa Nostra's point of view, the most worrying thing about Mattarella was his drive to free the system of awarding local government contracts of mafia influence. When Andreotti heard about a plan to kill Mattarella, according to the judges, he met with Bontate and other senior men of honour and urged them not to carry it through. After Mattarella's death, Andreotti again met Bontate, only to be told in no uncertain terms that Cosa Nostra considered itself to be beyond his influence. According to the judges' ruling, at no stage did Andreotti report any of this to the authorities, either to try and save Mattarella's life or to bring his killers to justice. When confronted with these findings by a journalist, Andreotti stressed the need to look at them in the context of the judges' ruling in its entirety.

What saved Andreotti from being convicted for this pattern of relationships with Cosa Nostra was the fact that Italy has a statute of limitations: it all happened too long ago. The judges commented only that Andreotti would have to 'answer to history' for what he had done. The former Prime Minister responded that, 'in a trial, I'm only interested in the final outcome. And in this case the outcome was positive. As for the rest, Amen.' His lawyers will now have to consider whether they will appeal to the Court of Cassation in an effort to rescue his reputation.

Both of these judicial rulings strongly indicate that, far from finding Sicily incomprehensible, Andreotti understood it well enough to stick by his political allies even when he was aware of at least some of the evils that they were committing. It is deeply worrying for Italian democracy that for so long so many electors were willing to place their trust in a man who, even before this trial, was strongly suspected of using the mafia, in the traditional way, as an instrument of local government.

In October 2003 the Court of Cassation brought an end to another protracted and controversial mafia case involving Giulio Andreotti. He had been accused of asking Cosa Nostra to kill a journalist who was blackmailing him – the murder took place in 1979. Three and a half years after first being committed to trial, Andreotti was judged to be innocent in September 1999. Then, in November 2002, a guilty verdict and a sentence of twenty-four years in prison were issued after an appeal by the prosecution. The Court of Cassation's definitive ruling was that the prosecution had failed to provide any evidence to back up its hypothesis. Thus, seven and a half years after the trial began, and over two decades after the murder had taken place, Andreotti's innocence was confirmed. He expressed relief that his nightmare was over, and claimed he was the victim of a political plot. The whole affair has done nothing to improve the reputation of Italy's political and judicial systems.

The years of the Andreotti trial have been silent ones for Cosa Nostra. Italy was shocked from its torpor by the atrocities of the early 1990s. It was then placated by the capture of Riina, Bagarella, and Brusca. And it seems now to have been put back to sleep by Andreotti's acquittal. When there are no prominent murders, Sicily can seem a long way away from Milan or Rome. But in the silence Cosa Nostra has begun to restructure. Since 'lo scannacristiani' was caught, Italy has set about letting a historic opportunity to defeat the mafia slip through its fingers.

Enter the Tractor

Bernardo Provenzano holds a record. He has been on the run, wanted for murder, since the day – 10 September 1963 – when he took part in an attack in Corleone on one of Michele 'Our Father' Navarra's remaining soldiers. An unparalleled forty years, and counting, as a fugitive from justice. And, like Riina before him, Provenzano has almost certainly spent most of that time in western Sicily. He is best known in Italy through a police identikit because the last photo of him shows him as an uneasy, brilliantined twenty-six-year-old – it was taken in September 1959. There is no clearer example of what mafia territorial control means in practice than Provenzano's continuing ability to evade capture.

For much of the last four decades Provenzano's role within Cosa Nostra was seriously underestimated; at one time it was even thought that he was dead. Indeed, one sign of how he has been misjudged is his nickname, 'the Tractor'. The world learned of it through the testimony of Antonino Calderone, one of the leading *pentiti* of the 1980s, who, from his distant viewpoint in Catania on the east of the island, thought that Provenzano was little more than a relentless killer, much less cunning than 'Shorty' Riina. Better-informed mafia defectors have now overturned that image; 'the Tractor' is more frequently known by the Corleonesi as 'the accountant' or 'zu Binnu' – 'Uncle Bernie'. They say that Provenzano has a much more astute business and political brain than Riina. Gioacchino Pennino, a doctor, DC politician, socialite, and man of honour who turned state's evidence in 1994, said that it was principally Provenzano who rode shotgun on 'pushy embezzler' Vito Ciancimino's political career. On one occasion in 1981, Pennino himself had been thinking out loud about switching out of Ciancimino's group on Palermo city council. He was summoned to meet Uncle Bernie who, without waiting for an explanation, told him in no uncertain terms to shut up and stay put.

For many years Provenzano operated in Riina's shadow. While Riina was busily engaged in a war on the state, Provenzano was quietly cultivating the networks of business and political friendships that have always provided the Sicilian mafia with its staple income. He began his business career as a debt collector for a loan firm set up by Luciano Leggio to recycle drug money, and has since specialized in health, construction, and – Tony Soprano would be curious to know – waste management. Like most of the Sicilian economy, these are businesses dominated by the public sector, and therefore by companies that have good links to politicians.

But Uncle Bernie is, of course, far from being a pacific character. As a long-term member of the Commission, he has racked up *in absentia* life sentences for some of the 'eminent corpse' murders, including Falcone and Borsellino, and for planning the 1993 bombing campaign on the Italian mainland. In the early 1990s, Provenzano took personal charge of a war between Cosa Nostra and a new federation of gangs based in southern and eastern Sicily that was originally formed by expelled men of honour; they called themselves the *stidda*, meaning both 'bright star' and 'bad luck'. Many of the victims of Provenzano's campaign – 300 in three years in the province of Agrigento alone – were teenage gunfighters bought cheap by the *stiddari*.

Since becoming boss of bosses after Leoluca Bagarella's capture in 1995, Provenzano has changed Cosa Nostra's strategy. The magistrates call his ploy 'submersion' because its key goal is to take Cosa Nostra below the radar of public discussion. Accordingly there have been no murders of prominent representatives of the state since Provenzano took charge. Those who are killed – significantly, they are almost all businessmen – die away from the big cities. Even petty crime in Palermo and Catania has dropped dramatically under Provenzano's leadership. Roberto

Scarpinato, a magistrate specializing in relationships between organized crime, business, and politics, argues that Uncle Bernie has grasped a fundamental rule of postmodern society: 'What does not exist in the media does not exist in reality.'

Former mafiosi who knew Provenzano say he is much more conciliatory in his management style than Riina, much more inclined to profit share. Within the mafia he is associated with the saying 'mangia e fai mangiare' – 'eat and let eat'. Some of the boss of bosses' business letters that have been intercepted give an idea of his approach: 'I'll end by saying that I'm at your complete disposal. I wish you the very best and send my dearest affectionate wishes to you and your father. May the Lord bless and protect you.' Cosa Nostra is still centralized, but no longer the dictatorship that it became under 'Shorty' Riina. Internal peace is Provenzano's priority.

Uncle Bernie's Cosa Nostra has also returned to cultivating its core business of protection rackets. The pressure on legal businesses to pay the *pizzo* has increased notably in the past few years. Protection rackets lend themselves well to the submersion strategy in that they rarely require the ultimate and conspicuous sanction of murder; a fire, a beating, or insistent targeted robberies are usually enough to convince anyone who displays any reluctance to put their hand in their pocket.

Protection is also the mafia's traditional ground-floor means of access to public works contracts. In July 2002, the national regulatory authority for public works published evidence to show that the system of blind bids, set up to prevent corruption, was being systematically subverted in Sicily. The Palermo chief prosecutor estimated that 96 per cent of government contracts were rigged in advance.

A large proportion of public spending in Sicily now comes from the European Union in Brussels rather than the Italian government in Rome. Agenda 2000 is the EU's plan to promote development in poorer parts of the Continent. The regional plan for Sicily envisages spending 7,586 billion euros over six years – from 2000 to 2006 – with a view to 'significantly and sustainably reducing economic and social disadvantage, increasing long-term competitiveness, and creating the conditions for full and free access to work on the basis of environmental values and equal opportunities'. Naturally the new, submerged Cosa Nostra does not share this vision of balanced, sustainable growth in Sicily, at least if the following bugged conversation from the summer of 2000 is anything to go by: 'They're advising everyone not to make a noise and attract attention because we've got to get our hands on all of this Agenda 2000.' It pays to remember that Salvo Lima had been a member of the European parliament for twelve years when he was shot dead.

There are no longer any heroin refineries in Sicily. The most recent trend is for the drugs to be produced where the poppies are grown. But Sicily is still a major point of access to the North American market. After eliminating the major drug-dealers in the *mattanza* in 1981–2, the Corleonesi immediately gave what they called a 'licence' to the remaining dealers to act on their behalf. There is evidence of narcotics business links between the Sicilian mafia and the emerging criminal organizations of Eastern Europe. Italian and Russian secret services heard of a first encounter between senior men of honour and members of the Russian mafia in Prague back in 1992. It seems that there was then a second meeting – again about drugs and the arms trade – in Switzerland at which American *mafiosi* were present too.

The profits from all of these illegal activities are now far easier to disguise, recycle, move and invest than they were in the days of Stefano Bontate, Totò Riina, and 'God's bankers'. The mafia has always been able to call on technical expertise, whether it be in citrus fruit dealing or international finance. And now, more than ever, the sons and daughters of men of honour are educated enough to become lawyers, bankers, and property dealers themselves.

Provenzano's major achievement has been to stem the tide of defectors from Cosa Nostra. The policy of exterminating *pentiti* and their families has ceased with a view to encouraging those who have turned state's evidence to retract and return to the fold. At the same time, Provenzano has also put the care of prisoners back in its traditionally high place on Cosa Nostra's list of priorities. During the chaos of the mid-1990s, many men of honour in custody were not receiving their salaries. Some idea of how bosses began to respond to the crisis emerges from the following extracts from letters written from prison by the captured boss of Brancaccio to one of his lieutenants:

There are 20 of our people who are ruined because of the trials. And they don't have the means to face the situation. The task is to come up with 3 or 4 apartments each so they can have a secure economic future – them and their families.

The guys in prison are always asking me why the monthly payment has been cut since I got arrested . . . I mean two million (£600) a month is hardly anything . . . I used to pay five million (£1,500) . . . I'm urging you to do at least as much as I did . . . When I was on the run we banked a basic of two hundred million (£66,000) a year plus between a billion and a billion and a half extra (£330,000– £500,000) . . . The builders who are on the move have got to produce those apartments . . . If anyone delays they've got to be made to pay. Anyone who takes advantage of the guys behind bars is dishonoured scum.

Under Provenzano, Cosa Nostra's common fund for prisoners, which is fed from a tax on incomes across the organization, has been reactivated. Consequently, as leading magistrate Guido Lo Forte says, 'Between the benefits offered by the state and those guaranteed by the mafia, prisoners are now choosing the latter.'

During the crisis of the mid-1990s, when it looked as if Cosa Nostra was on the verge of defeat, mafiosi fathers were reluctant to allow their sons to be admitted to the organization. Now initiations have resumed, albeit more selectively than before. Young men from families with long-established mafia histories behind them are being preferred in an effort to guard against *pentiti*. As Scarpinato says, 'Family ties are an antibody to collaboration with the state.'

Provenzano has gathered about him a generation of bosses

older than the young killers who tended to be close to Riina, Giovanni 'lo scannacristiani' Brusca being the emblematic case. Investigating magistrates sometimes refer to the Palermo Commission, now ruled over by Provenzano, as 'the Senate' because of the age of its members, who are with a few exceptions in their late fifties and sixties. Again, the fear of *pentiti* is driving this change. Older men of honour tend to have a long-term view: they have children to think of, and patrimonies to pass on to those children.

Communications within mafia Families and *mandamenti* have also become much more compartmentalized, with only a few chosen men of honour acting as channels of communication. It seems that it is now common practice for men of honour to conceal their status even from other mafiosi.

Provenzano's response to the crisis provoked by defectors from his organization has worked. There has only been one significant man of honour who has turned state's evidence since 1997 (about whom more below), and in the meantime legislators have sought to impose tight controls on the use of *pentiti*. *Pentitismo*, as it is called, has remained a controversial weapon in the magistrates' armoury. The verdict of the first Andreotti trial strengthened the arguments of those who consider *pentiti* inherently unreliable. There was controversy during the case when a key *pentito* killed another mobster while under police protection. The benefits that magistrates are able to offer mafia defectors in return for information have since been cut. And any evidence that *pentiti* provide more than six months after their capture is now considered invalid; the problem is that six months is not very long for a man of honour to provide detailed information on a lifetime of day-in, day-out criminal activity.

Provenzano has established a *pax mafiosa* while his organization rebuilds the support networks damaged during the 1980s and early 1990s. Because Cosa Nostra's guns have fallen silent for a while, some commentators have even been heard suggesting that the mafia is dying, that the new world of the internet and globalization is too modern for a semi-literate thug like

Provenzano to understand. But over the past century and a half the mafia has responded to all of the great challenges of modernity: to capitalism, to the emergence of the nation-state, to democracy, to the rise and fall of the great ideologies of Socialism and Fascism, to global war, to industrialization and deindustrialization. Nothing that the nineteenth or twentieth centuries could throw at the Sicilian mafia managed to stop it. There is little to suggest that, left to its own devices, Cosa Nostra will fail to meet the challenges of the twenty-first century either. Cosa Nostra will not decline of its own accord. Magistrate Scarpinato describes it as a 'collective brain, able to learn from its mistakes, to adapt and counter the different measures used to fight it'.

The fate of this 'collective brain' is still in the balance. Italy's law enforcement response to Cosa Nostra is now more co-ordinated and efficient than it has ever been. For example, in July 2002, by using global positioning system micro-beacons placed in suspects' cars, police arrested what they say was the whole of the Commission of Cosa Nostra for the province of Agrigento – fifteen men including one who is a doctor, nobleman, and member of the provincial council; the bosses had assembled – it is alleged – to elect a new *capo*.

But, as so often in the past, the Sicilian mafia's destiny will depend less on law enforcement than on politics, meaning both the organization's internal balance of power and its relationship with the people's elected representatives. Bernardo Provenzano faces one crucial political task. He has to find a way to settle a conflict of interests between the bosses who are still at large, and the historic leadership of the Corleonesi: men like Riina and Bagarella who have not turned state's evidence and are now nearly a decade into irreversible life sentences under a harsh prison regime. The bosses on the outside need peace and 'submersion' to implement a long-term rebuilding strategy. The bosses on the inside urgently need changes in legislation: first and foremost the reform of the prison conditions – known as Law 41 bis – that prevent them operating from captivity; but also changes to the laws on confiscation of mafia property, and even a reversal of the precedents established by the maxi-trial – perhaps through retrospective laws that weaken the value of evidence provided by *pentiti*. In other words, the demands that led to the attack on the state in the 1980s and 1990s have yet to be met.

And now, a decade after the deaths of Falcone and Borsellino and the bombs on the Italian mainland, some observers fear that Cosa Nostra has found someone in government who is prepared to give it what it wants.

The Major-Domo and the Ad Man

Antonino Giuffrè, known as 'Manuzza' ('Little Hand'), acting head of the Caccamo *mandamento* of Cosa Nostra, was captured on 16 April 2002. Giuffrè's nickname derives from his deformed right hand, which was mangled in a hunting accident. It is said he has since learned to load and fire a shotgun with just his left. In the abandoned farm building where Giuffrè was hiding (along with a loaded pistol, 6,000 euros in cash, and images of Padre Pio, the Sacred Heart and the Madonna) was a shopping bag full of letters to Bernardo Provenzano. Some entrepreneurs, it seems, were even writing to Uncle Bernie on company notepaper with requests for favours.

In June, feeling that he had been betrayed by his leader, Giuffrè started to talk to investigating magistrates: 'I was Provenzano's principal collaborator and my job was to try and restructure Cosa Nostra on a huge scale.' But his most startling claim was that in 1993 Cosa Nostra had 'direct contacts' with representatives of Silvio Berlusconi, Italy's famous perma-tanned media magnate with a crooner's smile.

That same year, 1993, it will be recalled, was the year of Cosa Nostra's bombing campaign on the Italian mainland. It was also the year when Berlusconi was in the process of forming a new political party to respond to the crisis brought about by the 'Clean Hands' corruption investigations. The subject of the meeting between Berlusconi's people and Cosa Nostra, Giuffrè claims, was an alliance between the mafia and Berlusconi's planned political party, soon to be baptized Forza Italia ('Come on, Italy!').

The following year Berlusconi led an alliance to victory in the general election. But the alliance proved fragile and collapsed before 1994 was out. Then in May 2001, a year before Giuffrè's capture, Forza Italia met with electoral triumph and Berlusconi became Prime Minister with a solid parliamentary majority behind him. The man who likes to be known as *il cavaliere* – 'the Knight' – is also the richest man in Italy with an estimated fortune of $10.3 billion at the time of the 2001 election; among many other things he owns the country's three major private television networks and a publishing empire. No one since Mussolini has had so much power over Italy or, indeed, over Sicily; the alliance led by Forza Italia holds all sixty-one of the island's parliamentary seats.

There are numerous indications that since 1994 men of honour have been directing their people to vote for Forza Italia candidates. Bearing in mind how the mafia has tended to operate over the past century and a half, there is nothing necessarily surprising or scandalous in this: politicians with power are inevitably the most vulnerable to pressure from organized crime. It is known that, because of its growing disenchantment with the DC in the 1980s, Cosa Nostra was on the lookout for a new political vehicle for its interests. In the late 1980s, overtures were made to the Socialist Party. Then in the early 1990s, 'Shorty' Riina began to discuss the possibility of a new Sicilian separatist movement with his business and political contacts in the Masons: 'Cosa Nostra is reviving the dream of becoming independent, of becoming the boss in a part of Italy, a state of its own, of our own,' said one defector at the time. It is believed that, in the minds of senior bosses within Cosa Nostra, the emergence of Forza Italia in 1993–4 offered an even better solution: a close relationship with the party that was set to be just as central to the national political scene as the DC had once been.

There are many reasons to be cautious about what 'Little Hand' says, and to fight shy of any equivalence between Forza Italia in Sicily and Cosa Nostra. Nobody in Italy would seriously claim either that Berlusconi is a mafioso or that his electoral victories are a direct reflection of mafia influence. The lessons of mafia history in that regard are clear: even at its apogee in the 1970s and 1980s, Cosa Nostra did not control nearly enough votes to achieve such a landslide for its favoured political party. Berlusconi's triumph owed more to dissatisfaction with his predecessors, effective campaigning, and public spending promises.

'Manuzza' Giuffrè's allegations could turn out to be fanciful, perhaps wishful propaganda fed by Cosa Nostra's leaders to the membership. Defence lawyers call what this latest *pentito* says 'an anthology of hearsay'. But the Palermo investigating magistrates take what Giuffrè says seriously because, they allege, it may reveal the outcome of a remarkable story from nearly three decades ago that potentially links one of Silvio Berlusconi's closest aides directly to Cosa Nostra.

In 1974, Berlusconi was looking for a groom and major-domo for his Arcore estate near Milan. He turned for advice to Marcello Dell'Utri who, after a prodigiously rapid rise through the Sicilian banking world, had recently moved to Milan to become Berlusconi's business factotum. (Dell'Utri later became the head of Publitalia, the highly profitable advertising arm of the Berlusconi business empire; it was he who came up with the idea of Forza Italia in 1993.) Dell'Utri's recommendation for the post of major-domo was a fellow Palermitan, Vittorio Mangano, who filled it for two years. Mangano died of cancer recently, a few days after being sentenced to life for two murders. This 'major-domo', it transpires, was a man of honour from the Porta Nuova Family of Cosa Nostra.

The story of the major-domo and the ad man is currently the subject of a case that has been dragging through the Palermo Court of Assizes for so long that most members of the Italian public have forgotten about it. (Berlusconi is not a defendant, it should be emphasized; his involvement is as a witness.) The prosecution alleges that Berlusconi's fears that his children would be kidnapped led Dell'Utri to approach Mangano for protection. Dell'Utri responds to these accusations by saying that he initially did not know about Mangano's criminal record, and that he dismissed him as soon as the truth came out. The prosecution asserts instead that this moment in 1974 was the beginning of a long-lasting relationship between Dell'Utri and the Sicilian mafia – an assertion that Dell'Utri vehemently denies. Still according to the prosecution, Dell'Utri has admitted to telling a business associate that he mediated between Berlusconi and Cosa Nostra to prevent his boss becoming the victim of a kidnapping, but he now claims this was merely an empty boast.

There is a long list of other charges running against Dell'Utri based around his supposedly regular dealings with men of honour; it is alleged that Dell'Utri recycled drug money and even that Stefano Bontate was considering initiating him into the mafia in 1980. Dell'Utri is also alleged to have mediated between Cosa Nostra and businesses in Berlusconi's group: in one direction he supposedly ensured the transmission of protection payments from Berlusconi-owned companies operating in Sicily; in the other direction, it is claimed, went mafia investment in Berlusconi-owned companies in Milan. Following the *mattanza* of the early 1980s, 'Shorty' Riina is alleged to have monopolized the mafia's links to Dell'Utri in the hope of taking advantage, through Dell'Utri, of Berlusconi's close relationship with the Socialist Party.

The prosecution also claims that Dell'Utri tried to extort 50 per cent of a sponsorship contract between a beer brand and the owner of Trapani basketball club in the early 1990s. He supposedly threatened the owner when he refused to pay: 'I advise you to think again. We have the men and the means to convince you to change your mind.' Dell'Utri, who refutes this allegation, is further accused of trying to persuade two mafia defectors to discredit investigating magistrates and three other *pentiti*; the alleged aim was to 'expose' a fictitious plot by judges to frame Berlusconi and Dell'Utri. This charge, like the others, is strongly disputed by the defence.

The Dell'Utri case is long and complex; it will turn on how the judges assess evidence that stretches back into the early 1970s and is far more extensive than Antonino Giuffrè's allegations. All the accusations are, of course, still being evaluated in court and may, at the end of that process, turn out to be unsubstantiated. But they have inevitably fuelled speculation about a verdict that, whichever way it goes, will be crucial. If Dell'Utri is judged to be innocent, many people will conclude that, as so often in the past, accusations of complicity with the mafia have been used as a political weapon – the real targets on this occasion being Berlusconi and Forza Italia. Such an outcome would inflict severe damage on the credibility of both the magistrates and the *pentiti*.

If Dell'Utri is guilty, then his notoriously close business and political relationship with Silvio Berlusconi will inevitably raise questions at the very least about the latter's judgement. If what Giuffrè says is right, then in 1993, through Marcello Dell'Utri, Cosa Nostra sought to obtain guarantees that Forza Italia when in government would prioritize the mafia's main demands: the maxi-trial verdicts, the law on confiscation of mafia wealth, and the harsh 41 bis prison regime. On this basis, some antimafia campaigners would conclude, perhaps hastily, that the venerable accord between the Sicilian mafia and the Italian political system has been renewed once more. At the very least, if Dell'Utri is convicted, the issue of whether Berlusconi knew about his ad man's dealings with the men of honour is likely to come onto the political and probably the judicial agenda.

But even if Giuffrè's claims about 'direct contact' between Forza Italia and Cosa Nostra in 1993 turn out to be baseless, and even if Dell'Utri is acquitted, Cosa Nostra had reason to rejoice when Forza Italia took power in 2001 because of Berlusconi's avowed hostility to those magistrates he regards as being overweening and politically biased. Berlusconi's involvement with the courts, over allegations that he bribed tax officials, engaged in false accounting, and committed fraud, has been much in the news. At the time of writing, he has just passed a law to make the five most senior figures in Italy's institutions, including the Prime Minister, immune from prosecution while in office. The law's first effect was to halt a trial in which Berlusconi himself was charged with paying massive bribes to judges in order to obtain a favourable decision in a privatization dispute. Berlusconi's view is that 'red' magistrates are conducting a concerted campaign to discredit him, using the same methods that he says they used to destroy democratically elected parties during the 'Clean Hands' investigations.

That is one reason why Forza Italia's top priority in government is to reform the judicial system. The policy programme announced by the Justice Minister Roberto Castelli argues that 'elements of the magistrature have tried in recent years to occupy terrain that belongs to politics', and have attempted to 'turn justice into a spectacle'. The Minister's plan is to 'bring responsibility for judicial policy, especially in the area of criminal law, back within the orbit of democratic sovereignty'. Berlusconi's opponents fear that the plan is to put justice under the control of the government.

In his struggle with the magistrates, Berlusconi's focus is on Milan, where his business interests are concentrated, rather than Palermo. Nevertheless, his justice policy may have important effects – even if unintended ones – at the other end of the peninsula. A number of measures are arguably likely to obstruct the hunt for Cosa Nostra's financial operations, notably a law making it much more difficult to get evidence from foreign bank accounts for use in domestic trials.

In addition to these legal reforms, the mafia finds Berlusconi's plans for public spending in the South highly appetizing, in particular the scheme to build a bridge linking Sicily and the mainland. Provenzano is apparently often heard to say, 'Fuck! If they build the bridge there'll be something for everyone.' Although Cosa Nostra has always been enthusiastic about public spending no matter who is in government, opponents of Berlusconi claim that some of the things his team have been saying have the effect of offering encouragement to Uncle Bernie. In August 2001, Pietro Lunardi, Minister for the Infrastructure, caused a storm when he remarked that Italy had to 'learn to live with the mafia; everyone should deal with the crime problem in their own way.'

Some members of Berlusconi's party have expressed hostility

towards mafia *pentiti*; they accuse them of being tools in the hands of politicized magistrates or of acting out a secret plan to destabilize Italy's political system. In the name of having a more humane prison system, other politicians from the parties within the governing coalition have floated the idea of offering mafiosi easier prison terms in return for 'dissociating' themselves from Cosa Nostra, but without turning state's evidence. There are reasons to believe that Provenzano's wing of Cosa Nostra would quite like to implement a deal along these lines. Pietro Aglieri, a boss who is studying theology in prison and who is known to be very close to Provenzano, wrote to antimafia prosecutors in March 2002 to ask for negotiations: his proposal was that men of honour would get less harsh penalties in return for recognizing both the existence of Cosa Nostra and the authority of the Italian state. Magistrates view such a scheme as a trap. They think Provenzano wants to resolve Cosa Nostra's internal conflict of interests by making merely symbolic concessions to the authorities. Although symbols are important in the world of Cosa Nostra, the likely upshot of 'dissociation' would simply be that the mafia would continue with its 'submerged' operations, confident in the knowledge that the public had been convinced that it was a thing of the past.

Irrespective of the Berlusconi government's intentions, Cosa Nostra undoubtedly likes many of the noises that have emanated from Rome since the last general election. But top bosses seem to have convinced the organization's grass roots, and perhaps even themselves, that they have a right to expect more than noises from a Forza Italia government, that firm promises have been given, that a government programme of legal changes will serve to heal the mafia's internal divisions.

Accordingly, Berlusconi's opponents are keeping a keen eye on his government to detect any hint of concessions to Cosa Nostra's headline demands. It is reassuring to report that there have been none so far. In fact the bosses were always likely to be disappointed in their expectation that they could skew the policy-making process to suit their own ends. Mafiosi have a great interest in finding friendly Italian politicians, but that does not necessarily mean that they understand Italian politics. What some of them may not appreciate is that even a hypothetical Prime Minister whose absolute priority was to do the bidding of the Sicilian mafia – and no one for a second believes that this is the case with Silvio Berlusconi – would have to face almost insurmountable obstacles. The spirits of Falcone and Borsellino stand guard over laws like 41 bis, and would exact a fearsome political price before they surrendered them. Any governing party that tried overtly to dismantle the pillars of Italy's antimafia legislation would be handing a colossal prize to its opponents and, just as importantly, to its coalition allies. (All government in Italy is coalition government, and the rivalry between coalition partners is nearly always just as fiery as the struggle between the ruling parties and the opposition.)

Whatever it was that encouraged some bosses to hope and expect so much when Forza Italia came to power more than two years ago, Cosa Nostra is now beginning to feel let down by a governing coalition it imagines, rightly or wrongly, to contain elements friendly towards it. For one thing, the 'dissociation' idea has not become policy. 'Dissociation' is thought to be Bernardo Provenzano's idea of a compromise, both between Cosa Nostra and the state, and between the mafiosi in prison and those still at large. In July 2002, Leoluca Bagarella, the man who was boss of bosses between 1993 and 1995 and who is thought to be hostile to any such compromise deal, showed that his patience had worn very thin; he used a court appearance to send out a warning that mafia prisoners living under the tough prison regime 41 bis were 'tired of being used, humiliated, oppressed and treated like merchandise by different political parties'. A man like Bagarella would never indulge in an aimless rant. Mafia-watchers interpreted his words as a threat, calibrated in its imprecision, and addressed perhaps to unknown members of the governing coalition, or perhaps to the government in general. In classic mafia fashion, anyone who was really meant to understand, would understand. In October 2002, the head of the Italian secret service said that there was a 'concrete risk' that Cosa Nostra, in its disappointment, would open up a new season of murders.

The end of 2002 saw a crucial decision go against the mafia when the Berlusconi government converted 41 bis from an annually renewed decree into a permanent law. A Forza Italia Senator, who has long argued in favour of inscribing 41 bis in the law books for good, commented that parliament had given the 'only possible response to Bagarella's worrying pronouncements'. In the eyes of men like Bagarella, however deluded they may be, Forza Italia has thereby scandalously failed to deliver on its most important commitment. No one had to wait very long for a sign of how Cosa Nostra felt about this setback. Soon after the parliamentary vote on 41 bis, magistrates were alarmed to see a banner appear during a football match at Palermo stadium; it read: 'We are united against 41 bis. Berlusconi has forgotten Sicily.' This was widely taken to be a warning directed at politicians in Sicily. The *pax mafiosa* may well be about to end. The paradox of these tense times in Sicily is that, if Cosa Nostra does start shooting again, then that will almost certainly be a sign that it is on the way to defeat. It is no wonder that the *pentito* Salvatore Cancemi has recently said, 'I find this silence more frightening than the bombs.'

In April 2000, at the age of seventy-two, Tommaso Buscetta died of cancer in his adopted American home. In the forty years spent serving Cosa Nostra, and sixteen spent trying to destroy it, he had taken on an estimated 200 pseudonyms. A few months before the end, in his last in-depth interview, Buscetta reflected on a unique life. The hopes that he and Giovanni Falcone had nurtured back in 1984 were now only a bitter memory:

At the end of my first interview, Giovanni Falcone and I deluded ourselves that this time the mafia would be defeated. That there would be no more mafia in our land. Now . . . I have to admit that my prediction was wrong.

Cosa Nostra, Buscetta concluded, has won: 'The mafia is inborn in all Sicilians.' Thus, in his pessimism, the man who made a unique contribution to exposing the falsehood that the mafia and the Sicilian character were the same thing ended his life reiterating it.

These are certainly worrying days for the mafia's enemies. But the time has not yet come to join in Tommaso Buscetta's fatalism. Even in a country as amnesic as Italy, what he revealed is unlikely to share the fate of the Sangiorgi report. The 'rustic chivalry' myth is dead. The secret that the Sicilian mafia managed to keep for so long, the secret of its existence, is out, and out for good. But through all that time, forces much more formidable than myth have kept the mafia strong. The next few months and years promise to determine which way Cosa Nostra will turn. No one outside the organization knows how deep the split between the bosses in prison and those outside runs; nor does anyone know the relative strength of the two factions. They may unite in a new offensive against the magistrates and in taking revenge on the politicians they imagine have let them down. Or they may collapse into civil war, bringing the whole organization back to the brink of destruction. Or Bernardo Provenzano may succeed in appeasing or isolating the bosses in prison. If he does, Cosa Nostra will continue quietly to restructure and reforge its pact with elements within the state, ready to enter a new phase of its savage history – a history that could, and should, have been brought to an end long before now.

Summer 2003

12

Ricotta Cheese and Ghosts

A Chronicle of Cosa Nostra since the Summer of 2003

On the morning of 11 April 2006, Italy was digesting the result of a general election when news broke that Bernardo 'the Tractor' Provenzano, boss of all bosses of the Sicilian mafia, had been captured. Television coverage of the two emerging stories switched between the indignant reactions of Silvio Berlusconi supporters (their leader had been voted out of office by a mere 26,000 votes), and the scenes in Sicily.

It soon emerged that Provenzano had been seized after a police surveillance operation on a tiny farm-cottage just outside the town of his birth. But the world had to wait until the early afternoon for its first glimpse of what a recent film had called 'the Ghost of Corleone'. A grey Alfa Romeo was shown pulling up outside Palermo police headquarters. Officers in black bullet-proof vests and balaclavas punched the air and cheered. A small, grey-haired man was ushered from the car, almost completely hidden by the scrum of police. Despite the shouts of '*Bastardo!*' and '*Assassino!*' from members of the public, his face, when it was finally glimpsed, was eerily calm. He peered into space over the rim of his bookish, metal-framed spectacles. After forty-two years and seven months on the run, Provenzano could now hide only behind the suggestion of a smile.

Six months on from his arrest, 'the Tractor' is now subject to the strictest solitary confinement regime available within Italian law. Even the bars on his window are flattened and angled to stop him looking out at the grim Umbrian steel town of Terni that lies beyond the walls of his maximum security prison. He spends his days peddling meaningless kilometres on his exercise bike, reading the Bible and, above all, writing. Provenzano likes to write. He used to rule Cosa Nostra with scribbled notes known as *pizzini*. Once in prison, he requested a dictionary so that he could begin to improve his comically bad Italian. All that he now lacks is subject matter. The boss of bosses has nothing to jot down but everything that happens: his meals, his medical checks, a few brief exchanges with the guards, the monthly visits from his wife and two sons, the delivery of yet another thick packet of legal documents.

For some men of honour in captivity, religion has become a conduit to a new life. The sham Catholicism that is integral to Cosa Nostra's value system can, with the encouragement of a patient confessor, be transformed into a credo that helps liberate the mind from subservience to organized crime. Provenzano is notoriously pious; and he receives regular visits from a priest. But few hold out any hope that he will turn his back on Cosa Nostra and collaborate with justice. Certainly, if he were to begin filling the pages of his diary with more than the details of his mind-numbing routine, then the history of the Sicilian mafia since the late 1950s would have to be rewritten. More light would be shed into the obscure corners of the organization's past. But even Provenzano cannot yet tell how historically significant his fall from power will be.

For all that many of the secrets of Cosa Nostra's history lie hidden behind Provenzano's half-smile, that history still haunts Sicily in many ways – above all with the spectre of mistrust. No sooner had the scenes outside Palermo police headquarters been broadcast around the country, than 'behindologists' were seeking out dark, underlying intrigues that explained Provenzano's capture. The Italian state's response to Sicilian organized crime was for so long so ambivalent that little it says or does is ever taken at face value.

Some early rumours suggested that the boss of bosses let himself be captured. Or that Cosa Nostra gave him up because he was no longer useful. Only a few days before the arrest, Provenzano's lawyer had claimed that his client was dead and that the authorities were chasing nothing more substantial than a ghost. There was speculation that this strange pronouncement hid a coded meaning: was Cosa Nostra saying that it knew its leader's time was up? But these stories almost certainly owe more to the myth of the mafia's omnipotence than they do to the reality of what happened.

The timing of Provenzano's capture, it was also widely said, was not coincidental. As Prime Minister, Silvio Berlusconi was openly hostile to the Palermo judiciary. In June 2003 he was quoted in a British magazine as saying, 'These judges are mad! . . . To do that job you need to be mentally disturbed, you need psychic disturbances.' Could it be that it had not been politically permissible to arrest Provenzano while Berlusconi was in power? Had the police waited outside Provenzano's Corleone hideout until the election result was in?

The extremely grave allegations implicit in these questions are without foundation. The man who coordinated the hunt for the boss of bosses, national chief antimafia prosecutor Piero Grasso, has explained the timing of the operation clearly enough: the police were only going to move in to seize the mysterious figure in the cottage when it was certain that he really was the man they were looking for, and that he was actually there to be arrested. The decisive moment came only when Provenzano's hand was seen reaching out for a bowl of ricotta cheese that had just been left outside his door.

That moment was the culmination of a hunt that had progressed in several important stages. The first serious blow to the system that kept Provenzano in hiding was when his trusted lieutenant, Nino 'Little Hand' Giuffrè, gave himself up and turned state's evidence in April 2002.

In October the following year, the mafia capo in charge of managing Provenzano's life in hiding was also put behind bars after a dawn raid on a small flat near the Palace of Justice in Palermo. Along with the usual pistols and large amounts of cash, some of Provenzano's now famous coded messages, or *pizzini*, were found in his hideout. At about the same time, disguised as a baker from Villabate, Provenzano went to Marseilles to have an operation on his prostate. The trip would turn out to be a serious error.

In January 2005, the net closed in even tighter with operation 'Grande Mandamento': a thousand police and *carabinieri* took part in the arrest of forty-six people centred on the mafia Family of Villabate, just east of Palermo. Provenzano's entire logistical structure had been dismantled, and he was forced to retreat to his home town of Corleone.

In February 2005 the story of Provenzano's operation in Marseilles broke, provoking great indignation: the mafia boss even sent the regional government the bill for his treatment. But when investigators from Sicily visited the French clinic, they were able to obtain some of the supreme boss's DNA. A new and more accurate photofit of Italy's most wanted man was also issued soon afterwards.

In October 2005, chief prosecutor Grasso reported on television that some 450 of Provenzano's supporters had so far been arrested and hundreds of millions of euros in property had been confiscated: 'Cosa Nostra is certainly paying a price for Provenzano's period in hiding.'

So when it finally came six months later, the capture of 'the Tractor' was not a surprise for Grasso. It was, as he said, primarily the product of patient old-fashioned police work, much of it involving young officers who believed in what they were doing so passionately that they did a great deal of unpaid overtime.

None of which stopped the rumour mill churning on 11 April 2006. Within hours of Provenzano's arrest, the few words he uttered were being scrutinized for secret messages. 'You can't imagine the damage you are doing,' he was reported to have said as police burst into his humble hideout. Did he mean that some secret agreement had been broken? Was he suggesting that, without him, Cosa Nostra would return to a war footing, and once again murder magistrates and place bombs in Italian cities? The leading historian of the mafia thought not. He dismissed Provenzano's quip as just the usual portentous claim to being a peacemaker in society. Mafiosi have been saying the same kind of thing since the middle of the nineteenth century.

Then there was the insult – '*Sbirro*' ('dirty cop') – that 'Shorty' Riina's son reportedly shouted at Provenzano when he arrived in jail for the first time. Among mafia-watchers you will often hear it said that Provenzano was actually an informer for the *carabinieri*; that back in January 1993 he sold 'Shorty' to the authorities so as to take supreme power within Cosa Nostra. And that, as part of this deal, the *carabinieri* delayed raiding Riina's hideout for long enough – eighteen days – to allow it to be cleared of information dangerous to other men of honour. According to 'Little Hand' Giuffrè, there are many in Cosa Nostra who share the same suspicion.

Evidence to back up that suspicion is lacking. It is now known that Riina's son did not shout anything at Provenzano. More-over, in February 2006, the secret serviceman and the *carabinieri* colonel who managed the operation to capture Riina in 1993 were resoundingly acquitted of any wrongdoing. The failure to raid Riina's Uditore villa was a mistake, rather than a crime, the judges ruled. But the theory that 'the Tractor' had other contacts within the *carabinieri* remains the least implausible of the many rumours that circulated in Palermo in the days follow-ing his arrest. We may never know whether the theory has any basis in fact.

A simple diet of ricotta cheese and chicory; a bed with blankets but no sheets; few possessions other than a Bible, spectacles, and clothes that would not have looked out of place on a peasant farmer: in hiding, the supreme boss of Cosa Nostra led a frugal life indeed. Of course the vast wealth that has already been confiscated from his many proxies make it clear that he could have lived in spectacular luxury if he were given the freedom to do so. But chief prosecutor Grasso argued that his 'poverty' was also a tactical choice, and a case of 'mafia ethics'. By living so simply, 'the Tractor' was giving an example of self-sacrifice – an important leadership gesture given how many bosses were living behind bars in conditions even more spartan.

Mediator, strategist, ethical example: Bernardo Provenzano was all of these things to Cosa Nostra in his years as its boss. And on 20 June 2006 it became clear that he was also the man preventing the organization from slipping back into civil war for the first time since the early 1980s. It turns out that Cosa Nostra is haunted by history too.

The morning of 20 June 2006 saw another brilliant police operation end in the arrest of forty-five suspected mafiosi, many of them of at least Family capo rank. Some of them were veterans of Falcone and Borsellino's maxi-trial – it was already well known that Provenzano had placed his trust in an older genera-tion of bosses.

Much of the information behind the arrests came when Provenzano's *pizzini* were decoded. The rest came from listening devices placed in an unassuming corrugated-iron garage in viale Michelangelo, which runs through one of the mafia-dominated *borgate* to the west of Palermo city centre. What investigators learned from these sources was that Provenzano had entrusted power within Cosa Nostra in Palermo to two men. Two men who were on the brink of going to war for the succession.

Salvatore Lo Piccolo and Antonino Rotolo were both already known to the authorities. Lo Piccolo has been on the run for over twenty years, and has long been touted as a possible successor to Provenzano. Rotolo was already an ally of the Corleonesi back in the days of Luciano Leggio. He was serving a life sentence at the time of his arrest, but he had managed to fake a heart condition and was given permission to serve out his sentence at home. The corrugated-iron garage bugged by the police lay adjacent to the garden wall of Rotolo's villa – close enough for him to hop over and attend meetings, where he would read Provenzano's *pizzini* out loud to his lieutenants. The investi-gating authorities contend that among the regular visitors to the garage were two men who allegedly ran Rotolo's day-to-day affairs. Both already have mafia-related crimes on their records, and their professional profile will only come as a surprise to anyone who still believes that the world of the mafia is only peopled by thugs: one is a construction entrepreneur and the other a neurologist.

Rotolo had been airing the idea of killing Lo Piccolo for some time, according to published snippets from the bugged garage summits. As he allegedly said to his neurologist friend: 'Lo Piccolo wants to get us all killed . . . he's stupid . . . we've got to put a noose round his neck first of all.' It seems that, when he was arrested, Provenzano was still mulling over a formal request from Rotolo to do away with Lo Piccolo. And Rotolo was evidently confident that permission would be granted: he had already acquired several barrels of acid.

Investigators looked to mafia history for an explanation as to why Rotolo and his clique were so nervous about Lo Piccolo, and why they thought him 'stupid'. In this case that history can be summarized in one name: Inzerillo.

Salvatore Inzerillo, cousin of New York boss Carlo Gambino, was one of the mafia's biggest drug dealers during the great transatlantic heroin boom of the 1970s. In May 1981 Inzerillo was murdered just before he could take delivery of a bullet-proof Alfa Romeo. It was by killing both him and the 'Prince of Villagrazia', Stefano Bontate, that the Corleonesi inaugurated the *mattanza* – the mass slaughter of men of honour that took them to undisputed power within Cosa Nostra. At that time, 'Shorty' Riina ordered that all of Inzerillo's vast network of relatives be exterminated. Fourteen of them died; the rest escaped to the United States. But now, a quarter of a century after the *mattanza*, with Provenzano's *pax mafiosa* in force, the fugitives are beginning to return. And they have received a warm welcome from Salvatore Lo Piccolo.

Antonino Rotolo is one of the last protagonists of the *mattanza* still able to exercise full power within Cosa Nostra. So he understandably feels vulnerable to revenge from the Inzerillo clan. The hidden microphones in his garage reveal his concerns: 'If they start shooting I will be the first to go down.' As one of Italy's leading commentators on mafia affairs remarked, 'The fugitives must seem like ghosts to the Corleonesi.' And the ghosts, it appears, were already spying on Rotolo's movements.

So the police have been stunningly successful in recent months against Cosa Nostra's Palermo leadership. But even before the world's media descended on Sicily to cover Provenzano's arrest, there was concern among some magistrates that too much attention was being focused on the boss of bosses and the other members of Cosa Nostra's military hierarchy. As one of them argued, the interest in Provenzano 'is like a lamp that casts a dazzling light on one side of planet mafia, yet obscures the other'. By the dark side of 'planet mafia' he meant the corrupt lawyers, entrepreneurs, doctors, financiers, civil servants and politicians who scuttled under cover during 'Shorty' Riina's war on the Italian state. Figures like these have been part of the mafia system since the beginning. Now they are back wielding their old influence within Cosa Nostra's affairs.

Perhaps ironically, the *pizzini* captured during the hunt for Provenzano have provided some of the clearest evidence to back up the magistrate's warning about the dark side of 'planet mafia'. In page after scrawled page of deal-brokering, 'the Tractor' hardly ever needed to threaten to obtain his protection money. As often as not, he would be approached for help. There is an iron commercial logic in these approaches. Client companies of Cosa Nostra can have huge competitive advantages, notably a short cut to public works contracts and quick access to capital. In the same way, client politicians can find it easier to be selected by party machines. The dire fact is that in some parts of Sicilian society there is a *voglia di mafia*: a demand or desire for the mafia (to quote the title of an excellent recent book).

The crime pages of Sicilian newspapers tell of familiar crimes in familiar places. January 2006 was just like any other month of *pax mafiosa*, of Cosa Nostra's submersion strategy. Yet, just like any other month, the small stories of violence and intimidation tell of an occult force whose methods and geography have not changed for a century and a half. On New Year's day in Borgo Molara, in what used to be Palermo's Conca d'Oro where the mafia was born amid the lemon groves, a campaigning priest found his tyres slashed and some bullet cases lying nearby. On 28 January, a man thought to have been asking for extortion money without authorization died of multiple gunshot wounds in Caccamo, once the electoral fief of Raffaele Palizzolo, chief suspect in the Notarbartolo case of the 1890s. The same day, in Corleone, where Bernardino Verro led his doomed struggle against the mafia before the First World War, a trade unionist had his car burned in yet another warning attack.

Episodes like these do not make the kind of international headlines that hail the arrest of a boss of bosses. Yet together they make for the most disturbing story of all: Cosa Nostra's hold over its territory is still strong. Sicily's shadow state ensures that this is a land unable to leave its past behind.

The judicial system too has been preoccupied with the past over the last three years. Unquiet spirits are continually being summoned up in the courtrooms. Spirits like Roberto Calvi, the 'God's banker' found hanging under Blackfriars Bridge in London in the summer of 1982. His case was reopened in both Britain and Italy in 2003, with the mafia boss Pippo Calò as one of the chief suspects. Spirits like the two courageous journalists, Mauro De Mauro, who vanished in 1970, and Mario Francese, murdered in Palermo in 1979. Totò 'Shorty' Riina is now accused of having ordered the death of De Mauro, 'Tractor' Provenzano that of Francese. Spirits like Vito Ciancimino, the 'pushy Corleonese embezzler'. Magistrates are still trying to track down the fortune he began to accumulate during the 'sack of Palermo' in the 1950s and 1960s. And spirits, finally, like Giovanni Falcone and Paolo Borsellino. The judicial quest to discover whether Cosa Nostra consulted mysterious senior figures in business and politics before going ahead and murdering the two heroic magistrates – as some mafia defectors maintain – is still open.

Of course not everyone is keen to summon up the ghosts of the past. If there is one man who embodies the ambiguities in the history of post-war Italian politics then it is seven-times

Prime Minister 'Uncle Giulio' Andreotti. In October 2004, the Court of Cassation finally set the seal on the Italian judicial system's view of his relationship with the Sicilian mafia by confirming what two earlier courts had ruled. Andreotti consciously aided the criminal organization until 1980. But in that year the murder of a senior Christian Democrat colleague led him to break off his ties. Because of Italy's statute of limitations, Andreotti's culpable involvement with the mafia took place too long ago for him to be convicted. Most of Italy does not seem to think that this verdict leaves a stain on the old man's reputation. In the spring of 2006 a smiling Andreotti starred in a mobile phone advertisement. As if to complete his rehabilitation, he then came within a handful of votes of being elected Speaker of the Senate.

Perhaps it is no wonder, given the public's willingness to forget, that some recent judicial rulings read like history lessons. Take the document that bears the date 11 December 2004 and the name of Marcello Dell'Utri, the ad-man aide to media magnate and Prime Minister Silvio Berlusconi. In 1,771 closely argued pages, the judges in the Dell'Utri case explain how Cosa Nostra engaged in a campaign of kidnappings on the Italian mainland in the early 1970s to raise capital for the drug business; how it sought to invest the vast profits of heroin in the mid-1970s; how, in the early 1980s, the Corleonesi exterminated the mafia establishment in the *mattanza*. How, when the Italian state finally began to fight back against Cosa Nostra's escalating savagery, the Corleonesi tried to find new political friends.

In going over all this old ground, the judges had an aim that was more than merely academic: to provide the background to their decision to find Dell'Utri guilty of giving 'a concrete, deliberate, conscious, specific and valuable contribution to maintaining, consolidating and reinforcing Cosa Nostra' over many years. According to their ruling, Dell'Utri 'collaborated in the activities of Cosa Nostra', and his collaboration was conducted primarily through Vittorio Mangano, the 'major-domo' and man of honour. Two of the key moments in the history of Dell'Utri's relationship with the mafia, as reconstructed by the judges, were the following. In May 1974, Dell'Utri helped arrange a meeting in Milan between Silvio Berlusconi and Stefano Bontate, the 'Prince of Villagrazia' who was, at the time, the most influential capo in the Sicilian mafia. In November 1993, Dell'Utri's diary records two appointments with Mangano, who subsequently told other senior mafiosi that Dell'Utri had promised that Berlusconi's nascent political party, Forza Italia, would help Cosa Nostra by relaxing some antimafia legislation. (The judges were at pains to point out that Dell'Utri's reported *promise* was why they found that he was willing to help Cosa Nostra in this instance. The promise was considered a criminal act, irrespective of whether anyone else in Forza Italia knew about it, or of whether the party's actions while in power conformed to what Dell'Utri had supposedly promised.)

Marcello Dell'Utri says he has not read the Palermo judges' ruling. It is likely that he would disagree with their version of Cosa Nostra's recent history: he is, after all, on record as stating that the mafia does not exist. But what is beyond doubt is that Berlusconi's close friend hotly contests the judges' view of his own career and the nine-year prison sentence that they based on it. Dell'Utri's appeal against a verdict he calls 'entirely political' began on 30 June 2006. Intriguingly, it seems that Silvio Berlusconi, who, according to the judges in the first trial, was the victim of mafia extortion for decades, may give evidence in the new hearings. Although Berlusconi himself made no comment at the time of Dell'Utri's conviction, senior figures in Forza Italia denounced it as a 'clamorous judicial error' and 'profoundly unjust'.

There are still many outside the Sicilian judiciary who feel a need for change rather than a desire for the mafia, who have a will to remember rather than a willingness to forget, who display a hunger for information rather than a refusal to understand. Documentaries on the mafia by leading television journalists continue to have a small but devoted following. In November

2004, well over eleven million Italians watched the concluding part of a dramatized life of Paolo Borsellino on television. In 2005, Giusy Vitale, a woman who acted as the boss of the Partinico Family of Cosa Nostra in her brothers' stead, turned state's evidence. Her story also looks set to be re-evoked in a film. (Women exercising such power by proxy is much more unusual in Cosa Nostra than it is in Italy's other, less hierarchically structured, criminal brotherhoods.)

On the morning of 29 June 2004, the citizens of Palermo woke up to find a slogan pasted on every available billboard and lamppost in the city centre: 'An entire people that pays protection money is a people without dignity.' It was the beginning of a grass-roots movement against Cosa Nostra's *pizzo* regime. Addiopizzo, as the movement is called, unites antimafia campaigners, businesses willing to make a public refusal to pay protection, and consumers keen to sponsor them. There is a long, long way for Addiopizzo to go: so far, only 127 Palermo businesses have made public their refusal to pay the *pizzo*, and few if any of them are in the suburban *borgate* where Cosa Nostra's territorial control is at its strongest. Yet Addiopizzo is a protest that will be nothing less than revolutionary for Sicily if it builds up sufficient momentum. If you are going to Palermo, visit the Addiopizzo website and make a point of showing your support.

Italy now has many pro-legality and antimafia organizations like Addiopizzo. Among them, special mention should perhaps go to Libera, which has taken on a particularly important role in managing the properties confiscated from mafiosi for socially useful ends. (The law regulating the confiscation of the profits of organized crime was updated in 1996 following a petition organized by Libera.) This summer, through Libera around one thousand young Italians spent their holidays working on confiscated mafia land in different parts of Italy.

In May 2006 the honorary president of Libera failed in a bid to be elected governor of Sicily. Her name is yet another sign of how history is constantly present in Sicily: Rita Borsellino is the sister of Paolo Borsellino, the magistrate who prepared the maxi-trial with Giovanni Falcone, and who was murdered soon after his friend and colleague in 1992. Rita Borsellino's victorious opponent in the Sicilian regional elections was Totò Cuffaro, a round-faced man with a permanent, beaming smile. According to the Palermo prosecutors, he comes from the dark side of 'planet mafia'. Cuffaro is now beginning a second term as governor of the island, and is also on trial for links to Cosa Nostra – charges that he disputes in the strongest terms. It was these charges that drew Rita Borsellino, a quietly spoken woman with little experience of public life, into the snake pit of Sicilian politics.

The election result was a clear success for the centre-right: Cuffaro won 53 per cent of the popular vote to Borsellino's 42 per cent. Observers from outside Italy might be tempted to view that result as a kind of referendum on the mafia issue. That would be a mistake. Rita Borsellino was not a one-issue anti-mafia candidate, and there were many perfectly legitimate reasons to vote for Cuffaro – not least his challenger's inexperience. Moreover it is far too early to draw any conclusions from the Cuffaro case: the governor confidently predicts that he will be found innocent, and voters may well turn out to be right to believe him rather than the prosecution. Yet his electoral victory, and even more the fact that an alliance of centre-right parties chose him as its candidate in the first place, are themselves cause for concern. Official charges of mafia involvement, however provisional, and however groundless they may turn out to be, would be electoral poison in any other European country. In Sicily, they are still manifestly not.

November 2006

Acknowledgements

Anyone who knows their way around the academic research on the Sicilian mafia that has been done over the last fifteen years or so will recognize the great debt I owe in these pages to the leading Italian experts in the field. I hope they will understand that, if I have chosen not to mention them in the text, it is only to avoid burdening a non-Italian readership with more names than is strictly necessary to tell the story. What first stirred in me the ambition to write *Cosa Nostra* was a desire to reproduce the intellectual excitement I had myself felt on reading the work of Alessandra Dino, Giovanna Fiume, Diego Gambetta, Rosario Mangiameli, Francesco Renda, Paolo Pezzino, Umberto Santino, and particularly Salvatore Lupo whose *Storia della mafia* is in many ways the single most important inspiration for what I have written here. I also derived great benefits from being able to discuss this project in person on several occasions with Salvatore Lupo and Giovanna Fiume. My fond hope is that they think the results of my labours worth while.

Meeting antimafia magistrates Antonio Ingroia, Guido Lo Forte, Gaetano Paci and Roberto Scarpinato left an impression on me and on *Cosa Nostra* that is far, far greater than is apparent from what is made explicit in the text. Francesco Petruzzella and Margherita Pellerano in the Palermo Palazzo di Giustizia were unfailingly considerate when I called on them for help.

Nino Blando deserves my special gratitude: he provided me with excellent company, crucial insights and indispensable guidance on a field trip in January 2003. I must also thank Nino's parents for a wonderful day in Gangi, Ina and Tullio for the welcome they gave me in Brancaccio, and Pippo Cipriani for sparing far more of his time than I had any right to expect in

461

Corleone – where Rosanna Rizzo was also kind enough to share the fruits of her research and experience with me. It would simply not have been possible to write this book without the hospitality of a number of other friends in Italy: Marina and Lorenzo in Milan, Hugo, Stefania and Savina in Rome, Igor and Alessandro in Palermo. My thanks are also due to Nick Dines and Antonio Orlando for their last-minute help with some illustrations, and to Alessandro Fucarini from the Labruzzo agency whose superb photographs deserve a much wider exposure.

Many of my friends read parts of the book at different stages and in so doing helped me undertake the difficult journey away from the conventions of academic writing towards a more readable style. The following will never have to prove their patience in any other way: Prue, Lucy, Clara, Rob, Rebecca, Doug, Emma, Nick, Sham, Claire, Dad, Sarah M., Dave, Jackie, Tommo, Jay, Claire H., Sam, Andrew H., Caz, Cat, Uncle John, Andy, Sarah, Charles, Irina, Rosie, Rosa, Naomi. I owe both Radoyka Miljevic and Robert Gordon a special debt of thanks for reading a complete final draft at very short notice. Sarah Penny cast an astute eye over the proofs. I was also lucky enough to be able to draw on the expertise of Mark Donovan, Christopher Duggan, Lucy Riall, Melvyn Stokes and Michael Woodiwiss. Gaia Servadio, Pino Adriano and David Critchley also provided useful information.

Ombretta Ingrascì did some fantastic work tracking down the illustrations. Her advice and criticism during the writing process have also been very precious. Readers should keep an eye open for her fascinating work on women and the mafia.

Since I first sat down to work on this book I have had almost constant discussions with John Foot. Whatever its faults, *Cosa Nostra* is far better than it could ever have been without his input and support.

The Italian Department at UCL and the Editorial Committee of *Modern Italy* deserve my gratitude for allowing me some time to write. The friendly and professional staff in Humanities 2 of the BL deserve a massive pay rise.

My editors at Hodder – Roland Philipps, Helen Garnons-Williams and Rupert Lancaster – have all been a joy to work with. Helen deserves particular thanks for some perceptive interventions at a crucial stage in the book's development. Everyone in the team at Hodder has been a model of cheerful professionalism. Catherine Clarke, my alchemical agent at Felicity Bryan, has helped make the whole process fun.

All the translations are my own unless otherwise stated.

This one's for Oscar and Beth.

Every reasonable effort has been made to acknowledge the ownership of the copyrighted material included in this volume. Any errors that may have occurred are inadvertent, and will be corrected in subsequent editions provided notification is sent to the author.

I would like thank the following for granting permission to quote from various published works: Rubbettino Editore for Commissione parlamentare d'inchiesta sul fenomeno della mafia e sulle altre associazioni criminali similari, *Mafia, politica, pentiti*; Enrico Deaglio for the interview with Andrea Camilleri in *Diario*; R.C.S. Libri S.p.A. for Giovanni Falcone and Marcelle Padovani, *Cose di Cosa Nostra*, and for Saverio Lodato, *Venti anni di mafia*; Tullio Pironti Editore S.r.l. for Lucio Galluzzo, Franco Nicastro, Vincenzo Vasile, *Obiettivo Falcone*; Edizioni La Zisa S.r.l. for Alessandra Dino, *Mutazioni. Etnografia del mondo di Cosa Nostra*, and for Dino Paternostro, *L'antimafia sconosciuta. Corleone 1893–1993*; Editori Riuniti for Corrado Stajano, *Mafia. L'atto d'accusa dei giudici di Palermo*.

Picture Acknowledgements

1. Reproduced by permission of *La Repubblica*, Rome, and the British Library (Newspaper Library). 2. Copyright unknown. 3. Olympia, Milan. 4. John Dickie. 5. Reproduced by kind permission of Baron Alessandro de Renzis Sonnino. 6. John Dickie. 7. From *L'Ora*, 3–4 May 1901 reproduced by permission of the Biblioteca Nazionale, Rome. 8. Private collection. 9. Biblioteca Nazionale Braidense, Milan. 10. Archivio di Stato, Palermo. 11. Palladium/Tipografia Ferdinando Cortimiglia, Corleone. 12. Rubettino, Soveria Mannelli (CZ). 13. Copyright unknown. 14. From the *New York Herald*, 16 April 1903, reproduced by permission of the General Research Division, the New York Public Library, Astor, Lenox and Tilden Foundations. 15. Copyright unknown. 16. Dario Flaccovio Editore, Palermo. Reproduced by permission of the British Library, YA1990.a.12670. 17. Olympia, Milan. 18. S.A.C. spa, Milan. 19. Labruzzo, Palermo. 20. Labruzzo, Palermo. 21. Copyright unknown. 22. John Dickie. 23. Labruzzo, Palermo. 24. Labruzzo, Palermo. 25. Copyright unknown. 26. Labruzzo, Palermo. 27. Labruzzo, Palermo. 28. Labruzzo, Palermo. 29. Reproduced by kind permission of Giovanni Impastato. 30. Labruzzo, Palermo. 31. Olympia, Milan. 32. Copyright unknown. 33. Copyright unknown. 34. Labruzzo, Palermo.

Bibliography

General

General studies

The following books have been my constant companions during the writing of *Cosa Nostra*:

Aymard, M., and Giarrizzo, G. (eds), *La Sicilia*, Turin, 1987

Cancila, O., *Palermo*, Bari, 2000

Gambetta, D., *The Sicilian Mafia*, London, 1993

Lupo, S., *Storia della mafia*, Rome, 1993 and 1996

Mangiameli, R., *La mafia tra stereotipo e storia*, Caltanissetta, 2000

Pezzino, P., *Una certa reciprocità di favori: mafia e modernizzazione violenta nella Sicilia postunitaria*, Milan, 1990

Pezzino, P., *Mafia: industria della violenza*, Florence, 1995

Renda, F., *Storia della mafia*, Palermo, 1997

Santino, U., *La mafia interpretata*, Soveria Mannelli, 1995

Santino, U., *Storia del movimento antimafia*, Rome, 2000

Testimonies by pentiti

Brusca, G., and Lodato, S., *Ho ucciso Giovanni Falcone*, Milan, 1999

Buscetta, T., and Arlacchi, P., *Addio Cosa Nostra*, Milan, 1994

Calderone, A., and Arlacchi, P., *Gli uomini del disonore*, Milan, 1992

Cancemi, S., *Riina mi fece i nomi di . . .*, Bolsena, 2002

Commissione parlamentare d'inchiesta sul fenomeno della mafia e sulle altre associazioni criminali similari, *Mafia, politica, pentiti: la relazione del presidente Luciano Violante e le deposizioni di Antonio Calderone, Tommaso Buscetta, Leonardo Messina, Gaspare Mutolo*, Soveria Mannelli, 1993

Bibliography

Archival sources

Most archival sources are listed below under the appropriate sections
of the book. However, the papers of the first parliamentary commission of inquiry were important for many periods of the Sicilian
mafia's history:

Commissione parlamentare d'inchiesta sul fenomeno della mafia in
Sicilia, *Documentazione allegata alla relazione conclusiva della
Commissione parlamentare d'inchiesta sul fenomeno della mafia
in Sicilia*, 34 vols, Rome, 1976–1985 (hereafter referred to as
Documentazione allegata)
*Testo integrale della Relazione della Commissione Parlamentare
d'inchiesta sul fenomeno della mafia*, 3 vols, Rome, 1973

Newspapers and magazines

Avanti! (Milan)
Corriere della Sera (Milan)
Diario (Milan)
Domenica del Corriere (Milan)
Giornale d'Italia (Rome)
Giornale di Sicilia (Palermo)
Illustrazione Italiana (Milan)
L'Ora (Palermo)
La Nazione (Florence)
New York Herald (New York)
Il Precursore (Palermo)
La Repubblica (Rome)
Resto del Carlino (Bologna)
Sicilia Nuova (Palermo)
Il Teatro Illustrato (Milan)
The Times (London)
La Tribuna (Rome)
L'Unità (Rome)

Interviews with antimafia magistrates
Antonio Ingroia
Guido Lo Forte
Gaetano Paci
Roberto Scarpinato
All carried out April 2002, Palazzo di Giustizia, Palermo

Prologue/Introduction/Men of Honour

Bianconi, G., and Savatteri, G., *L'attentatuni*, Milan, 1998
Capellani, N., *Vita di Giovanni Verga*, Florence, 1972
Catanzaro, R., *Il delitto come impresa*, Padua, 1988
Dino, A., *Mutazioni*, Palermo, 2002
Falcone, G., and Padovani, M., *Cose di Cosa Nostra*, Milan, 1991
Flury, R., *Pietro Mascagni: a Bio-Bibliography*, London, 2001
Fulvetti, G., 'Tra silenzio e collusione', in *Novecento*, 5, 2001
Lewis, N., *The Honoured Society*, London, 1964
Lo Forte, G., 'L'atteggiarsi delle associazioni mafiose sulla base
    delle esperienze processuali acquisite: la mafia siciliana',
    unpublished paper, 1996
Mascagni, P., *Epistolario*, vol. 1, Lucca, 1996
Niceforo, A., *L'Italia barbara contemporanea*, Milan, 1898
Siebert, R., *Le donne: la mafia*, Milan, 1994
Stille, A., *Excellent Cadavers*, London, 1995

1 The Genesis of the Mafia 1860–1876

Abba, G. C., *Da Quarto al Volturno*, Bologna, 1960
Alatri, P., *Lotte politiche in Sicilia sotto il governo della Destra
    (1866–74)*, Turin, 1954
Biundi, Giuseppe, *Dizionario siciliano-italiano*, Palermo, 1857
Brancati, E., and Muscetta, C., *La letteratura sulla mafia*, Rome, 1988
Carbone, S., and Grispo, R. (eds), *L'inchiesta sulle condizioni sociali
    ed economiche della Sicilia (1875–1876)*, 2 vols, Bologna, 1968–9

Bibliography

Crisantino, A., *Della segreta e operosa associazione*, Palermo, 2000

D'Alessandro, V., and Giarrizzo, G., *La Sicilia dal Vespro all'Unità d'Italia*, Turin, 1989

Da Passano, M. (ed.), *I moti di Palermo del 1866: verbali della Commissione parlamentare di inchiesta*, Rome, 1981

Davis, J. A., *Conflict and Control*, London, 1988

De Mattei, R., 'L'inchiesta siciliana di Franchetti e Sonnino', in *Annali del Mezzogiorno*, 1963

Di Bella, S., *I mafiusi della Vicaria di Palermo*, Cosenza, 1991

Dumas, A., *The Garibaldians in Sicily*, London, 1861

Fiume, G., *Le bande armate in Sicilia (1819–1849): violenza e organizzazione del potere*, Palermo, 1984

Franchetti, L., *Condizioni politiche e amministrative della Sicilia*, vol. 1 of L. Franchetti and and S. Sonnino, *Inchiesta in Sicilia*, 2 vols, Florence, 1974

Franchetti, L., *Politica e mafia in Sicilia*, Rome, 1995

Hay, D., *Albion's Fatal Tree: Crime and Society in Eighteenth-Century England*, Harmondsworth, 1975

La Motta, M., 'Le inchieste del 1875–76 nell'opinione pubblica siciliana', in *Nuovi Quaderni del Meridione*, 51–2, 1975

Loschiavo, G. G., *Cento anni di mafia*, Rome, 1962

Lupo, S., *Il giardino degli aranci*, Venice, 1990

Lupo, S., 'Nei giardini della Conca d'Oro', in *Italia Contemporanea*, 156, 1984

Maison, É., *Journal d'un volontaire de Garibaldi*, Paris, 1862

Mangiameli, R., 'Banditi e mafiosi dopo l'Unità', in Mangiameli, R., *La mafia tra stereotipo e storia*, Caltanissetta, 2000

Maurici, A., *La genesi storica della rivolta del 1866 in Palermo*, Palermo, 1916

Morvillo, A., *Storia e processo della tortura del sordo-muto Antonio Cappello*, Palermo, 1864

Nievo, I., *Lettere garibaldine*, Turin, 1961

Novacco, D., 'Considerazioni sulla fortuna del termine "mafia"', in *Belfagor*, 14, 1959

Onofri, M., *Tutti a cena da don Mariano: letteratura e mafia nella Sicilia della nuova Italia*, Milan, 1995

Pezzino, P., *La congiura dei pugnalatori: un caso politico –
guidiziario alle origini della mafia*, Venice, 1992

Recupero, A., 'Ceti medi e "homines novi": alle origini della mafia',
in *Polis*, 1 (2), 1987

Riall, L., *Sicily and the Unification of Italy: Liberal Policy and Local
Power, 1859–1866*, Oxford, 1998

Santino, U., *La cosa e il nome: materiali per lo studio dei fenomeni
premafiosi*, Soveria Mannelli, 2000

Sciascia, L., *Il mare colore del vino*, Turin, 1973

Sonnino, S., *I contadini in Sicilia*, vol. 2 of L. Franchetti and
S. Sonnino, 2 vols, *Inchiesta in Sicilia*, Florence, 1974

Sonnino, S., *Lettere ad Emilia Peruzzi, 1872–1878*, Pisa, 1998

Thompson, E. P., *Whigs and Hunters: the Origin of the Black Act*,
London, 1975

Traina, A., *Nuovo vocabolario siciliano-italiano*, Palermo, 1868

Trevelyan, G. M., *Garibaldi and the Thousand*, London, 1909

Trevelyan, G. M., *Garibaldi and the Making of Italy*, London,
1920

Turrisi Colonna, N., *Pubblica sicurezza in Sicilia nel 1864*, Palermo,
1988

2 The Mafia Enters the Italian System 1876–1890

Alongi, G., *La maffia nei suoi fattori e nelle sue manifestazioni:
studio sulle classi pericolose della Sicilia*, Turin, 1886

Alongi, G., *Manuale di polizia scientifica*, Milan, 1898

Archivio Centrale dello Stato, Direzione generale affari penali;
misc., 1863–1925, b. 44, f. 558. 1877: reports by chief prosecutor
to Minister of Justice.

Atti Parlamentari: Camera dei Deputati, Sessione 1874–75, Rome

Berselli, A., 'Il governo dei moderati e la Sicilia', in *Quaderni del
Meridione*, 1, 1958

Bonomo, G., *Pitrè, la Sicilia e i siciliani*, Palermo, 1989

Buttitta, A., *Ideologie e folklore*, Palermo, 1971

Caico, L., *Sicilian Ways and Days*, London, 1910

Cardullo, F., *Le vie dello zolfo in Sicilia: storia ed architettura*, Rome, 1991

Colacino, T., 'La Fratellanza: associazione di malfattori', in *Rivista di Discipline Carcerarie*, 5–6, 1885

Cutrera, A., *La mafia e i mafiosi*, Palermo, 1900

De Nicolò, M., *Trasformismo, autoritarismo, meridionalismo: il Ministro dell'Interno Giovanni Nicotera*, Bologna, 2001

Genco, M., *Il Delegato*, Palermo, 1991

Gentile, G., *Giuseppe Pitrè*, Florence, 1940

Lestingi, F., 'L'associazione della Fratellanza nella provincia di Girgenti', in *Archivio di Psichiatria, Scienze Penali ed Antropologia Criminale*, 5, 1884

Lombroso, C., *L'uomo delinquente*, 4th edn, Turin, 1889

Lombroso, C., *La donna delinquente, la prostituta e la donna normale*, Turin, 1893

Marino, G. C., *L'opposizione mafiosa 1870–1882*, Palermo, 1964

Pezzino, P., 'Stato violenza società: nascita e sviluppo del paradigma mafioso', in Pezzino, P., *Una certa reciprocità di favori: mafia e modernizzazione violenta nella Sicilia postunitaria*, Milan, 1990

Pezzino, P., '"La Fratellanza" di Favara', in Pezzino, *Una certa reciprocità di favori*, Milan, 1990

Pitrè, G., *Usi e costumi, credenze e pregiudizi del popolo siciliano*, 4 vols, Palermo, 1889

Russo, N. (ed.), *Antologia della mafia*, Palermo, 1964

Seton Watson, C., *Italy from Liberalism to Fascism, 1870–1925*, London, 1967

3 Corruption in High Places 1890–1904

Archivio Centrale dello Stato, DGPS, aa.gg.rr. Atti speciali (1898–1940), b. 1, f. 1, 'The Sangiorgi Report'

Barone, G., 'Egemonie urbane e potere local (1882–1913)', in Aymard, M., and Giarrizzo, G. (eds), *La Sicilia*, Turin, 1987

Barone, G., 'Il tramonto dei Florio', in *Meridiana*, 1991, 11–12, pp. 15–46

Dizionario Biografico degli Italiani, Rome, 1960: entries on the Florio family

Candela, S., *I Florio*, Palermo, 1986

De Felice Giuffrida, G., *Maffia e delinquenza in Sicilia*, Milan, 1900

Ganci, S. M., *Il commissariato civile per la Sicilia del 1896*, Palermo, 1958

Lentini, R., and Silvestri, P. (eds), *I Whitaker di villa Malfitano: seminario di studi – Palermo 16–18 March 1995*, Palermo, 1995

Lupo, S., '"Il tenebroso sodalizio": un rapporto sulla mafia palermitana di fine Ottocento', in *Studi Storici*, 2, 1988

Marchesano, G., *Processo control Raffaele Palizzolo & C. Arringa dell'avv. G.M.*, Palermo, 1902

Nicolosi, P., *Palermo fin de siècle*, Milan, 1979

Notarbartolo, L., *Memorie della vita di mio padre*, Pistoia, 1949

Poma, R., *Onorevole alzatevi!*, Florence, 1976

Renda, F., *Socialisti e cattolici in Sicilia (1900–1904)*, Caltanissetta, 1972

Sanderson Whitaker, R., *Whitaker of Hesley Hall, Grayshott Hall, Pylewell Park and Palermo*, London, 1907

Trevelyan, R., *Princes Under the Volcano*, London, 1972

4 Socialism, Fascism, Mafia 1893–1943

Andreucci, F., and Detti, T., *Il movimento operaio italiano: dizionario biografico (1853–1943)*, Rome, 1976–8

Anselmo, N., *La terra promessa: vita e morte di Bernardino Verro e del movimento contadino nel feudo*, Palermo, 1989

Anselmo, N., *Corleone Novecento*, 4 vols: vol. 1, Corleone, 1998

Archivio di Stato di Palermo, Prefettura Gabinetto 1906–25, b. 267, fasc. 'Omicidio Verro Bernardino', Rapporto del Capitano dei RR.CC., del Delegato di P.S. e del Commissario di P.S., Corleone, dated 4 November 1915

Archivio di Stato di Pavia, *Carte Mori*, 'Relazioni, pubblicazioni, studi e discorsi (8)'

Bibliography

Blok, A., *The Mafia of a Sicilian Village, 1860–1960: a Study of Violent Peasant Entrepreneurs*, Oxford, 1974

Calderone, A., and Arlacchi, P., *Gli uomini del disonore*, Milan, 1992

Cappellini, A., *Polesani illustri*, Genoa, 1938

Cararrubea, G., *I fasci contadini e le origini delle sezioni socialiste della provincia di Palermo*, Palermo, 1978

Cicala, A., 'Il movimento contadino in Sicilia nel primo dopoguerra (1919–1920)', in *Incontri Meridionali*, 3–4, 1978

Colletto, G., *Storia di Corleone*, Siracusa, 1936

Duggan, C., *Fascism and the Mafia*, London, 1989

Loschiavo, G. G., 'Il reato di associazione per delinquere nelle province siciliane', in *100 anni di mafia*, Rome, 1962

Lupo, S., 'L'utopia totalitaria del fascismo (1918–1942)', in Aymard, M., and Giarrizzo, G. (eds), *La Sicilia*, Turin, 1987

Mangano, S., *Bernardino Verro socialista corleonese*, Palermo, 1974

Marchese, A. G., *Inventario corleonese*, Palermo, 1997

Marino, G. C., *I padrini*, Rome, 2001

Mori, C., *Tra le zagare oltre la foschia*, Florence, 1923

Mori, C., *Con la mafia ai ferri corti*, Milan, 1932

Mori, C., *The Last Struggle with the Mafia*, London, 1933

Paternostro, D., *L'antimafia sconosciuta: Corleone, 1893–1993*, Palermo, 1994

Paton, W. A., *Picturesque Sicily*, London, 1898

Petacco, A., *Il prefetto di ferro*, Milan, 1975

Porto, S., *Mafia e Fascismo*, Palermo, 1977

Raffaele, G., *L'ambigua tessitura*, Milan, 1993

Renda, F., *I Fasci siciliani (1892–94)*, Turin, 1977

Rizzo, R., *Bernardino Verro e il movimento contadino a Corleone*, unpublished thesis, University of Palermo, 1998

Romano, S. F., *Storia dei fasci siciliani*, Bari, 1959

Rossi, A., *Un italiano in America*, Milan, 1892

Rossi, A., *L'agitazione in Sicilia*, Milan, 1894

Spanò, A., *Faccia a faccia con la mafia*, Milan, 1978

5 The Mafia Establishes Itself in America 1900–1941

Albini, J. L., *The American Mafia: Genesis of a Legend*, New York, 1971

Archivio di Stato di Palermo, Archivio Generale – Questura di Palermo, b. 1584, f. 196, f. 352, police reports on Petrosino murder

Asbury, H., *The Gangs of New York*, Garden City, NY, 1928

Blok, A., *East Side, West Side: Organizing Crime in New York 1930–1950*, Cardiff, 1980

Carey, A. A., *Memoirs of a Murder Man*, Garden City, NY, 1930

Deaglio, E., 'Se vince lui, ma forse no', interview with A. Camilleri in *Diario* at: http://www.vigata.org/rassegna_stampa/2001/Archivio/Int09_Cam_mar2001_Diario.html

Gabaccia, D. R., *From Sicily to Elizabeth Street: Housing and Social Change among Italian Immigrants, 1880–1930*, Albany, NY, 1984

Gentile, N., *Vita di capomafia*, Rome, 1993

Gildeer, R. W., 'The housing problem – America's need of awakening,' *The American City*, 1, 1909

Haller, M. H., 'Illegal enterprise: a theoretical and historical interpretation', in *Criminology*, 28, 2, 1990

Henderson, T. M., *Tammany Hall and the New Immigrants*, New York, 1976

Landesco, J., *Organized Crime in Chicago*, Chicago, 1968

Lawes, L. E., *Life and Death in Sing Sing*, Garden City, NY, 1928

Lupo, S., 'Cose nostre: mafia siciliana e mafia americana', in P. Bevilacqua *et al* (eds), *Storia dell'emigrazione italiana*; 3 vols, vol. 2, *Arrivi*, Rome, 2002

Maas, P., *The Valachi Papers*, London, 1971

Nelli, H. S., *The Business of Crime: Italians and Syndicate Crime in the United States*, New York, 1976

Nelli, H. S., *From Immigrants to Ethnics: the Italian Americans*, Oxford, 1983

Petacco, A., *Joe Petrosino*, Milan, 2001

Pitkin, T. M., and Cordasco, F., *The Black Hand: a Chapter in Ethnic Crime*, Totowa, NJ, 1977

Reid, E., *Mafia*, New York, 1964

Rossi, A., *Impressioni italo-americane*, Rome, 1907

Rossi, A., 'Per la tutela degli italiani negli Stati Uniti', in *Bollettino dell'Emigrazione*, 16, 1904

Rossi, A., 'Vantaggi e danni dell'emigrazione nel Mezzogiorno d'Italia', in *Bollettino dell'Emigrazione*, 13, 1908

Sciarrone, R., *Mafie vecchie, mafie nuove*, Rome, 1998

Smith Jr, D. C., *The Mafia Mystique*, New York, 1975

Sori, E., *L'emigrazione italiana dall'Unità alla seconda guerra mondiale*, Bologna, 1979

Stokes, M., 'The gangster cycle, the impact of the Depression, and cultural struggles of the early 1930s', in *Le crime organisé à la ville et à l'écran*, Tours, 2002

Weissman Joselit, J., *Our Gang: Jewish Crime and the New York Jewish Community, 1900–1940*, Bloomington, 1983

Woodiwiss, M., *Organized Crime and American Power: a History*, Toronto, 2001

6 War and Rebirth 1943–1950

Adriano, P., *Indagine conoscitiva dell'Archivio della Commissione Alleata di Controllo – Governo Militare Alleato in Italia*, unpublished report, 2001

'Allied to the mafia', BBC2 *Timewatch* documentary, first transmitted 13 January 1993

Campbell, R., *The Luciano Project*, New York, 1977

Casarrubea, G., *Salvatore Giuliano*, Milan, 2001

Di Lello, G., 'La vicenda di Salvatore Giuliano', in Violante, L. (ed.), *La criminalità*, Turin, 1997

Di Matteo, S., *Anni roventi: la Sicilia dal 1943 al 1947*, Palermo, 1967

Gaja, F., *L'esercito della lupara*, Milan, 1962

Harris, C. R. S., *Allied Military Administration of Italy 1943–1945*, London, 1957

Kezich, T., *Salvatore Giuliano*, Rome, 1991

Lumia, L., *Villalba, storia e memoria*, Caltanissetta, 1990

Mangiameli, R., 'Gabelloti e notabili nella Sicilia dell'interno', in Mangiameli, R., *La mafia tra stereotipo e storia*, Caltanissetta, 2000

Maxwell, G., *God Protect me from my Friends*, London, 1957

Meyer, K., and Parssinen, T., *Webs of Smoke*, New York, 1998

Montanelli, I., *Pantheon minore (incontri)*, Milan, 1955

Naro, C., *La chiesa di Caltanissetta tra le due guerre*, Caltanissetta and Rome, 1991

Pantaleone, M., *Mafia e politica 1943–1962*, Turin, 1962

'Relazione sull'indagine sui casi di singoli mafiosi', in *Testo integrale*, vol. 1

Renda, F., *Salvatore Giuliano*, Palermo, 2002

Romano, S. F., *Storia della mafia*, Milan, 1963

Sicily. Zone Handbook (Foreign Office), London, 1943

7 God, Concrete, Heroin, and Cosa Nostra 1950–1963

Barrese, O., *Complici*, Milan, 1973

Biagi, E., *Il Boss è solo*, Milan, 1987

Bonanno, J., *A Man of Honour: the Autobiography of a Godfather*, London, 1983

Chubb, J., *Patronage, Power and Poverty in Southern Italy*, Cambridge, 1982

Farinella, M., *Diario Siciliano*, Palermo, 1977

Kennedy, R. F., *Robert Kennedy in His Own Words*, London, 1988

Pantaleone, M., *Mafia e droga*, Turin, 1966

'Relazione sull'indagine sui casi di singoli mafiosi', in *Testo integrale*, vol. 1

Santino, U., and La Fiura, G., *L'impresa mafiosa*, Milan, 1990

Stabile, F. M., *La Chiesa nella società siciliana*, Caltanissetta, 1992

Stabile, F. M., *I consoli di Dio*, Caltanissetta, 1999

Sterling, C., *The Mafia*, London, 1990

Thomas, E., *Robert Kennedy. His Life*, New York, 2000

Bibliography

8 The 'First' Mafia War and its Consequences 1962–1969

Blando, N., 'Di cosa parliamo quando parliamo di Regime mafioso?', unpublished conference paper, 2002

Deaglio, E., *Raccolto rosso: la mafia, l'Italia e poi venne giù tutto*, Milan, 1995

Di Lello, G., *Giudici: cinquant'anni di processi di mafia*, Palermo, 1994

Nisticò, V., *Accadeva in Sicilia*, Palermo, 2001

'Relazione sull'indagine sui casi di singoli mafiosi', in *Testo integrale*, vol. 1

Sciascia, L., *Il giorno della civetta*, Turin, 1961

'Sentenza, emessa il 22 dicembre 1968 dalla Corte di Assise di Catanzaro, nei confronti di Angelo La Barbera ed altri, imputati di vari omicidi, sequestri di persone, violenza privata ed altri reati', in *Documentazione allegata*, vol. 4, tomo 17

Servadio, G., *Angelo La Barbera: the Profile of a Mafia Boss*, London, 1974

Tranfaglia, N., *Mafia, politica e affari, 1943–2000*, Rome-Bari, 2001

9 The Origins of the Second Mafia War 1970–1982

Anselmo, N., *Corleone Novecento*, 3 vols: vol. 3, Corleone, 2000

Arlacchi, P., *Mafia Business*, London, 1986

Bartolotta Impastato, F., *La mafia in casa mia*, Palermo, 1987

Dalla Chiesa, C. A., *Michele Navarra e la mafia corleonese*, Palermo, 1990

Dino, A., 'Ritorno a Mafiopoli', in *Meridiana*, 40, 2001

Galluzzo, L., Nicastro, F., and Vasile, V., *Obiettivo Falcone*, Naples, 1989

Parlagreco, S., *L'uomo di vetro*, Milan, 1998

Pistone, J. D., *Donnie Brasco*, New York, 1989

Russo Spena, G., *Peppino Impastato: anatomia di un depistaggio*, Rome, 2001

Santino, U., 'Peppino Impastato: la memoria difficile', in *Meridiana*,
40, 2001
Silj, A., *Il malpaese*, Rome, 1994
Stajano, C. (ed.), *Mafia: l'atto d'accusa dei giudici di Palermo*,
Rome, 1986
'Testo della requisitoria consegnata alla Commissione dal dottor
Giovanni Pizzillo, Procuratore della Repubblica presso il
Tribunale di Palermo', in *Documentazione allegata*, vol. 1
Vitale, S., *Nel cuore dei coralli*, Soveria Mannelli, 2002

10 Terra Infidelium 1983–1992

Caponnetto, A., *I miei giorni a Palermo*, Milan, 1992
Caruso, A., *Da cosa nasce cosa*, Milan, 2000
Corte Suprema di Cassazione, *Sentenza sul ricorso proposto da
Corrado Carnevale*, Rome, 30 October 2002
Ginsborg, P. (ed.), *Le virtù della Repubblica*, Milan, 1994
Ginsborg, P., *Storia d'Italia 1943–1996: Famiglia, Società, Stato*,
Turin, 1998
La Licata, F., *Storia di Giovanni Falcone*, Milan, 2002
Lodato, S., *Venti anni di mafia*, Milan, 1999
Pansa, G., *Carte false*, Milan, 1988
Schneider, P. and J., 'Il caso Sciascia', in J. Schneider (ed.), *Italy's
'Southern Question'*, Oxford, 1998
Sciascia, L., *La Sicilia come metafora*, Milan, 1979
Sciascia, L., *A futura memoria*, Milan, 1989
Stille, A., *Excellent Cadavers*, London, 1995

11 Bombs and Submersion 1992–2003

Alajmo, R., *Un lenzuolo contro la mafia*, Palermo [no date]
'Antimafia', special issue of *Meridiana*, 25, 1996
Buscetta, T., and Lodato, S., *La mafia ha vinto*, Milan, 1999
Caselli, G. C., and Ingroia, A., *L'eredità scomoda*, Milan, 2001

Catanzaro, R., 'Un anno di svolta nella mafia e nell'antimafia', in
  S. Hellman and G. Pasquino (eds), *Politica in Italia '93*, Bologna, 1993
Corte d'Appello di Palermo. Presidente Scaduti. Sentenza nei
  confronti di Giulio Andreotti. 2 maggio 2003. (Secondo grado.)
Deliziosi, F., *Don Puglisi*, Milan, 2001
Dino, A., 'La mafia del Gattopardo', in *Micro Mega*, 4, 2001.
Grasso, P., and Lodato, S., *La mafia invisibile*, Milan, 2001
Jamieson, A., *The Antimafia: Italy's Fight against Organized Crime*,
  London, 2000
Lo Forte, G., 'L'evoluzione della "politica" di Cosa Nostra dal 1996
  ad oggi', unpublished paper, 2001
Lupo, S., *Andreotti, la mafia, la storia d'Italia*, Rome, 1996
Oliva, E., and Palazzolo, S., *L'altra mafia*, Soveria Mannelli, 2001
Procura di Palermo, Direzione Distrettuale Antimafia, *L'onore di
  Dell'Utri*, Milan, 1997
Torrealta, M., *Ultimo*, Milan, 1995
Torrealta, M., *La trattativa*, Rome, 2002
Tranfaglia, N., *La sentenza Andreotti*, Milan, 2001
Tribunale di Palermo. Presidente Ingargiola. Sentenza nei confronti
  di Giulio Andreotti. 23 ottobre 1999. (Primo grado.)

12 Ricotta Cheese and Ghosts

'Ecco perché il padrino viveva da povero', *Corriere della Sera*,
  15 April 2006.
Bellavia, E., and Palazzolo, S., *Voglia di mafia. Le metamorfosi di
  Cosa Nostra da Capaci a oggi*, Rome, 2004. An illuminating
  interview with chief prosecutor Grasso took place at the launch
  of this book hosted by the antimafia organization Cuntrastamu.
  A recording of the interview can be downloaded from:
  www.cuntrastamu.org
Bolzoni, A., 'Dagli Usa tornano gli "scappati" e edesso tremano i
  Corleonesi', *La Repubblica*, 21 June 2006.
Bolzoni, A., 'Bibbia, pizzini e una cyclette. Ecco la giornata del
  padrino', *La Repubblica*, 21 July 2006.

Johnson, B., and Farrell, N., 'Forza Berlusconi', the *Spectator*, 6 September 2003.

Lupo, S., interview, 'Zu Binnu? Non è il superboss', in *Narcomafie*, April 2006.

Scarpinato, R., 'Mafia e potere', paper from *Mafie d'Italia nel nuovo millennio: analisi e proposte*, papers of the Seminario di formazione di Libera held in July 2003, and downloadable from www.libera.it.

Tribunale di Palermo. II Sezione penale presieduta da Leonardo Guarnotta. Sentenza nei confronti di Dell'Utri Marcello e Cinà Gaetano.

Corle Suprema di Cassazione, seconda sezione penale presieduta da Giuseppe Maria Cosentino. Sentenza sui ricorsi proposti dalla Procura Generale presso la Corte d'Apello di Palermo e da Giulio Andreotti. 15 ottobre 2004. Published in *Segno*, 262, February 2005.

The following internet sites are among the best sources of information on contemporary developments:

http://www.antimafiaduemila.com
The website of the magazine *Antimafia 2000*.

http://www.interno.it/dip_ps/dia/home.htm
This includes the Direzione Investigativa Antimafia's six-monthly reports to parliament.

http://www.centroimpastato.it/index.php3
The website of Centro Siciliano di Documentazione 'Giuseppe Impastato', run by Umberto Santino and Anna Puglisi, has a regularly updated record of mafia-related crimes and other issues.

http://www.addiopizzo.org
The website for the grass-roots antimafia movement Addiopizzo.

The proceedings of the ongoing parliamentary commission of inquiry into the mafia are on the following sites:

Bibliography

http://www.liberliber.it/biblioteca/i/italia/verbali_della_commissione_
parlamentare_antimafia/html/

http://www.camera.it/_bicamerali/antimafia/home.htm

Notes on Sources Quoted

Prologue/Introduction/Men of Honour, pp.xiii–18

p.xix Falcone and Padovani, p.41.
p.6 Buscetta and Arlacchi, p.20.
p.6 Falcone and Padovani, p.49.
pp.6–7 Buscetta and Arlacchi, p.155.
p.11 *La Repubblica*, 15 September 1998.
p.13 Dino, *Mutazioni*, p.78.
pp.13–14 Brusca and Lodato, p.84.
p.18 Bianconi and Savatteri, pp.280–4.

1: The Genesis of the Mafia 1860–1876, pp.19–64

p.29 Carbone and Grispo, vol. 2, p.1002.
p.35 Brusca and Lodato, p.33.
pp.36–7 Crisantino, pp.85–6.
pp.40–1 Turrisi Colonna, p.43.
p.42 Turrisi Colonna, p.47.
p.43 Sonnino, *Lettere* p.231.
p.46 Da Passano, pp.130–2.
p.49 Quotes in this paragraph, from Franchetti, *Condizioni*, pp.3–4, 56.
p.53 Franchetti, *Condizioni*, p.98.
pp.59–60 Alatri, p.95.

2: The Mafia Enters the Italian System 1876–1890, pp.65–91

p.69 *The Times*, 21 June 1875.
p.69 *The Times*, 9 June 1875.
pp.70–2 Tajani's speech is in *Atti Parlamentari: Camera dei Deputati, Sessione 1874–75, Discussioni*, 11–12 June 1875.
p.73 Pezzino, 'Stato: nascita e sviluppo del paradigma mafioso', in Pezzino, *Una certa reciprocità*, p.112.
pp.73–4 Carbone and Grispo, vol. 2, p.1137.
p.82 Colacino, p.180.
p.83 Falcone and Padovani, p.31.
p.84 Caico, pp.176–7.
p.88 Alongi, *La maffia*, pp.55, 58.
p.89 Carbone and Grispo, vol. 2, p.1008.
p.89 Alongi, *La maffia*, pp.72–3.
p.90 Pitrè, vol. 2, p.292.

3: Corruption in High Places 1890–1904, pp.93–152

p.99 Cancila, p.237.

p.106 Archivio Centrale dello Stato, Sangiorgi report, p.117.

p.108 Sangiorgi report, pp.120–1.

p.114 Trevelyan, *Princes Under the Volcano*, p.223.

p.115 Sangiorgi report, p.38.

p.117 Sangiorgi report, p.137.

p.118 Sangiorgi report, p.137.

p.120 Sangiorgi report, p.193.

p.120 Sangiorgi report, p.37.

p.122 Sangiorgi report, pp.335–6.

pp.123–4 Sangiorgi report, p.1.

p.125 Barone, 'Egemonie urbane', p.317.

p.125 *Giornale di Sicilia*, 20–1 May 1901.

p.126 *Resto del Carlino*, 30–1 October 1901.

p.130 Notarbartolo, p.276.

p.135 *Avanti!* 18 November 1899.

p.137 *Avanti!* 18 November 1899.

p.139 Notarbartolo, p.339.

p.140 *Avanti!* 24 November 1899.

p.141 *The Times*, 22 December 1899.

p.143 *Avanti!* 28 September 1901.

p.146 *Giornale d'Italia*, 1 August 1902.

p.147 *The Times*, 1 August 1902.

p.149 Marchesano, pp.294–5.

p.151 Lupo, *Storia della mafia* (1996 edn), p.133.

4: Socialism, Fascism, Mafia 1893–1943, pp.153–191

pp.155–6 Rossi, *L'agitazione*, pp.81–2.

p.156 Paton, *Picturesque Sicily*, p.179.

p.158 Rossi, *L'agitazione*, p.82.

pp.158–9 Rossi, *L'agitazione*, p.84.

p.159 Rossi, *L'agitazione*, pp.86–7.

pp.159–60 Rossi, *L'agitazione*, p.84.

p.160 Rossi, *L'agitazione*, pp.125–6.

p.168 Paternostro, p.166.

p.174 Spanò, p.44.

p.174 Spanò, p.43.

p.174 *Sicilia Nuova*, 10–11 January 1926.

p.175 Petacco, *Il prefetto*, p.100.

p.176 Calderone and Arlacchi, pp.14–15.

p.177 Porto, p.22.

pp.181–2 Lupo, 'L'utopia totalitaria', p.394.

p.183 *Giornale di Sicilia*, 28–9 July 1925.

p.184 Mori, *The Last Struggle*, p.22.

p.186 Marino, *I padrini*, p.113.

p.188 Raffaele, p.205.

pp.189–90 Mori, *Con la mafia*, p.84.

p.190 Archivio di Stato di Pavia.

5: The Mafia Establishes Itself in America 1900–1941, pp.193–232

p.195 *New York Herald*, 26 April 1903.

p.197 Gildeer, p.34.

pp.199–200 Reid, pp.131, 139, 143.

p.203 Carey, p.120.

p.208 Nelli, *The Business of Crime*, p.75.

p.210 *New York Herald*, 26 April 1903.

p.215 Deaglio, 'Se vince lui'.

p.219 Gentile, *Vita di capomafia*, p.91.

p.231 Calderone and Arlacchi, p.158.

6: War and Rebirth 1943–1950, pp.233–268

p.236 Pantaleone, *Mafia e politica*, p.63.

p.239 *La Repubblica*, Palermo, 11 June 2000.

p.242 'MAFFIA, Aug–Dec. 1943', Allied Commission Control 10106/143/28 Bob. 689C Scat. 140, quoted in Adriano, p.4.

p.243 *Sicily. Zone Handbook*, part 3.

p.243 'Allied to the mafia'.

p.244 Romano, *Storia della mafia*, p.302.

pp.252–3 Montanelli, pp.282–3.

p.253 Marino, *I padrini*, p.246.

pp.265–6 Quoted in Renda, *Salvatore Giuliano*, pp.101–2.

7: God, Concrete, Heroin, and Cosa Nostra 1950–1963, pp.269–301

p.285 Farinella, p.25.

p.287 Quoted in Stabile, *La Chiesa*, p.265.

8: The 'First' Mafia War and its Consequences 1962–1969, pp.303–328

p.322 Commissione parlamentare d'inchiesta sul fenomenc della mafia in Sicilian, *Documentazione allegata*, vol. 5, pp.375–642; p.375, dated 29 October 1975.

9: The Origins of the Second Mafia War 1970–1982, pp.329–375

pp.332–3 Calderone and Arlacchi, p.91.

p.341 Galluzzo, Nicastro, and
      Vasile, p.106.

p.341 Galluzzo, Nicastro, and
      Vasile, p.107.

p.343 Stajano, p.14.

p.350 Vitale, p.53.

p.350 Bartolotta Impastato, p.30.

p.354 Russo Spena, p.170.

p.355 *La Repubblica*, 11 April
      2002.

p.358 Sterling, p.295.

p.359 Pistone, p.388.

p.364 Leonardo Messina in
      Commissione parlamentare
      d'inchiesta, *Mafia, politica,
      pentiti*, p.523.

p.364 Leonardo Messina in
      Pezzino, *Mafia*, p.346.

p.369 Stajano, p.23.

p.370 Stajano, p.19.

pp.371–2 Gaspare Mutolo in
      Commissione parlamentare
      d'inchiesta, *Mafia, politica,
      pentiti*, p.1232.

pp.372–3 Buscetta and Arlacchi,
      p.219.

10: Terra Infidelium
1983–1992, pp.377–403

p.381 La Licata, p.77.

p.381 La Licata, p.77.

p.385 Lodato, p.107.

pp.386–7 Lodato, p.132.

p.387 Caponnetto, p.24.

p.388 *La Repubblica*, 30
      September 1984.

p.390 *La Repubblica*, 8 August
      1985.

p.396 Sciascia, *La Sicilia*, p.74.

p.398 Leonardo Messina in
      Commissione parlamentare
      d'inchiesta, *Mafia, politica,
      pentiti*, p.542.

11: Bombs and Submersion
1992–2003, pp.405–443

p.409 Lo Forte, interview with the
      author.

p.410 *La Repubblica*, 26 May
      1992.

p.414 Dino, *Mutazioni*, p.183.

p.419 Gaspare Mutolo
      interviewed in Commissione
      parlamentare d'inchiesta,
      Mafia, politica, pentiti,
      pp.1255, 1288.

p.430 Dino, 'La mafia del
      Gattopardo', p.206.

p.432 Scarpinato, interview with
      the author.

p.435 Leonardo Messina in
      Commissione parlamentare
      d'inchiesta, *Mafia, politica,
      pentiti*, p.522.

p.437 The charges in the
      paragraph beginning, 'The
      prosecution also claims
      that . . .' are as outlined in *La*

Repubblica, http://
www.repubblica.it/online/fatti/
utri/accuse/accuse.html

My assumption is that this article
is a fair and accurate summary.
p.442 Buscetta and Lodato, p.14.

Index

DC = Democrazia Cristiana
PCI = Partito Comunista Italiano
Sicilian towns and villages have been selectively indexed.

Addiopizzo 458
Adowa, battle of (1896) 98
Aglieri, Pietro 440
Agrigento (town) 48–9, 69, 79,
    189, 217, 219, 223, 427;
    capture of Brusca 10, 417;
    Favara Brotherhood trial 81
Alaimo, Rosario 82, 83
Albanese, Giuseppe 71–3
Alexander, General Sir Harold 241
Alongi, Giuseppe: *The Mafia . . .*
    Manifestations 88–90
AMGOT (Allied Military
    Government of Occupied
    Territory; WWII) 241–4, 246,
    250, 262
Anastasia, Albert 216, 217
Andreotti, Giulio ('Uncle Giulio')
    4, 418, 419, 420–5, 43, 456
Andronico, Giovanni 274–5
'Antimafia' enquiry 321–4, 332,
    337, 355, 384, 422
Antiochia, Roberto 389
Aprile, Andrea Finocchiaro 244,
    246, 275

Atlanta Federal Penitentiary (US)
    212
Atria, Rita 41
Avanti! (newspaper) 147

Badalamenti, Gaetano ('Tano';
    also 'Sitting Bully') 351, 421;
    Commission evolution 297,
    337, 349–50, 371; drug dealing
    300, 337, 349; death of
    Impastato 351, 354–5; US links
    356, 359, 372, 373; mafia
    factions 368, 370–1
Bagarella, Calogero 337
Bagarella, Leoluca 414–15, 417,
    425, 427, 432, 441–2
Banca Romana 97–8
Banco di Sicilia 129, 130, 134,
    136–7, 166, 281
Batista y Zaldívar, Fulgencio 294
Bergman, Ingrid 367
Berlusconi, Silvio ('the Knight')
    4, 434–42, 447, 449, 456–7
Biagi, Enzo 272–3
Boldini, Giovanni 112

Bologna 180: railway station massacre 345

Bonanno, Giuseppe ('Joe Bananas'): New York Family 256, 289, 359; *A Man of Honour* (book) 289–90, 291; return to Sicily and Sicilian Commission 289–90, 292, 293, 294–8, 300–1, 338, 358, 423; meeting with Buscetta 291–2

Bontate, Stefano ('Prince of Villagrazia') 384, 437, 453, 457; Commission member 337–8, 362, 368, 370; humiliated by Riina 370–1; Masonic connection 372; drug dealing 372–3, 429; murder and gang war 373–5; Andreotti connection 421, 423–4

Bonventre, Giovanni ('John') 295

Bordonaro, Lucio Tasca 243–4, 246, 262

Borgnine, Ernest 201

Borsellino, Agnese 415

Borsellino, Paolo: murder xx, xxi, 411, 413, 415, 416, 427, 455; Palermo maxi-trial 5, 343, 452, 459; joins antimafia team 387; upbringing and character 391; accused of careerism 394–5; CSM investigation 399, 400

Borsellino, Rita 458–9

Brancaccio (township) 305–6, 374, 416

Brando, Marlon 332, 338

'Brotherhood' ('Fratellanza'; criminal gang; Favara) 76, 80–5, 87, 88, 89, 101

Brusca, Davide 10–11

Brusca, Enzo 14

Brusca, Giovanni ('lo scannacristiani') 13–14, 369, 414, 431; Falcone murder xiv, 10; capture 10–11, 417, 425; defection 17; initiation 35–7; war on state 414–15

Buchalter, Louis ('Lepke') 231

Buscemi, Giuseppe ('Pidduzzo') 108–10

Buscetta, Tommaso 9, 326; defection xviii, xix–xx, 4, 5–7, 11, 12, 82, 101, 294, 295, 343, 387–8, 421; Palermo maxi-trial and 'Buscetta theorem' xx, xxi, 343, 393, 394, 397, 398, 402, 413, 417; on mafia origins 25, 271–2; comments on Orlando, Aprile and Giuliano 184, 244, 262, 275; appearance and character 272–4; opinion of Genco Russo 275; joins Porta Nuova Family 275–6; comments on Gioia, Ciancimino and Lima 279, 281, 418, 422; meeting with Bonanno 291–2; drug and tobacco trafficking 292, 300, 356, 357, 360, 368; Commission involvement 297, 298–9, 300, 338, 349; Ciaculli car bomb 308; role in first mafia war 313–16, 318, 325,

328; right-wing plotting 345;
comment on Riina 370, 413;
leaves Italy for Brazil 372–3,
374; meeting with Contorno
375; fate of sons 417; death
442–3

Caccamo (town) 96, 129, 131,
136, 324, 434, 455
Cagney, James 230
Calderone, Antonino 17, 175,
176, 188, 356, 397, 426
Calderone, Pippo 371
Caltanissetta (province) 48, 79,
241, 246, 249, 371
Calvi, Roberto 363, 455
Camilleri, Andrea 215–16
Cammarata, Angelo 249
Camorra (criminal group;
Naples) 1, 75, 218
Cancemi, Salvatore 416–17, 442
Capaci (town): Falcone murder
xiv–xv, xvii, 10, 11, 410–11,
416
Capone, Al ('Scarface Al') 1,
221–2, 216, 226–7, 229, 316
Caponnetto, Antonino 387–8,
397, 399
Caporetto, battle of (1917) 54,
178
Cappello, Antonio 57, 58–9
Cappiello, Nicola 207–8
Carnevale, Judge Corrado 398,
402, 409, 421
Carollo, Benedetto 28–33
Carollo, Giuseppe 135, 142

Caronia, Don Stefano 171
Caruso, Giuseppe 115–16, 117
Cascio-Ferro, Don Vito 185–6,
204–5, 211
Caselli, Gian Carlo 412
Cassa Agricola San Leoluca
(Catholic fund) 166–7
Cassarà, Ninni 389
Castellammare del Golfo (town)
229, 289, 295, 359
Castellammarese war 223–8,
290
Castelli, Roberto 439
Castiglia, Francesco (aka Frank
Costello) 221, 222, 230, 293
Castro, Fidel 294
Catania (town) 15, 17, 175, 235,
371
Cattanei, Franco 323
Cavataio, Michele ('the Cobra')
315, 316, 328, 337, 338, 344
cento passi, I (film) 354
Chinnici, Rocco 386, 387
Christian Democracy
(Democrazia Cristiana) *see* DC
Churchill, Winston 241
CIA (Central Intelligence Agency)
239, 243
Ciaculli (town) 171; Greco war
254–9, 297, 305; car bombs
305–8, 312, 313, 314, 315, 318,
321, 336
Ciancimino, Vito 280–5, 322,
338, 383, 388, 422, 426–7, 455
Cinisi (town) 297, 348, 359; car
bombs 312, 349

'Clean Hands' (corruption investigations) 412, 421, 434, 439

Colonna, Nicolò Turrisi, Baron of Buonvicino: *Public Security in Italy* (report) 39, 40–2, 44, 46, 56, 60, 63; attempted assassination 39, 42–3; political activities 39–40, 68, 75; suspected mafia connections 43–6, 63, 120; link with Giammona 43–6, 119–20, 122

Commission, the (*also* Cupola; 'the Senate'): structure xix–xx; evolution 228–9, 271–2, 290, 297–9, 300–1, 337, 349–50, 360–1, 371; first mafia war 311, 315–16, 317, 320; dissolution and reconstitution 318, 328, 337–8, 349–50; domination by Corleonesi 340, 371, 372; Palermo maxi-trial 398, 402; Agrigento commission 432

Communist Party (Partito Comunista Italiano) *see* PCI

Conca d'Oro (Palermo) 102–3, 106, 138, 186, 455

Connors, Francis 200

Consentino, Louis 222

Contorno, Salvatore ('Totuccio') 83, 374–5

Coppola, Francis Ford xiii, 331

Corleone ('Tombstone'; town) 155–6, 157, 171, 185, 196, 201, 331, 333, 338, 450, 455

Corleonesi (mafia group) xviii, xx, 10, 91, 161, 300, 311, 331–2, 356, 388, 429, 432, 452; rise to power 333–9; role in second mafia war (*la mattanza*) 367–75, 453, 456

Corriere della Sera (newspaper) 313, 347–8, 394–5

Cosa Nostra *see* mafia

Cosenza, Vincenzo 125, 138, 142

Costanzo, Maurizio 415

Crispi, Francesco 98

Croce Verde Giardini (village): Greco war 254–8, 305

CSM (magistrates' governing body) 399–400

Cuba 294

Cuccia, Don Francesco 182, 187

Cucco, Alfredo 174, 190

Cuffaro, Totò 459

D'Alba, Antonino 109–11

D'Alba, Vincenzo 106–9

D'Aleo, Tommaso 109–10, 126

D'Andrea, Anthony 223

d'Annunzio, Gabriele 112

Dalla Chiesa, General Carlo Alberto 384–5, 386

Dannemora (prison; US) 238

Dante Alighieri (battleship) 182

DC (Democrazia Cristiana; political party): land reform (Sicily) 250, 251–2; opposition to PCI 250–1, 286; mafia involvement 250–2, 279–80, 281, 283, 284–5, 289–90, 309, 319, 335, 365, 418–19, 420, 426; death of Vizzini 253; growth in power 264–5, 280, 379; Russo as DC politician 275; prosecution of Ciancimino 285; murder of Lima 285, 419; support of Church 286–8; alliance with Socialist Party 287, 320, 379; Moro kidnapping 347; controversial support of PCI 350–1; Sindona case 362; hostility towards Dalla Chiesa 385; Orlando's opposition to mafia 392, 400–1; decline of mafia influence 408–9, 419, 435; party's demise 412; Andreotti 420, 423, 456; murder of Mattarella 423

DEA (Drug Enforcement Administration; US) 272, 358

defectors (*pentiti*) xi, 5, 11, 18, 119, 175, 340, 429–30; on Lima's death 419; state use of 431, 440

Dell'Utri, Marcello 436–8, 456–7

De Mauro, Mauro 319, 342, 383, 455

Dewey, Thomas E. 231, 238

DIA (Direzione Investigativa Antimafia) 401–2, 412

Di Cillo, Rocco 410

Di Cristina, Giuseppe 367–70, 371, 373

Di Forti, Don Filipo 171

Di Lello, Giuseppe 387

Di Maggio, Balduccio 413

Di Maggio, Giuseppe 264

Di Matteo, Giuseppe 10, 11, 12–13, 417

Di Matteo, Santino 10

Di Pisa, Calcedonio 311, 315

Di Primo, Giuseppe 202, 203, 212

di Rudinì, Antonio 139

Di Sano, Emanuela 106, 107, 108

Di Sano, Giuseppa 104–9, 110, 120, 124, 126

Di Stefano, Salvatore 122

'Dissociation' policy: Cosa Nostra/state compromise 440–1

Divine Comedy (Dante) 351

DNA (Direzione Nazionale Antimafia) 401–2, 412

Dolci, Danilo (the 'Sicilian Gandhi') 288

d'Ondes Trigona, Baroness Giovanna 117–18, 142

drugs trafficking 272, 290, 292, 293–4, 295–6, 297, 298, 300, 316, 360, 368, 429; first mafia war origins 311, 359–61, 372–3; revenues 356, 358, 362, 456; Pizza Connection case (US) 357–8

EU (European Union): Agenda 2000 (Sicily) 428–9

Falcone, Giovanni: murder
xiv–xv, xvii, xx, 409, 410–11,
416, 427, 455; early career
xviii; 'Falcone method' xviii,
362, 365–6; upbringing and
character xviii, 380–2, 391;
investigations and defections
xviii, xix–xx, 5, 12, 175, 272,
292, 338, 356, 442;
observations on mafia xxi, 6,
15, 46, 359, 373, 392; as
Director of Penal Affairs 362,
401–3, 408–9, 412, 413, 423;
Salvo investigation 365–6;
joins antimafia team 387; post
maxi-trial opposition 398–401;
attempt on life 400 *see also*
Buscetta, Tommaso; Palermo
maxi-trial
Fanfani, Amintore 279, 280,
281
Farrarello, Gaetano ('King of the
Madonie') 173
Fascists *see* Partito Nazionale
Fascist
FBI 290, 293, 317, 358
Federal Bureau of Narcotics (US)
293
Filipello, Matteo 149
Flegenheimer, Arthur ('Dutch
Schultz') 231
Florio, Franca (née Franca
Jacona di San Giuliano) 112
Florio Jr, Ignazio 111–17, 125–6,
134, 146
Florio, Vincenzo 114, 117

Fondo Laganà, murders at
103–4, 111, 116–17
Fontana Nuova (criminal group;
Misilmeri) 76
Fontana, Giuseppe: Notarbartolo
murder and trial 140–1, 143–4,
146, 148, 170; emigrates to US
152, 204–5; Petrosino murder
211, 212
Forza Italia (political party) 4,
434–6, 438, 439, 440, 441,
442, 457
Franchetti, Leopoldo 43, 44, 45,
47–54, 61, 72; *Political and
Administrative Conditions in
Italy* 46, 49–50, 51–4, 63, 73
Fratuzzi (mafia group; Corleone)
160–1, 164, 166, 168, 170–1
Freemasons *see* Masonic societies
'Fuse Burners' ('Stuppagghieri';
criminal group; Monreale) 76,
77

'G' Men (film) 230
Galante, Camillo ('Carmine') 295
Galati, Dr Gaspare 81; memo to
Interior Ministry 32–3, 34, 38,
43, 63, 67, 73, 89, 101;
Giammona and Fondo Riella
takeover 27–33, 44, 68, 120
Gambino, Carlo 357, 359, 453
Gambino, John 374
Gangi (Sicily), siege of 172–5,
176, 184, 185, 186
Garibaldi, Giuseppe 21–2, 23, 39,
50, 57, 74, 76, 159, 179

Garofalo, Frank 295

Garufi, Pancrazio 134

Gelli, Licio 364

Genco Russo, Giuseppe ('Zu
    Peppi'; aka 'Gina
    Lollobrigida') 189, 236, 251,
    252, 275, 296

Gennaro, Don Giorgio 171

Genovese, Vito 216

Gentile, Cola (*also* Nick) 214–16,
    217–20, 222–9, 230, 231–2,
    243, 296, 299

Getty III, Eugene Paul 368

Giammona, Don Antonino 38,
    60, 63, 126, 310, 311, 414;
    initiation ritual 34, 36:
    relationship with Colonna
    44–6, 68, 96; war with Siino
    119–23; Sangiorgi prosecution
    124–5 *see also* Galati, Dr
    Gaspare

Gioè, Nino 17–18

Gioia, Giovanni ('the Viceroy')
    279–80, 281, 282, 283, 323, 420

Giornale di Sicilia (newspaper)
    147, 353, 384, 391, 415

Giuffrè, Antonioni ('Little Hand')
    434–5, 437, 438, 449, 451

Giuliano, Salvatore ('King of
    Montelepre') 259, 260–6,
    267–8, 275, 307, 311, 419

Godfather, The (film) xiii, 331

Grand Hotel des Palmes
    (Palermo): US/Sicilian mafiosi
    meetings 295–7

Grassi, Libero 402

Grasso, Piero 449–51

Greco, Antonina 255

Greco, Michele ('the Pope')
    258–9, 371, 421

Greco, Piddu ('the Lieutenant')
    255, 256, 257, 258, 309, 371

Greco, Pino ('the Shoe') 375

Greco, Rosalia 255

Greco, Salvatore ('Little Bird')
    297; Sangiorgi report 254; the
    Commission 300, 316; first
    mafia war 309, 311, 312, 314,
    318, 328, 339; and trial 325;
    right-wing plotting 345

Greco war (family feud) 254–9,
    297, 305

Gregorio (mafioso) 380–1

Grifò, Giovanni 264

Gualterio, Marquis Filippo
    Antonio 59–61

Guardia di Finanza (tax police)
    360

Guarnotta, Leonardo 387

Guevara, Ernesto ('Che') 294

Harlem Inn (brothel; US) 222

Hawthorne Smoke Shop
    (gambling den; US) 222

Hennessy, David 195

Hoffa, Jimmy: Teamsters Union
    317

Hoover, J. Edgar 293, 317

Horowitz, Henry 221

Hotel Sole (Palermo) 250

Humphreys, Murray ('the
    Camel') 221

Hunt, Sam ('Golf Bag') 221
Illustrazione Italiana (magazine) 102–3
Impastato, Felicia Bartolotta 350, 351, 353, 354–5
Impastato, Giuseppe ('Peppino') 292, 348–9, 350–5
Impastato, Luigi 350, 351, 355
International Longshoremen's Association (ILA) 217
Inzerillo, Pietro 201, 212
Inzerillo, Salvatore ('Totuccio') 359, 362, 368, 369, 372, 373, 375, 384, 453

John Paul II, Pope 415, 416

Kefauver, Senator Estes 293, 295, 319
Kelly, Paul (*earlier* Paolo Antonio Vaccarelli) 206–7
Kennedy, Robert 216, 316, 317

La Barbera, Angelo 309–10, 311–13, 314–15, 316, 317, 325, 339, 419
La Barbera, Salvatore 309, 311, 314, 316, 419
La Fata, Vincenzo 264
La Guardia, Fiorello 230
La Licata, Francesco 380–2
La Mantia, Vito 243
La Torre, Pio 384, 386
Lampedusa, Giuseppe Tomasi di: *The Leopard* 288
Lansky, Meyer ('Little Man') 221

Lanza, Giovanni 71–2, 73, 75
Lanza, Joseph ('Socks') 238
Lascari, Serafino 264
Law 41 bis (prison conditions legis.) 432, 438, 441, 442
Leggio, Luciano ('Scarlet Pimpernel') 91, 427; first mafia war 311; appearance and character 332–3, 371; origin of nickname 334; murder of Rizzotto 334, 336; war against Navarra 335–7; the Commission 337–8; right-wing plotting 345; mafia factions 368–9, 371; kidnapping 370–1; Palermo maxi-trial 392–3, 397; death 413
Lercara Friddi (town) 74, 221, 335
Li Causi, Girolamo 246, 247–8, 265, 323
Libera 458
Lima, Salvo: sack of Palermo 280–5, 309; at Ministry of Finance 323; connection with Salvo cousins 365, 423; Andreotti connection 418–21, 422, 423; as MEP 429
Lipschultz, Louis 222
Little Caesar (film) 230
Lo Forte, Guido 409, 430
Lo Piccolo, Salvatore 452–3
Lo Porto, Vincenzo 115–16, 117M
Lombroso, Cesare 87–8
Long, Senator Huey 230

Luciano, Charles ('Lucky'; *earlier* Salvatore Lucania) 1, 216; early years 221, 222; Castellammarese war 226–7, 289; and Commission 228, 229; political links 230; imprisonment 231, 237–8; WWII activities 237, 238; expulsion from USA and career evolution 238, 295, 299–300, 318; US/Sicilian mafiosi meetings 295–6; death 317, 350

Lunardi, Pietro 439

Madonia, Benedetto 202
mafia centres (Palermo) xix; Acquasanta 100, 109, 120; Falde 100, 120; Olivuzza 39, 100, 111, 113, 115, 117, 120, 278; Passo di Rigano 36–7, 100, 119, 120, 369; Perpignano 100, 119, 120; Piana dei Colli 100, 119, 120; Malaspina 27, 100, 119, 120; Uditore 30, 31, 32, 34, 38, 63, 81, 100, 101, 120, 311, 314
mafia (*also* Cosa Nostra): rules and command structure xi, xix, 3, 5–7, 50–1, 338; background xvi, 1–8, 27, 40–1, 46, 51–3, 62–4, 90, 99, 229, 271–2, 290–1; origin of mafia/ Cosa Nostra names xix, 24–5, 43, 55–6, 59, 60–1, 144, 189, 216, 271; Sicilian-American relationship xx, 358; codes of honour, loyalty and silence 4–7, 9–10, 11, 13–15, 16–18, 42, 69, 82–3, 183, 355; initiation rites 12, 34–8, 44, 81–2, 161, 342; attitude to women and children 12–13, 14–15, 355; religious parallels 15–17; first mafia war 305–16, 317, 318, 320, 325–8, 361; second mafia war (*la mattanza*) 332–9, 356, 367–75, 384, 453, 456; at war with state 385–6, 414–15; on verge of defeat 417, 430; re-emergence 429–33, 440, 442–3; common fund for prisoners 430

mafiusi di la Vicaria, I (play) 55–6
Magaddino, Stefano 229, 289, 295, 359
Magistratura Democratica (legal reform group) 347
Malausa, Lieutenant Mario 305, 306
Mangano, Vincenzo 216, 217
Mangano, Vittorio 436, 456
Mano nera ('Black Hand'; extortion gangs) 207–8
Manzella, Cesare 349, 352
Maranzano, Salvatore 224–9, 289
Mascagni, Pietro: *Cavalleria rusticana* (opera) xiii–xiv, xv–xvi, 90–1, 420
Masonic societies 37, 57, 69, 75, 163, 346, 364–5, 372, 435; P2 (Propaganda 2) 364

Masseria, Joe ('Joe the Boss') 216, 220, 224–6, 227, 228, 229, 289
Mattarella, Piersanti 423–4
Mazzini, Giuseppe 159
McKinley, President William 202
Meli, Antonino 399
Millunzi, Don Gaetano 171
Mistretta (town) 187–9
Monreale (town) 71, 171, 261
Montana, Beppe 388–9
Montinaro, Antonio 410
Morello, Giuseppe ('Piddu') 199; Morello gang (NY) and body in barrel murder 201, 202, 204–6, 211, 220; counterfeiting conviction 212; death 224
Mori, Cesare 172–5, 176–8, 180–1, 184–7, 189–91, 204, 346; *Among the Orange Blossoms Beyond the Mist* (book) 181
Moro, Aldo 347
'Moustache Petes' (*also* 'greaseballs'): purge 227–8
Muro Lucano, Bishop of 241
Mussolini, Benito: Fascist movement 157, 172, 179–81, 183, 435; war on mafia 174, 175–6, 181–2, 183–4, 187; deposed 241
Mussomeli (town) 189, 236, 251, 275, 296
Mutolo, Gaspare 413

Naples 21, 300
Narcotics Control Act (1956; US) 293

narcotics *see* drugs trafficking
Navarra, Michele ('Our Father') 333, 335–6, 337, 373, 426
Nazione, La (newspaper) 147
'Ndrangheta (criminal group; Calabria) 1, 402
New York Herald (newspaper) 195, 204, 207, 209, 210
New York: trade links with Sicily 26, 195, 204; Elizabeth Street 197, 205; Mulberry Bend 198; Little Italy 198, 202, 206, 209, 230; gun licences 204; East Harlem 205, 212, 221, 224, 231; mafia leadership 205–6, 219, 225, 226; non-mafia gangs 206–7; Brooklyn 212, 217, 219, 289, 311, 358, 362; City Democratic Club 217; docks and longshoremen 217; East Side 217; Newark 231; drive against organized crime 230–1; Pizza Connection 357–8
NGI (Navigazione Generale Italiana) 111–12, 134, 137, 138, 142, 144, 148, 150
Niceforo, Alfredo: *Contempory Barbarian Italy* xvi
Nicotera, Giovanni 74–6
Nixon, President Richard 357
Normandie, SS (liner) 238
Northern League (political party) 401
Notarbartolo, Emanuele (Marquis di San Giovanni) 411; murder 128–33, 155, 307,

383; first trial 133–42; second
trial 142–7; quashing of
verdicts 147–8; retrial and
acquittals (Palizzolo and
Fontana) 148–51, 170, 204, 209
Notarbartolo, Leopoldo 128, 129,
130–1, 135, 137, 138–52
Noto, Francesco 113, 115–16, 126
Noto, Pietro 113, 115–16, 126

O'Dwyer, William 231
'Operation Husky': Allied
occupation of Sicily (WWII)
235–7, 239, 240–1, 249, 333
see also AMGOT
Ora, L' (newspaper) 146, 150,
319, 336, 342, 383, 386–7
Orlando, Leoluca 392, 400
Orlando, Vittorio Emanuele
183–4
Ortoleva, Antonino 187–8
OSS (Office of Strategic Services;
US) 243, 249
Osservatore Romano (Vatican
newspaper) 415

Pacino, Al xiii, 9, 331
Palace of Justice (Palermo;
'Poison Palace') 400
Palermo maxi-trial xx, xxi, 5,
101, 343, 392–4, 397–8, 402,
417, 419, 452, 459; Court of
Cassation appeals xx, xxi, 398,
402, 409, 413, 416, 418, 419
Palermo: Garibaldi and liberation
21; description of city 23–4;

'stabbers' conspiracy 57–8;
'sack of Palermo' 277–85, 290,
455; 'Palermo spring' 392;
antimafia demonstrations
410–11
Palizzolo, Don Raffaele 91, 95–7,
99, 122, 127, 148, 150, 209,
341, 455 *see also* Notarbartolo,
Emanuele
Panepinto, Lorenzo 168
Pantaleone, Michele 239, 245–8,
324
Pappalardo, Cardinal Salvatore
392, 393
Partito Nazionale Fascist
(political party) 157, 172, 174,
175–6, 179–82, 186, 189,
190–1, 240
Pay or Die! (film) 201
PCI (Partito Comunista Italiano):
mafia opposition 244–6, 248;
Li Causi and Villalba incident
247–8, 323; political
manoeuvring 251, 263, 287,
320, 344–5, 350–1, 379, 401;
Portella della Ginestra
massacre 263–4; Church
opposition 287; calls for mafia
inquiry 319, 320; murder of La
Torre 384
Pecoraro, Lorenzo 283–4
Pelloux, General Luigi 98–9,
123–4, 127, 138, 139
Pennino, Gioacchino 426–7
pentiti see defectors
Petrosino, Adelina (née Salino) 209

Petrosino, Joe (aka Guglielmo De Simoni) 199–203, 209–11, 220, 293, 383

Petto, Tommaso ('Ox') 203, 212

Piazza Fontana (Milan): massacre 344

Pisciotta, Gaspare 266, 267–8

Pistone, Joseph D. (aka Donnie Brasco) 358

Pitrè, Giuseppe 90–1, 144, 148

Pope, Frankie 222

Portella della Ginestra: massacre 263–4, 265, 286–7; and trial 266, 267–8

Progresso Italo-Americano, Il (US newspaper) 155

'Pro Sicilia' (protest group) 148, 150

Profaci, Joe 256, 296

Provenzano, Bernardo ('the Tractor' *also* 'Uncle Bernie'): religious sentiment 15, 448; as killer 337, 368, 455; as fugitive 369, 426; Riina connection 371, 451; Palermo maxi-trial 392; war on state 414; mafia leadership 426–33, 434, 439, 440; 'disassociation' policy 441; capture 447–52

P2 (Propaganda 2) *see* Masonic societies

Public Enemy (film) 230

Publitalia (advertising company) 436

Puglisi, Father Pino 416, 417

Puzo, Mario: *The Godfather* 214, 322, 332

Radio Aut (local radio station) 351, 352, 353

Raging Bull (film) xiii

Red Brigades (terrorist group) 345, 347

Repubblica, La (newspaper) 239, 419

Resto del Carlino (newspaper) 147

Ricciardi, Giuseppe 326

RICO measures (Racketeer Influenced and Corrupt Organizations; US) 386

Riina, Totò ('Shorty') 10, 338, 356, 368, 371–2, 416–17, 426, 451, 455; initiation of Brusca 35–6, 369; second mafia war (*la mattanza*) 332, 370, 375; the Commission 340; Palermo maxi-trial 392, 402, 419; wealth confiscation 407–8; war on state 409, 411, 418, 427, 454; capture 413–14, 425, 432; attitude towards defectors 416–17; Andreotti connection 421; proposed separatist movement 435; Dell'Utri connection 437

Rizzotto, Placido 334, 335, 336

Roman Catholic Church 15–16, 166–7, 240–1, 286–8, 319, 363, 415–16

Rosario, Father: 'Tertiaries of Saint Francis of Assisi' 30

Rose, John Forester 74–5, 76

Rosi, Francesco: *Salvatore Giuliano* (film) 260–1, 264, 266

Rossellini, Roberto 367

Rossi, Adolfo 155–6, 157, 158–61, 196, 198

Rotolo, Antonino 452–4

Ruffini, Ernesto, Cardinal Archbishop of Palermo 286–7, 288

Russo, Joseph 243, 249

Sacra Corona Unita (criminal group; Puglia) 1

Saetta, Antonino 402

Salvo, Ignazio 365, 388, 422, 423

Salvo, Nino 365, 370, 372, 388, 422, 423

Sangiorgi, Ermanno 99; report on mafia 100–27, 254, 298, 311, 325, 328, 443; Notarbartolo trial 138, 140–1, 144, 145, 150, 170

Sant'Elia (nobleman) 57–8

Santapaola, Nitto ('the Hunter') 15, 371

Santino, Umberto 354

Saturnia, SS (liner) 311

Scaglioni, Pietro 383

Scarface (film) 230

Scarpato's (restaurant; Coney Island) 226

Scarpinato, Roberto 428, 430, 432

Scelba, Mario 265–6

Schifani, Rosaria 410, 411

Schifani, Vito 410

Sciascia, Leonardo 61–2, 397; *The Day of the Owl* 320, 394–6

Scopelliti, Antonio 402

Scorsese, Martin xiii

Senate Special Committee to Investigate Crime in Interstate Commerce (US) 293

Servadio, Gaia 310

'Sheets Committee' (antimafia organization) 411

Sicilcasa (building company) 283, 284

Sicily: psyche and culture xiv, xvi–xvii, 90, 443; early history 21–3, 50–3, 59; poverty 24–5, 155–6; citrus trade 26–7, 195, 249; sulphur industry 79–80, 84–5; Fasci (peasant movement) 157, 166, 169, 179, 196; post-WWI mayhem 177–9; emigration to US 189, 195–9; post-WWII separatist movement 243–5, 250, 262; cattle and grain trade 249

Siino, Filippo 120–1

Siino, Francesco 119–23, 125

Sindona, Michele 362–3, 364, 422

Sing Sing (US prison) 202, 203, 121

Slavonia, SS (liner) 210

Socialist Ideal, The (news-sheet) 349

Socialist Party (Italy): political manoeuvring and demise 263, 287, 320, 379, 412; mafia overtures 435; Berlusconi link 437

Sonnino, Sidney 43, 44, 45, 47–9, 61, 72

Spadaro, Tommaso xviii
Spampinato, Giovanni 319
Spanò (Sicilian restaurant) 291, 297
Spatola, Alfonso 36
Spatola, Rosario 362
St Valentine's Day massacre 222
Stella, Don Constantino 171
Stromboli (film) 367
Sullivan, Tim ('Dry Dollar') 207
supergrass *see* defectors

Tajani, Diego 70, 307
Terranova, Cesare 384
Terranova, Ciro 212, 217
terrorism, right-wing: 'strategy of
     tension' 57–8, 344, 345–6, 347
Times, The 69, 74, 141, 146–7
tobacco trafficking 356–7, 360–1
Torretta, Pietro 311, 314, 325, 338
Trapani basketball club 437
Tribuna, La (newspaper) 155
Truman, President Harry S. 263

Ucciardone (prison; Palermo)
     268, 273, 274, 340, 392
United States of America xx,
     1–2; Sicilian immigration 189,
     195–9; New Orleans 195, 204,
     230, 231; Democratic Party
     197, 207, 230; mafia mobility
     205–6; mafia 'trademark'
     control 207, 208; Prohibition
     213–14, 220, 222, 223, 224,
     230, 292; Kansas City 217, 219,
     220; Philadelphia 218, 219;
     Pittsburgh 218, 219; San

Francisco 219; Williamsburg
     221; Chicago 221, 223, 226,
     230, 309; Las Vegas 292;
     Detroit 297, 317, 349 *see also*
     New York
Ustica (prison; Italy) 83

Valachi, Joseph 317: *The Valachi
     Papers* 216, 224
Vassallo, Don Ciccio 370
Verga, Giovanni 90–1
Verro, Bernardino 157–61, 162–9,
     170–1, 196, 333, 334, 455
Verro, Giuseppina Pace Umana
     169
via dei Georgofili (Florence): car
     bomb 415
via dei Gladiatori (Rome): bomb
     415
via Palestro (Milan): bomb 415
Villa Deliella (Palermo) 277–8
Villabate (town) 96, 131, 140,
     149, 242, 256, 305–6, 307,
     449–50
Villalba (town) 254, 256;
     'Operation Husky' 235–7,
     239–41; wounding of Li Causi
     245–8
Vitale, Giusy 458
Vitale, Leonardo 340–3, 367, 388
Vizzini, Don Calogero ('Zu
     Calò'; US codename 'Bull
     Frog') 275, 296, 323, 324, 334,
     338, 419; 'Operation Husky'
     235–7, 239, 240–1; Miccichè
     (estate) takeover 245–53

Vizzini, Monsignor Giovanni
235
Vizzini, Raimonda 245

Wagner, Richard : *Parsifal* 295
Whitaker, Audrey 113, 114, 115,
125

Whitaker, Effie 114
Whitaker, Joseph ('Pip') 114
Whitaker, Joshua ('Joss') 113–14,
125, 295

Zaza, Michele ('Mad Mike')
356–7, 361